The Harp and the Eagle

The Harp and the Eagle

Irish-American Volunteers and the Union Army, 1861–1865

Susannah Ural Bruce

NEW YORK UNIVERSITY PRESS

New York and London

NEW YORK UNIVERSITY PRESS
New York and London
www.nyupress.org

Library of Congress Cataloging-in-Publication Data
Bruce, Susannah Ural.
The harp and the eagle : Irish-American volunteers and the Union
Army, 1861-1865 / Susannah Ural Bruce.
p. cm.
Includes bibliographical references and index.
ISBN-13: 978-0-8147-9939-0 (cloth : alk. paper)
ISBN-10: 0-8147-9939-6 (cloth : alk. paper)
ISBN-13: 978-0-8147-9940-6 (pbk. : alk. paper)
ISBN-10: 0-8147-9940-X (pbk. : alk. paper)
1. United States—History—Civil War, 1861–1865—Participation,
Irish American. 2. United States. Army—History—Civil War,
1861–1865. 3. Irish American soldiers—History—19th century. 4.
Irish Americans—History—19th century. 5. Catholics—United
States—History—19th century. I. Title.
E540.I6B78   2006
973.7'410899162—dc22   2006016125

New York University Press books are printed on acid-free paper,
and their binding materials are chosen for strength and durability.

Manufactured in the United States of America
c 10 9 8 7 6 5 4 3 2 1
p 10 9 8 7 6 5 4 3 2

For "my boys": Bo, Robby, and Gus
Thanks for making my life such a grand adventure

and

Renée Susan Wyser-Pratte, 1971–2005
I miss you, Ren

Contents

Acknowledgments   ix

Introduction   1

1   "An Irishman Will Not Get to Live in This Country":
     The Irish in America, 1700–1860   7

2   "Remember Your Country and Keep Up Its Credit":
     Volunteering for Ireland and America   42

3   "We Are Slaughtered Like Sheep, and No Result
     But Defeat": The Decline of Irish-American Support
     for the War in 1862   82

4   "The Irish Spirit for the War Is Dead! Absolutely
     Dead!": Battles Raging in the Field and at
     Home, 1862–1863   136

5   "Hordes of Celts and Rebel Sympathizers":
     The Decline and Consequence of Irish-American
     Support for the War   190

6   "Father Was a Soldier of the Union": Irish Veterans
     and the Creation of an Irish-American Identity   233

     Conclusion   263

     Notes   265

     Bibliography   285

     Index   293

     About the Author   309

Acknowledgments

I like to read biographies of writers I admire because I want to copy their routines and style to improve my skills, and I think a dark part of me likes to know that they suffer, too. But I learn something else from their work. No author would ever get published without a lot of help along the way. In a sense, this book is as much the work of my friends and colleagues as it is mine. Well, at least the good parts.

This began as a doctoral dissertation, though it has changed tremendously from that first incarnation. The core of the project was shaped by my doctoral adviser, Donald J. Mrozek, professor of history at Kansas State University, who remains a valued mentor and treasured friend. Contributing to this, as well, were my committee members Peter B. Knupfer, Lou F. Williams, and Sue Zschoche of the K-State History Department and Harald E. L. Prins, K-State professor of anthropology. All of them remain friends and supporters to this day, and Harald, in particular, has been wonderful about debating the finer points of this work as I polished my arguments. While researching and writing the dissertation, I taught as a full-time lecturer in the Department of History at Sam Houston State University and earned a tenure-track position there when I received my Ph.D. My colleagues supported the project in every way possible and it is a privilege to continue working with them today. I would like to thank especially Jim Olson and Robert Bruce, who read and offered valuable suggestions on the manuscript, as well as Caroline Crimm, Charlann Morris, and Nancy Sears for their constant support. I am grateful, too, to my students, including one of our best graduate students, Justin Baxley, who dug up some outstanding nineteenth-century articles that contributed to this work. Thanks go to the SHSU Newton Gresham Library staff, especially Betty Craig, as well as the Kansas State University Library staff, especially John Johnson and Lori Fenton. Travel funds from the SHSU history department, directed first by Jim Olson and later by Terry Bilhartz, helped with the research, as did a generous grant from the Irish American Cultural Institute, its president John Walsh, and the Friendly Sons of St. Patrick.

Over the years, the dissertation evolved into a book and that manuscript evolved into a much stronger one. Many of the final revisions were thanks to the suggestions of Kerby Miller and I am forever indebted to him for directing me to a wealth of Irish soldiers' letters and helping me to embrace the complexity of this work. Similar guidance came from Randall Miller, another reader of the manuscript and a scholar who aided it tremendously with his detailed suggestions for revisions. Both Kerby and Randall remain postdoctoral mentors who push my understanding of Irish-American history and the U.S. Civil War to new levels. I would also like to thank the additional anonymous reader of the manuscript for his or her helpful suggestions.

Guiding this evolution, too, was Carol Reardon. I can't recall exactly when we first met, but my first extended contact with her was during her Civil War battlefield staff rides while I was a West Point Summer Fellow in 2002. The entire fellowship was outstanding, but Carol's contributions at Manassas, Antietam, and Gettysburg were unforgettable. She hasn't been able to shake me since. Throughout this work Carol served as a sounding board for my ideas. She took time out of her schedule to return with me to Antietam and Gettysburg to make sure I had the Irish units in the right place, and then she read and reread the sections of the manuscript relating to those battlefield discussions. And she's never made a penny for all of that work. True, there have been the odd dinner or two, but I will never be able to repay my debt. Thank you, Carol. In addition to Kerby, Randall, and Carol, I would like to thank the following colleagues who shared sources or helped strengthen my arguments: Ruth-Ann M. Harris, Lawrence Kohl, Bruce Vandervort, Larry Bland, Arnold Schrier, Dennis Showalter, the late Russell F. Weigley, Jeffrey Grey, and Chris Samito.

As you research a book, the material doesn't always take you where you think it will. This, of course, is good and the way historians should work, but it means that a lot of archivists and librarians have to be ready to help you along the way as you request just one more box to fill in the missing piece of your story. For their help in this part of the journey, I would like to thank the staff at the National Archives and Records Administration and the Library of Congress in Washington, DC, Dan Rolph and Kerry McLaughlin at the Historical Society of Pennsylvania, Shawn Weldon at the Philadelphia Archdiocesan Historical Research Center, Derek W. Weil and Beth Becker at The Civil War and Underground Railroad Museum of Philadelphia, and Jim Mundy, Director of the Library and Historical Collections at the Union League in Philadelphia. Thanks go to Michael Comeau and John Hannigan at the Massachusetts State Archives and Kim Nusco and Kate DuBose at the Massachusetts Historical Society. In New York I had the pleasure of working in a number of repositories, but would like to especially thank Chris Karpiak at the New York State Library in Albany and Bill Cobert and the outstanding staff at the American Irish Historical Society in New York City, as well as Henry F. White, Jr., historian of the Society of the Friendly Sons of St. Patrick in the City of New York, whose papers are held at the American Irish Historical Society. While I was visiting the city, authors Peter Quinn and Terry Golway were kind enough to take time from their busy schedules to discuss my work and offer their suggestions. In Illinois, I would like to thank Chuck Cali, John Reinhardt, and David A. Joens of the Illinois State Archives, Leigh A. Gavin, Debbie Vaughan, and Rob Medina of the Chicago Historical Society, and Cheryl Schnirring of the Abraham Lincoln Presidential Library. Thanks go to John White and Devon Lee of the Southern Historical Collection at the University of North Carolina at Chapel Hill, Miriam Meislik and Michael J. Dabrishus of the Archives and Special Collections Department of the University of Pittsburgh, and Ryan Meyer at the U.S. Army Military History Institute at Carlisle Barracks, Pennsylvania.

When I needed to make sure my analysis of Irish soldiers on Civil War battlefields was right, certain people, in addition to Carol, played an essential role in directing me to resources or walking the ground with me. Thank you Jeff Prushankin, Keith Alexander, Keith Bohannon, and Kelly O'Grady, as well as John Heiser, Scott Hartwig, Eric Campbell, and Tim Orr at Gettysburg National Military Park, Jim Burgess at the Manassas Battlefield Park, Bob Krick at the Richmond National Battlefield Park, Don Pfanz and Frank O'Reilly of the Fredericksburg and Spotsylvania County National Military Park, and Ted Alexander at the Antietam National Battlefield. John, Scott, Eric, Jim, and Frank all read and offered advice on portions of the manuscript and saved me from some embarrassing mistakes. Any that remain, I'm afraid, are entirely my fault. Don Ernsberger and Mike Kane helped clarify details about the Irish 69th Pennsylvania, and Joe Gannon and Gerry Regan of "The Wild Geese" and the late Lieutenant Colonel Ken Powers, historian of the 69th Regiment Veterans Corps, directed me to some wonderful material pertaining to the Irish Brigade. Thanks go to the late Mr. Robert Fitzgerald, Mrs. Ruth Fitzgerald, and Mr. Michael J. Langhoff for allowing me to quote from their ancestors' letters in this book.

Across the Atlantic, I would like to thank Elizabeth M. Kirwan, Ciaran Mc Eniry, and Gerry Lyne of the National Library of Ireland, A.M. McVeigh of the Public Records Office of Northern Ireland, and Gregory O'Connor and Eamonn Mullaly of the National Archives of Ireland.

When I could not track down items myself, Joan Phillipson of Historical Research Associates in Belfast was a tremendous help. Special thanks to Mr. Timothy Woulfe of County Limerick and William and Ruth Irvine of County Armagh for sharing information about their ancestors who fought in the Union Army and for allowing me to use it in this book, and to Irvine Collins for helping me to locate the Irvines in Ireland and sharing their photograph of Abraham Irvine.

For their assistance with providing the photographs for the book, I would like to thank Lynn Libby of Enola, Pennsylvania, who reproduced all but one of these images, and William F. Ural, M.D., of Southport, North Carolina, for reproducing the Lord Lieutenant of Ireland Proclamation of 1864. Special thanks go to Joe Gannon, too. As the editor of "The Wild Geese Today" (www.thewildgeese.com) Joe made me aware of the early-twentieth-century postcard that illustrates the cover of this book. I cannot thank him enough for loaning it to NYU Press and especially for giving it to me in celebration of this project. For detailed editing, patience, and unwavering support for this project, I am indebted to my editor, Debbie Gershenowitz. I cannot thank you enough for your faith in me and this book. I am also grateful to Despina Papazoglou Gimbel, managing editor of NYU Press, who masterfully directed the final states of production. Thanks go to my copyeditor, Emily Wright, and my indexer, Martin Tulic, as well.

If I had known when I started this project just how difficult it would be, I am not sure I would have gone down this road. Working-class Irish Catholic immigrants and their children did not leave as many records as we might hope. Still, their tale is there if you are willing to dig for it, but the work is frustrating. Fortunately, I had friends and family who routinely stepped in to keep me going. Even if their repeated proddings of "So, is the book done yet?" became a little annoying, I couldn't have done this without them. I'd like to thank in particular Jon and Jennifer Ural, "Aunt" Carol and "Uncle" Jim Fitzgerald, John, Bonnie, and Tom Wolfe, Pat Sheehan, Drs. Willa M. Bruce and J. Walton Blackburn, Joe, Carol, and Josh Bruce, as well as Leslie (Hegman) Sproat and Olinda Cardenas, who were and are fabulous nannies for our son when work kept my husband and me away. To the women who helped keep me together, I can never thank you enough: Renée Wyser-Pratte, Ann-Marie Vannucci, Kelli Shonter, Randi Tinkleman, Valeri Pappas, and Lisa Kiniry. In the end, though, it all comes down to the four people who have influenced me most. My parents, Dr. William F. and Mrs. Sue C. Ural, deserve credit for giving me the confidence to start this journey, the love to keep me going, and the discipline to complete it. My husband,

Robert "Bo" Bruce, is a fellow historian and author and was a tremendous asset with this project. I suppose I would have done this without him, but, like the thought of my life without him, it just wouldn't have been any fun. Thanks, dear friend, for sharing this crazy life with me. Finally, our son Robby, who came along at the end of this project and nearly had it at a standstill, deserves my thanks for the constant reminder of what is most important in life.

Introduction

William O'Grady braced himself against the cold. It was early December 1861 and he was alone in New York City. Just two years before he had been a second lieutenant with the British Army in India, but to the outrage of his Irish-born father, a colonel also serving in India, O'Grady had inexplicably resigned his commission and gone to America. Now the son was determined to prove that he was no coward. He could fight, and would fight, for causes he believed in. For William O'Grady, like so many other Irishmen already fighting in America, the cause of union was inextricably linked to that of Irish independence.[1]

As he stepped off the boat and onto the dock, a mass of soldiers, recruiters, and other immigrants whirled around O'Grady. Wandering into the city, he encountered a fellow Irishman named Colonel Dennis Burke recruiting men for his Irish 88th New York Infantry Regiment, which became part of the Irish Brigade, one the most celebrated Irish units of the American Civil War. Burke regaled young O'Grady with tales of the glory and honor of serving in an Irish regiment fighting for the causes of America and Ireland. As a man proud of his heritage, O'Grady knew of the historic traditions of other Irish units like the Irish Brigade of France, celebrated for its bold bayonet charge that turned the tide at the Battle of Fontenoy in 1745.[2] He believed this was his chance to show his father "what he was made of." He signed his name and joined the 88th New York. William O'Grady had been in America for only two hours.[3]

Before the war was over a ball would rip through O'Grady's shoulder at Antietam and another would graze his hip at Fredericksburg. By 1864 his vision would begin to fail him and he would require a guide to lead him through camp and on the march. The war would take its toll on O'Grady, but he could tell his father that he had remembered the martial tradition of his Irish ancestors and continued the ancient struggle for liberty.[4]

William O'Grady's experiences were fairly common among Irish and Irish-American Catholic volunteers in the Union Army during the Civil War. While many served in nonethnic units, others joined Irish regiments and marched and camped with their friends and countrymen. When explaining the motivation behind their enlistment in these Irish units, they routinely linked their service in America to their past in Ireland and their future as Irish-Americans. The experiences of these men and the way these events shaped their understanding of the war are the basis of this work.

This is not an ethnic history of Irish-American Catholics in the nineteenth century, nor is it a traditional battle narrative. The tale of these men and their families lies at the crossroads between the battlefield and the home front. By focusing our attention there we can learn why these men volunteered to fight for the Union when so many of them were not born in America or had been in the country for less than a decade. Similarly, we can investigate the way their families understood their service and the way the views of Irish-American soldiers and civilians changed as the war progressed, casualties rose, and Union war aims evolved.

Nearly 150,000 Irish and Irish-Americans served in the Union Army between 1861 and 1865, and there are numerous studies of the Irish Brigade, books on other Irish-American regiments, biographies of famous Irish-American soldiers, examinations of Irish Catholic soldiers in particular Union units, published letters, diaries, and memoirs of Irish-American veterans, and a few sweeping studies of ethnic soldiers in general. What we lack, however, is a broad examination of the way Irish Catholic men and their communities understood this service in the Union Army. That is what I offer with *The Harp and the Eagle*.

For some Irish men, especially the radical Irish nationalists in America known as the Fenians, military service offered experience they could apply to their anticipated war for an independent Ireland.[5] Others referred to the opportunities they had found in America and spoke of their hope to save the Union as an asylum for future Irish refugees. Some served to challenge nativist prejudice and prove their loyalty as Americans, hoping their sacrifices would lead to new opportunities in postwar America. For other Irishmen, military service was not necessarily based on ideology or heritage, but rather on a basic need for the money, clothing, food, and shelter they could earn in the Union Army, though at a tremendous risk.

Scholars have offered various arguments as to the primary factor or few factors that inspired tens of thousands of Irish and Irish-Americans to don the Union blue between 1861 and 1865.[6] It is a difficult concept to grasp, however, since the motivations of Irish-American Catholic volunteers and their families are as varied as their own communities. This is an essential point to understand if we are to have a fuller sense of Irish-American participation in the northern war effort. An Irish man's decision to join the Union Army, and the support or criticism he received from his family regarding this decision, was shaped by his and their religion, economic background, age, duration of time in the United States, birthplace, location in America, and many other factors. In addition, there are a limited number of records from these soldiers and their families to help us understand why they joined the Union Army, why they stood their ground on the battlefield, and how their views about the war evolved. Despite these challenges, I believe a broad examination of the role of Irish-American Catholics within the Union war effort deserves further consideration. I am reaching beyond the ideological studies of Civil War soldiers that focus predominantly on the Protestant, native-born experience to shed new light on these men and their families, who remain a mystery despite their popularity.

After years of research, I began to unravel a common thread running through the myriad of motivations behind Irish-American views of war for union. Irishmen routinely explained their actions in terms of their Irish and their American heritage, more often than not in that order. Sometimes they were explaining themselves to family in Ireland who did not understand their service in an American war. At other times, they defended decisions to oppose the Union war effort or clarified their dedicated service in the war against nativist attacks. When they volunteered, fought, or refused to continue fighting, they did so on the basis of the way the war affected their communities in America or in Ireland, or sometimes in both places. This does not mean that the vast majority of Irish volunteers were so focused on their Irish heritage that they were all Fenians. They were, however, aware of their heritage since most Irish or Irish-American Catholic volunteers were either recent immigrants or American-born children of immigrants who maintained strong ties to family and memories in Ireland or Irish-American communities in the United States.

When Irish men in New York, Boston, or Philadelphia rushed to fill the ranks in 1861, for example, they spoke of a loyalty to their families in America and Ireland, and cited proudly the historic traditions of Irish men who fought for an independent Ireland or served as the famous Wild Geese, warriors who fled English rule in Ireland to serve in foreign armies, always hoping to return and liberate their homeland.[7] Initially, the U.S. Army and native-born Americans accepted, and even encouraged, this ethnic pride. Communities held parades to celebrate the formation of Irish units, ladies' organizations donated green silk banners to Irish regiments, and American officers claimed to have some "fighting Irish" heritage of their own.[8]

Problems arose, however, when the interests of Ireland and the Union came into conflict. By 1863, thousands of Irish-American soldiers were dead or wounded, and their communities began to question the cost of this war. Expressing these sentiments, a leading Irish-American paper lamented, "How bitter to Ireland has been this rebellion! It has exterminated a generation of its warriors."[9] President Abraham Lincoln's announcement of the Emancipation Proclamation in the fall of 1862 had also contributed to these sentiments. Many Irishmen envisioned millions of former slaves reaching an equal status with them at the bottom of the northern economy, which could then transfer into comparable power throughout the social structure. The national draft announced in the spring of 1863 fanned these fires of frustration, with Irish leaders criticizing the exemption clause within the draft legislation that allowed the wealthy to avoid service by purchasing a substitute at a price most immigrant laborers could not afford. Large numbers of Irish-Americans across the North concluded by 1863 that the cause of union no longer supported their interests as Irishmen, and they began to abandon their support for the war.

In response to these developments, native-born Americans stopped cheering Irish military traditions, fighting abilities, and other examples of ethnic pride, and they returned to the antebellum descriptions of the Irish as "disturbing characters" who upset the "community order."[10] While many Americans saw this declining Irish support as a betrayal, most Irish-Americans saw no change in their approach to the war. Indeed, they considered their actions to be examples of loyalty and honor because they remained faithful to their original goals even if this meant abandoning the Union cause. A sense of responsibility to their families in America and Ireland had inspired Irishmen to wear Union blue, and it was this same sense of concern for their communities that led large numbers of Irishmen to oppose that cause.[11] Theirs was a balancing act of competing loyalties, one quite old to Ireland, and the other new to America, and they shifted between these depending on the demands of each situation. It was a complex process, and *The Harp and the Eagle* is the story of that tumultuous relationship at war.

Irish-American Catholic soldiers and their families at home suffered from higher illiteracy rates than native-born Americans, causing Irishmen to leave fewer records for historians.[12] Still, the material is there in the letters and diaries, memoirs, government and church records, and in the community newspapers, which we can be fairly confident, given their popularity, expressed the general opinions of their readership. Though limited and scattered, the evidence became like threads that I wove together, row by row, to create a tapestry that relates the story of these soldiers and their countrymen.

Of the available material, most of it relates to the Irish Brigade, but there is a significant quantity of sources on Irish and Irish-American Catholic volunteers and their countrymen outside this unit. The majority of my source material focuses on cities with the largest Irish-American populations in 1860, which include New York, Philadelphia, and Boston (See table 1.1 in chapter 1). Still, there were significant numbers of Irishmen in towns and cities across the Midwest and the western United States, and to show how views can change on the basis of geographic experiences, I incorporated examples of Irish-Americans in communities from Cincinnati, Ohio, to San Francisco, California, and countless towns in between. These sources include the views of soldiers and civilians, men and women, Catholics and Protestants, and Irishmen in America and Ireland. I found, for example, that Protestant Irish-Americans were more likely to support the northern war effort than Catholics, and that the Irish Catholics of the Midwest and West appeared less radical and victimized by anti-Irish prejudice than those in the eastern United States. Despite differences like these, the common link between their experiences remained: Irish and Irish-American volunteers routinely cited their own lives and experiences as Irishmen and Americans when explaining their support for a war for union but their opposition to Emancipation, a draft, and the appalling casualties the war inflicted on their communities.

Due to the fact that native-born Protestants dominate studies of Civil War soldiers' motivations for service, motivations in combat, and postwar experiences, I wanted my book to focus on the experience of Irish Catholic volunteers.[13] It should be noted that because the focus of this study is on Catholic Irish and Irish-Americans, general references to Irishmen or Irish Americans in the text should be understood to refer to Catholics. References to Ulster Irish, Ulstermen, or Scots Irish would naturally refer to Protestants, and in any other discussion of Irish Protestants, they are identified specifically as such.

With regard to the military aspects of this war, my analysis primarily focuses on the way Irishmen viewed a particular battle or other major military event, government policy relating to the war, or what was happening to their families in America or Ireland, and the way these issues influenced their view of the war and their service in the army. I do not address the experiences of every Irish unit at every battle of the Civil War. That is not the purpose of this work. There are certain battles, though, that are essential to understanding Irish-American military service in this conflict. The story of the Irish Brigade at Fredericksburg, for example, has come to dominate the memory of that battle. Similarly, the image of Father William Corby blessing the Irish Brigade or Colonel Patrick "Paddy" O'Rorke's leadership of the 140th New York have become such a part of the history and memory of the Battle of Gettysburg that they must be discussed in a study like this.

It should be noted that the spelling and grammar in some of the letters and diaries of Irish and Irish-American soldiers and their families could be seriously distracting from their message. Rather than have hundreds of quotations filled with "sic" and brackets, or distracting spelling errors that misrepresent an intelligent, thoughtful author, I have made minor corrections to spelling and grammar where necessary, while never altering the meaning of the original statements. If any readers would like an exact transcription of a particular letter, I will be happy to provide that or direct them to the appropriate archive.

In the end, I hope I convince the reader of what I discovered through years of detailed reading and research. Dual loyalties to Ireland and America influenced the actions of Irish Catholic volunteers in the Union Army during the American Civil War. Even when economic necessity led them into a Federal uniform, they still considered how this would affect their families in America and Ireland, and explained their decisions to both. In the postwar period, they would insist on inserting their service into the larger American memory of a war that redefined the nation, and thus claimed for themselves a unique place in American history. These observations are not necessarily surprising, but no one has ever presented an examination of the motivations and experiences in a sweeping study of the Irish Catholic volunteer for American union. That is what I offer here.

1

"An Irishman Will Not Get to Live in This Country"

The Irish in America, 1700–1860

The history of the Irish in America is both long and complex, involving the immigration of Protestants and Catholics, skilled laborers and peasants, rebels and farmers. Understanding why Irish men volunteered for the Union Army in 1861 and why their families supported or challenged this decision requires an understanding of the generations preceding them. In achieving this understanding, one can examine what the Irish hoped to find in America, how they went about accomplishing their goals, and how these factors influenced their actions during the American Civil War.

In the decades before the war, most Irish immigrants settled in or near the cities of Boston, New York City, and Philadelphia. Irish immigration from before the Great Famine of 1845 through 1855 involved Irish Protestants of varying means, but few fit the destitute image so commonly associated with the "huddled masses." Even so, they did not always find life in America as successful as they had hoped, nor did many colonists, and later Americans, find the Irish a particularly positive addition to their "city on the hill."

Ulster Irish were the backbone of Irish immigrants to the British colonies in America and the late-eighteenth-century United States. In the early seventeenth century, Presbyterian Scotsmen had settled in Northern Ireland, encouraged by an English government hoping to pacify rebel Ireland and encourage the development of a Protestant ruling class. Some of these Ulster Scots or Ulster Irish, as they came to be known, chose to continue their westward journey and traveled to North America as part of the "Great Migration" of 1717–1775. Sharp fluctuations in the Irish linen industry, combined with industrial depressions and the resulting changes within Ulster society, inspired some of the departures. Increasing rents due to rising prices or competition for land were also to blame, and Irish farmers looked toward America for better opportunities. For others still,

Anglican discrimination against the Ulster Irish Presbyterians' belief drove them to the United States. Motivated primarily by these economic and religious factors, nearly 250,000 Ulstermen migrated to the American colonies.[1]

When the Ulster Irish arrived in America, large numbers of them settled in New England, especially in the growing town of Boston, where they soon became the focus of hostility. Puritan city leaders resented the Ulster Irish loyalty to Presbyterianism while other Bostonians focused on economic issues, primarily the number of destitute immigrants depleting the town's limited charitable resources that, many believed, should not be wasted on noncitizens. The 1730s brought an economic recession to the already tense ethnic situation and witnessed several riots as Bostonians organized to harass the Ulster Irish and encourage a second migration—out of Boston. City leaders even went so far as to forbid one ship's captain from landing his Irish "Transports."[2]

Ulstermen who settled in Pennsylvania and areas farther south found more success, usually due to their ability to dominate sparsely populated areas or to their settling in colonies with greater religious tolerance. The western hills of Virginia and the Carolina backcountry had plenty of free land and economic opportunities. Even here, though, the Ulster Irish had difficulties with colonial governments, most commonly regarding the Irishmen's relationship with the local Indian peoples. Colonial leaders frequently complained of their endless efforts to mend relations with Indians as the Ulstermen pushed farther and farther into the frontier and onto lands that colonial governments had secured for the Indians. All was not perfect in Pennsylvania either, as Ulstermen complained that the Quaker-dominated assembly was corrupt and tyrannical and enforced excessive taxation. In protest the Ulster Irish led a march on Philadelphia while their fellow Ulstermen in North Carolina voiced opposition to the colonial government's tyranny, as Ulstermen saw it, in the "Regulation" movement that dominated the backcountry in the 1770s. Neither group found much success, though, especially the Regulators, whose defeat at the battle of Alamance in 1771 included the execution of their leaders.[3]

Despite these conflicts, by the time of the American Revolution most Ulster Irish were successfully adapting to American society, and many of their children defined themselves as Americans with little interest in celebrating their ethnic heritage.[4] In fact, the rare moment when they sought to document their lineage occurred only when they sought to differentiate themselves from later-arriving groups of Irish in America. Ulstermen adopted the title "Scots-Irish" to demonstrate that unlike the destitute Irish Catholics pouring into mid-nineteenth-century America, the Ulster Irish were skilled Presbyterian Scotsmen and were only Irish by virtue of a brief period of settlement in Ireland before they moved on to the United States.[5]

The number of Irish Catholics entering America was limited during the "Great Migration" of Presbyterian Ulstermen. Most Catholics lacked the money for the journey from Ireland and the majority of those who did come arrived as indentured servants or convicts. After serving out their time of servitude or bondage, these Irish Catholic laborers and convicts migrated to the frontier, settling in the Appalachian Mountains where land was inexpensive. Unlike among the Ulster Presbyterians, religion was not an essential component of these immigrants' identity. Many had left Ireland as nonpracticing Catholics, having been born into the faith with little understanding of it and no real devotion to it. For that reason many Irish Catholics settling on the Appalachian frontier in the eighteenth century converted to the Protestant evangelical faiths popular during the Great Awakening or adapted to the traditions of the Ulster Presbyterians on the frontier.[6]

Irish emigration to America slowed during the Napoleonic Wars (1796–1815) and the War of 1812. Both conflicts made transatlantic travel dangerous, and Irish emigration to the United States between 1783 and 1814 is estimated at only 100,000 to 150,000.[7] The next wave of Irish immigration occurred between 1815 and 1845, bringing nearly one million migrants to North America. This nearly doubled the total Irish emigration of the previous two centuries, and by the mid-1830s the majority of this group was arriving in the United States. The primary catalyst for this movement was the economic recession following the Napoleonic Wars that led to the consolidation of estates and the evictions of thousands of Irish tenants, sparking a period of social and economic upheaval as small Protestant landowners and the Irish Catholic tenancy sought control over their increasingly chaotic lives.[8]

News from America also contributed to this rise in immigration. Ulstermen living in Pennsylvania, Virginia, and the Carolinas spoke of the plentiful land and opportunities, and increasing numbers of Irish, Catholic and Protestant, were listening to what emigrant John Bell called the "whisperings of ambition."[9] One Ulsterman living in Philadelphia advised his friends that the "young men of Ireland who wish to be free and happy should leave it and come here as soon as possible. . . . [T]here is no place in the world where a man meets so rich a reward for good conduct and industry as in America."[10] Some Irish Catholics would make this journey, too, but they hesitated to leave home. The peasants were tied to the land by traditions of history, religion, and language, and it would take the dramatic events of the next few decades to convince them to break their economic and cultural ties to Ireland.[11]

The 1820s marked a turning point in the demographics of Irish emigration to America. Although the linen industry improved in the late 1820s and 1830s, it did so in ways that decreased the cottage employment on which spinners and weavers in southern and western Ireland had come to depend. With the additional pressures from declining prices for farm products, an increasing population, and continued religious persecution, Irish Catholics joined those searching for work in England and then moving on to opportunities in America, and between 1820 and 1850 they came to dominate the migration from Ireland.[12]

The reception the Irish received was not welcoming, though not quite as hostile as it would become by the 1840s and 1850s. In the first three decades of the nineteenth century, nativism existed in America, but it was not the organized national movement that it would become by mid-century. Anti-Catholic sentiment, however, existed throughout the young nation, especially where immigrants settled in large numbers and seemed to threaten the Protestant traditions that dominated American life. By the mid-1820s and 1830s, native-born American frustration with the growing Catholic population had increased dramatically.

In 1824, for example, New York City was wracked with the violence of the Greenwich Village Riot of July 12. This was Orange Day, when Irish Protestants celebrated the triumph of the armies of Protestant William of Orange over the Catholic forces of King James II at the Battle of Boyne in 1690. The day began with Irish Protestant laborers marching through Greenwich Village waving orange flags to commemorate the anniversary, a tradition brought with them from Ireland. A determined group of Irish Catholic weavers confronted them and demanded that the Orangemen lower their flags. The ensuing riot injured dozens of Irish Protestants and Catholics, including a pregnant Catholic woman determined to play a role in the defeat of the Orangemen.[13] Arrests and newspaper editorials indicated that each side shared blame, but the punishments handed down were unbalanced. Dozens of Irish Catholics were among those arrested following the riot, but not a single Protestant joined them in jail or at the subsequent trials.[14] As nativism, which had always included a strong anti-Catholic element, intensified, the focus of the protest narrowed beyond the Irish generally to target Irish Catholics in particular.

The 1830s brought continued anti–Irish Catholic activities by the city leaders of New York, Boston, and Philadelphia, who bemoaned issues ranging from the horrible burden of the Irish poor on the cities' charity to the amount of urban property owned by the Catholic Church. In Boston, the famous artist and inventor Samuel F. B. Morse advised Americans that the only way to curb the flow of Catholics, most of whom were Irish, into America was to end immigration. "Awake! To your posts!" warned

Morse. "Place your guards . . . shut your gates!" Joining him were radical Protestant ministers organizing associations to warn the public of the growing Catholic menace. The *Boston Recorder,* the *New York Observer,* and the *Christian Spectator* raged against what they deemed the blasphemy of the Roman Catholic Church, the immorality and idolatry it taught, the cruelty disseminated by its priests, and the submissiveness demanded by the Pope of his minions. Contributing to this was Reverend Henry Ward Beecher, father of Harriet Beecher Stowe and leading northern abolitionist. Beecher raged against the growing Catholic threat to America, and he called on Protestants to rise and meet this menace within the nation.[15]

In 1834, tension erupted into a fiery inferno when a popular account appeared reporting torture and debauchery in a Boston convent. That year Rebecca Reed published *Six Months in a Convent,* which was a fabricated tale of harrowing experiences and escape from the Ursuline convent in Charlestown, Massachusetts, just outside Boston. Nativists had long been suspicious of the activities of the nuns working in the convent school that educated the daughters of some of the city's wealthiest families. In actuality, the young women were exposed to little Catholicism at the convent, where the Ursuline superior Sister Edmund St. George had adjusted religious services and classroom instruction to accommodate the largely Protestant student body.[16] Reed's tale, however, reinforced the nativist public's worst fears, and it quickly became the year's best-selling novel. Within the first week of publication, over ten thousand copies were sold. By the end of the first month a horrified and insatiable public had purchased two hundred thousand copies.[17]

In late July 1834 the events came to a terrifying climax. One Ursuline nun suffered a nervous breakdown and was found wandering through the streets of Charlestown until sisters from the convent located her at her brother's home, where the nun agreed to return to the convent. As the story spread through the city, though, the events evolved into tale of oppressive Catholicism and compromised women. Anti-Catholic activists twisted the nun's experience into a tale of capture and torture in their belief that her experience was like that of Rebecca Reed. Rumors circulated through Boston of the kidnapping of young innocent girls who were forced to remain within the convent against their will, ordered to accept papal doctrines, and subjected to unthinkable violations.

Into this tempest arrived Reverend Lyman Beecher on a speaking tour. In a series of sermons delivered on Sunday, August 10, 1834, Reverend Beecher called Bostonians to arms, demanding that they meet this Catholic menace with resolve and deliver innocent Americans from the papal conspiracy. The following evening a mob of nearly fifty laborers stormed the convent, smashing windows and doors and donning nuns' habits until fire forced them into the gardens. There the men danced around the court-yard and watched, along with fire companies who refused or were too frightened to douse the flames, as the Ursuline convent burned to the ground. While many leading Bostonians later denounced the violence, they applauded the motivations of the mob and their determination to confront the Catholic threat in America.[18]

By the 1840s, similar violence was common in Irish Catholic areas of New York, Boston, and Philadelphia. On May 6, 1844, Protestant com-munity members met in the Irish Catholic–dominated Kensington district of Philadelphia to discuss their fears of the growing Irish Catholic burden on their community and the increasing influence of Catholics in America. The meeting turned violent as members confronted Irish Catholics in the area, and it erupted into a bloody riot lasting three days. The local militia brought an end to the fighting, but the destruction was staggering. Ken-sington was a mess of shattered glass, burning churches, and bleeding men. Two Catholic churches, St. Michael's and St. Augustine's, were de-stroyed, dozens of Irish Catholics had lost their homes in the fires set by the Protestant mob, and sixteen Catholics lay dead. Two months later, similar events occurred in Southwark, followed by smaller incidents in other Irish Catholic sections of Philadelphia. This violence was focused on *Irish* Catholics in particular. Protestants passed several German Catholic churches in the rioting in Kensington and left them unscathed, focusing instead on Irish Catholics, whom they viewed as the most impoverished, lazy, and criminal in America.[19]

Robert Smith, an Ulster Irishman living in Philadelphia, recalled the violence that year with outrage. He had found some success in America and by 1844 worked as a customs house official, one of only three Irish men to hold such a position among the two hundred officials employed, and he insisted that his position was the result of merit and his close per-sonal ties to President John Tyler. That summer, the Protestant Smith wit-nessed the ethnic violence in Philadelphia and expressed outrage at the attacks because he saw them as a blow to all foreigners. "Our city," he told his family in County Antrim, "has been nothing but the scene of bloodshed." The root of the problem was "native [born] American citi-zens forming themselves into a body to deprive all the foreigners of their rights and privileges guaranteed to them by the Constitution." Most of the nativists' rage, Smith explained, was focused

upon the Irish Roman Catholics and at one of their meetings the Irish rose against them and there was a great number shot on both sides. There was a great many Roman Catholic churches and nunneries burned in this city and as many as fifty killed in one riot. There were 20 cannons discharged in one night by the military and mob, and the military was called in from every part of the state to the amount of 20,000, and a great many of them were shot like dogs. . . . [The violence] was horrible, and many a widow and orphan were left by the scene.[20]

Despite attacks like these, or perhaps in determined response to them, many Irish Catholic immigrants remained loyal to their faith and their heritage and this turmoil, in Ireland and the United States, would influence the way they viewed the American Civil War. Survival taught them to protect their own interests, and their support for a cause would, by necessity, depend on how it affected their homes, their families, and their dreams for Ireland or America, or both. These lessons emerged not only in eastern cities with their increasing Irish Catholic populations, but in the West as well.

For the Irish in cities like St. Louis, Missouri, the adjustment to life in America varied. In the antebellum period, the city had a large Irish Protestant and Catholic population, and by 1860 the Irish would comprise nearly the largest immigrant group in the city, with nearly 20 percent of the population of St. Louis, comparable only to Germans. Irish immigrants arriving in the city in the 1830s through the 1860s found active

TABLE 1.1
Irish-born Populations in Major U.S. Cities, 1860

City (Ranked in Order of Largest Irish-born Population)	Total City Population	Total Irish-born City Population	Irish-born as Percentage of Total City Population
1. New York, NY	793,186	203,740	26%
2. Philadelphia, PA	543,344	95,548	18%
3. Brooklyn, NY	262,348	56,710	22%
4. Boston, MA	175,579	45,991	26%
5. St. Louis, MO	157,476	29,926	19%
6. Chicago, IL	108,305	19,889	18%
7. Cincinnati, OH	157,313	19,375	12%
8. Albany, NY	40,099	14,780	37%
9. Newark, NJ	70,654	11,167	16%
10. Lowell, MA	36,786	9,460	26%
11. San Francisco, CA	55,626	9,363	17%
12. Pittsburgh, PA	48,063	9,297	19%
13. Buffalo, NY	80,320	9,279	12%
14. Jersey City, NJ	28,891	7,380	26%
15. Rochester, NY	47,794	6,786	14%
16. Detroit, MI	44,216	5,994	14%
17. Milwaukee, WI	45,140	3,100	7%

SOURCE: *Statistics of the United States (including Mortality, Property, etc.) in 1860; Compiled from the Original Returns and Being the Final Exhibit of the Eighth Census; Under the Direction of the Secretary of the Interior* (Washington: GPO, 1866), lvii–lviii.

Protestant and Catholic organizations that welcomed them, many directed and run by natives of the Emerald Isle. Both groups ran private schools, hospitals, churches, and charitable agencies, and were ready to help immigrants find work in St. Louis. Mother Angela Hughes, sister of New York archbishop John Hughes, for example, helped found the Catholic Orphans' Association in St. Louis in 1841, while Irish-American Jesuit Father George Carrell rose to the presidency of St. Louis University, becoming the institution's first leader of Irish ancestry, in 1842. That same year, George Maguire, a native of Omagh, County Tyrone, became St. Louis's first foreign-born mayor.[21]

Similarly, in San Francisco, Irish immigrants faced a noticeably warmer welcome than that experienced in the more established eastern cities. Part of this difference related to their significant population in San Francisco from its early roots. In early 1848, the city's population numbered just under a thousand, but by 1852 San Franciscans included over forty-two hundred Irish immigrants and fourteen hundred Irish Americans born in the United States. Both Catholics and Protestants comprised these numbers, but many were of the Famine era who had settled in a region noted for its relative tolerance of Catholics. When Terence Bellew McManus, an Irish nationalist exiled to the British penal colonies, escaped and made his way to San Francisco in 1851, the city welcomed him with a large celebration that included the mayor and other leading members of city government. Indeed, the area become a rather common welcome point for escaped Irish exiles, with Patrick O'Donohue arriving in June 1853 and John Mitchel following shortly thereafter. Again, they were welcomed as heroes of the cause of Irish nationalism, not only by Irish Catholics in the city but also by leading members of San Francisco's government.[22]

In Chicago, Illinois, Irish Catholics dominated the city's ethnic population, growing from several hundred in the 1830s to over six thousand by 1850, and through the 1860s, that population would triple. The Chicago Irish found themselves in the interesting position of, along with German-Americans and other immigrants, dominating the native-born population of the city. They tended to cluster not in the ethnic ghettos seen in the East, but rather in parish neighborhoods spread throughout the city. As a result, the acculturation process for the Chicago Irish was more rapid than that seen in other ethnic communities, due to these pockets of Irish life heavily influenced by their surrounding native-born neighbors. Irish-Americans in Chicago clung firmly to their religious and nationalist tradition, indeed becoming more devout Catholics in the United States than many of them had been in Ireland. At the same time, however, they integrated into the larger American society by adapting to the political, economic, and some of the social traditions of the Midwest.[23]

This is not to say that American cities west of the Appalachians were immune to the nativist rumblings of the late 1840s and 1850s, for those fires reached all the way to the Pacific. Indeed, as early as 1836 Elijah Lovejoy, later made famous as a martyr to the abolitionist cause, departed St. Louis insisting that he was a "victim of popular violence" perpetrated by local Catholics, not slave holders. His exodus resulted, he explained, "especially for honestly endeavoring to open the eyes of my countrymen to the danger which threatens their civil and religious rights, from the workings of a foreign despotic influence, carried here by its appropriate instruments, the Jesuits."[24]

Similarly, an immigrant majority in Chicago did not stop the American-born citizens from decrying the onslaught of the foreign-born and supporting the nativist movement of the 1850s. They focused most of their wrath on Irish Catholics, who were strongly united by their faith in Chicago, even more than by politics or nationalism.[25] In 1855, the Republican Chicago *Tribune* sponsored the mayoral Know Nothing candidate and focused most of their demands for reform, including temperance, on the local Irish Catholic population. The *Tribune* argued, "The great majority of members of the Roman Catholic Church in this country are Irishmen. The fact is peculiarly true in this city." The editors continued, "Who does not know that the most depraved, debased, worthless and irredeemable drunkards and sots which curse the community, are Irish Catholics? Who does not know that five-eighths of cases brought up every day before the Mayor for drunkenness and consequent crime, are Irish Catholics?"[26] On average, however, Irish immigrants experienced more tolerance in the 1830s and early 1840s in the Midwest and West than in regions in the eastern United States.[27]

Much of this changed with the Great Potato Famine, which ushered in the largest emigration of Irish Catholics in American history and changed the character of both nations. By the time the famine ended in the early 1850s, over one-quarter of the population of Ireland was either dead or departed. Some historians have estimated Irish deaths by starvation or disease resulting from the Famine at 1.1 to 1.5 million persons, and between 1845 and 1855 nearly 1.5 million Irish (mostly Catholics) traveled to the United States, approximately 340,000 sailed to British North America, another two to three hundred thousand settled elsewhere in Great Britain, and thousands more went to Australia and other parts of the world. It was as though an entire generation had left Ireland: only one in three Irish males born around 1831 died in Ireland of old age, and in communities like Munster it was only one in four.[28]

Given the activities of American nativists on the eve of the Famine migrations, it is little wonder that these immigrants, overwhelmingly

Catholic, received a mixed reception in America, particularly in the eastern regions but also throughout the country. In some cases, there were exceptions to this hostility as citizens responded with surprising sympathy. The Americans had, after all, sent doctors and food for Irish relief, to the extent that the Society of Friends of Ireland recalled, "The chief source whence the means at our disposal were derived was the munificent bounty of the citizens of the United States. The supplies sent from America to Ireland were on a scale unparalleled in history."[29]

Contemporary accounts from Irish-American newspapers note, too, the charity that Americans demonstrated at this time. Cincinnati, Ohio's *Catholic Telegraph* observed, "All the unhappy questions, political and religious, which occasionally add bitterness to life, have been as if by common consent, suppressed," as the fighting subsided between nativists and Catholics in that community.[30] Boston's Irish-American paper the *Pilot* noted,

> Never have the annals of humanity and civilization recorded a more striking exemplification of the devotion of mankind to the cause of human happiness, than in the present grand demonstration in behalf of suffering Ireland. . . . In America, Catholics and Protestants, all without distinction of party or creed have come to the rescue of their starving fellow beings.[31]

Charity was soon overwhelmed, however, by the suffering masses appearing daily in American harbors from Boston to New Orleans, and then other cities throughout the nation.

By the late 1840s, nativist warnings began to resonate more widely. The Boston *Daily Advertiser* complained, "The increase in foreign-born pauperism in our midst is an evil . . . the consideration of which we adjourn until it will, perhaps, be too late to apply a remedy."[32] The reverend Theodore Parker described the Boston Irish as "idle, thriftless, poor, intemperate, and barbarian,"[33] while editorials in the Boston *Advertiser* discussed the rise of juvenile crime, the result of nearly three thousand children, "vicious, criminal, profligate, and abandoned," reduced to begging, stealing, and other "degrading practices." Nativist Bostonians explained that it was primarily the fault of Irish immigrants, "who imported their vile propensities and habits from across the water" and passed such traits on to their "wretched offspring."[34]

The New York and Philadelphia Irish did not find a much warmer welcome. Ellis Paxson Oberholtzer, an historian at the University of Pennsylvania in the 1850s and member of Philadelphia's upper class, described the Irish Catholic immigrants' "revolting vicious habits. Being of the lower order of mankind, they were repellent to those who were further advanced in the social scale."[35] Such descriptions made common appearances in local newspapers.

By the mid-1850s, the Irish of St. Louis experienced the force of rising nativism as well, and Catholic and Protestant Irish failed to maintain the significant level of cooperation that had defined their role in the city in earlier years. As one historian explained, "From 1854 forward, to be Irish in St. Louis meant to be Catholic," while the Protestant Irish blended into the majority of the population.[36] That very year, for example, so many Irish Catholic women worked as domestics in private homes that St. John the Evangelist Parish established a mass at 5:00 A.M. every morning so the girls could attend services before their households awoke and they had to be at their duties.[37] Two years earlier, a local mob, fearing the potential influence of local Irish Catholics in the election of Democrat Franklin Pierce, indicated their rage at not only the recently arrived immigrants but also the more established Irish Catholics, capable of voting and holding at least a level of respect in St. Louis. They ransacked homes and businesses throughout the more prominent Irish sections of town, and targeted at least one church as well.

When the rioters arrived at St. Louis University, they were puzzled to find Father John Baptist Druyts, a Belgian-born Jesuit, who, through his confident pacing before the gates of the school, quietly reciting the Psalms, convinced the mob the school must be so heavily defended that they should depart. It was a bluff, but it worked. Two years later, in August 1854, a judge insisted on carefully checking the naturalization papers of every voter in the Irish Fifth Ward on election day. As the lines grew along with the summer heat, tempers boiled over into another riot. They mayor sent in local soldiers who reestablished calm, but they did little to repair the prejudices between Irish Catholics and their nativist neighbors.[38]

These divisions existed not just between native-born Americans and immigrants but also within the Irish population itself as the old tensions between Protestants and Catholics surfaced in communities like Iowa City, Iowa. In the spring of 1856, Irish-American Henry Allen, a Presbyterian minister, commiserated with an old friend in Dublin. "The opposition you speak of as existing in the city of Dublin is even here," Allen wrote.

> "Fullness of bread and abundance of idleness"—worldly pride and the monster Romanism are all here. If Rome is losing ground in Europe she is moving heaven and earth to plant and cultivate her heresy in America. Every new place here in the west that is likely to be a place of importance she is occupying, and by those arts known only to her, she is laboring to disseminate her dogmas.[39]

The pinnacle of American nativism was the Order of the Star-Spangled Banner, also called the American party but most well known as the Know Nothings for their habit of denying all knowledge of the secret organization's traditions. Tracing their roots to the 1830s and having evolved through several political titles, the Know Nothings rose to prominence in the 1850s, riding the tide of nativism. They characterized themselves and their purpose as "Anti-Romanism, Anti-Bedinism, Anti-Pope's Toeism, Anti-Nunneryism, Anti-Winking Virginism, Anti-Jesuitism, and Anti-the-Whole-Sacerdotal-Hierarchism with all its humbugging mummeries. Know Nothingism is for light, liberty, education and absolute freedom of conscience."[40] At its core, this movement was comprised of native-born white Protestants viewing immigrants, most particularly Catholics and their beliefs, as gravely threatening to the United States and its Protestant cultural traditions.[41] It is significant to note that the Know Nothings never supported the idea of closing the doors to immigrants, but rather advocated extending naturalization periods and employing other methods to ensure that the foreign-born were fully Americanized before exercising the rights of citizenship. As native-born Americans experienced the onrush of immigration in the mid–nineteenth century, particularly that of Irish and German Catholics who clung to their religious roots rather than adopting the predominant Protestant habits of the United States, the Know Nothings' popularity increased. They showed impressive returns in the elections of 1854 and 1855 throughout New England and the north Atlantic states, with their greatest victories occurring in Massachusetts, where nativists controlled the governor's office and both houses of the state legislature. These were major results considering the fact that one of the country's largest immigrant populations lived in Boston, Massachusetts, and the nativists made enormous advances in the Northeast despite, and in response to, its large number of immigrants.[42]

In the midst of this struggle between the nativists' hopes for the future and those of Irish Catholics, some families split on the issue. Brothers William and Michael Shaughnessy of County Limerick immigrated to the United States separately, Michael in 1836 and William in 1849. While Michael and his family settled in Granville, Wisconsin, William preferred the climate of Jackson, Mississippi, and by the 1850s, both men and their families enjoyed financial security in America. While adjusting to the economic, political, and social traditions of the country, they remained fiercely loyal to the Irish heritage and their Catholic faith. When their brother George immigrated to America, probably in the late 1840s or early 1850s, he settled in Wisconsin and married a Protestant woman. When George converted to the Methodist faith, William raged against his brother's determined abandonment of Catholicism. He declared George "a downright imposter, an infidel," after George made such claims as, "The Popish Priest has a charter in his pocket that by blowing and spitting on bread and wine he can create a little Jesus Christ every time he pleases." William burned the letter and insisted that he would receive no more from his brother.[43]

While George appears to have embraced the traditions of nineteenth-century native-born Americans by marrying a Protestant and adopting her faith, William and Michael remained staunch defenders of their Catholic traditions and their heritage. In 1856, they commiserated over the fact that both were dropping the "O" from the front of their surname. Upon learning that Michael was "determined to prefix" his name with an "O" in the future, William insisted this was "perfectly right." The two men even corresponded occasionally in Gaelic, and William noted, "when you wrote to me last year in the Irish language, I saw that the name could not be spoken without prefixing O. . . . [A]nyone may know that the Irish is older than the English language. . . . [W]hy should we adopt England's policy to our own destruction."[44] The divisions between nativists and foreign-born cut deeply in the 1850s, but it is significant to note that they divided the Irish community as well, not just between families but within them, and in the case of the Shaughnessys, the feud appears to have been permanent.

Across the country, Irish Catholic immigrants felt the nativists' disapproval, and as slavery became an increasingly divisive and defining quality of the 1850s, it did not help matters that northern Know Nothings, who attracted large numbers of Free-Soilers and antislavery activists, linked Irish Catholics with the proslavery movement.[45] As one Know Nothing lodge in Massachusetts asserted, "There can be no real hostility to Roman Catholicism which does not embrace slavery, its natural co-worker in opposition to freedom and republican institutions."[46] Meanwhile in Ohio, Know Nothing President Thomas Spooner asserted, "Americanism [i.e., Know Nothingism] and Freedom are synonymous terms. . . . Foreignism and Slavery are equally so, and the one is antipodes of the other." Similarly, Know Nothings in Hartford, Connecticut, insisted, "we contend for Freedom as well as Americanism. We oppose the extension of slavery as well as the spread of Romanism. We are as hostile to the march of the slave oligarchy as we are to the control of a foreign potentate over free America."[47] As the turmoil of the early 1850s grew, so too did nativists' support of the Know Nothings, and their actions challenged the ease with which Irish Catholics adjusted to life in America.

Nativists were not alone, though, in understanding the power of politics. Irish Catholics may have arrived in America with few skills, but among them was a valuable understanding of the power and economic

opportunities that could be acquired through politics. Much of this understanding was acquired through centuries of resistance to British laws and
had been most recently developed by Irish nationalist Daniel O'Connell's politicization of the Irish people. O'Connell mobilized the Irish for
political action and taught them to organize locally and work toward
their goals within a resistant Anglo-Saxon Protestant system. As Irishmen
arrived in America, they applied this knowledge to the Anglo-American
Protestant system.[48]

Irishmen had other advantages in the American political system. Politics and politicians were not celebrated nor particularly respected in the
United States. Wealthy Americans encouraged their sons to enter careers
in business, law, or medicine, not politics, which was viewed as a sordid
arena necessary to the workings of democracy but not something in which
a gentleman involved himself.[49] Political positions, especially at the local
level, were often left to those unable to secure more desired employment.
Naturalized Irish-Americans would use these positions and the established
system of graft and favoritism, combined with later activities in labor
unions and the church, to climb the socioeconomic ladder of America.

Most of the Irish in America belonged to the Democratic party and had
done so for generations. For the Ulster Irish of early immigration, the
party of choice was the Democratic-Republicans. This preference was not
the result of an active recruitment of the Irish by the party of Jefferson.
Rather, it stemmed from the fact that the Federalist party was the one calling for stricter naturalization laws, which culminated in the 1798 Alien
and Sedition Acts, and exhibiting an Anglophilia characterized in their
support of the Jay Treaty and favorable trade policies with Britain. The
Federalists reminded many Irish-Americans, Protestant and Catholic, of
the British Tories, as did the Federalists' Whig successors, who were reminiscent of a wealthy, propertied, Protestant class with continued anti-
immigrant sentiments.[50]

By the 1820s the Irish supported the new Democratic party. Jackson
was popular with the Irish because of his Scots-Irish ancestry and his bril-
liant defeat of the British at New Orleans in 1815. The Whigs would
retain the anti-immigrant stance of the Federalists, and when the Republican party was born in the 1850s, it included a sizable membership of former Whigs, Free Soilers, and the nativist Know Nothings.

It was not, however, merely a matter of exclusion that led the Irish into
the Democratic party. Just as the Federalists and Whigs contained elements opposed to immigrant interests by the 1840s, so the Democratic
party actively courted immigrants and, in particular, Irish Catholics. In
1848 the Democrats characterized this outreach effort with a call on "our
naturalized fellow citizens, . . . Frenchmen, Germans, Irish, English" to

contemplate the impact of a Whig victory. The Whigs were "the party that passed the infamous alien law—the party who would never permit you to become citizens of this land of liberty, . . . the party that openly leagues with the proscriptive native Americans to overthrow the democracy who stand by your rights and privileges." The Democrats closed by reminding the Irish in particular that the Whig Zachary Taylor was "the favorite candidate of the Native American organizations . . . for President. . . . Let Irish citizens think well of this matter, before giving one vote to the party of American Orangemen."[51]

Not all Irish Catholics saw the increasing political participation of their friends and neighbors as a positive sign. Michael Doheny, who would later help to found the Irish nationalist Fenian movement, fled Ireland for his role in the failed 1848 uprising and consciously resisted an active role in American politics. To him, the American political system held little hope for Irishmen. He saw Whigs as direct descendents of the old Federalists and trusted nothing they said, but he did defend the Democratic party against the accusation that it was a defender of slavery. He insisted when speaking with old friend and fellow nationalist William Smith O'Brien that the Democratic party was first and foremost the defender of equal rights. The Republicans, he argued, were simply the result of an unholy marriage between the Whigs and the Know Nothings, and offered nothing for the Irish in America.

Despite his defense of the Democrats, Doheny remained disgusted with the political activism of his fellow Irishmen. He believed "success has become their God, and morality is acquiring it—utterly despicable. They are mimickers of gigantic swindling. In virtue of being somebody in public estimation every other virtue is absorbed." Within politics, "they aspire to places precisely in proportion to their ignorance and rascality. In this of course they are countenanced by the American politician who uses their subordinate gains as a lever to raise himself."[52]

However it was gained, the Irish vote within the Democratic party became so powerful that this was a frequent warning in northern Know Nothing speeches. Later in the 1850s, many Republicans blamed Irish-Americans for John C. Fremont's presidential defeat in 1856 and considered the Irish their "uncompromising foe." *Harper's Weekly* noted this as well, warning that "the Irish race in the United States is very powerful, far more so than its numbers justify. It rules most of the large cities, not only on the seaboard, but in the interior also."[53] Irish-born Patrick Dunny, who arrived in Philadelphia in 1854, gleefully agreed with that assessment. He explained, "there never was excitement in America before at an Election" like that of James Buchanan in 1856. "Nor [had] the Americans never got a home blow before the Irish came out victorious," he added, and now they "claim as good a right here as Americans themselves." As to how a man who left Ireland in 1854 managed to vote in that election, Dunny offered only hints: "I am not here two years until next spring and I had the honor of voting at the last two elections which I got through the very best of interest," and without these connections, he explained, "I would have to wait five years for other ways and what those I allude to will have to do."[54]

The Know Nothings and others might have been outraged by such illegal activities, but Dunny saw it as one of the wonders of America and as part of exercising the kind of power that would earn him respect in his new life. "It won't do," he explained to his parents, to arrive in America and say, "I had such and was such and such at home. . . . Strangers here, they must gain respect by their conduct and not by their tongue."[55] While many native-born Americans and dedicated civics educators of the day would have been horrified with the concept of using illegal voting to earn legitimacy—completely missing the focus on constitutional law and the responsibilities of citizenship—Dunny preferred to skip straight to the act of casting the ballot. He, like many antebellum Americans, understood this act to be one of the key tenets of respectability and power.

Fellow Philadelphian James Dixon may have agreed with Dunny's methods, but he was far less positive on the wonders of America. An Irish Catholic who appears to have emigrated in the late 1840s, Dixon made his living as a merchant seaman and by the mid-1850s had traveled extensively between Philadelphia, New York, and Jamaica, as well as having spent several years living in California. By 1855, disappointed with "dull" business in the East, he was considering returning that November to California, where economic reports indicated business was "never more promising than . . . at present and I find I can do as much better there than any where I have been yet."

Even so, he warned his family against emigration to any part of America. As he explained to his sister living in County Wexford, Ireland, "Affairs are becoming fearful in this country, the Know Nothings have murdered a number of Irishmen in Louisville and destroyed their property, and [the] feeling continue[s] as it is on the increase. An Irishman will not get to live in this country." Even in Ireland, Dixon argued, "if people are poor . . . they will be protected from murderers like the Louisville affair."[56] Despite his frustrations, Dixon appears to have remained in America, though he settled in California, which had a reputation for greater tolerance for Irish Catholics.

The Irish of Chicago experienced similar gains in political power during this time period. Because they comprised nearly one-fifth of the city's population and exercised significant and unified political participation, the Chicago Irish wielded considerable power within the Democratic party in the 1830s, 1840s, and 1850s. They faced a minor setback during the height of nativism in 1855, but quickly reclaimed the city from a Know Nothing mayor after one year in 1856. Nativists continued to speak out against their political power, but numbers and activism worked in the favor of the Irish. In the 1850s, for example, Irish-Americans held positions on the city council, and by 1860, they comprised 46 percent of the Chicago police force.[57]

With their growing political influence, increasing numbers of Irish Catholics challenged some of the Protestant traditions in American public life, and they did so with the growing power of the Catholic Church in America. Archbishop John Hughes of New York dreamed of uniting the Catholics of America to improve the church and their lives in this nation.[58] With increasing influence, Irish Catholic leaders demanded an end to Bible readings in the public school system, largely because they were conducted via the Protestant King James Bible. In Maryland, New York, Ohio, and Pennsylvania, Catholics lobbied state legislatures to provide public funds for the parochial schools teaching Catholic doctrines. Nativists warned that Catholics had "been taught to idolize the Pope of Rome as an incarnate God . . . and [had been] trained in the unrepublican habit of passive obedience and non-resistance to a foreign *Hierarch* who claims the right to think for them," and nativists pointed to the recent demands by the Irish Catholic community as evidence of this.[59]

Catholic leaders in St. Louis, Missouri, however, lacked a large Irish population to promote their goals. Catholic Church leaders saw the years of Protestant influence within the public schools as the real problem. In the 1850s, quiet young Father James Henry marched his pupils from St. Lawrence O'Toole's Catholic school in a procession past the local public schools in protest of the bias against Catholicism he saw within public education. The debates in St. Louis never became quite as heated as those in the East, but they still divided the community in the antebellum period.[60]

The Irish Catholics of San Francisco had a similar experience. While the extremists on both sides of the debate fought aggressively, there were enough moderate options to make the education debate in San Francisco one of the least controversial of the debates in America's major cities with a significant Catholic population. This was partly due to the approach of leading politicians and partly to the influence that Irish Catholics carried in a community that lacked a powerful, established Protestant base. In 1851, for example, city leaders allowed public funds to support private Catholic schools. While this ended a year later with the nativist movement of that decade, and the Know Nothings controlled seven of the eight wards of San Francisco by 1854, the following year saw city leaders consciously employing Catholic teachers in the public school system, and even arranging for Catholic teachers to work in Protestant parochial schools and Protestant educators to serve in the Catholic parish schools. While this angered the radicals on both sides, such gestures pleased the general public in antebellum San Francisco as a suitable compromise, and that year Democrats took back four of the eight wards. The city possessed its conservative Protestant leaders, including members of the powerful Committee of Vigilance, organized in the 1850s to bring law and order to San Francisco, who often overlooked legal methods to accomplish their goals and frequently targeted the Irish Catholics in the city. The evidence indicates, however, that due to their relatively large population, political organization, and the lack of a historic, Protestant base in the community, the San Francisco Irish exercised more power and fell victim to less powerful prejudice than those in the East.[61]

In some of the eastern sections of the country, however, and even at the national level, other groups saw the importance of reaching out to the nation's growing immigrant population. Some political leaders recognized their potential power and sought out their support. In a gesture to potential immigrant voters, the Republicans revised their party platform in the election of 1860, pledging to oppose

[a]ny change in naturalization laws or any state legislation by which the rights of citizens hitherto accorded to immigrants from foreign lands shall be abridged or impaired; and in favor of giving a full and efficient protection to the rights of all classes of citizens, whether native or naturalized, both at home and abroad.[62]

By this time, however, the problems between many immigrants, especially Irish Catholics, and the Republican party reached beyond their anti-immigrant roots. Many Irishmen also opposed the radical wings of the Republican party, especially the abolitionists.

Ironically, in the early 1840s a series of events indicated that the Irish might have chosen to support the abolitionist cause as one similar to their own. These events concerned the relationship leading abolitionist William Lloyd Garrison formed with Irish nationalist Daniel O'Connell, who was at the height of his power in the Irish Repeal Movement, calling for peaceful agitation to demand home rule for Ireland. O'Connell had found success and fame using similar methods to secure Catholic emancipation in Ireland a decade earlier, and he was recognized in Ireland and America as a leading advocate of Irish freedom and the emancipation of American slaves. As early as 1829, O'Connell chastised America for retaining this institution and pledged that he would not visit the country so long as slavery remained.

Given these views, he was a natural choice for the American abolitionists in their effort to recruit numbers to their movement. When they read O'Connell's pledge and antislavery statements to Irish- and native-born American audiences, however, the results were disappointing. At first, Bostonians at Fanieul Hall seemed to support O'Connell's call: "Irishmen and Irishwomen! *Treat the colored people as your equals, as brethren. By your memories of Ireland, continue to love liberty—hate slavery*—CLING BY THE ABOLITIONISTS—and *in America you will do honor to the name of Ireland.*"[63] The crowd responded enthusiastically to each refrain of O'Connell's speech. Some later noted that few Irish attended the rally, and those Irish who read the speech in the morning paper were not in support at all.

Irish-American papers throughout the Northeast were quick to respond. The Boston *Pilot* had already characterized abolitionism as "thronged with bigoted and persecuting religionists; with men who in their private capacity, desire the extermination of Catholics by fire and sword." Now the paper argued that Irishmen would never ally with a group whose policies would "bathe the whole South in blood" and only weaken America as a whole. In fact, the *Pilot* continued, that was the entire problem with abolition. Irish-Americans should not view it as a reform focused on freeing slaves as Ireland had tried to free itself from British rule. Rather, argued the *Pilot,* this was all part of a British strategy to weaken the one nation that offered salvation to so many Irish. The *Pilot* asked, "Can the exiled victims of British oppression relinquish the hate they bear the oppressor, and lend their influence for the furtherance of his subtle schemes?"[64] Similarly, the Boston *Catholic Diary* recognized slavery as unjust, but feared more the "zealots who would madly attempt to eradicate the evil by the destruction of our federal union." The *Catholic Diary* announced further that O'Connell had "no right to shackle the opinions of the Irishmen of America. . . . We can tell the abolitionists that we acknowledge no dictation from a foreign source."[65]

Archbishop Hughes thought the speech a fabrication, but added that if it was not, he thoroughly disapproved of O'Connell's statements. As a central leader to the Irish of New York and as the figurehead of Irish Catholic America, Hughes proclaimed it

[t]he duty of every naturalized Irishman to resist and repudiate the address with indignation. . . . I am no friend of slavery, but I am still less friendly to any attempt of foreign origin to abolish. The duty of naturalized Irishmen or others, I consider to be in no wise distinct or different

from those of native born Americans. And if it be proved an attempt has been made by this address, or any other address, to single them out on any question appertaining to the foreign or domestic policy of the United States, in any other capacity than that of the whole population, then it will be their duty to their country and their conscience, to rebuke such an attempt come from what foreign source it may, in the most decided manner and language that common courtesy will permit.[66]

Many other Irish Americans agreed with Archbishop Hughes.

Irish miners in Pottsville, Pennsylvania, rejected the idea of African-Americans being their "brethren." Furthermore, they resented a foreigner, even an Irishman, criticizing an American domestic policy, and one that they believed was a legacy from British rule. Here they saw themselves as at least as much American as Irish, and perhaps more American than Irish, proclaiming, "We do not form a distinct class of the community, but consider ourselves in every respect as CITIZENS of this great and glorious republic" and "we look upon every attempt to address us, otherwise than as CITIZENS, upon the subject of abolition of slavery, or any subject whatsoever, as base and iniquitous, no matter from what quarter it may proceed."[67] Just as other Irish-Americans had done and would continue to do, the Pottsville miners were shifting between their American and Irish identities depending on the situation, and in this case they insisted on being viewed as Americans.

As if this result were not bad enough, abolitionists faced a new problem. Southern slaveholders were announcing their support of O'Connell's Irish Repeal Movement, and American branches of O'Connell's Loyal National Repeal Association (LNRA) were accepting their donations and public support. Southern politicians and public leaders offered their support, the most prominent being Robert Tyler, President John Tyler's son. The young Tyler endorsed the LNRA, announcing, "All I know is that I love Irishmen and hate tyranny in every form."[68] Garrison was horrified. Not only had the American Irish failed to heed O'Connell's call to abolition, but they were also joining with the slave South to support O'Connell's Repeal Movement.

The Irish leader eventually denounced the support of slaveholders and all Irish-Americans who associated with them, proclaiming, "Over the broad Atlantic, I pour forth my voice, saying, Come out of such a land, you Irishmen; or, if you remain, and dare countenance the system of slavery that is supported there, we will recognize you as Irishmen no longer."[69] O'Connell realized that this might be the end of Irish-American financial support so crucial to his Repeal efforts, and he was right. Irish

South Carolinians announced, "as the alternative has been presented to us by Mr. O'Connell, as we must choose between Ireland and South Carolina, we say South Carolina forever!"[70] Not all Irish-American Repeal associations reacted so strongly, but the general consensus held that O'Connell's demands were too high. Irish-American support for abolition required them to embrace the very group that decried the plight of the slave while ignoring the suffering of Irish laborers in the northern mills and factories.

In addition, O'Connell and the American abolitionists' actions appeared, to many Irish-Americans and Americans alike, as a violation of the U.S. Constitution. Irish editors and community leaders argued that America and its institutions were the last great hope for the Irish and that any call to reject or disobey American political doctrines was a blow struck at Irish salvation here on earth. As the Boston *Pilot* argued, "the Union of these States is the Alpha and Omega of [Irishmen's] hopes for the future, as it has been their shield and protection during the past."[71]

One final factor prevented many Irish Catholics from joining the abolitionist cause. Many Protestant reformers emerged from the Second Great Awakening religiously committed to moral and social reform. They shifted the traditional Christian emphasis away from original sin and replaced it with a focus on personal involvement in improving human society and, in the process, actively choosing salvation.[72]

This was in sharp contradiction to the beliefs of much of the American Catholic community. The *Catholic Telegraph and Advocate,* the Cincinnati diocesan newspaper, expressed this dichotomy in 1852:

There will always be sickness, poverty, grief, weeping, in the world. The world is cursed—and the malediction of God—the necessity of redemption—will remain on it to the end of time. . . . Any doctrine of progress that teaches us to look for happiness in this world is false and to be rejected even without examination.[73]

The Baltimore *U.S. Catholic Magazine* warned fellow Catholics of this age of reform and its

[f]atal doctrine of humanitarianism and socialism, which pretend to do more for man than the gospel itself, and promise him perfection and a paradise on earth. . . . The present life is but a journeying, through many trials, dangers and sufferings, to a higher state of existence, . . . the government and ministry of the church have for their object only to prepare man for these better enjoyments of a future world.[74]

Thus in the 1840s and 1850s, high points in the Protestant American reform movement, the controversial issues that divided a nation also clarified the division between Protestants and Catholics in America.

The discussions surrounding slavery, temperance, women's rights, and the various reform movements of the mid–nineteenth century captured this division. The temperance movement was particularly unpopular with German and Irish immigrants in America, who saw the call to prohibit the sale of liquor on Sundays, or altogether, as a direct attack on one of the few pleasures of the working poor. The movement was also viewed as a nativist attack on their foreign traditions and served as another example of the disparity between Protestant natives and Catholic immigrants in America.

In 1851 Baltimore's *Catholic Mirror* captured the range of this immigrant indignation by arguing, "The pulpit, not in the legislative halls, is the place to inculcate temperance," while Cincinnati's *Catholic Telegraph and Advocate* declared the temperance laws to be "a scheme as ridiculous as ever emanated from the fanatical brain." Similar warnings came from the Boston *Pilot* and the New York *Irish-American*, who worried about the fanaticism behind the temperance legislation, arguing that such zeal was more threatening to American institutions than intemperance could ever be.[75]

In 1842, Philadelphia rioters released their frustrations on the issue by attacking temperance reformers. Ulster Irish immigrant Robert Smith, who would be outraged by nativist attacks on Irish Catholics in 1844, participated in this riot against African-American temperance reformers. "The Negroes were walking in a temperance procession," Smith noted in 1842, "with their banners displaying what we did not like" and of the "one to two thousand colored people in the procession about 12 o'clock a.m., and about 2 o'clock p.m. there was not the face of a single colored person to be seen in either our city or county. There was estimated about 5,000 whites in the mob, and the massacre was dreadful." Admitting that he was with the mob for most of the violence, Smith insisted he was not there for all of the attacks. "I thought it a pious notion to keep clear of such scrapes," he explained. "The white mob burned the first night property belonging to the colored people to the amount of 25,000 dollars, consisting of their hall and one of their churches, which I think was a shame for them to molest the temple of the Lord."

It is significant to note the complexity of this situation within the Irish-American community. Robert Smith was Protestant, and not particularly fond of Catholics or African-Americans. As he explained, "We have had a serious time lately with the colored people and the whites, the Catholics being the worst of the two." For Smith, this fight crossed religious lines into an attack on a cultural pleasure. He saw temperance as the primary evil in this situation and focused his attention on the African-American marchers.[76]

Thus in the end, this was a complicated situation involving the traditions of various groups that did not always get along. The overarching argument between Protestants and Catholics in America often involved their interpretations of the Christian faith. Sometimes, though, Irish Protestants and Catholics in America, who strongly disagreed on such matters, could cooperate on an issue they saw as attacking their ethnic traditions.

Within Irish-American Catholic communities, though, their conservatism on the reform issues, especially the most controversial subject of slavery, was grounded in their religious beliefs. As historian Francis Hueston explained, many Catholic editors and Irish Catholic leaders

> believed that since legitimate civil power came from God, one must obey laws and constituted authorities, unless they patently contradicted another law of God. In accordance with papal announcements, the editors condemned the slave trade. Slavery itself, they argued, was undesirable, but not unjust *per se* (not intrinsically immoral) and, therefore, laws supporting it had to be obeyed.[77]

For large numbers of Irish Catholics, therefore, slavery was a political issue that did not contradict their religious beliefs or practices.

This difference of opinion was a problem Irish Catholics faced with other groups as well, including political organizations that would seem to appeal to many Irish-Americans. Groups such as the Free Soilers were calling for greater economic freedom for workingmen and the end to economic systems (slavery, for example) that threatened such freedom. The theory might have been very attractive to poor Irish laborers, but instead they opposed the Free Soilers' resistance to the restraints and order many Irish-Americans perceived as necessary for a well-ordered society. They viewed Free Soiler beliefs as a violation of the laws of God and nature. Catholic editor Orestes Brownson captured this in his declaration that

> we see not in Free-Soilism a single redeeming element. It is wild, lawless, destructive fanaticism. The leaders of the party that sustain it are base and unprincipled men, whose morality is cant, whose piety is maudlin sentiment, and whose patriotism is treason. A more graceless set of deluded fanatics or unmitigated hypocrites could not be found, were we to search the world over.

Brownson then went so far as to argue that

> no religious man, no loyal citizen, can, after the developments the party has recently given, any longer adhere to it, or afford it the least conceivable countenance. Whoever continues to support it can be excused from treason only on the ground that he is insane, or else that he stands too low in the scale of intelligence to be responsible for acts.[78]

Protestant American reformers responded in kind, arguing that Catholics were friendly to slavery and hostile to freedom, and Republican leader George William Curtis pointed out that "American civilization, in its ideal, is historically, the political aspect of the Reformation. America is a permanent protest against absolutism." Republican John P. Hale concurred, explaining that Catholicism was inherently a threat to American traditions that could "only be maintained . . . on the principle of Protestant liberty."[79]

These difficulties within the political system were echoed in Irish efforts to succeed in the labor market. More than any other immigrant group in mid-nineteenth-century America, the Irish arrived without labor skills. The Irish being a largely agricultural people, very few of them made it to the western farmlands of the United States or even those in upstate New York and western Pennsylvania and Massachusetts. Upon arrival most of the Famine Irish were so poor that immediate further travel was economically and physically impossible. Some Irish managed to escape the tenements of New York to travel to the smaller cities like Albany, Buffalo, and Rochester.[80] Non–Irish Catholics and those with some labor skills had much more success in moving beyond New York, with as many as 60 percent staying only a few weeks in New York City before settling in the interior of the United States.[81] Most of the Irish poor were unable to move beyond their first homes in America and other may not have wished to. American farming involved far more land than these peasants were accustomed to working, and the homes in rural America were separated by vast spaces. For the rural Irish, visiting with neighbors and participating in activities within their local community were parts of everyday life. The cities of America were not only frequently the sole choice for the Famine Irish, but they also held Irish neighbors, a parish community, and relief organizations that offered security in this new and foreign world.[82]

With few labor skills and little understanding of labor organization, the Irish found jobs that were routinely the lowest paying and worst in the city, located along the docks and near the tenements they now called home. Without labor skills and with as many as one-third to one-half the Famine Irish speaking Gaelic, they were twice as likely as fellow German immigrants to take positions as common laborers. Some historians estimate that in 1850s Boston 22 percent of German immigrants compared to 6 percent of Irish immigrants found nonmanual jobs. Fifty-seven percent of Germans found positions as skilled laborers compared to 23 percent of the Irish immigrants. For a time, free Blacks in Boston were economically and socially more secure during the late 1840s and 1850s than the Irish. New York City and Philadelphia offer similar statistics. Many of the Irish immigrants who did arrive with some labor skills found their employment ability decline as they aged, because they were skilled in crafts whose demand was fading in an industrializing nation. Each passing year saw Irish stevedores reduced to longshoremen and Irish building contractors, to common laborers.[83]

Irish women, however, did find work. Most white Americans considered domestic service belittling and refused to take positions commonly held by free or enslaved African-Americans. Irish immigrant women were not as selective, and they came to dominate the service industry by the middle of the nineteenth century. For those who could not find or hold positions as domestics, their story was much more like that described above. Many had to find work in the growing factories and mills in northern American cities, and the most destitute resorted to prostitution. In 1850s New York City, Irish women dominated prostitution, and like the Irishmen who found work as indentured servants and common Irish laborers, they were frequently referred to as "white slaves" and "white niggers," indicating the proximity of their socioeconomic condition to that of free or enslaved African-Americans.

Irish-Americans labored in the worst jobs because of their desperate need and lack of skills, which was caused in part by and contributed to the fact that many native-born Americans saw them as valueless compared to native-born white and even slave labor. Irish-Americans desperate for other opportunities to improve their socioeconomic condition often joined the military. It offered a steady income with room and board and afforded an escape from oppressive urban squalor. In the 1850s, foreign-born soldiers comprised the majority of army personnel. Between 1850 and 1851, for example, 3,516 immigrants entered the United States Army, and of these 2,113 came from Ireland.[84] These incentives may not have been sufficiently enticing to attract large numbers of native-born Americans, but they offered significant financial opportunities for poor, unskilled immigrants and a chance to learn American customs and traditions, which could lead to more employment options. Some scholars have failed to recognize this fact, and emphasize instead the low pay and poor conditions of military service, concluding that few would have voluntarily sought such a life. Examining military service from an immigrant, unskilled laborer's perspective makes its significant benefits more apparent.[85] During the American Civil War these opportunities continued to attract Irish volunteers, who could earn impressive sums from enlistment bounties by the final years of the war.

Immigrant representation in the military had increased steadily since the 1820s. Almost immediately, this growing ethnic representation in the military became a concern for the U.S. Army, and as early as the late 1820s, military leaders took steps to limit immigrants' enlistment. The U.S. Army developed new restrictions, initially insisting that all recruits must be U.S. citizens and later amending this to a policy where "[n]o foreigner shall be enlisted in the army without special permission from general head-quarters." In addition, the adjutant general of the Army, Robert Jones, opened an investigation to determine the impact of immigrant restrictions on recruiting and to ascertain whether foreign or native soldiers were more likely to enlist. The study revealed that there had been a serious decline in the number of recruits coming from eastern cities, which were centers of large immigrant populations and traditionally the most successful areas for enlistments. Studying immigrants' versus native soldiers' character and general skill, investigators concluded that they were generally of equal quality, though the authors did conclude that some foreign soldiers were of "turbulent character and intemperate habits." Lieutenant Colonel Enos Cutler, superintendent for the Eastern Department and a chief member conducting the study, concluded that he preferred not to have immigrants in the U.S. Army unless commanders could renew the punishment of flogging, which Congress had outlawed in 1812. Other investigators challenged this view of immigrant disobedience by pointing out that foreigners were less likely to desert than native-born soldiers. Cutler's call had some support, however, because the practice of flogging was reinstated in 1833 for cases of desertion, but then outlawed once again and permanently in 1861 (flogging was outlawed in the U.S. Navy in 1850).[86]

The committee summarized its findings with the comment that whatever problems some personnel might have with immigrant servicemen, manpower demands required removal or serious reduction in restrictions against foreign enlistments. Secretary of War John C. Spenser responded in 1842, proposing that the U.S. Army accept immigrants intending to become naturalized American citizens. Within another five years, all conditions on immigrant enlistments were dropped, with the single exception that all recruits have a "competent knowledge of the English language."[87]

Several possibilities explain high rates of enlistment among immigrants. Many were tempted by the steady paycheck. In the 1840s, army recruiters informed men that over a five-year enlistment they could save up to seven hundred dollars in wages and that they had the opportunity, in theory at least, to earn more as they rose through the ranks in a system based on merit rather than class. While the pay was lower on average than that which many common laborers could earn in mid-nineteenth-century America, other incentives balanced these economic discrepancies.

On average, common laborers could earn $272 annually in 1850s America if they worked consistently for six days a week throughout the year.[88] This was not, however, a common immigrant experience. Even if Irishmen could find economically competitive work, it was usually for short periods of time, followed by long stretches when their wives or the poor houses supported them.

In contrast, the base annual income for enlisted personnel in the U.S. Army ranged from $132 to $252 in the 1850s. The average pay for un-skilled labor was higher than army pay, but the provisions that accom-panied military salary made this alternative quite attractive. Recruiters reminded Irishmen that their work in the military was steady, not spo-radic as with many jobs available in the cities. More importantly, supple-ments included housing, regular meals, clothing, and free medical care by trained professionals. From this perspective, enlistment in the U.S. Army was an attractive alternative.[89]

Some recruiters went so far as to offer additional incentives, including a twenty-dollar signing bonus (although that was abolished in 1833 for encouraging the "wrong sort" into service) or a hundred acres of western farmland and free transportation to the frontier. The Irish responded. By the 1850s, when foreigners comprised two-thirds of the army's strength, Irish-Americans constituted nearly 60 percent of the total.[90]

Immigrants who did enlist found the army quite different from the recruitment posters. Irish soldiers learned quickly that nativist prejudice infested the army as well. Many officers viewed all enlisted men, native and immigrant, with disdain because of their generally poor, working-class backgrounds and their lack of education. A U.S. Army doctor in the 1840s warned recruiters,

> In its illimitable resources, this country insures to every variety of talent and to every effort of industry, an ample return. Where, then, a man is reduced to the necessity of enlistment to secure subsistence, there may be reason to believe that his habits are not good, or that some physical infir-mity prevents his earning an adequate support; or he is urged to find in the service what an imbecile mind could not elsewhere procure.[91]

That same year, Colonel George Croghan noted that the Irish "(a few hon-ourable exceptions to the contrary) are the very bane of our garrisons."[92]

Thus immigrant enlisted men found the prejudice against their working-class background compounded by nativism. Much of the animosity they encountered focused on their ethnic traditions and their unfamiliarity with or unwillingness to adjust to American customs. Religion was a key issue, especially in the late 1840s as the relationship between the United States and Catholic Mexico grew tenuous. As the number of Irish Catholics in the U.S. Army increased, military leaders felt unprepared to deal with religious diversity. Prior to the Mexican War, all army chaplains were Protestant, and during the war only two Jesuits were added for the ministry. Most soldiers were Protestant and saw no problem with this, nor did much of the nation. Some evangelical chaplains, officers, and men may have been just as offended by mandatory religious attendance at services conducted by Episcopalian priests, who dominated among army chaplains, as were Catholic soldiers. But most Americans were not interested in accommodating the needs of Catholics, insisting instead that immigrants abandon their religion for new American traditions, including Protestantism.

Some Catholics in the military disagreed. In the 1840s, for example, Catholic lieutenant John P. J. O'Brien refused to march his men to a Protestant service. His commander and devout Catholic John DeB. Walbach insisted on the supremacy of army regulations despite their shared faith and arrested O'Brien. The matter was finally resolved when President John Tyler ordered O'Brien released and excused him from future church attendance, but within a few years it was clear that the problem of religious freedom within the army continued. In 1846 one Catholic soldier complained to the New York *Freeman's Journal* of regulations that forced him to attend Protestant services directed by a minister "whose words are mainly directed to insulting, calumniating and abusing the Catholic Church."[93]

Catholic soldiers were not alone in noticing this prejudice. Some native-born officers worried about its impact on the army's overall morale. Captain E. Kirby Smith worried that such slurs as "Mick," "Paddy," or "croppie" would lead to increased desertion rates. General Zachary Taylor, commanding the American forces bordering Mexico in the spring of 1846, ordered the end of such epithets and bias against Catholic and foreign-born soldiers. Some officers commanding units with a large Catholic representation or who posted near a heavily Catholic population developed similarly liberal religious policies.

The controversy was more complex, however, than a simple case of anti-Catholicism. Catholics occasionally enforced the Protestant religious regulations in the army on fellow Catholics. It was not that the army was particularly anti-Catholic, but rather it resisted any group or individual who refused to subordinate his beliefs to overall army policy. For example, most U.S. soldiers were not active in their faith, and some non-Catholics resented the mandatory services just as much as Catholics did. West Point cadet Ulysses S. Grant described the practice as "not exactly republican," and other non-Catholic officers lodged formal complaints. When West Point instructor Simon Bolivar Buckner, a non-Catholic, protested mandatory services as a violation of constitutional rights, he found himself in trouble more for challenging the status quo than for challenging any particular religious position. Those censured for religious matters in the U.S. Army were not only Catholics but also Methodists, Baptists, Unitarians, or agnostics.

Those going about their religious beliefs quietly, however, were quite often left alone. William T. Sherman, for example, was baptized Catholic, and though he was never devout, his wife was very active. This did not, however, appear to have any impact on his advancement in the prewar army. In the late 1840s and 1850s, when nativism peaked in America, many army commanders tried to appease Catholic soldiers. In 1857 department commander David Twiggs attended a consecration ceremony at a San Antonio church, while a decade earlier Lieutenant Colonel Gustavus Loomis found himself criticized by the adjutant general for anti-Catholicism, anti-constitutionalism, and intolerance for prohibiting a priest from preaching at a post chapel.

On the other hand, when Oliver O. Howard joined the Methodist Church in Tampa, Florida, he noted, "some of the officers said that I had disgraced the uniform; others that I was half crazy; but a few sympathized with me and were my friends." Similarly, when a young officer considered increasing his involvement in a high-church faction of the Episcopal Church, fellow officer Robert E. Lee advised against it. Religious involvement to the extent of regular church attendance was expected, but Lee discouraged the man from taking a radical position on any matter. Mistreatment of Catholics in the U.S. Army was rooted in multiple factors, including their working-class condition, their status as immigrants, and their unwillingness to subjugate their religious beliefs to army traditions.[94]

Private George Ballentine, a Scotsman and veteran of the British Army, noted the animosity toward immigrant soldiers and theorized about its effect on the U.S. Army:

The barbarous treatment which foreign soldiers . . . received from ignorant and brutal officers, and non-commissioned officers on that campaign, were I to relate it in minute detail, would seem almost incredible. I have frequently seen foolish young officers violently strike and assault soldiers on the most slight provocation, while to tie them up by the wrist, as high as their hands would reach, with a gag in their mouths, was a common punishment for trivial offenses. In fact, such a bad state of feeling seemed to exist between men and officers throughout the service that I was not surprised that it should lead to numerous desertions.[95]

Numerous officers, including George Meade and Ulysses S. Grant, joined Smith, Taylor, and Ballentine in recognizing the need to eliminate the prejudiced treatment of immigrant and Catholic soldiers. During the Mexican-American War mistreatment of immigrant Catholics plagued the army throughout the conflict and led to one of its most infamous cases of mass desertion.[96]

Despite General Taylor's orders, immigrant desertion rates, traditionally lower than those of native-born soldiers, continued to rise during the war. This may have occurred because Taylor's orders had no effect or because of the highly publicized fact that Catholic soldiers in the U.S. Army were expected to fight fellow Catholics. The most famous example of this dilemma involved the San Patricios, or the St. Patrick's Battalion, formed by American deserters who joined the Mexican Army. News of the unit shocked Americans, who came to see the desertions as another reminder of the warnings of nativists, who had long questioned the loyalty of Catholics to America, arguing that someday papists would have to choose between the Catholic church and America. Lost on many Americans was the fact that most of the San Patricios were not Irish, like their leader John Riley, a native of County Galway, but rather were of diverse origins. While many were Catholic immigrants, their organization had more to do with offers of land and money from the Mexican government and the deserters' mistreatment in the U.S. Army than any inner conflict over fighting a Catholic nation.[97]

The Irish-American community offered little support for Riley and his seventy-two compatriots found guilty of desertion. Irish leaders struggled to illustrate that by no means was the St. Patrick's Battalion comprised entirely of Irish Catholics and even tried to argue that John Riley was a fictional character manufactured by the nativist press. Irish-American editors tried to switch the focus to the service of loyal Irish soldiers. The Boston *Pilot* asked, "Instead of stirring anti-Irish and anti-Catholic rancor by dwelling upon this imposter [Riley], why do not the nativist papers pay attention to another Riley, the brave and gallant colonel, who has distinguished himself so valiantly?"[98] Colonel Bennet Riley was one of the most famous Irishmen in the American Army at that time. Ulysses S. Grant described him as "the finest specimen of physical manhood I had ever looked upon . . . 6'2" in his stocking feet, straight as the undrawn bowstring, broad shouldered with every limb in perfect proportion, with an eye like an eagle and a step as light as the forest tiger." Riley was born in America, but grew up with the shanty Irish and was seen as a poor Irishman who had found success in this land.[99]

Another example of a loyal Irish-American was artillery lieutenant John Paul Jones O'Brien, one of the first Catholics to graduate from West Point. Though he was born to economically successful Irish immigrant parents in Philadelphia, and thus not seen as of true impoverished immigrant stock, the Irish community celebrated him for his support of Catholic religious freedoms. It was, after all, O'Brien who faced a court-martial for refusing to force the Catholics in his artillery company to attend Protestant services.[100]

The Irish community in America was also quick to point out that of the more than five thousand Irish who served with the U.S. Army in Mexico, the majority remained loyal. The Irish who served in the San Patricios, they argued, were not accurate representations of the Irish in America or of their long-standing contributions to the army. Nevertheless, nativist groups clung to claims by John Riley himself that 70 percent of his men were Catholic, citing this as a clear demonstration that Catholics could never truly be loyal Americans because their primary devotion was to the church. They would always be a threat to Protestant America, the weakest strands in the national fabric. Indeed, the era of the San Patricios, combined with the dramatic increase in Irish Famine immigrants to America, signaled a rising period of nativism in the country.

While the Irish-American community and nativists drew various lessons from the San Patricios, so too did the U.S. Army. Recognizing the dissatisfaction of many Catholic soldiers, the army allotted four permanent positions for Catholic chaplains. There were several salary increases, including a significant supplement in 1854. In addition, the army reduced imposition of its most severe punishments. Flogging was a rarity by the 1850s, and in 1861 the War Department abolished it completely. David Twiggs, who carried out the punishment of Riley and some of the San Patricios, would a decade later, as noted above, appease the Catholics in his ranks by attending a consecration ceremony in a San Antonio Catholic church. Thus in the years following the Mexican War, the army and its commanders worked to diminish any sense among its soldiers that they would be persecuted for their Catholic faith, indicating instead that the San Patriocios were punished for their disloyalty to the United States rather than for any of their religious beliefs.

This did not end the frustrations of some Irish-Americans within the army. In 1858, Irish-born John Thompson was serving in the 1st U.S. Infantry, stationed at Fort Duncan, Eagles Pass, Texas. It appears that Thompson left Ireland while still actively serving as a lieutenant in the

2nd Royal Lanark Militia of the British Army, traveled to the United States without his father's consent, and there joined the U.S. Army. By 1858, a terrified and repentant eighteen-year-old tearfully contacted his father to beg his assistance in leaving the U.S. Army. Not only was he homesick, but he had endured at least three days lost on the open Texas plains with only one companion, where they fought off an Indian attack before finally making it back to camp. Thompson declared, "You cannot imagine my feelings . . . I am a private soldier in the United States Army. The hardships I go through will kill me. A private in the Queens Service has a better life even than the subalterns of this Army." A sympathetic American officer informed Thompson that if his father and other respectable witnesses could testify that the boy was not yet twenty-one years old, they could secure, with the help of the U.S. consul in Ireland or England, Thompson's release from military service. His father, Reverend Skeffington Thompson, worked with the consular office in Belfast and managed to achieve his adventurous son's release and insisted that he return at once.[101]

Despite the anti-Irish prejudice within the antebellum army, some officers noted, in another form of prejudice, positive attributes of Irish troops. While condemning the treasonous actions of groups like the San Patricios, several commanders could not help but note how well Riley and his men had fought. Their comments reveal the racial beliefs of the day, in that the Irish "race" was comprised of great men who love a good fight. These opinions indicate, too, a level of respect of Irish fighting ability and a desire to channel that ability toward loyal American service in the future. This would indeed be the case in 1861 as the president of the United States and others worked to make sure immigrants knew their service and support was desired and encouraged it through the formation of similar ethnic units, only these with a fierce loyalty to the United States.

While recognizing the benefits and detractions of Irish service in the U.S. Army, radical Irish nationalists like Michael Doheny found other aspects of America's strong military tradition enticing. A veteran of the failed 1848 Irish uprising, Doheny was living as an exile in America in the late 1850s, planning for his return and the liberation of Ireland. As a future founder of the Fenian Brotherhood, the American-based counterpart of the Irish Republican Brotherhood, Doheny was conscious of the movement's need for weapons, experienced soldiers, and funding, and he found these in state military organizations, as well as local militia units. "I saw material for an army here and not only the means of organizing it but every facility afforded by the state governments." Early in the 1850s, Doheny boasted that he had organized nearly twenty-five thousand "of as brave fellows as you need wish" and could have them ready for service within four years. Infighting among the Irish nationalist leaders, however, and lack of funds, military leadership, and transportation caused many of Doheny's recruits to disappear before they could be used. He insisted that they would reorganize quickly as long as he could demonstrate a clear chance for success. Doheny believed that they would reassemble "any day were there means of transportation [to Ireland] and men to command them. . . . If a sure careful blow were struck in Ireland Fifty Millions sterling would be raised here in two months; but to prepare for such an event you could not raise fifty cents."[102]

Doheny's numbers seem a little bold, but there is similar evidence from other Irish-Americans organizing and joining these organizations. Ten years earlier, in 1848, an Irish-American named Thomas Reilly was living in upstate New York. That year found him positively miserable in America, "very sad, very lonely" and claiming that "nothing save death could lull the storm which is raging in my mind." He informed his friends in Dublin that he was "friendless, deserted, and lonely" and hoped only for the chance to return to Ireland.

He worked toward that goal by joining a group of volunteers preparing for the liberation of Ireland. "There are Irish Volunteers preparing in America to invade Ireland in case of an emergency," Reilly explained. "My name is enrolled on the list and we are drilling ourselves for the occasion. Perhaps I will return to Ireland with the green flag flying above me. I care not if it becomes my shroud. I have no regard for life while I am in exile." Their numbers, according to Reilly, were actually larger than those quoted by Doheny: "We expect to muster 50,000 men in a short time, god send them soon. If that force were thrown on the southern coast of Ireland we would quickly march to the city of Dublin and set it in a blaze."[103] While their plans may seem grandiose, the British government treated reports of these organizations with great interest. In 1849, British colonial secretary Lord Elgin learned from an informant that the New York Irish Republican Union was already exporting military surplus materials from the Mexican War to Ireland and that a force prepared to train an "army of liberation" was en route to Ireland that summer.[104]

Thus there were several motivations behind Irish-American military service, both in the U.S. military and in state and local militia units. Doheny was an exception to the rule among Irish-Americans, most of whom lacked his fervent and active dedication to Irish nationalism. Still, he touched on a popular sympathy within the immigrant population, the desire for a free Ireland, and in that sense his motivations reveal a larger, though unreliable, trend among Irish-American soldiers in the United States.

As one might expect, it did not help Irish-Americans trying to portray an image of loyalty when news leaked that Irish militia units might be more interested in securing Irish interests than in securing those of America. One of the most famous examples of such tensions erupted in 1854 in Boston, Massachusetts. Contributing to the turmoil that year was the Fugitive Slave Act, which allowed for the forcible return of runaway slaves to their owners and required the assistance of local police or military forces. While many northern whites came to oppose the law forcing them to support the institution of slavery, at least tacitly, Irish Catholics remained outspoken supporters of the Fugitive Slave Act. They argued that the rights of slave owners were protected by the Constitution and emphasized respect for the rule of law.

That year a famous case involving runaway slave Anthony Burns erupted in Boston and in newspapers across the country. When Burns was captured, he was marched out of the city amid huge crowds, some supporting the decision and others opposing it as inhumane. Conspicuous among the troops escorting Burns to the ship that would return him to slavery was the Columbian Artillery, a local Irish Catholic militia unit. Seeing Irish-Americans in such a prominent role supporting the institution of slavery caused abolitionists and nativists alike to increase their efforts to restrict the rights and power of the Irish in America.[105] The leading Irish paper in the city, the Boston *Pilot,* denounced the crowd supporting Burns as "anarchists" and applauded the role of the Columbian Artillery for returning him to his "rightful owner," all of which exemplified a "perfect triumph of law and order."[106] Native-born Bostonians, however, saw things differently.

Congregationalist minister Eden B. Foster compared the forced removal of Burns to the days when British soldiers controlled the streets of Boston, an analogy that must have infuriated members of the Columbian Artillery and Boston's Irish Catholic population. Foster cried from his pulpit in Lowell,

> Never before since British hirelings stood in the streets of Boston and shot down unarmed and unoffending citizens, has that city been under martial law and military siege. Never before, since the blood of the Revolution was shed, have the streets of Boston been blockaded, and the business of Boston suspended, and the free expression of opinion coerced by cannon and sword, by the menace and the terror, and the death-dealing power of the military arm.

It was all part, Foster insisted that afternoon in a separate sermon, of the larger plot involving the Kansas-Nebraska Act. That legislation "renders aid to the plottings of the Romish hierarchy," he claimed:

Everything indicates that there is a struggle coming on in this country between the principles of Protestant liberty and Romish power. . . . But what I wish especially to remark in this connection is, the alliance between Slavery and the Roman Catholic religion in this strife. Their spirit is one, the spirit of bigotry and intolerance in Church and State, the spirit of dictation over the conscience and our politics.[107]

By the following year, so many Bostonians agreed with this position, supported by their interpretations of corrupt Irish Catholic involvement in politics, opposition to social reforms, and abuse of militia power, that they turned much of the city power over to Know Nothings and disbanded organizations like the Columbian Artillery as unsafe and disloyal. Indeed, just as their power rose in many states across the country in the mid-1850s, Know Nothings came to dominate the city of Boston, the Massachusetts governorship, and the state legislature.[108] Groups like the Columbian Artillery collapsed under this rising nativism.

As the nation inched toward Civil War, many northern Irish-Americans saw a new opportunity. Just as their united activism in political, social, and religious organizations was improving the conditions of thousands of Irish-Americans, so too could military service. Large numbers of Irishmen would seek such service for the financial opportunities it offered, and others would serve more for the experience it provided Irish nationalists for a future war to liberate Ireland. Significant numbers of Irishmen saw the Civil War and military service in terms of their lives as both Irishmen and Americans. By saving America, they argued, the war would preserve a safe haven for future generations of Irishmen. Others still saw an opportunity to prove their loyalty through military service, and hoped such demonstrations would improve their lives in America.

As they viewed different aspects of American life, whether politics, economics, or social change, Irish-Americans viewed this war in terms of the way it would impact their own communities. The difficult period of the 1840s and 1850s had taught them to expect few handouts from the native-born populace. If they were to make better lives for themselves during the Civil War era, Irish-Americans would do this by sticking together and maintaining their focus on their own communities' needs. They would view the war through Irish lenses, and so long as their goals and the union cause remained united, large numbers of Irishmen would volunteer for Civil War service in the Union Army. As those interests diverged, however, Irishmen would have to choose between Irish America and the United States.

2

"Remember Your Country and Keep Up Its Credit"
Volunteering for Ireland and America

With the election of Abraham Lincoln and the creation of the Confederacy, Americans north and south were forced to take a stand on the issues that were driving the country toward war. Irish-Americans, too, would make important choices during this time, and concern over their interests in America and in Ireland would shape these decisions.

In the election of 1860, Irish Catholics remained overwhelmingly loyal to the Democratic party. This decision was not particularly complex for them. The Republicans contained abolitionists whom many Irish-Americans saw as more concerned with the plight of southern slaves than with the plight of poor Irish laborers. Republicans had also earned the reputation as the party of nativists. Boston's Irish newspaper the *Pilot* characterized the ranks of the Republicans as "scattered and broken forces of the Know Nothing party" that represented "hatred and prejudice and injustice to the Irish particularly."[1] Days before the election, the *Pilot* reminded its readers of the nativists' efforts to lengthen naturalization periods and limit immigrants' rights in America. "Remember that every vote cast for a Republican is an endorsement of the two year amendment. A naturalized citizen who would vote for a party who proscribes his race, does not deserve the rights of citizenship."[2]

For every criticism of the Republicans and Lincoln, whom the *Pilot* described as a "very weak man intellectually," Irish leaders presented resounding praise for Stephen Douglas.[3] Reporting on the nation's response to his nomination for president, the *Pilot* described "irrepressible bursts of enthusiasm from the hearts of the people—the Union-loving people in every section of this wide extended country."[4] Much of the Irish-American support for Douglas was tied not only to his emphasis on union but also to his opinions on the Constitution. Irish-Americans grounded much of their opposition to abolitionists and other radicals in their interpretation of the American Constitution and the sacred power of its protections.

When abolitionists challenged the wisdom of the Constitution, character-izing it as "a covenant with death and an agreement with hell," many Irish-Americans were horrified. It was the Constitution that guaranteed the few rights they managed to maintain, and it was through that docu-ment that the Irish would continue their struggle for equality in America. Take away the Constitution, the Irish argued, and the knots binding America together would unravel and destroy all future hope for the Irish in America and in the old country. To most Irish-Americans, Douglas was the candidate who best represented these beliefs. "No other statesman," professed the *Pilot,* "has done as much for securing the constitutional rights of the South as Mr. Douglas has done, and that too, without im-pairing a single right of the North."[5]

Large numbers of Irish-Americans also feared the economic impact of a Lincoln victory. James Gordon Bennett's *New York Herald* warned work-ers, "if Lincoln is elected you will have to compete with the labor of four million emancipated Negroes."[6] This was a frequently discussed dread within the Irish-American community. The abolition of slavery, warned the *Pilot,* would precipitate a black exodus to the North, where former slaves would, "by overstocking the market of labor do incalculable injury to white hands."[7] Similarly, Philadelphians told stories of Irish protecting their own labor through sabotage. Diarist Sidney G. Fisher related the experience of an acquaintance who "discharged an Irish servant and in his place employed a Negro. Shortly after, his garden was trespassed on, plants and shrubbery destroyed and a paper stuck on one of the trees, threatening further injury if he did not send away the Negro." Fisher went on to note that the "Democrats have industriously represented that the Republicans intend to emancipate the Negroes and make them the equals of the whites; also, that when the slaves are free, there will be a great emi-gration of them to the North to the injury of the white workingmen." The Irish, "who are all Democrats," Fisher pointed out, "implicitly believe" such information and vote accordingly.[8]

Irish nationalist Richard O'Gorman agreed with these concerns, but saw the tensions as the result of a crisis in economic philosophy. In April 1861 he warned friend and fellow Irish revolutionary William Smith O'Brien, "I think we shall have war. Nothing less can ever purify this land of the corruption arising from the too sudden activity of commerce. We have been going all wrong and nature is asserting her violated Laws."[9] Oddly, O'Gorman sounds quite similar to the most radical abolitionists, whom he vehemently opposed, in his interpretation of the war as a neces-sary penance to purge the sins of America.

The divisions between Irish America and the native-born population became particularly sharp in the month preceding the election of Lincoln.

"Reception by the people of New York of the Sixty-ninth Regiment, N.Y.S.M., on their return from the seat of war, escorted by the New York Seventh Regiment, July 27, 1861." *Frank Leslie's Illustrated History of the Civil War* (1895). Originally appeared in *Frank Leslie's Illustrated* during the American Civil War, specific date unknown. Photograph research courtesy Mr. John Wolfe, Southern Pines, NC. Photograph reproduction courtesy Lynn L. Libby, Enola, PA, 2005.

Americans throughout the Northeast and along the Atlantic seaboard anticipated the visit of the Prince of Wales, son of Queen Victoria and future ruler of Great Britain, with great enthusiasm. Not everyone, however, was thrilled. As famed New York City diarist George Templeton Strong observed, "The protest of certain militia companies of Irishmen against parading to do honor to a Saxon and an oppressor of Ireland is the single exception" to the otherwise unanimous celebration of his visit. These companies were part of the 69th New York State Militia regiment, comprised almost entirely of Irish-born and first-generation Irish-Americans. Their commander was Irish exile Colonel Michael Corcoran, who was also a high-ranking member of the Irish Republican Brotherhood in America, an Irish nationalist organization commonly known as the Fenians.[10] While the reaction of most of New York City caused Strong to note that the Prince of Wales's visit "has occasioned a week of excitement beyond that of any event in my time, and pervading all classes," Corcoran and the 69th carried out a conscious act of protest.[11]

It began with prominent New Yorker W. B. Fields's offer to send Corcoran tickets for a ball honoring the prince, and tensions increased when their division commander announced that the 69th was one of the units selected to participate in a parade for the city's guest. Corcoran and many of the men were dedicated Irish patriots, who saw their loyalty to America as equal or secondary to their work toward Irish freedom. Corcoran's activities along these lines had forced his escape to America, and many of the men in his unit had similar histories. They would not honor the Prince of Wales, the future leader of a nation that Corcoran and his men saw as the oppressor of Ireland. For them, England insisted on its right to rule Ireland, but had done nothing to aid its people during the Great Famine, an event many of the men believed was the result of England's anti-Irish bigotry.

Adopting as democratic a system as possible, the men of the 69th N.Y.S.M. voted to excuse themselves from the parade. On October 6, 1860, Corcoran took care of the first problem by explaining to Fields that he was "not desirous of joining in the Festivity" of honoring the Prince of Wales, and thus required no tickets. The issue of removing the regiment from the parade, however, would prove more difficult.[12] Colonel Corcoran decided that civil disobedience was their best policy, and on the day of the parade the 69th simply did not appear. When called upon to explain these actions, Corcoran stated that his men had participated in the legally required number of ceremonies that year, and thus had the right to withdraw from this occasion. Technically, this was true. Militiamen had to pay dues to cover the expenses of their uniforms and held jobs in addition to the time required for training and regimental duties. To prevent excessive expense and time requirements on the men, state legislatures had passed a law that militia generals could only request the men of their command to parade a certain number of times per year. Once a regiment had fulfilled these requirements, it could refuse any additional orders to parade.[13]

Despite their creative defense, Corcoran's commanders and native-born community leaders were not amused. Military authorities arrested Corcoran on charges of disobedience and ordered him to face a court-martial. Again he defended himself by citing the limit on the number of parades, as well as presenting an ideological case against the prince, arguing,

> Although I am a citizen of America, I am a native of Ireland. . . . [I]n the Prince of Wales I recognized the representative of my country's oppressors, . . . [and] in my opinion no change of circumstance should efface the memory of the multiplied wrongs of fatherland, and . . . in honoring that personage, I would be dishonoring the memories, and renouncing the principles of that land of patriots.[14]

It was a passionate defense, but the native-born Americans in the city were not moved. They continued to demand Corcoran's punishment and the disbanding of the regiment.

Such actions were not unusual. Five years earlier, Massachusetts governor Henry Gardner disbanded "all military companies composed of persons of foreign birth." When one Irish militia commander refused and challenged the governor to court-martial him, Gardner avoided the issue and achieved his goal by reorganizing all militia regiments so that there was no place available for Irish companies.[15] In 1858, similar nativism led to the disbanding of the predominantly Irish 9th New York State Militia regiment.

As *Harper's Weekly* explained following the Prince of Wales incident, New Yorkers were more than willing to take similar action against the 69th. "As militiamen and soldiers they have not infrequently been an absolute nuisance," the editors of *Harper's Weekly* argued:

> It is not worth while to repeat the story . . . of the Irishmen who deserted from our army and constituted the battalion of San Patricio, in the Mexican War. . . . The spectacle of the ignominious surrender of the Irishmen in Lamoriciere's army, who had volunteered to assist the Pope in keeping down his Italian subjects, has not yet been forgotten. Before our Irishmen thrust themselves anew under the public notice they should allow the effluvia of this transaction to pass away.[16]

Throughout the country, *Harper's Weekly* continued, Irish-Americans had proven an equally large nuisance. The editors reminded readers of the tens of thousands of Irishmen pouring into the country every year and pointed out that most native-born Americans accepted the immigrants, even welcoming them with land "almost for nothing; employment at far better wages than they could have at home; and political rights equal to those which are enjoyed by the sons of the best and noblest Americans," and the country even "let them have their priests and their churches" and defended Irishmen from attacks by nativists. Despite all of these advantages, the Irish had proven to be incapable of civilized behavior, *Harper's Weekly* insisted. The Irish in America "have so behaved themselves that nearly seventy-five percent of our criminals and paupers are Irish; that fully seventy-five percent of the crimes of violence committed among us are the work of Irishmen," and through "the incapacity of the Irish for self-government," the American democratic system and universal suffrage "has fallen into discredit." Despite all of this, the editors noted, native-born Americans had never even considered legislation directed against Irish-Americans. American had not shown any thought of denying them their political rights, nor had they sought to protect themselves against the Irish proclivity toward "misconduct." True, the editors noted, some radical Protestants were an exception, but on the whole native-born Americans had been exceedingly tolerant.[17]

This outrage over perceived Irish-American ingratitude was found in many of the Republican and other native presses throughout the city. In the face of these criticisms, Corcoran and his fellow officers in the 69th tried to strengthen their defense. Captain Thomas Francis Meagher, fellow Irish patriot and exile, explained that Corcoran's actions and those of the regiment should not indicate disloyalty or disobedience to America. This nation won its independence from Britain, Meagher argued, and as befits the victor America should be magnanimous when visited by a representative of its defeated enemy. The situation is different, though, Meagher explained, for the exiled sons and daughters of Ireland. If Irish-Americans had participated in the parades honoring the Prince of Wales, Meagher argued, these

> would have furnished a forcible argument to those who deny that Ireland has any mischiefs growing out of her political condition to complain of— who contend that her people are satisfied with their relations of subserviency [sic] to England—and who flippantly assert that the explosions of disaffection, which now and then take place in the country, are occasioned only by the vicious ambition of men who must produce disorder to achieve renown."[18]

Meagher went on to explain that had there been no legal support for their refusal to participate in the parade, the regiment would have appeared to honor the prince regardless of its members' personal beliefs. As soldiers who swore an oath of loyalty to the United States, they must obey their orders no matter how unpleasant. The Irish-Americans of the 69th and the Irish-American community of New York would have "grievously compromised [themselves] in the presence of the law" and the nation. Having the legal right to refuse participation, however, Irish-Americans would have been equally wrong to join the ceremonies.[19]

The theme of dual loyalties would be repeated frequently over the next several years. It was a dangerous argument to make in nineteenth-century America, when few native-born citizens were patient with immigrants' desires to preserve their cultural heritage. Irish-Americans' determination to maintain their Catholic faith, for example, had already proved exceedingly unpopular among many native-born Americans, not only due to the anti-Catholicism that was common throughout the nation but also because this loyalty to customs of the Old World was interpreted as a lack of

Captain David P. Conyngham of General Thomas Francis Meagher's staff, Irish Brigade, and author of *The Irish Brigade and Its Campaigns*. Photo taken in Bealton, Virginia. Courtesy of the Library of Congress. Photograph reproduction courtesy Lynn L. Libby, Enola, PA, 2005.

loyalty to America. A common theme in nativists' complaints of the immigrants of the mid–nineteenth century, which included most Irish-Catholics and future Union Army Irish soldiers, was that they resisted adaptation to American society. Whereas past immigrants had adopted American customs quickly, the Know Nothings and other nativists argued, members of the mid–nineteenth century's "Great Migration" were "determined that neither themselves nor their children shall ever conform to American manners, American sentiments, or the spirit of American institutions." The Know Nothings were sensitive particularly to immigrants' habit of clustering in ethnic neighborhoods and organizations, which they argued prevented them assimilating to "form one great people—one great nationality." Thus when Corcoran and the 69th N.Y.S.M. refused to march for the Prince of Wales and defended this action with arguments rooted in their Irish heritage, an already outraged American public saw proof of how disloyal immigrants could be toward their nation.[20]

The tensions between the Irish and native-born communities of New

York continued to build that fall as Michael Corcoran awaited his trial, but he never questioned his position on the issue. For Corcoran there was no doubt that much of his loyalty would always lie with Ireland. A passion for Irish freedom had led Corcoran to take many stands on the basis of principle, within and outside the law, as had his family for generations. Born in Sligo, Ireland, in 1827, Michael Corcoran traced his ancestry to Patrick Sarsfield, the earl of Lucan. A brigadier general serving under King James II, Sarsfield was an Irish hero of the Williamite War from 1688 to 1691, known for his courage and leadership.[21]

Growing up in Ireland, Michael Corcoran attended one of the new national schools, where he received an English education. At the age of nineteen he joined the Revenue Police and aided their efforts to find and arrest outlaw distillers in the Irish countryside. While stationed in Donegal, Corcoran carried out his orders and upheld his oath to the Crown in Ireland, but as the Great Famine took its toll on the Irish people Corcoran had increasing difficulties understanding the purpose of arresting men who were using whatever means necessary to feed their families. By 1848, Corcoran realized he had more empathy for the men he was chasing than for his comrades on the force, and he joined the Ribbonmen, a small secret agrarian society waging a campaign of terror along the Irish countryside. They burned barns and haystacks, maimed cattle, and damaged other property of the landlords and their agents. It was all part of a larger effort to avenge the Protestant domination and persecution of Irish Catholics that had been the policy in the land for centuries.[22] By 1849 the Revenue Police suspected Corcoran's involvement with the Ribbonmen, and he fled to the United States fearing his execution for treason should he be captured.

A cold rain welcomed Corcoran to New York City in October 1849. He had no contacts, no family, no job, and not a penny to his name. He found men like himself, though, at Hibernian Hall, a tavern that doubled as a Democratic district polling area and Irish-American gathering place. Here Corcoran became active with fellow Irish nationalists in America and joined their organization, known as the Fenian Brotherhood. This was the American counterpart to the Irish Revolutionary Brotherhood in Ireland, and the Fenians were particularly active in New York, Boston, and Philadelphia, the three major American cities with the largest Irish populations in 1860 (see table 1.1 in chapter 1).[23] In addition to joining this Irish nationalist movement in the United States, Corcoran became involved in local Democratic party politics.[24] In the fall of 1851, Corcoran joined the newly formed all-Irish 69th New York State Militia, which included a number of Fenian members, where he quickly rose through the ranks. By the time of the Prince of Wales incident, Corcoran had married his boss's niece, Elizabeth Heaney, and remained busy as the commander of the 69th and a leader in the Fenian organization.

As the foreign- and native-born of New York debated the events that found Corcoran in prison that fall, other momentous developments captured their attention. November brought the election of a new president as well as growing political controversy. Abraham Lincoln's victory strained political divisions to the breaking point, especially in radical South Carolina, which voted to secede from the union that December 1860. Irish-American leaders in the North encouraged their supporters to accept Lincoln's election, but continued to offer their sympathies to the South.

Like many northern Democrats, they were caught between supporting southern criticisms of the Republican party and their own loyalty to the union, and they expressed this frustration with outbursts directed at the new administration. Torn by divided loyalties, they made statements that frequently contradicted each other. Radical Irish nationalist Michael Doheny, living in New York City after escaping Ireland after the failed 1848 uprising, was a strong supporter of Ireland's push for independence from the British Empire, and he feared what Civil War would do to America and Ireland. Should the union dissolve, Doheny warned his friends in Ireland, "then assuredly anarchy would follow and after anarchy despotism."[25]

Other Irish-Americans in Boston agreed. They regarded with "unqualified displeasure the attitude of the South," the *Pilot* explained, though they understood that "all this great . . . sorrow and shame has been evoked by the malign, brutal conceit of the ignorant parvenus of the North."[26] Even so, the editors clarified, Irish-Americans must pledge to "stand by the Union; fight for the Union; die by the Union."[27] Within another two weeks, leading elements of the Boston Irish community seemed to reverse their position again, challenging the governor's call for the state militias to prepare for war. "Why do not the people say," cried the *Pilot*, "'we shall stack our rifles and not an inch shall we move when you command us to march to a fratricidal war!'"[28] The Boston Irish were not alone in their confusion.

The New York *Irish-American* argued, "We deprecate the idea of Irish-Americans—who have themselves suffered so much for opinions' sake not only at home but *here even*—volunteering to coerce those with whom they have no direct connection."[29] Even the future leader of the Irish Brigade sympathized with the South. Thomas Francis Meagher defended the rights of southern secessionists, even going so far as to challenge the use of the term "rebel" as disrespectful to Confederates. "You cannot call eight millions of white freemen 'rebels,'" Meagher argued, preferring the more respectable term "revolutionists."[30] Similar sentiments were expressed in Philadelphia, not only in the Irish-American communities but among the native-born populace as well.[31]

It should be clarified that there were variations to this Irish response. Beyond the Catholic population, devout Irish Protestants like Samuel Nimiks hoped the war could be avoided, but if it proved necessary, he predicted the North would win and was openly antislavery. He thought it would be "a very unnatural war" because in "many Cases it will be the father against the Son and Brother against his Brother and each one believing that the[y] are carrying out the true spirit or meaning of the Constitution of America." Still, the Protestant Irish immigrant explained, "I am not so much concerned as we have the right cause by the end," and insisted that the war may be "the only effectual speedy way of setting the coloured population at liberty."[32] As an antislavery, Protestant Irish-American, Samuel Nimiks is an exception to this study, which is focused overwhelmingly on Irish Catholics in America, but his views are worth noting to highlight the textured response of Irishmen to the crisis in the United States.

When Confederate forces under General P. G. T. Beauregard fired on Federal Fort Sumter, however, this mixture of emotions was clarified. For one Irish-American, serving with Company E, First U.S. Artillery inside the fort, the position had long been clear. As Irish-born John Thompson explained to his father, "in spite of all their bluster I am almost sure [the Confederates] never will fire a shot at us, indeed I think they are only too glad to be let alone." He insisted, "we are confident and contented because we all see the strength of our position and know that the <u>chivalry</u> of South Carolina are effectually scared to attack the frowning fortress the possession of which they so much desire."[33]

Two months later, he admitted the error in that prediction, but took pride in the resistance he and the other U.S. troops demonstrated inside the fort.[34] Despite his obvious loyalty to the First U.S. Artillery and clear opposition to the Confederate forces outside their position, Thompson did not see a role for himself in this war. After returning to New York in August 28, 1861, while thousands of native-born and Irish-American, as well as other immigrant groups, were enlisting, Thompson left the U.S. Army and does not appear to have ever served again.[35]

Once Confederate forces fired on the Federal arsenal at Fort Sumter, South Carolina, however, Irish-American opinion in the North swung solidly behind a union. Meagher came to believe that his loyalty to the United States was as significant as his work for Irish freedom. In this respect, he captured the feeling of many Irish-Americans who did not support the abolitionists, nor the Republicans, and yet could not remain inactive during a conflict that threatened to destroy the nation. Note, however, the way he linked directly the cause of America with that of Ireland:

> Duty and patriotism prompt me to [support the Union]. The Republic, that gave us an asylum and an honorable career,—that is the mainstay of human freedom, the world over—is threatened with disruption. It is the duty of every liberty-loving citizen to prevent such a calamity at all hazards. Above all is it the duty of us Irish citizens, who aspire to establish a similar form of government in our native land. It is not only our duty to America, but also to Ireland. We could not hope to succeed in our effort to make Ireland a Republic without the moral and material aid of the liberty-loving citizens of these United States. That aid we might rely upon receiving at the proper time. But *now,* when all the thoughts, energies, and resources of this noble people are needed to preserve their own institutions from destruction—they cannot spare either sympathy, arms, or men, for any other cause.[36]

Meagher and the Irish-American communities throughout the North were overwhelmingly Irish born. They saw themselves as being as much Irish as American. In viewing the role they would play in this conflict, Irish-American leaders routinely saw the war in terms of dual loyalties and described it that way to their immigrant audiences. They would remind Irishmen to fight as much out of gratitude to America for serving as a refuge for Irish exiles as to preserve the nation because Ireland's old enemy Great Britain wished to see it destroyed. As the war continued, native-born Americans would become increasingly frustrated that Irishmen would not simply fight to save the union, but rather continued to see the conflict in terms of their Irish and American heritage.

On occasion, Irish-American leaders worked to explain the war from a purely loyal American perspective. The Boston *Pilot,* for example, viewed the secession of southern states with little sympathy, arguing that they could not overlook that southerners had failed to use the tools within the governmental system to reach their goals. Southern leaders never tried to pass a constitutional amendment protecting slavery, argued the *Pilot,* which made secessionists a group that "preferred fighting to the practice of statesmanship." Under such circumstances, the *Pilot* supported the federal government's right to "sustain itself by all the military strength at its command."[37] By the end of May, Boston's Irish-American leaders were concluding that their original belief that abolition was the source of dissolution was incorrect. It was, in fact, the leaders of the Deep South who simply used the abolitionists as a means to their disloyal ends. "It is now evident," declared the *Pilot,* "that the cotton states have been hatching treason for a long time; and if abolitionism had never been they would have revolted."[38]

The New York *Irish-American* concurred with this opinion, and by that summer the editors rallied their community to prepare for war, declaring that the Union flag "shall never be trailed in the dust if Irish-American hearts and heads can keep it gloriously aloft."[39] In Philadelphia leading Irish-Americans followed a similar pattern, and April 1861 found them recruiting within their communities to serve the Union cause. Some Philadelphians, as in New York following the Prince of Wales incident, recalled the San Patricios of the Mexican War. General Winfield Scott, veteran and hero of that war and now general-in-chief of the U.S. Army, determined to refute that image of Irish service by publishing a letter in the Philadelphia *Inquirer* attesting to the loyalty and dedicated service of the vast majority of Irish soldiers who had fought in his army in Mexico.[40]

Other Irish-Americans in Philadelphia offered similar statements and encouraged Irish service. Prominent Philadelphia lawyer Daniel Dougherty used his talents as a public orator to call the Irish to arms. Commodore Charles Stewart, a hero of the U.S. Navy with close ties to Ireland, wrote a lengthy article calling for Irish denunciation of southern secession and their rallying to the cause of union.[41] Just as in other communities throughout the northern United States, increasing numbers of Philadelphian Irish-Americans were reversing their apathy toward the war and rallying to the banner.

In the process, the Irish-Americans of the Union states found themselves in the strange situation of siding with abolitionists and Republicans, and against the southern states whose rights they had previously supported. As Joseph B. Tully, quartermaster for the 69th N.Y.S.M. explained, in the end, the Irish had to side with the Constitution and union:

> War is always a great calamity, but the destruction of national greatness and free institutions is greater, and, therefore, while we shall regret the necessity, we shall endorse the policy that maintains the laws, cost what sacrifices of life and property it may. The 69th regiment is composed of men who have always stood by the South in a constitutional way. They have never had any affiliation with abolitionism, but their regard for the South is far from equaling their love for the Union. The latter "must and shall be preserved," if the blood of ourselves and all who feel as we do can effect that preservation.[42]

As increasing numbers of Irish-Americans came to see this, they answered President Lincoln's call by volunteering in astonishing numbers. Many of them sought the opportunity to contribute to the war effort in a way that would draw attention to their ethnic background, once again revealing dual loyalties that would be problematic with many native-born Americans.

Some of these men were Fenians, looking to gain military experience for a future revolution to free Ireland. Others fought to save America as a powerful nation that would continue to offer hope and security to future generations of Irish refugees. Others still included unemployed Irish seeking a signing bonus and a steady pay check. These men frequently joined regular units, caring little for ethnic loyalties. Still, some of these individuals combined financial need with their interests as Irishmen and sought military service in one of the many Irish units being formed in 1861.[43]

Few Irish-Americans saw the war purely as Americans. The vast majority of military-age Irish-American males were recent immigrants who had spent the majority of their lives in Ireland, and many did not see their journey to America as one taken by choice but rather as a matter of exile. Recruiters and Irish-American community leaders recognized this and commonly mentioned dual loyalties to encourage military service.

Peter Welsh, of Irish descent and Canadian birth, is an excellent example of the ideologically motivated Irish-American soldier. Welsh was visiting family in Boston, Massachusetts, in the summer of 1862 when he found himself in the middle of domestic disputes. Welsh sought an escape in the pubs of Irish Boston, but what started as a way to let off steam turned into a full-blown spree, and when he recovered his senses he found himself without a penny and too ashamed to return home to his wife in Charlestown. He sought penance and a financial solution in Company K of the 28th Massachusetts Volunteer Infantry. Military service would provide a steady source of income for his wife and family and, he hoped, reclaim some of the honor he had lost.[44]

By the summer of 1863, now a veteran and color sergeant, Welsh saw his service as much more than a means of earning a living and a punishment for misdeeds. "America is Irlands [sic] refuge Irlands last hope," Welsh explained to his wife's father, who lived in Ireland and did not understand Welsh's desire to serve in this American war.

Destroy this republic and her hopes are blasted If Irland is ever ever [sic] free the means to accomplish it must come from the shore of America. . . . [T]o this country Irland owes a great deal how many thousands have been rescued from the jaws of the poorhouse and from distress and privation by the savings of the industrious sons and more particularly by the daughters of Irland who have emigrated here. . . . When we are fighting for America we are fighting in the interest of Irland striking a double blow cutting with a two edged sword For while we strike in defence of the rights of Irishmen here we are striking a blow at Irlands enemy and oppressor England hates this country because of its growing power and greatness She hates it for its republican liberty and she hates it because Irishmen have a home and a government here and a voice in the counsels of the nation that is growing stronger every day which bodes no good for her.[45]

Welsh was fighting as much for one nation as the other, and he expected his father-in-law, a fellow Irishman, to accept or at least understand his service when viewed in the light of dual loyalties.

For Fenians and other Irish nationalists in America, the Civil War served as a training ground to prepare for war against England. Even Peter Welsh, who was not a Fenian, described the Civil War as "a school of instruction for Irishmen and if the day should arrive within ten years after this war is ended an army can be raised in this country that will strike terror to the Saxons [sic] heart."[46] For Thomas Francis Meagher the inspiration was similar. Explaining his loyalty and duty to America, Meagher saw a clear link to his duty for Ireland. Meagher explained,

It is a moral certainty that many of our countrymen who enlist in this struggle for the maintenance of the Union will fall in the contest. But, even so; I hold that if only one in ten of us come back when this war is over, the military experience gained by that *one* will be of more service in the fight for Ireland's freedom than would that of the entire ten as they are now.[47]

Meagher's stance was not surprising considering his position within the Irish nationalist movement throughout the previous decades. Thomas Francis Meagher was born in the port city of Waterford in Southern Ireland on August 23, 1823, and his early life was steeped in Irish nationalism. His father was active in Irish nationalist Daniel O'Connell's Catholic emancipation and home rule campaigns in Ireland, and the young Meagher saw his father become the first Catholic mayor of Waterford since the seventeenth century and a member of Parliament, where Thomas Meagher, Sr., argued for the restoration of the Irish Parliament in Dublin.

In addition to this early instruction in nationalism, Thomas Francis Meagher received an excellent education at Clongowes Wood, a Jesuit-run boarding school in Kildare. Meagher honed his skills as an orator, surpassing all of his classmates in English composition and rhetoric. After graduating and leaving for the English College of Stonyhurst, Meagher wrote a history of the Clongowes Debating Society that came to the attention of Daniel O'Connell, of whom the great Irish nationalist prophesied,

"The genius that could produce such a work is not destined to remain long in obscurity."[48]

Equally impressive was Meagher's work at Stonyhurst, where again he excelled in oratory and won awards for his composition. He took some of his first stands on Irish nationalism, beginning with his refusal to play his clarinet in the band's 1840 celebration of the 25th anniversary of the Battle of Waterloo. In later years, he took equal pride in winning a long struggle with an English professor determined to relieve Meagher of his "detested Irish brogue." Meagher saw his brogue as a symbol of his Irish heritage and fought to retain it, and would proudly proclaim his victory years afterward.[49] These events at Stonyhurst marked the beginning of his long journey down the road of Irish nationalism, a cause he would later link with American union.

After graduation and a summer tour of the continent, Meagher returned to Waterford and prepared to travel to Dublin to study law. During that summer of 1843, however, he became involved in Daniel O'Connell's continued efforts to achieve the return of Parliament to Ireland and the renewal of home rule. Meagher began making closing speeches at O'Connell's "monster rallies," where the great Irish nationalist, now affectionately known as the "Liberator," hailed Meagher. The young Meagher developed friendships with men of similar thinking who would later become famous in the Irish nationalist movement around the world: John Mitchel, Thomas D'Arcy McGee, Richard O'Gorman, Charles Gavan Duffy, and Smith O'Brien. They became known as Young Ireland, and by the late 1840s they had tired of rallies and speeches, arguing that peaceful protests were not enough and insisting that they were prepared to use force to gain their freedom.

This was a direct challenge to O'Connell's approach, which had pledged to achieve their goal through peaceful methods. After O'Connell was imprisoned for one of his rallies despite calling it off under the demands of British officials, the Young Irelanders decided to take matters into their own hands. In 1846 Meagher delivered the speech that made him famous. When Meagher rose to speak that day at Conciliation Hall on July 27, he challenged O'Connell and the peaceful agitators with a demand to achieve Irish independence by any means necessary.

Rising from his seat and turning toward the crowd, Meagher directed his words to the lord mayor of Dublin, openly challenging any opposition to armed resistance:

I do not abhor the use of arms in the vindication of national rights. There are times when arms will alone suffice, and when political ameliorations call for a drop of blood, and many thousand drops of blood. . . . The man

that will listen to reason—let him be reasoned with, but it is the weap-
oned arm of the patriot that can alone prevail against battalioned despotism. . . . Then, my lord, I do not condemn the use of arms as immoral,
nor do I conceive it profane to say, that the King of Heaven—the Lord of
Hosts! the God of Battles! bestows His benediction upon those who
unsheathe the sword in the hour of a nation's peril. . . . Abhor the sword
—stigmatize the sword? No, my lord, for, at its blow, a giant nation
started from the waters of the Atlantic, and by its redeeming magic, and
in the quivering of its crimson light, the crippled Colony sprang into the
attitude of a proud Republic—prosperous, limitless, and invincible![50]

Again and again Meagher cried, "Abhor the sword—stigmatize the
sword?" challenging such an approach. Ireland had tried peaceful agitation and England refused to listen. Now, Meagher argued, was the time
for the sword. The speech earned him the nickname "Meagher of the
Sword" and shaped the image of the Young Irelanders and Irish nationalism for the mid–nineteenth century.

However popular Meagher was with the crowd before him, members
of the Repeal Association were not pleased, especially Daniel O'Connell's
son, who recoiled at the challenge to his father's leadership. The Repealers
insisted that the Young Irelanders act within the goals of peaceful reform
or leave. Meagher and the Young Irelanders chose to leave.

The Young Irelanders had support from an Irish populace frustrated
with the tedious process of peaceful agitation coupled with the third year
of the potato famine. Indeed, the Famine had exposed the union debate's
fatal flaw. If Ireland and England were one country, the suffering Irish
asked, why does England do nothing to aid Ireland and insist that the
island find its own solutions?[51] After the worst year of the Famine, known
as Black '47, more and more Irishmen were with "Meagher of the Sword"
and ready to strike a blow for freedom.

But Young Irelanders lacked both the organization and the funding to
wage a successful rebellion. In July, inspired by the revolutions of 1848 on
the continent, they tried to start their own revolution. It never expanded
far beyond some shooting at the home of a widow named McCormack,
and their enemies would mockingly refer to this Irish revolution's one
skirmish as "The Battle of Widow McCormack's Cabbage Patch."[52]

No matter how small their revolution, Meagher and his comrades had
still participated in an act deemed treasonous by the high courts, and
they were arrested and faced trial that fall. As the trials came to a close
and Meagher realized he would probably receive the death penalty, he
took the opportunity to make a statement before hearing the court's decision. He asked for neither leniency nor mercy, but boldly restated his

dedication to Irish freedom, declaring, "I am here to regret nothing I have ever done—to retract nothing I have ever spoken."[53] The court was hardly amused and handed down a death sentence on Meagher and his comrades. The leaders of the movement, including Meagher, received the traditional English sentence for treason: to be hanged, quartered, and their remains disposed of according to Her Majesty's wishes.[54] The plight of the convicted revolutionaries was so celebrated in America and Europe, however, that Queen Victoria responded to strong diplomatic pressure by commuting their sentences to banishment to Van Diemen's Land (Tasmania). Their internment was rather loose, however, and Meagher escaped to San Francisco in early 1852 and then traveled on in May to New York City, where he received a warm welcome from an Irish-American community that had been riveted by the Young Irelander's uprising, trial, and sentencing, covered in Irish newspapers as well as private letters from family in Ireland.

Meagher tried his hand at several professions ranging from journalism to law to business, but nothing seemed to inspire him like his work for Irish nationalism. In November 1855, he married Elizabeth Townsend, daughter of a wealthy New York merchant and Republican who thoroughly disapproved of the match, especially when his daughter converted to Catholicism. Through 1861 Meagher made his living as editor and owner of the *Irish News* and on a lecture circuit throughout the eastern United States to secure interest and donations for the cause of Irish nationalism. The following April, with the firing on Fort Sumter, Meagher began organizing an Irish Zouave company to join the 69th New York State Militia. Meagher's Zouaves joined the fighting that July at Manassas and returned with the regiment to the city to muster out in August.

Thus Meagher's explanation of serving the Union cause in terms of the way it would affect Ireland is not surprising. Fellow Irish native and Fenian Michael Corcoran expressed similar sentiments. While supporting the cause of union and liberty, Corcoran's statements in the spring of 1861 revealed a dedication to the Fenians that would have proven true the criticisms of many native-born Americans who questioned his loyalty. On April 21, Corcoran addressed the New York Fenian Brotherhood, urging all members who were not part of the 69th N.Y.S.M. to *avoid* service in that unit or any other. He explained that it was more important that the Fenians in America continue to focus on Ireland and avoid anything that might diminish their ranks and weaken their potential military strength. Corcoran argued that there were plenty of Irish serving in the 69th who were not Fenians and thus there was no need to deplete that organization's force. For those joining him, however, Corcoran believed, "we will not be the worse for a little practice, which we engage in, with the more heart because we feel it will be serviceable on other fields."[55] This was a peculiar stance for a man who would be heralded as a great American patriot in the Civil War. Indeed, Corcoran and Meagher are excellent examples of the dual loyalty to Ireland and America, most particularly in that order, that motivated Irish-Americans to serve in ethnic units. They would train together and serve together under Irish officers and beside fellow Irishmen, gaining experience for a future war that was equally as important as, if not more important than, that facing them presently.

Some Irish-Americans explained their service in ethnic units as an attempt to draw attention to Irish sacrifices and, in the process, prove their value to America and earn the respect of fellow citizens. Charles G. Halpine, an Irish native who served in the 69th New York and later as a staff officer for Union general David Hunter, became famous for his creation of the fictional Irish-American soldier Miles O'Reilly. Halpine submitted letters to northern newspapers throughout the war, often signing them as O'Reilly, whom Halpine portrayed as an ignorant Irish private loyal to the cause of union. Halpine and his O'Reilly character became famous when he published these during and after the war in two books, *The Life and Adventures of Private Miles O'Reilly* (1864) and *Baked Meats of the Funeral* (1866).[56] Halpine captured in O'Reilly and the other Irish-American figures in his stories all of the complex emotions and hopes that motivated them to serve the cause of union. Central to these, Halpine explained to his Irish-born and native-American audience,

> was the thought that [the Irish-American soldier] was thus earning a title, which hereafter no foul tongue or niggard heart would dare dispute, to the full equality and fraternity of an American citizen. Ugly and venomous as was the toad of civil strife, it yet carried in its head for the Irish race in America this precious, this inestimable jewel. By adoption of the banner, and by the communion of bloody grave trenches on every field, from Bull Run to where the Chickamauga rolls down its waters of death, the race that were heretofore only exiles, receiving generous hospitality in the land, are now proud peers of the proudest and brave brothers of the best.[57]

Some Irish-Americans in Boston agreed. "When the next generation records with flushed cheeks . . . this heroic age," wrote the *Pilot*, "they can say with proud consciousness 'we too, are Americans, and our fathers bled and died to establish this beloved country.'" Even so, the editors showed little faith that this devotion would be recognized. "Let no Irishman think that because . . . he has lost an arm, an eye, or a leg," the *Pilot* warned, "he will be treated decently henceforward."[58]

Quartermaster Joseph B. Tully of the 69th New York was happy to have the chance to serve as both an American and an Irishman. Despite the tragedy of the war, Tully explained, Irish-Americans felt a certain amount of "gratification that now an opportunity was at hand to demonstrate their devotion to the Union, their pride in the character of their race and fatherland, and their own courage, fortitude and fidelity."[59] Colonel Corcoran agreed with this sentiment, encouraging those who insisted upon serving to "go with [your] own countrymen [rather] than have [your] services unappreciated, and [your] national identity lost among strangers."[60] Tully and Corcoran's comments, however, still reveal an Irish pride in their "race" and a desire to ensure that the Irish nationality be recognized in service to the Union. Thus, the dual identity remained even here, and it would prove troublesome as casualties mounted, war aims changed to include abolition, and increasing numbers of Irish-Americans saw themselves as having less and less in common with the Union.

These Irishmen, even those who expressed their desire to fight to save the Union, linked that service with their dreams of Irish freedom. Their viewing the war in this manner would frustrate increasing numbers of native-born Americans suspicious of the idea of dual loyalties and would create problems for Irish-Americans, leading them to question whether it was worthwhile to preserve America as a future refuge for Ireland and a hope for Irish freedom. To many native-born Americans this would be shocking evidence of Irish disloyalty.

In addition to the motivations of Irish freedom, American union, and demonstrations of gratitude and loyalty, Irishmen also volunteered from basic economic need. The steady paycheck the U.S. Army advertised in the midst of a depression in the early period of the war, which was followed by inflation as the fighting continued, attracted these soldiers to military service. In the spring of 1861, the American economy became unstable as southern states seceded and the nation marched steadily toward war. Times were so difficult by April that the New York *Irish-American* theorized that many of the Irish volunteers for the war were in fact unemployed workers who served only because their situation had become "almost disastrous." The findings of the New York Association for Improving the Condition of the Poor supported this, estimating that unemployment rates in 1861 were "at least 25 per cent greater" than in the years following the desperate panic of 1857.[61]

In Boston, Irish-American Maurice Sexton cautioned his family in Ireland that the economy was indeed poor, warning that this was not a good time to come to America. "It is certainly deplorable to think what ruin [the war] has brought the majority of the working people to," he wrote. "The business of the country is wholly prostrate. Nothing doing in any line of business or other industrial improvement, and all the people who have lived by their labour and only from hand to mouth, as a general thing, are gone to the war." Sexton saw no end in sight to the bloodshed: "I am sorry to say that it has made many a widow and orphan to deplore the loss of their fond parent and affectionate husband, and yet there is no prospect of peace."

Despite his frustrations, Sexton was positive that one thing could reunite the nation, and that was a threat of European aggression toward the North and South. Seeing conflict in this light, he forgot all talk of warning family away from potential military service, as well as his own concerns for avoiding a potential draft. If European powers interfered with the war, attacking both parties while distracted in an internal conflict, "the whole population of the United States would rise up in arms, and lay down their lives, their honors, and their riches at the altar of liberty and sacrifice the whole from the laws and Constitution of the United States, the best and most liberal government in the world." Sexton prophesied, "You may be assured there would be a general stampede of both native and foreign, rich and poor, not distinctions" and insisted "it would not be a war aggravated as it is now by means of a few republican fanatics of the North, varying or interfering with the institutions of the South, which in like manner has excited the seceding fanatics of the South."[62]

Sexton's idea of a European alliance led by the British and French against a divided America is a bit fanciful, but the way it immediately shifted the tone of his letter is significant. While personally opposed to the war, or at least disappointed with northern leadership and somewhat sympathetic to the southern position, Sexton demonstrates a fierce loyalty to America once the enemy is Britain or France, or some foreign power. He has a clear dedication to the country, but he defines it according to his interests, as both an Irishman and an American.

Just as Sexton described the financial incentives inspiring enlistments in Boston in 1861, similar factors encouraged midwesterners to serve. Irish-born Henry O'Mahoney had found work as a machinist in Illinois until the ship where he worked burned down. Military service offered steady employment, so O'Mahoney and his friend Pat Sullivan, who had grown up near O'Mahoney in Ireland, went to Chicago to enlist in the U.S. Navy. He makes no mention of ideological beliefs or his views as an Irish-American when discussing the motivations behind his enlistment. The sole focus for both men appears to have been a regular salary and the two-hundred-dollar bonus promised upon their honorable discharge from the service.

Despite dreams of serving at sea, O'Mahoney found himself on river gunboats along the Mississippi performing such brutally difficult labor that he "often thought, when sick and worn out . . . that death by leaping overboard would be preferable." The men were disgusted by the poor rations of beef "that was blood red when crumbled with the finger," and "hardtack which when broken open was full of bugs." Complaining of paymasters who cut their rations and efforts by officers to find something with which to dishonorably discharge sailors so they would be ineligible for their bounty, O'Mahoney spent the majority of his time at war learning to stay out of trouble in order to secure that two-hundred-dollar bounty.[63]

Immediately following the firing on Fort Sumter and President Lincoln's call for seventy-five thousand volunteers to suppress the rebellion, the 69th N.Y.S.M. held a vote and overwhelmingly agreed to offer their services to the Union. Corcoran presented his men to the governor of New York, who recognized the 69th as one of New York's few regiments with the discipline and training to offer immediate assistance to the nation's capital, now surrounded by Confederates and their sympathizers. Two prominent New Yorkers, businessman James Bowen and politician Thurlow Weed, concurred, calling on Governor Edwin Morgan to "quash at once the court martial on Col. Corcoran." He agreed finally and ordered Corcoran to return to his regiment and prepare to embark for Washington within three days.[64]

This did not allow Corcoran much time. He had fallen ill during his trial and was only now recovering. Still, he was determined to show the Irish-American community, New York, and the nation that the Prince of Wales incident was not an indication of Irish disloyalty to America. Corcoran saw their immediate service as perfect proof. Meeting with his men shortly after his release, Corcoran announced, "The commandant feels proud that his first duty, after being relieved from a long arrest, is to have the honor of promulgating an order to the regiment to rally to the support of the Constitution and the laws of the United States."[65]

As the one thousand members of the 69th N.Y.S.M. departed the city, their march to the pier was crowded with tens of thousands of well-wishers. The men had gathered that morning for a presentation of the colors, forming in Great Jones Street as Maria Lydig Daly, wife of Irish-American judge Charles Patrick Daly, presented the Irish regiment with a silk American flag. Colonel Corcoran pledged that Mrs. Daly's flag would "never suffer a stain of dishonor while a man of the 69th remained alive to defend it," again emphasizing Irish loyalty to the United States.[66]

At midafternoon, the regiment formed to march to the pier. Carrying their new American flag next to the green silk regimental banner, a gift to the regiment for their famous snub of the Prince of Wales, the 69th N.Y.S.M. marched past old St. Patrick's Cathedral and Hibernian Hall among throngs of Irish-Americans. Their cheers were deafening, recalled one observer, and were accompanied by "flags and banners streamed from the windows and the house-tops" while "ladies waved their handkerchiefs from the balconies, and flung bouquets on the marching column." At the head of the procession Colonel Corcoran rode in a carriage, too weak from his illness to ride a horse. Nearby a sign rallied the men and defined their dual causes: "69th, remember Fontenoy" and "No North, no South, no East, no West, but the whole Union."[67]

The mention of the Battle of Fontenoy spoke to the numerous comparisons that day between the 69th and other Irish regiments that had served loyally in other nations' wars. It was a symbol of the historic tradition of Irishmen serving for causes other than those of Ireland, though indirectly related to that island's freedom. In 1745 Irish exiles serving in the French Army had formed into *le Brigade Royal Irlandois* (the Royal Irish Brigade) and earned their fame in a daring bayonet charge against the English that turned the tide at Fontenoy for France.[68]

These Irishmen were part of the tradition of the "Wild Geese," whose roots date back to 1688, though the tradition of Irishmen serving in foreign armies against the English dates back much farther and would continue for generations to come. As each man escaped from Ireland, hidden away and registered in ships' manifests as "Wild Geese," their tradition became part of the memory of Irish resistance and the hope of Irish freedom. With the Irish volunteers, the American Civil War became part of that tradition.[69]

With this dual dream of Irish freedom and American patriotism, the 69th N.Y.S.M. marched down to the pier and aboard the steamer *James Adger* that would take them to Annapolis, from where they would march to Washington, DC. Public support of the 69th came not only from the Irish-American community but also from elements of the native-American public. The *New York Times* reported that spring on the massive turnout of Irish-Americans hoping to serve in this famous Irish regiment. "The 69th Off to War—Five Thousand Men More Than Required" read the headline, and the reporter pointed out that men from as far away as Boston, Hartford, and New Haven, Connecticut, had come to the city in the hope of joining Corcoran and his men on the road to war.

Few if any disparaging comments appeared about the Irish hoping to serve together, nor was there any reference to the Prince of Wales incident or the disloyalty of the San Patricios. The *Times* and the general public seemed interested only in the rush to service by these Irish-Americans. Many native-born Americans also commented with approval on the fact that members of the Irish and native-born community were organizing a fund for the families of the regiment, noting that over fifteen hundred dollars had already been contributed, including $250 from members of the stock exchange. "Such contributions are very much needed," noted the *Times,* "as a majority of the soldiers of this Regiment leave large families in very poor circumstances."[70]

The *Times*'s coverage of the 69th continued on a positive note, painting a picture of unified support of the regiment. "Long before the troops made their appearance," they stated, "the neighboring thoroughfares were completely choked up with people eager to catch a glance—perhaps a last one—of the familiar faces of friends before they should embark." Once again the *Times* reminded readers of the outpouring of support the 69th had received to its call for volunteers. "The rush for positions in the regiment was tremendous," they wrote, "and thousands who have been enrolled, were left behind, in consequence of the orders of the Major-General, that not more than a thousand men, all told, should be taken from the City."[71] The *Times* continued, recording the celebration of the men and even embracing the link between the causes of Ireland and America:

> When Sergeant-Major Murphy, bearing the magnificent national standard of the Regiment, and the Color Sergeant, with a splendid silk Star-Spangled Banner, also the property of the Regiment, appear [sic] in Great Jones Street and unfurled the united standards of Old Ireland and Young America, the enthusiasm of the soldiers and of the surrounding masses was wholly indescribable. All along Broadway the multitude shouted their huzzas, and from windows and housetops waved flags and handkerchiefs; the members, as they recognized familiar faces, raising their hats and responding enthusiastically. So densely packed was the route that the regiment were [sic] obliged to march in file. Some five hundred persons who had been left out, determined to stick by their favorite regiment as long as possible, and accompanied them the whole way to the boat.

Even at the pier, the crowd was astonishing. "In every direction people had clambered into the rigging of the vessels," wrote the *Times.* "They covered the tops of the pier-sheds and houses, and every place where a view could be obtained."[72] This clear demonstration of Irish-Americans' willingness to sacrifice for union may have convinced native-born New Yorkers to overlook the Prince of Wales affair and forget some of their prejudices in the face of looming conflict. The question, however, was how long their support for Irish volunteer units would last, especially when they included so much non-American imagery. Also, it remained to be seen if Irish-Americans, along with the rest of the North, could sustain this enthusiasm for the war.

For now, though, reactions to the departure of the 69th New York within the Irish-American audience was enthusiastic, with frequent mentions of Ireland and the importance of maintaining Irish honor. Michael Cavanagh, author of Thomas Francis Meagher's memoirs and an active Fenian, recalled that day and the "commingled feelings" of the Irish as they expressed their cheers and their sorrow. Irish nationalist Michael Doheny compared the departure of the 69th with the "Sailing of the Wild Geese," seeing in the event a blending of pride in his fellow Irish and sorrow that once again they were off to fight for a cause other than their own.

Cavanagh recalled that the most frequent comments from the crowd focused on this as well, while others reminded the soldiers to "remember your country, and keep up its credit, boy!" and it seems fitting that among all the references to a dual history and loyalty it was unclear whether the speaker was referring to Ireland or the United States. Recalling the mood that day, Michael Cavanagh explained that there were three motivating factors for Irish military service that were obvious in that April crowd:

> Honest pride in their adopted country; a feeling of gratitude which intensified their sense of duty to that country in its hour of peril, and an abiding hope of being *some* day—if God spared them—enabled to devote their soldierly experience to the liberation of the land of their birth and first love,—these constituted their actuating motives, and nerved them for whatever fate was in store for them.[73]

These motivations carried the men aboard the *James Adger* and on to Washington, where the 69th took up residence at Georgetown College. Most native-born New Yorkers, and large numbers of Americans generally, showed patience that spring for such expressions of dual loyalty among Irish-American troops.

The citizens of Washington were immensely relieved by the arrival of the 69th N.Y.S.M. and other regiments after the capital's period of isolation and vulnerability to a Confederate attack. Despite some frustrations over assignments and supplies, the units were infected with the excitement as well and overlooked many past differences in their new focus on a greater threat, just as New Yorkers had, during the recruitment and departure of the 69th, forgotten the Prince of Wales incident.

During a visit to the regiment's headquarters at Georgetown, the correspondent from the *New York Times* noted that the 69th had already had visitors from the 5th Massachusetts. All of the antagonism behind the Protestant sons of New England and the perceived "Papal Army" of America seemed to have disappeared, and he was thrilled to see such "an exciting scene . . . [of] Puritan New Englanders and Catholic Irishmen thus fraternizing." General Runyon, commanding a New Jersey brigade, commented similarly, "The common danger appears to have made native and foreigners common friends." It is interesting to note, too, that there was little reference to the fact that the Irishmen were staying at a Catholic institution. Some papers referred to the priests on campus, but the nativist tones were missing that would have been more apparent in reports from a decade earlier and perhaps even later in the war.[74]

Once again, native-born Protestants seemed willing to overlook the religious and ethnic qualities of the 69th New York now that these Irish Catholics were so dedicated to the American cause. Similarly, these Irishmen and their families at home seemed quick to display this loyalty and willingness to serve, and even Catholic leaders like Archbishops John Hughes in New York and John Purcell in Cincinnati, Ohio, became involved in blessing the flags of Union units as they marched off to war. For a brief time, the causes of American Protestantism and Irish-American Catholicism cooperated with astonishing efficiency. It would be a fragile relationship, though, that had long-term ramifications for the Irish in postwar America. The service of Irish-Catholic volunteers would reflect directly on their communities, and if this rush to the colors faltered, the spirit of cooperation would not only die, but it would also leave bitter resentments between the two groups for years to come.[75]

During the stay at Georgetown, Colonel Corcoran received orders from the War Department to increase his force by three hundred men. Included in these numbers would be the newly formed Irish Zouaves, commanded by Captain Thomas Francis Meagher. Corcoran and Meagher had discussed plans for organizing this unit from the hundreds of men Corcoran had left behind when the 69th N.Y.S.M. met its maximum muster of a thousand men. On the day before the 69th left New York, Meagher began recruitment. He called for only Irish volunteers, again keeping in mind Corcoran's well received argument that if Irish were to serve they should do so together to ensure that their valor was recognized. Meagher called "Young Irishmen to Arms!" and within a week, he had filled the ranks of the Irish Zouaves with a hundred Irish-Americans who would become Company K in the 69th N.Y.S.M. Awaiting transport to Washington, the new recruits met at the corner of Tenth Avenue and Broadway to drill in the billiards hall of a Captain Phelan. By May 22, the Irish Zouaves and an additional two hundred Irish-Americans were ready to fill the ranks of the 69th, and they departed for Washington.

Their arrival in the capital was marked with much fanfare despite the late hour. Marching down Pennsylvania Avenue, the regimental band struck up a tune as Meagher and his fellow officers led the column toward Georgetown College, filing past Willard's Hotel and the White House.[76]

Meagher and his Irish recruits joined the 69th N.Y.S.M. at Georgetown and followed them across the Potomac to Arlington Heights, where the men began construction on their new headquarters.

The 69th constructed its new home with amazing speed, pausing only for visits from Washington dignitaries. These included President Lincoln and his cabinet members, who made a point of visiting the Irishmen of the New York 69th, perhaps another example of Lincoln's understanding of the need to secure the support of the various constituencies of the North, including Irish-Americans. News of the president's visit reached New York, and other papers throughout the North. The *Herald* proudly proclaimed that this was not the first visit by these politicians, who had earlier visited the 69th at Georgetown, and after witnessing a dress parade, the president, cabinet members, and visiting generals were "loud in their praises of the efficiency of the men in drill."[77]

If it was a conscious strategy, Lincoln's efforts seemed to be paying off. By the end of May 1861, reports of new support for the president were emerging from previous Confederate sympathizers in areas like St. Louis, which included a large Irish-American community. "A great change seems to be coming over the spirits of the people," noted one reporter, "[t]hose who a week ago were loud for 'Governor Jackson and secession' being now daily and hourly enlisted in the government's service, and especially is this true of the Irish population."[78]

Upon completion of the fort, the men announced that it would be christened Fort Seward in honor of the New York secretary of state, but the War Department insisted on honoring the regiment's labors by naming it for its colonel. The celebrations of completion included the controversial baptism of a Fort Corcoran cannon by the 69th's chaplain, Father Thomas Mooney. Though Mooney was popular with the men for such martial enthusiasm, Catholic leaders were not pleased. Archbishop Hughes supported the idea of Irish service in this war, but he realized that Irishmen's actions would reflect, fairly or not, on Irish Catholics across the nation. He had defended Mooney against previous complaints about his enthusiastic behavior from Catholic leaders, but this unorthodox application of a sacrament, along with comments that appear to have included a call for the men to "flail" the enemy, forced Hughes to return Mooney to St. Brigid's in New York. While he would always be quick to chastise the Lincoln administration or the media for failing to recognize Irish sacrifices in this war, Hughes was equally quick to rein in any member whose actions might reflect poorly on American Catholics. He was well aware of the spotlight on his flock.[79]

Early June found the soldiers, Federal and Confederate, anxious for a fight. The night air frequently filled with the sound of shots and alarms ringing out as pickets exchanged fire. On June 2, an alarm rang around midnight when bugles of the 5th, 28th, and 69th New York Regiments sounded the officers' call. Visiting civilian Judge Daly and active Fenians John O'Mahoney and Richard O'Gorman grabbed their revolvers and located Colonel Corcoran to ascertain the threat, while Captain James Haggerty led the 69th out of the fort at a double quick and down Fairfax Court House Road. As with so many other alarms, there was no oncoming assault by the Confederates, but rather a brief exchange of shots between rebel pickets and outposts of the 28th New York. The men settled back into their routine of preparing and waiting for war.[80]

As July began, U.S. military leaders accepted the need for a battle despite the lack of training and organization that still plagued the army. General-in-Chief Winfield Scott was among those hoping for additional time for preparation, but President Lincoln insisted that they move before the three-month enlistment terms of the northern volunteers expired. The press echoed Lincoln's position, but this was not necessarily supported by the general public. Irish-American Judge Daly noted, "The impatience for the capture of Richmond is limited to the paper Generals of the [New York] *Tribune* whose personal security from all danger makes them naturally blood-thirsty and eager for the fighting of battles."[81]

Even Daly, though, was worried about the three-month enlistments, and he contacted Corcoran to see if they should begin recruiting a new batch of volunteers. Corcoran seemed as concerned as Daly, but determined not to publicly recognize the potential problem. "I have to say," Corcoran explained, "that, just now, it would be premature for me, or for anyone, to say what the 69th will do on the expiration of their three month's [sic] term of service. Their action will be determined by events, and this is all I am authorized, or feel justified in saying at this moment."[82]

Daly and Corcoran were not alone in these fears. All across the North men had answered President Lincoln's call for volunteers after the attack on Fort Sumter, pledging their service for three months, but those terms were nearing their end. The Lincoln administration and military leaders throughout the North hoped the enthusiasm that had led to large enlistments that spring would inspire men to reenlist. The cause of liberty and union had been especially popular in Irish-American communities, where Irishmen throughout New York City and the state rapidly filled the ranks. The 37th New York Infantry (the "Irish Rifles"), for example, filled their ranks in a single week.[83]

Similarly enthusiastic responses came from Irish-American communities all over the North. In Boston, Irish-born Thomas Cass received permission from the governor to organize a regiment of Irishmen to answer

Lincoln's call for volunteers. The ranks of the 13th Massachusetts Volunteer Militia filled quickly, many of them having served together in the Columbian Artillery, the Irish militia unit dissolved before the war due to nativist hostilities. Undaunted, the Irishmen had later met unofficially, supplying their own uniforms and arms. When Cass sent out his call, it was primarily these men and other Irishmen who responded, again indicating a desire to call attention to their service by enlisting in an Irish unit. While these Irishmen would receive significant support from the community, a sizable portion of the native-born population still saw the Irish militiamen as trouble and remembered broadsides that had called the community to arms just a few years earlier to face the militia group of "vagabond Irishmen" that was prepared "to shoot down the citizens of Boston." While many Bostonians had forgotten such animosity in the face of a common enemy in the spring of 1861, others were clearly displeased that Cass had reunited the Columbian Artillery, referring to his new regiment as a "load of Irish rubbish."[84]

Despite their quickness to volunteer, the soldiers of the 13th Massachusetts Volunteer Militia demonstrated a few problems. The regiment's captain, M. H. MacNamara, explained, "Not having a proper place of security for the recruits, many of them, growing restless, would become invisible,—some for a time, some forever,—leaving you the genial employment of liquidating sundry board bills, and mentally reckoning the brokerage value of sundry little loans."[85] Despite their difficulties with recruiting, MacNamara took pride in the service of this Irish militia regiment that would later become the Massachusetts 9th Infantry Regiment. After the war he wrote a history of the "Irish Ninth" to remind "the world how well the Irishmen, exiled from their native land by the ruthless system of English law practiced in Ireland, . . . [served] their adopted country in the day of her trial."[86]

Here again was an Irish-American who understood his Civil War military service in terms of both Ireland and America. MacNamara saw an opportunity to record the history of Irish military service that would improve native-born Americans' perception of Irish-Americans. Rather than seeing them as lazy and downtrodden, the reader would be shown how "Irish soldiers turn the 'horrors of war' into the most enjoyable of festivities." Regarding service in an Irish unit, MacNamara recalled that many of his comrades were motivated by old memories of Ireland's Wild Geese and the historic Irish Brigade of France that "won so much glory and shed so much blood."[87] Finally, MacNamara explained that an inability of the Irish to love America as much as they loved Ireland did not dim their affinity for their new homeland. "They could fight for it as bravely," he argued, "and shed their blood for it as freely, as any 'to the manor born.' "[88] While reinforcing anti-Irish stereotypes, MacNamara's work offers excellent documentation of what Irish-Americans hoped to gain from military service in the war.

James McKay Rorty fought for a combination of these reasons and others. In part, he reenlisted after his initial term of service in the spring of 1861 because army life seemed to strengthen him. This may seem surprising, considering that Confederates captured Rorty during the Battle of First Bull Run and he barely survived a bold prison escape that year. Still, as he explained to his disapproving parents in the fall of 1861, "I joined the 69th a shy, morose, and gloomy being, weak in body and with fluctuating health." Now a veteran of one battle and a disciplined soldier, Rorty was stronger, free of the asthma and consumption that had plagued him, and rid of his nervous habits. In addition, through this new army life, he "benefited by acquiring a more thorough knowledge of the world, and of my countrymen in particular: more tact, address and general information, which will be useful to me in any path of life."

For Rorty, though, there were other factors as well. In addition to his "attachment to, and veneration for the Constitution, which urged me to defend it at all risks," he fought for Ireland. He was a dedicated Fenian and hoped "that the military knowledge or skill which I may acquire [in the American Civil War] might thereafter be turned to account in the sacred cause of my native land." Still, he clarified, he fought for America, too. A permanently divided America "would close forever the wide portals through which the pilgrims of liberty from every European clime have sought and found it. Why? Because at the North the prejudices springing from the hateful and dominant spirit of Puritanism, and at the South, the haughty exclusiveness of an Oligarchy would be equally repulsive, intolerant and despotic." For Rorty the answer was simple: "Our only guarantee is the Constitution, our only safety is the Union, one and indivisible."[89] For men like Rorty and MacNamara, dual loyalties to America and Ireland shaped their decision to serve and their explanations to their families at home.

Despite this rush to service by Irish-Americans, and an apparent peace between native-born Protestants and Irish Catholics, evidence of nativist frustration with ethnic regiments, and Irish service in particular, surfaced in several northern communities that summer. In Illinois, one recruiter warned that no one should trust Irishmen to be loyal soldiers, shouting "D——n the man that relies on Paddies," and some Illinois communities acted on this prejudice by hesitating to supply newly recruited Irish companies with weapons. Quartermaster General S. E. Lefferts of the Wisconsin State Militia declared to an Irish militia company offering its services to the war effort, "There are enough young Americans to put down this trouble inside of ninety days and we do not want any red faced foreigners." The reaction from the Irish-American community is noteworthy. While later wartime and postwar accounts would frequently portray Irish-Americans as avoiding service, here they insisted on their right to fight for American union. Lefferts barely escaped a beating when the Irishmen charged at him, and later he denied ever making the statement.[90]

These actions represent the fragility of the temporary truce between Irish Catholics and native-born Protestants in America. The warmth demonstrated between the two groups in the East broke in these midwestern Irish-American communities. The Wisconsin Irishmen had all been members of the Hibernian Guard, and despite their reaction to Lefferts, following the incident they returned their weapons to their armory and voted to disband. This case is particularly noteworthy since Irish-Americans seemed to face less prejudice in midwestern and western communities than in the eastern, more established cities. Perhaps, though, cities like New York, Boston, and Philadelphia contained sufficiently large Irish communities to offer overwhelming demonstrations of loyalty to union that small groups of midwestern Irishmen could not, and thus nativists' suspicions could continue to thrive in the Midwest. Also, the unusual warmth between the two groups speaks to the fact that many of these ethnic and religious tensions were simply eclipsed by contagious enthusiasm for the war. The experiences of these midwestern Irishmen, while the exception to the rule in 1861, remain significant in their foreshadowing of tensions that would reemerge once the excitement of war gave way to its grim realities.

Indeed, even during this early phase of congeniality between native-born Protestants and Irish Catholics, there are indications that all was not well. The case of the 13th (Irish) Massachusetts Volunteer Militia in May 1861 is a good example. Shortly after they left the city for training on Long Island in Boston Harbor, Governor John A. Andrew of Massachusetts began receiving a flood of complaints of violence and disobedience among these new recruits. He decided to send an investigator to assess the situation. George D. Wells reported back to the governor that the Irish were good soldiers but lacked proper leadership, without which they were practically wild. Wells warned the governor that he must not order the 13th M.V.M. to Washington for fear that their behavior might reflect poorly on the state and his leadership.

For example, Wells explained, the men "care nothing for authority," and he recently observed an Irish sentry "patrolling with bare feet [and] a pipe in his mouth." Formation of an entirely Irish regiment may not have been wise, Wells summarized. "[T]he sweepings of our jails" are now representing the state and electing "officers of their own stripe." It was one thing to have Irish soldiers, but quite another to cluster them together under Irish leadership where the native Bostonians would lose control over this rabble. Perhaps, suggested Wells, the governor could assign a new officer to the regiment or disband it and disperse the Irish companies within other units. In this manner, the men would "be overcome by superior force [and] feel that they *must* obey," a theory rather similar to the nativists' call to scatter immigrants throughout native-born communities to foster full acceptance of American traditions.[91]

Despite the concerns of men like Wells, New England was not alone in witnessing the Irish-American rush to volunteer. In April 1861, James A. Mulligan, an Irish-American and active member of the Democratic party in Chicago, began organizing an Irish unit and his success challenges the idea that the experiences of midwestern Irish-Americans detailed above spoke for the entire region. Within a week Mulligan's ranks had swelled to twelve hundred men, but so many other regiments had already organized to meet the state quota that Mulligan had to secure a letter from President Lincoln to accept the Irish regiment from Chicago. Their fellow Illinoisan agreed, and the 23rd Illinois, popularly known as the "Irish Brigade" in a reflection of Mulligan's sense of history, was mustered into service.[92]

April 1861 found Major Joseph W. Burke, a native of Ireland and exile of the 1848 uprising, raising a similar Irish regiment in Cincinnati. Though the ranks filled quickly with Irishmen living in Ohio, Burke turned command of the regiment over to native-born William Haines Lytle, a common move when ethnic unit commanders feared they would not gain state support and funding, fiercely competed for among the many new regiments, without a native-born element to their command. As a prominent member of the Ohio bar, participant in local and state politics, and veteran of the Mexican War, Lytle was much more likely to receive support than the Irishman Burke.[93] It was a significant decision, considering the support many Irish regiments were receiving in the spring of 1861, and reflects that while the general native-born response to ethnic units was positive, some lingering prejudice and questions of loyalty remained.[94]

Irish-Americans were also rushing to volunteer in Philadelphia. Preexisting Irish militia companies, with names like the Irish Volunteers, the Hibernia Greens, and the Meagher Guards, formed the 2nd Philadelphia Regiment of State Militia while proudly proclaiming their ethnic heritage. In April 1861 the men elected Welsh-American Joshua T. Owen their colonel, Dennis Heenan as lieutenant colonel, and Irish-born Dennis O'Kane their major. The 2nd Philadelphia R.S.M. mustered into service as the 24th Pennsylvania Volunteers in the spring of 1861. They saw little service that summer, though the men took pride in their willingness to serve beyond their three-month enlistment period to secure the upper Potomac until replacements could arrive. The unit mustered out of service in August, but many of its members reenlisted in a new and largely Irish regiment that fall, the 69th Pennsylvania, patterned after the Fighting Irish of the 69th New York right down to their regimental number.[95]

The leading Irish-Americans of Philadelphia, many of them members of the Irish charitable organization the Friendly Sons of St. Patrick, were outspoken in their support of the Union cause. In June 1861, the Friendly Sons presented several resolutions proclaiming their "unalterable devotion and attachment to the government of the United States, and the Constitution." They made a conscious effort to inform the community that their views reflected those of all Irish-Americans in Philadelphia. The Irish men and women of the city were devoted entirely to the cause of union, the Friendly Sons explained, and they "will yield not in loyalty to the country which they have adopted as their own, the Government, Constitution, and Laws of which it is not less their duty than their inclination and determination to uphold, defend and obey."[96]

Members of the Friendly Sons backed this up with action. The Society's president, Major General Robert Patterson, and both of his sons, Colonel Francis E. Patterson and Colonel Robert Emmet Patterson, were already in service by June 1861. Unfortunately, the family's record would not be the finest of the war. Their first embarrassment came with General Robert Patterson's failure to prevent Confederate general Joseph E. Johnston's reinforcement of General P. G. T. Beauregard at the battle of First Bull Run. Later scandals surrounded his son, Francis Patterson, who commanded a non-Irish regiment from Philadelphia at the beginning of the war and later reached the rank of brigadier general. In November 1862, the young Patterson was charged with executing an unauthorized retreat based on false rumors. When the matter came before General Ambrose E. Burnside, then commander of the Army of the Potomac, Patterson died before any rulings could be made when he accidentally shot himself with his pistol.[97]

The leadership of the Friendly Sons of St. Patrick, despite their claims, did not necessarily speak for all of the Irish. The Patterson men were not really interested in commanding Irish units, despite their dedication to serve in the war and their conscious membership in the Friendly Sons of St. Patrick. Perhaps their situation matched that once criticized by New Yorker and leading Fenian Michael Cavanagh, who grumbled that the Friendly Sons in New York were Irish "in name—not in heart" and were "in the habit of toasting the health of the British Queen!" at their annual meetings. Members of an Irish New York militia regiment put an end to this on St. Patrick's Day 1852, when Captain John Broughaw led his men in reversing their glasses during the year's toast and "gave expression to the universal indignation of his outraged countrymen in language so scathing," recalled Cavanagh, "that the flunkies were abashed" and the custom was never again repeated. From then on the pro-British members of the Friendly Sons slowly resigned, and the organization became increasingly Irish nationalist and Catholic.[98] Cavanagh's characterization of the Friendly Sons may not compare exactly with the experience in Philadelphia, but that city's members were certainly a reflection of the more successful Irish, many of whom were of Protestant and of Scots-Irish heritage.

The Friendly Sons may not have represented all of the Irish in Philadelphia, but many of the wealthy as well as the impoverished Irish in the city demonstrated loyal support of the Union that spring. St. John the Baptist Parish in Manayunk, a mill town just upriver from Philadelphia, had organized its own militia unit, the Jackson Rifles, with members of the congregation. They mustered into service on April 29, 1861, as Company A, 21st Pennsylvania Infantry Regiment. The company was almost entirely composed of Irish-Americans, many of whom remained with the unit when it was reorganized that fall and joined the 98th Pennsylvania Volunteers. Though that regiment was comprised primarily of German-Americans, the original Company A remained intact as an Irish unit, another demonstration of support for Colonel Corcoran's hope that Irish-Americans would serve in Irish units to call attention to their sacrifice and loyalty. In the case of Company A, 98th Pennsylvania Volunteers, it worked. Over one hundred years later, as parish members gathered their history, they focused detailed attention on the Irish and German-American Catholic veterans from their community, including Medal of Honor winner First Sergeant Peter McAdams of the Irish Company A.[99]

While the Irish-American turnout all over the North was tremendous that spring, it was the 69th New York that saw the most significant action in the first battle and came to represent the early contributions of Irish-American Catholics. Their actions at the Battle of First Bull Run, the first engagement of the war, proved to many native-born Americans that Irish soldiers could serve loyally and bravely in this conflict and behave well under fire, which could not be said of many Union forces that July day.

June 1861 found Brigadier General Irvin McDowell in command of nearly thirty thousand Federal forces organized to put down the Confederate rebellion. Both he and General-in-Chief Winfield Scott agreed that the men were not ready for an offensive, but President Lincoln insisted that the army had to move before most of their force's three-month enlistments expired and before inaction came to characterize his government.

Following these orders, McDowell laid out a plan to attack Confederate general P. G. T. Beauregard's 20,000-man force at Manassas Junction, Virginia. The only other Confederate forces in the area were the twelve thousand men stationed as Harper's Ferry, (West) Virginia, under the command of General Joseph E. Johnston. McDowell ordered the aging Irish-native Philadelphian and president of the Friendly Sons of St. Patrick, General Robert Patterson, to use his 18,000-man state militia force to hold Johnston in the Shenandoah Valley and prevent him from reinforcing Beauregard.

Patterson had served as Winfield Scott's second-in-command in the Mexican War, but the assignment in 1861 required independent command, which he had never exercised, over inexperienced and poorly trained troops, who would have challenged even an experienced commander. Patterson was not pleased or comfortable with the assignment. He constantly sought the opinions of his staff, even less experienced than he, and failed to act decisively in the assignment. Patterson's mistakes allowed Johnston to slip past his force and rush toward Manassas Junction to reinforce the Confederates at midday.[100]

Actions leading to these events began much earlier for the 69th N.Y.S.M. Assigned to Colonel William Tecumseh Sherman's 3rd Brigade of Brigadier General Daniel Tyler's 1st Division, the 69th New York prepared for battle as they approached the middle of July. In the days before the first battle, some of the men were planning to leave camp, believing that their three-month enlistments were up. While this may have been in part due to cowardice or lack of genuine support for the war for some of the soldiers, many of the men explained that they had not yet been paid and desperately needed to return to New York to support their families. When Colonel Corcoran discussed these matters with Sherman, he consulted the War Department. They clarified that the ninety-day period began when a man mustered in, not when he enrolled in the unit. Corcoran and many of the men accepted this and enthusiastically anticipated the battle, but some Irishmen, Sherman noted, were not pleased with the decision and continued to complain.[101]

Sherman's problems increased as the men were marching toward Centerville, Virginia, on July 13. Outside Fairfax Court House, they spotted Confederates and prepared to engage them, but the rebels retreated before any shots were fired. Shortly afterward a loaded musket slipped from a stack of arms, fired, and hit Captain John Breslin of Company F. Despite Breslin's obvious pain, Sherman refused to allow him to return to Washington and insisted that he go on with the regiment with the ambulances in the rear. It was a decision that earned Sherman a terrible reputation with many of the men and Meagher in particular, who described

Sherman as "a rude and envenomed martinet" who was "hated by the regiment."[102]

Sherman, Corcoran, and the 69th saw little fighting the morning of July 21, staying in their position near the Warrenton Turnpike on the opposite side of Bull Run from the Confederates. Near the Stone Bridge, they fired intermittently at rebel skirmishers, trying to divert attention away from Colonel David Hunter's 2nd Division moving toward Matthews Hill from Sudley Ford to the northwest. By 11 A.M. Union and Confederate forces were heavily engaged on Matthews Hill, and General McDowell ordered Tyler to advance across Bull Run and reinforce Hunter. With the 69th New York in the lead, Sherman's 3rd Brigade forded the stream about a half-mile above the Stone Bridge and moved up the hill on the opposite bank.

Advancing slowly to avoid confusion from the fact that over two of their companies were clad in gray uniforms, they came against Louisiana Zouaves, many of whom were fellow Irish Catholics recruited from the docks of New Orleans.[103] Mistaking the New Yorkers for Confederates, the Zouaves allowed the 69th to advance within close range only to be surprised when the Irish New Yorkers fired a massive volley that ripped through the Zouaves' lines. As the wounded Louisiana Irish retreated from the field, the 69th's acting lieutenant-colonel James Haggerty tried to ride down a rebel, but the man turned and fired and Haggerty fell from his saddle mortally wounded. While mourning this loss, some of the men may have noticed a larger tragedy for the Irish in America. Many of the Louisiana and the New York Irish had entered the ranks with the same hopes of providing for their families, protecting their communities and their adopted homelands, and gaining military experience that could be used to free Ireland from British rule. Despite their related motives, that hot July day found them on opposite fields of battle, killing each other for similar goals.

Joining with Colonel Andrew Porter's Brigade of Hunter's Division and Samuel P. Heintzelman's 3rd Division as they prepared for the assault on Henry Hill, the 69th New York fell in line behind the 2nd Wisconsin and the Scots-Irish 79th New York. Corcoran and his Irish New Yorkers watched as the 2nd Wisconsin failed in two desperate attacks, followed by another heroic but equally unsuccessful assault on the hill by the 79th New York. Sherman ordered the 69th forward, and the regiment rushed into the battle. Many of the men were bare-chested, having stripped down in the heat of the summer and the battle, and as Colonel Corcoran led his men into the fray, a journalist from *Harper's Weekly* captured the scene with a romantic sketch of the 69th for his paper, describing how the Irishmen had "stripped themselves, and dashed into the enemy with the utmost fury. The difficulty was to keep them quiet."[104] The image contrasted sharply with the one of disloyal Irishmen *Harper's Weekly* had painted just nine months earlier following the Prince of Wales incident. For now at least, Irish bravery in service to America was wiping away past prejudice and improving the image of the Irish among native-born Americans. This sketch of dedicated Irish service at First Bull Run was reprinted in papers throughout the North as native-born and Irish-Americans alike celebrated the stereotype of a rugged Irish "race" in their favorite element, a good fight. A certain level of prejudice remained in references to Irishmen as "natural" fighters, an image of violence that had plagued them in the 1840s and 1850s, but now the Irish were using such stereotypes to their advantage.

The 69th made two separate assaults on the Confederate position that day, but in the end they, too, failed to take the hill. As the 69th New York retreated along the Warrenton Turnpike, Corcoran noticed rebel cavalry and ordered the men into a square formation, which they managed quite well despite the chaotic situation around them. As they neared the woods, however, they had to shift back into column, and while they were doing this two regiments racing toward the rear swept through the Irishmen and the 69th was caught up in the flow. Private James McKay Rorty of Company G in the 69th New York blamed Sherman for this disaster. He argued that Sherman "told the men to get away as fast as they could as the enemy's cavalry were coming" and thus the Irishmen were not to blame for the panicked retreat.[105]

Colonel Corcoran waved the national banner to rally his men and returned some order to the unit, but few stopped to join him. Those who did quickly found themselves surrounded, and along with Corcoran, were taken prisoner. Major Meagher similarly tried to rally the men around the green silk banner given the unit after the Prince of Wales incident, shouting, "Boys, look at that flag—think of Ireland and Fontenoy." Shortly thereafter rebel forces managed to tear the 69th's emerald banner from its standard, much to the horror of the men who were standing their ground. Whatever order remained was weakened by this and then crushed as Meagher's horse was shot from under him and he fell to the ground unconscious. It was only the sharp eye of a trooper of the 2nd U.S. Cavalry who spotted Meagher and carried him to safety that prevented his capture.[106]

In small groups the 69th stumbled back toward Washington and Fort Corcoran, arriving around 3:00 A.M. on July 22. Thirty-eight of their friends and comrades were dead on the field near Bull Run, while another fifty-nine lay wounded. Ninety-five Irishmen were missing in action, some captured while others who had seen enough of war were gone for good. Despite their losses and flawed exit from the field, the advance of the 69th

N.Y.S.M. and the rest of Sherman's Brigade contributed to the Confederate withdrawal from Matthews Hill and when retreating from Henry Hill, the 69th handled themselves better than most of the Federal units that day.[107]

As the Irishmen assessed their losses and their first performance in battle, so too did Irish Catholic and native-born New Yorkers. The day after the battle the *New York Herald* reported, "the 69th (Irish) regiment [is] reported to have behaved most gallantly in their fight."[108] As the days continued, though, reports came in of the death of acting lieutenant-colonel Haggerty and of Colonel Corcoran's capture, while several papers mistakenly reported Meagher and Colonel Robert Nugent among the dead, and still others reported a spreading rumor that Meagher's fall from his horse was the result not of gunfire but of drunkenness.

Maria Lydig Daly worried over these reports, the impact of this loss, and its effect on the war.[109] The New York *Irish-American* agreed, arguing that the Federal defeat at First Bull Run "will be found small in comparison with the detriment which we are likely to suffer from the prolongation of a struggle which a decisive victory in the present instance would have virtually reduced within terminable limits."[110]

Despite the loss, many New York Irish-Americans remained positive about the conduct of the 69th New York. The *Irish-American* proudly quoted a report from the *New York Times* praising the actions of the 69th at First Bull Run. Others spoke of the role played by Father O'Reilly, the 69th's chaplain, who cared for the wounded Irishmen amid the battle and escaped capture by lying among the dead when a Confederate patrol passed by. A great sigh of relief met reports that Captain John Wildey of the New York Fire Zouaves had recovered the regiment's Prince of Wales flag and returned it to the 69th's camp following the battle. Little public mention was made of the embarrassing capture of the United States flag that Maria Lydig Daly had presented the regiment. Daly heard that "the ensign dropped it in his retreat, and as he escaped unhurt, has not dared to show his face. The Regiment declared that he shall be shot if he does." Most of all, the Irish-American community anticipated the return of the regiment to the city, planning a massive turnout to demonstrate their support of the men.[111]

The response from the native-American press also celebrated the heroism of the 69th New York, but congratulations were mixed with surprise and condescension. The *New York Times* gave the Irish veterans a front-page headline: "Our War-Worn Heroes—Return of the 69th Regiment." The article, though celebratory, carried a heavy paternalistic tone, as though the master of a house were rewarding the services of a dedicated servant. To be fair, though, part of this may have also reflected a naiveté about war. Shock over the condition of the returning veterans revealed how much the nation would learn in the coming months and years of the toll and unromantic nature of war. Much of the piece, however, reveals a continued prejudice against Irish-Americans. The same report that calls the men of the 69th N.Y.S.M. heroes refers to the Irishwomen in the crowd as "Biddy," the generic and derogatory term used for Irish domestic servants. The *Times* explained that many "a Biddy" was there against direct orders from their employers, having already received two holidays as the city awaited the return of the delayed regiment. The *Times* then went on to note that the veterans of the 69th "presented a rather disheveled appearance," but excused this by noting the "eager gladness in their eyes which compensated for defects of toilet." Despite some continued prejudice, other aspects of the *Times* report suggested that native presses were revising their image of Irish-Americans, and this revision was based largely on that groups' dedicated battlefield service. The *Times* reported that "so unquestionable [the 69th's] valor, so complete and heroic its willing self-devotion, that the first word of qualified praise has not yet reached our ears."[112]

Many Irish-Americans took similar pride in the improving image they shared due in part to the bravery of the 69th New York at the First Battle of Bull Run. Inspired by the unit's record and hoping to claim similar praise for themselves, Irish-Americans in the city formed another regiment of their countrymen into the 3rd Irish Volunteers and contacted Meagher to request that he command them. "The glorious example set to the Irish adopted citizens by the gallant 69th," explained Lieutenant Colonel P. D. Kelly, "induced the formation of the 3rd Irish Volunteers, and its principles are the same as theirs—if the Irish perform a brave act, let *them* get the credit of it."[113]

Similar reports in the *New York Herald* proudly announced that despite their tremendous losses, the spirit of the "Fighting 69th" was as strong as ever:

> The President and Secretary Seward visited the quarters yesterday, and had an interview with the 69th, which has been terribly cut up, and whose Colonel (Corcoran) was wounded and is still missing. The term of the 69th has expired, but upon Mr. Lincoln—who complimented them upon their valor and valuable services—asking them to reenlist, they declared, with loud cheers, their determination to do so to a man, and see the fight out.[114]

In the midst of this praise, however, came concerns from distant family members. On the day after the battle, July 22, 1861, Matilda Sproul wrote to her son Andrew from Ireland. Andrew J. Sproul emigrated to America in the 1840s and was living with his wife Frances in Fredericksburg, Ohio, when the letter arrived. His mother Matilda had expressed concern in a previous letter over "troublesome times in America" and now repeated her fears: "I am uneasy when I hear of so many going out of Philadelphia to the army."[115]

As the summer came to a close and the North regrouped, communities assessed this first stage of the war. It was obvious to almost everyone now that this was going to be a much longer and larger conflict than expected. After this first taste of war, some northerners had had enough and would choose against reenlisting. Many Irish and native-born northerners, however, responded to their defeat in Virginia as the 69th had, reorganizing their efforts, calling upon their countrymen to rally to the flag, and forming Irish companies, regiments, and brigades. Each hoped to capture some of the glory of the 69th New York, support the interests of the Irish in America, and make their contribution to the cause of union. Some hoped that Irish service would reflect well upon their countrymen and would challenge the negative stereotypes of "Bridget" and "Pat" in America. Their strongest motivations, however, continued to be tied to Ireland and their immediate needs in America: the Fenians seeking military experience, many Irishmen fighting to save a united America as a home for themselves and future Irish refugees, and other Irish-Americans enlisting for the steady paycheck and bonuses.

As the weeks progressed, Irishmen seemed to be achieving these goals as training camp slowly turned them into soldiers and as they mailed some of their pay home to their families. It even appeared that Irish volunteering was improving their image among some native-born Americans. The Lowell (Massachusetts) *Advertiser,* a native press, reported on the formation of the 9th Connecticut Volunteers. The report explained that the regiment was comprised almost entirely of Irishmen and made repeated reference to the bravery, patriotism, and fearlessness of the soldiers. While prewar reports offered few kind words to describe Irish commanders of militia regiments, the native press described the Irish-born colonel of the 9th Connecticut as possessing "superior accomplishments and genius" and the major as a "profound scholar, a polished gentleman, and distinguished young lawyer." The native-born women of New Haven, Connecticut, presented the regiment with national and state colors, the latter bearing an Irish harp.[116] The gift, representing the dual loyalties of Irish-American soldiers, signified that many native-born Americans approved of this motivation for service, and it suggests that their prejudice against Irish-Americans was diminishing. For this trend to last, however,

Irish-Americans would have to continue supporting the same goals and issues that inspired native-born American elites.

As the nation organized new regiments that fall and winter of 1861, Irish-American military service was improving the image of Irishmen among native-born Americans. The strongest motivations for Irish volunteering, however, remained tied to the interests of Irish America. As long as these remained linked to the goals of the Union war effort, Irishmen would continue to serve in large numbers and earn the praise of native-born Americans. The Union cause, however, would change in the following year to include emancipation. At the same time, Irishmen would be realizing what a massive physical toll the war was demanding from them, as thousands lay dead and wounded on the battlefields of Virginia and Maryland. They would soon choose between the interests of America and those of Irish America, and many of them would support the latter.

3

"We Are Slaughtered Like Sheep, and No Result But Defeat"

The Decline of Irish-American Support for the War in 1862

The year 1862 would be marked by the rise of the new Irish Brigade and its growing fame for tenacity at Malvern Hill, Second Bull Run, Antietam, and Fredericksburg. By the end of the year Union commanders agreed that the Irish Brigade was one of the best in the Army of the Potomac, and the unit to be called upon to take the most difficult objectives. In battle after battle the Irishmen proved not only their ability as soldiers but also their loyalty to the United States, even if that was not necessarily a goal. Such a reputation had a price, though, and lengthening casualty lists and pensions too small to support the widows and orphans left behind tested Irish-Americans' willingness to sacrifice for abstract goals of duty and honor and American union. Similarly, a conflict that was training Fenians was killing and wounding so many that some Irishmen wondered if anyone would be left to fight Ireland's next war.

The fall of 1861 found the Irishmen of the 69th New York State Militia home in New York, weary from the first battle of the war but confident that, though First Bull Run had been a defeat for the Union forces, the 69th had performed reasonably well. As David Power Conyngham, a staff officer in the future Irish Brigade and historian of that unit, reflected, "the disaster at Bull Run, when properly considered, seemed natural and almost inevitable. Raw troops who had never been in a battle were hurled against strongly intrenched [sic] positions, well manned and gunned." The 69th New York, he argued, "had by desperate fighting succeeded in driving the enemy from some of their strongest lines." Conyngham dismissed their panicked retreat as more reflective of the inexperience and lack of discipline of the raw troops than any great flaw in the Irishmen. The rout, he argued, "was first commenced by the teamsters and civilians; and the militia, not knowing much more about a battle, became infected, and thus it spread to the whole army. Such a thing could not happen with an army six months in the field. . . . It was, after all, but a training-school to open men's eyes to the real necessities and responsibilities of war."[1]

Fenian Michael Cavanagh, who wrote *The Memoirs of Gen. Thomas Francis Meagher,* agreed. The men of the 69th New York, he explained, "did not feel themselves beaten, and would not accept the shame of a defeat for which they, at all events, were not responsible."[2] Tied to this confidence was the men's desire to return to the seat of war. Even before the 69th N.Y.S.M. mustered out of service on August 3, 1861, the officers discussed reorganizing the regiment for three years' service. The Lincoln administration supported this idea and at the end of the month, the War Department gave Thomas Francis Meagher, now a colonel, permission to reorganize the unit into the 69th New York Volunteers and to direct the organization of four additional regiments to form a brigade, the commander of which would be named by the War Department.[3]

Meagher went to work immediately to make this an Irish brigade whose men came from the Irish communities in New York, Massachusetts, and Pennsylvania. Prominent New York Catholic Irish-Americans organized a committee to raise funds for the brigade, while Meagher went about contacting Irish-Americans in Boston and Philadelphia regarding the formation of Irish regiments there. The Boston regiment was to be the 28th Massachusetts, commanded by Colonel Mathew Murphy, while the Irishmen of Philadelphia and neighboring communities rushed to form a similar regiment from that state. In New York City, the 3rd Irish Volunteers, who had organized in the hope of attracting positive attention to the Irish in America through gallant service, joined the brigade as the 63rd New York Volunteers, led by Colonel Felix E. O'Rourke. The 69th New York joined the brigade under the leadership of Colonel Robert Nugent, followed by the 88th New York Volunteers under Colonel Henry Baker.[4]

That fall of 1861 found Thomas Francis Meagher once again using his talents as an orator and leader to recruit Irish-Americans to the newly formed Irish Brigade. At the 69th New York's festival in Jones' Woods, organized to raise money for the regiment's widows and orphans, Meagher spoke of the sacrifices the Irish had already made, but called on them to continue the fight. He asked his audience,

Will the Irishmen of New York stand by this cause—resolutely, heartily, with inexorable fidelity, despite of all the sacrifices it may cost, despite of all the dangers into which it may compel them, despite of all the bereavements and abiding gloom it may bring upon such homes as this day miss the industry and love of the dead soldiers of the Sixty-ninth . . . ? *For my part, I ask no Irishman to do that which I myself am not prepared to do.*

My heart, my arm, my life is pledged to the national cause, and to the last it will be my highest pride, as I conceive it to be my holiest duty and obligation, to share its fortunes.[5]

Meagher had not forgotten his audience's dual loyalties to Ireland and Irish America, and his discussions frequently emphasized not only sacrifice but also the link between the causes of Ireland and the war in America. Contacting a friend in Boston, Meagher called on Irish-born B. S. Treanor to work toward filling the ranks of a regiment of Boston and Massachusetts Irish. Meagher explained that these men would be not only serving "the friendliest government Irishmen have ever known" but also saving the United States from England's "evil scheme" of helping the Confederacy to destroy the American republic. Let the Irish of Boston know, Meagher declared, that "every blow dealt against the great conspiracy beats back the insolence and base plots of England."[6]

More representative of the dual theme was Meagher's speech at the funeral of Irish nationalist Terence McManus in September 1861. When a speaker at the gathering mentioned the service of the 69th at First Bull Run, someone from the audience called for three cheers for Meagher, followed by cheers for Corcoran and the men of the 69th. Meagher then rose from his seat and asked for another round of cheers "for the two brave sons of John Mitchel, who are fighting as bravely on the other side." John Mitchel was an Irish nationalist who served a sentence, like Meagher, in Van Dieman's Land (Tasmania) after the 1848 uprising. At the outbreak of war both of his sons chose to fight with the Confederacy. Despite serving for their military foe, many northern Irish-Americans still felt a loyalty to Mitchel, his sons, and southern Irish-Americans for their shared heritage. John Mitchel, who celebrated Irish service north and south, shared these sentiments and saw the war more in terms of a training ground for Irish patriots than a struggle between secession and union. Pleased with reports of the 69th's service at Bull Run, Mitchel reflected, "I imagine the men who faced Beauregard's artillery and rifles until Bull Run ran red, will not be likely to shrink on the day (when will it dawn, that white day?) that they will have the comparatively light task of whipping their weight of red-coats."[7]

Perhaps because of this loyalty to Ireland, Meagher was extremely sensitive to Irish criticisms of Irish-American involvement in the Civil War. In his mind, the two causes were directly related, and it was the United States that needed the assistance of its Irish citizens. He railed against those who would "with their raw notions of liberty and democracy endeavor to wean the Irish-born citizens of the American Union from their duty to the laws, the magistracy, and the sovereignty of the Republic from which they derive the only political consequence they have ever as yet possessed."[8]

While Irishmen in New York formed regiments that would join Meagher's Irish Brigade, Irishmen in other northern communities organized similar units. The 24th Pennsylvania Volunteers, a largely Irish infantry regiment, had seen little battlefield experience during its three-month existence in the summer of 1861. Even so, the volunteers had suffered from insufficient food and clothing, and their return to Philadelphia that July had made quite the impression as the men insisted on wearing overcoats in the oppressive heat rather than reveal their tattered uniforms. Despite this, most of the men mustered out of the 24th Pennsylvania quickly reorganized into a new three-year regiment designated the 69th Pennsylvania Volunteers, again comprised largely of young Irishmen.[9]

For Irish-Americans like Patrick Dunny in Philadelphia, the loss at Bull Run did not dampen his enthusiasm for the war. That October, he described the battle in great detail to his family in Ireland. Though a civilian, Dunny had acquired numerous details of the battle, and discussed in particular the struggle between the 69th N.Y.S.M.—"a nobler set of men there was not in the world"—and the Louisiana Tigers—"as good Irish as any one." He declared their struggle for control of the 69th's colors the most deadly on that day, with "more lives lost over that flag than any one object on the field," and concluded that the loss of Irish lives on both sides was "grievous to every Irishman." Despite these tragic reports, Dunny reminded his family that an Irishman was in charge of the army now (referring to General George B. McClellan) and that "there is a great times here enlisting now," with "a great many whole regiments of Irish going almost daily."[10] This rapid response was not, however, the norm in all northern Irish communities.

In Boston, the call went out in September 1861 for three-year enlistments in the 28th Massachusetts. Despite enticements of serving in the Irish Brigade with famed commanders like Thomas Francis Meagher, the organizers had trouble filling the unit. Perhaps Irish Catholics in the city viewed the war as Maurice Sexton did. In November 1861, he told his family in Ireland of the "ruin" the war "brought the majority of the working people." He seemed convinced, however, that much of Boston's working class had already departed for service, and warned his male relatives against emigrating to America until hostilities had ended, for they "would not get a thing to now except to go to the war out to Virginia, and perhaps get shot."[11] It was not until December that recruiters had sufficient numbers to muster the regiment into service, and even then they were still adding companies in the field.[12]

In Wisconsin that fall many immigrant companies, let alone regiments, had difficulty recruiting sufficient numbers and had to settle for an Irish-German immigrant mix to their unit.[13] Similar problems faced the organizers of the Irish 35th Indiana Volunteer Infantry Regiment. In spite of attractive recruiting advertisements in the local paper explaining that service in the 35th brought a one-hundred-dollar bounty, 160 acres of land upon mustering out of service, and a weekly allowance of one dollar for each man's wife and fifty cents per child in addition to the husband's regular pay, the citizens of Lafayette, Indiana, had not been able to form two Irish companies. That September, preparing to march out of town to train at Camp Tippecanoe, Captain John Balfe revealed his frustrations over limited recruiting success and equally poor attendance at muster when he decided to consolidate companies and reminded the men that "full attendance is urgently required" at all regimental affairs. By September, the 1st Irish, 35th Indiana had to open its ranks to native-born American volunteers to fill the unit.[14] This necessity may have been partly due to the limited number of Irish-Americans of military age in these communities. Another factor may have been the fact that by the fall of 1861, the initial romantic rush to war had faded and more sober minds now considered the decision to volunteer.

Exactly what changed remains unclear, though a final factor appears to be continued, or renewed, prejudice against the Irish by native-born Americans. This complaint surfaced in Iowa and Michigan in September 1861. Irishmen in Iowa protested that even though they had filled their regiments with fellow Irish-Americans, field commands were being given to non-Irish officers. Other Irishmen complained that they were not being provided with sufficient clothing or food and that after months in service, they had received no pay. Some of them argued that this was a reflection of official army prejudice against ethnic units, while others pointed to religious discrimination. Irish soldiers in Michigan made similar complaints, pointing out that they lacked a sufficient number of Catholic chaplains. "No provision whatever is made for [Catholic soldiers'] spiritual care," wrote the *Detroit Daily Tribune*, "while Protestants are amply provided for as regards their spiritual wants."[15] Father Peter Paul Cooney of the 35th Indiana noted, "the great evil is [that there is] not one chaplain in the army for twenty that are needed." In particular, Cooney worried about Catholics mixed in predominantly Protestant regiments, where the Catholics' religious needs were "entirely neglected."[16]

Some Irish-American leaders believed the solution was to avoid service in ethnic units. Irish-born Dennis Mahoney, a Democratic newspaper editor in Dubuque, Iowa, had been addressing this issue for months. In August 1861 he argued against Irish units and even challenged the entire principle that Irish military service would somehow improve the standing of these immigrants with native-born Americans. The old hatreds would appear in "insult and derision of the Irish, whether . . . considered as the subject of a Police Court brawl or as the heroic defenders of the Star Spangled Banner. It is all the same," Mahoney argued. Similarly, if the Irish enlisted in ethnic units, they would call attention to their unique heritage and their pride in this past. Americans, explained Mahony, would see this as a rejection of native traditions in favor of past loyalties. If they wanted to become accepted in this country, Mahony argued, the Irish must serve in American units.[17]

In other cases, Irish leaders warned their countrymen against units that were Irish in name only. William G. Halpin took out an ad in the *Cincinnati Daily Enquirer* to warn Irishmen of the recruiting methods of the 15th Ohio. Apparently, recruiters made a handsome profit by enrolling Irishmen who were informed that they would be joining a totally Irish unit, when in fact the unit was only part Irish, native-born officers commanded it, and the new recruits were treated "with the utmost indignity . . . [and] most contemptuously." As a result, many of the men threatened revolt while others simply walked out of camp and returned home disgusted by the entire process.[18]

One of the most violent encounters between native and Irish Union troops occurred in September 1861 after Irish soldiers at Camp Cairo, Illinois, raged through camp on a drunken spree that did not end until guards had fixed bayonets and made it clear they would use them. One Irishman fought off ten soldiers before finally being subdued. Native-born soldiers witnessing the event had their negative stereotypes of the Irish confirmed, and one prophesied that at some future point the tensions would erupt in "a hells [sic] own mess between the hibernian [sic] guards and union guards." The feeling seemed to be mutual, as James Swales of the Native Union Guard recalled the Irishmen in camp calling the Americans "the scum of hell [and] other mean names." Whoever started it, the Native Union Guards pledged to finish the debate, claiming that at "the very first opportunity we are just going to simply clean them out."[19] In the early months of the war, such problems were set aside in the face of a common enemy. After the bloody fighting of 1862, however, the casualties and defeats exacerbated ethnic strife and caused some Irishmen to question the value of military service.

Despite these problems, the recruiting abilities of Thomas Francis Meagher had attracted sufficient numbers to muster the regiments of the new Irish Brigade into service, though they were still under strength, and send them to Fort Schuyler along Long Island Sound, where their training began. As one veteran recalled, this is where the brigade "learned its A B C of military tactics." As the 69th's ranks filled and they prepared to march to Washington, their departure was marked with a ceremony at which they and the other New York regiments of the Irish Brigade (63rd N.Y.V. and the 88th N.Y.V.) received their colors, though only the 69th had sufficient numbers to depart the city. The 63rd and the 88th would remain at Fort Schuyler awaiting additional recruits and join the 69th later that year.

The turnout for the November 18, 1861, ceremony was tremendous. Each speaker took the opportunity to remind the men of their historic role as Irish soldiers of an Irish Brigade, as well as their new role as loyal citizens of the United States. One speaker, prominent New Yorker and Irish-American Judge Charles Patrick Daly, included a heavy emphasis on discipline and dedication in his talk. The theme comprised nearly half his speech as Daly reminded the men that the Irish Brigade of old "achieved its historical renown not through the admitted bravery of its members merely, but chiefly by the perfection of its discipline." It would be only through this generation of Irishmen's ability to imitate this discipline "that you will or will not be known hereafter. The selection of such a name only renders the contrast more glaring in the event of inefficiency and incompetency," Daly expounded.[20]

Daly may have revealed underlying qualms he had about Irishmen's response to the call for volunteers and their new commander. Despite Meagher's efforts, two of the three New York regiments lacked sufficient numbers to depart for the South. Some of this may have had to do with the ongoing discussion of who would command the Irish Brigade and of Meagher's role in its organization.

The brigade's command was expected to go to James Shields. The former U.S. senator, currently stationed in California, was a veteran of the Mexican War and perhaps the best-known Irish-American officer in the country. That fall, however, some questioned whether Shields would accept the position, and it appeared to others that Meagher was working to secure it for himself. In fact, Shields declined the offer for a variety of reasons, most stemming from his rank of major general in the Mexican War and his desire to seek a similar rank in this conflict, rather than accepting the lower brigade command.

When Shields denied the honor in the hope of securing a higher command, the next logical choice was Meagher, who had been so critical in the brigade's organization and to Irish-American participation in the war. The Irishman's lack of command experience, however, worried several people, as did his personal ambition. Maria Lydig Daly, wife of Judge Daly, was a sharp critic of Meagher. Both she and her husband were heavily involved with fund raising for the brigade and were close friends of Michael Corcoran, then languishing in a Confederate prison. Maria Daly saw Meagher as a usurper of Corcoran's work with ambitions that could harm rather than serve the Irish-American effort. Declaring Meagher "double-faced," Daly recalled how "Tuesday last, he said nothing would induce him to be a brigadier; on Saturday last, he begged Mr. [John] Savage to push the matter with some influential men in Washington." Even when Judge Charles Patrick Daly, a leading Irish-American in New York, tried to dissuade Meagher from accepting such a high rank, Meagher seemed determined to secure at least a colonelcy. Judge Daly was shocked at Meagher's failure to comprehend that he could not handle such a responsibility.[21]

All of this could just be one woman's jealousy. Maria Lydig Daly did not like Meagher or his wife, whom Daly believed was envious of her fundraising work for the Irish Brigade. Maria Daly was not alone, however, in voicing her frustration over Meagher's filling the vacancy left by Michael Corcoran's capture. Most complaints surfaced following reports that Meagher had been drunk at the battle of First Bull Run and negligent in his duties. London *Times* correspondent William Howard Russell was sharply critical of most Union regiments and despised for his coverage of the battle, and it was he who started the rumors of Meagher's intoxication. Some Irish-Americans denied such reports, including Father Bernard O'Reilly on his travels in Ireland following his work as regimental chaplain for the 69th N.Y.S.M. He reassured Meagher's family, friends, and supporters by rejecting all such claims.[22]

As the months passed, however, a vocal minority within the Irish-American community began making accusations similar to Russell's, claims that could not be attributed to anti-Irish prejudice of London or northern newspapers. A Lieutenant Connolly, who had been held with Corcoran in a Confederate prison and recently exchanged, visited Judge Daly with several other Irish-American officers on February 5, 1862, the same day Meagher officially assumed command of the Irish Brigade. During the battle of First Bull Run, Connolly explained, he and Colonel Corcoran had seen nothing of Meagher after the initial assault and assumed that he had died. When Corcoran was captured, one of his first requests was that a Confederate soldier "look for poor Meagher's body, and have it sent through the lines to his wife." Later, however, Connolly and Corcoran learned from other captured Irishmen that "Meagher was intoxicated" from the start of the battle "and had just sense and elation enough to make one rush forward and afterwards fell from his horse drunk," where he remained until a U.S. Army trooper spotted his unconscious body and carried him to safety.[23]

Despite the frustrations of these officers and some Irish-Americans, significant elements of the community rallied to Meagher's calls to war.

Many Irishmen could not believe these rumors of cowardice and assumed they were examples of anti-Irish prejudice. Meagher had proven his valor in the uprising of 1848 in Ireland, during his trial, and in his escape from Van Diemen's Land. His speeches at recruiting rallies and in camp that winter portrayed a hero of Ireland and America. Meagher of the Sword, Irishmen claimed, would lead them to glory in America and again in Ireland.

Thus northern Irish-American opinion on the war in the spring of 1862 was mixed, though leaning toward support of the Lincoln administration and Irish involvement in the conflict. On one hand, Meagher, Judge Daly, and other prominent leaders, whatever their differences, were very vocal in calling for Irish support for the war. As for Meagher, many individuals, officers and civilians, questioned his ability, but other military men strongly supported him, sending President Lincoln a petition to ensure Meagher's command of the Irish Brigade. The 63rd and 88th New York lacked sufficient numbers to join the 69th New York when it departed for the capital in November 1861, but they did reach sufficient strength to join their comrades shortly after Christmas. There appeared to be similar recruiting problems among the Irish in the Midwest, but this may have been due more to the smaller size of the Irish-American population there and unreasonable recruiting expectations than to a disinterest among the Irish population. Still, complaints of renewed anti-Irish prejudice in these regions played a role in this as well.[24]

Whatever the various factors, there were fissures in Irish support for the war as early as the fall of 1861, and some of the men used this anxiety to their advantage. In the early months of war it was common for President Lincoln to appoint "political generals," men whose commands were not based on military experience as much as their influence with constituents whose support was critical to the administration. This was true of several Democratic generals, including Benjamin Butler and Nathaniel Banks, as well as such immigrant commanders as German-born Franz Sigel and Carl Schurz, and Irish-born Thomas Francis Meagher and Michael Corcoran.[25]

Irish-Americans across the North learned quickly that local and state officials shared the president's need for broad-based support. Such was the case when Dr. Charles D. B. O'Ryan contacted Illinois governor Richard Yates to offer his services as surgeon for the 23rd Illinois Infantry Regiment, also known as the Irish Brigade. Originally organized the previous summer, the 23rd Illinois experienced its first heavy fighting when Confederate General Sterling Price's forces besieged their position in Lexington, Missouri, in September 1861. After holding out for several weeks and taking significant losses, Colonel James A. Mulligan, a first-

General James A. Mulligan, commander of Mulligan's Irish
Brigade (23rd Illinois Volunteer Infantry Regiment). Courtesy
of Chicago Historical Society.

generation Irish-American, surrendered his force, all of whom were paroled except Mulligan himself, who refused and was taken prisoner. He
was finally exchanged for a Confederate officer and returned to Chicago
in November, where hundreds of people gathered to greet him.[26]

That winter Mulligan worked to reorganize the 23rd Illinois, which
had officially disbanded after all of its officers were captured. With the approval of General George B. McClellan and President Lincoln, the Irish
Brigade was reformed with the same regimental title of the 23rd Illinois,
and many of the Irishmen who filled its ranks had served under Mulligan
at the Battle of Lexington. Irishmen from native units also contacted Mulligan to request transfers to the 23rd Illinois, frequently citing anti-Irish
and anti-Catholic bigotry in native units as the reason for their request.[27]

In some cases Irish-Americans would use the possibility of nativism, and the threat to report such charges in their home communities, to secure coveted positions within Irish units. Dr. Charles D. B. O'Ryan, for example, contacted Governor Yates to appeal his case and reminded the governor of the problems that disgruntled Irishmen could cause should state and federal leaders reveal any sign of the previous decade's nativism. Informing Yates of his desire to serve with the Irishmen of the newly reorganized 23rd Illinois, O'Ryan hinted that "so long as our rulers act with the same impartiality toward [the Irish] as towards all other citizens without distinction of country or creed, which has not been the case heretofore, as in the days of Native Americanism and lately of Know Nothingism, which . . . left an impression on the minds of the Irish," these leaders should be able to maintain united Irish support. Still, warned O'Ryan, he had heard that Governor Yates was "suspected of harboring unfriendly feelings toward Irishmen." If this was true, O'Ryan encouraged the governor to "alter [his] sentiments and by a just and an honorable cause, to make [the Irish] your friends instead of your foes, and I will assure your Excellency that you shall never have cause to regret having done so." Dr. O'Ryan then went on to suggest actions the governor could take, actions that would "gratify the Irish not only of Chicago," he advised the elected official, "but throughout the States, as it will be regarded as a compliment to them to have one of their countrymen appointed to such an office." A refusal to appoint O'Ryan, however, could have the disastrous effect of reviving "the old feeling of defiant Know-Nothingism." With one final attempt to clarify his argument, which by now read like something between astute advice from a political strategist and outright blackmail, O'Ryan insisted that his appointment must appear to be a voluntary act by the governor. Otherwise his Irish constituents might think it a favor to others rather than a compliment to their service.

Despite his frustration with "this rampant doctor," Yates saw the wisdom in O'Ryan's arguments. The governor responded promptly, strongly insisting that he "never <u>was</u> a Know-Nothing," that he had "not the least feeling against the Irish," and that it was he who encouraged Colonel Mulligan to protest Halleck's decision to Washington, giving Mulligan a "strong letter" of endorsement to support his arguments to the president. Yates then promised to do all in his power to appoint O'Ryan as surgeon to the 23rd Illinois.[28]

O'Ryan's appeal to Yates could be used as an example of Irish-Americans trying to use military service to demonstrate loyalty and improve their condition in postwar America, but it also illustrates the confidence with which some Irish-American leaders used this process. O'Ryan employed forceful arguments to convince the governor of Illinois that he must act according to O'Ryan's interests or face the political consequences that the Illinois Irish-American community was willing and able to create. His argument may have involved some self-aggrandizement on O'Ryan's part but is also a significant example of a growing confidence among some Irish-Americans in their positions and their ability to take firm stands.

Other examples of clever maneuvering to secure Irish-American interests appeared the following year. In 1862, Governor Yates was pulled into another debate within the second Irish regiment from Illinois, the 90th Illinois Volunteers, known as the "Irish Legion." Formed that summer, the regiment was riddled with political infighting as Mexican War veteran, Democrat, and Irish-born American William Snowhook struggled against Captain Timothy O'Meara to secure leadership of the unit. O'Meara had several advantages over Snowhook, including strong backing from one of the most prominent Irish-American leaders in the war, Colonel Michael Corcoran, and an active advocate in Father Dennis Dunne, vicar general and then bishop of the Diocese of Chicago. Snowhook, on the other hand, had bipartisan support for his campaign, but the influential John G. Haines, close advisor to Governor Yates, shifted his support to O'Meara and the Chicago Diocese announced its hesitancy to support Snowhook due to his Protestant wife. Added to this was a regimental election directed by Father Dunne's followers while Snowhook was out of camp, at which time O'Meara was unanimously elected in part due to warnings to the men that without O'Meara, the regimental chaplains would not be Catholic.

When Snowhook tried to challenge his rival's unanimous election to Governor Yates, Father Dunne reminded Yates of several important factors. First, Snowhook was seeking to change the 90th Illinois from an all-Irish-Catholic regiment to include native-born Americans and Protestants, essentially opening the ranks to any who wished to join. In a lengthy discussion with Governor Yates and his advisers, Father Dunne and other O'Meara supporters reminded Yates how important it was to keep the Irish happy if he hoped to secure their support for the war. Another warning came from a Captain P. O'Marsh, Company B, 90th Illinois, who had heard that certain parties in Chicago were trying to convince the governor to oppose O'Meara's election by withholding his regimental commission. He warned Yates that such actions would slow the recruiting process and create disorder among the men.[29]

John G. Haines, active in Chicago's political world and a close friend of the governor, agreed with O'Marsh's warning and carried the argument further, cautioning that such unrest could reach beyond the regiment to the Irish-American community of Chicago and to native-born Americans generally. Haines was especially fearful of the impact of Snowhook's suggestion to open the regiment to all recruits, Irish and native born, Catholic and Protestant, and of any sign that the governor supported such actions. "The regiment as you know," warned Haines, "is wholly Irish Catholic and it would raise a row on both sides to consolidate with it any other companies not Irish and Catholic." The only answer, Haines theorized, was to back O'Meara. Any other action "will do you . . . much harm," argued Haines. In large part, this was due to the attention Father Dunne and O'Meara had already received among Irish Catholics across the northern United States. These men were known from Chicago to New York, where the news of Dunne's recruiting of an Irish regiment was placarded all over New York City and Brooklyn, and where Irish-born New Yorker Michael Corcoran had hand picked O'Meara to command the new unit.[30] If Yates wished to appease his Irish constituents and fill the state's recruiting quotas, he realized he must support Dunne and O'Meara and keep the 90th Illinois purely Irish Catholic. Yates followed these suggestions and secured Irish political support.[31]

Despite recruiting difficulties and ethnic tensions, many Irish regiments and the most well known "Irish Brigade," commanded by Thomas Francis Meagher, prepared to enter the war in the spring of 1862. They had spent that winter in camp near the nation's capital, where the Army of the Potomac's new commander, General George B. McClellan, drilled them incessantly and instilled the discipline and order that would carry the army through the war.

Despite the men's anxious anticipation of the coming battles, that winter and spring were not particularly pleasant. Lieutenant Colonel Robert Guiney of the Irish 9th Massachusetts Volunteers, like many of the men in camp that year, was amazed and depressed by the soupy mud into which everything seemed to sink. Men walking through camp reminded Guiney of flies "endeavoring to walk through a dish of molasses." Father William Corby, Catholic chaplain to the 88th New York, recalled similar conditions. Long after the war, he was frequently amused by historians' efforts to give a poetic beauty to the camp rather than tell readers of the harsh realities of that first winter of war. "Everyone who campaigned in Virginia will agree with me," Corby reflected, "that the Virginia mud, after winter rains, is the worst mud he ever encountered."

For many Irishmen and Union soldiers in general, this winter began the slow destruction of their romantic notions of war. As Father Corby described, "imagine a man living in a tent all winter, with less accommodations than lumber-men find in the wilds of Minnesota! No beds except some army blankets placed on boards." Within the tents, all heat and meals were fueled by "green pine, which, in many cases, furnished more smoke than heat; so that frequently we were obliged to . . . turn back a

Members of the Irish Brigade, Harrison's Landing, Virginia. Father William Corby, C.S.C., chaplain of the 88th New York Volunteer Infantry Regiment, is seated on the far right. Courtesy of the Library of Congress. Photograph reproduction courtesy Lynn L. Libby, Enola, PA, 2005.

flap of the canvas at either end of the tent, and let the cold, damp wind of Virginia pass through and dispel the pungent vapor." As Corby was quick to point out, this was nothing compared to the future discomforts they would face on the march and in battle, but it was part of what historian Reid Mitchell has discussed as the hardening process, whereby the young boys of the Midwest and manufacturing centers of New York, Massachusetts, and Pennsylvania learned the basics of soldiering.[32]

It was also a time that revealed the strengths and weaknesses of Irish-American involvement in the war. The men's discomfort led to some fights, but also camp activities that made the Irish famous for their gaiety and their excitement about the coming battles. In late January 1862, for example, Captains Gallagher and Mahan of the Irish 9th Massachusetts Volunteers were on the verge of a duel before other officers stopped them. Major Patrick Guiney proudly noted his role in preventing the affair, but seemed to take equal pride in the fact that the men were so passionate in their anger and sense of honor. "They were blood to the eyes!" Guiney recalled, adding "Who wouldn't be an Irishman?"[33] Apparently, Guiney was not alone in taking pride in his ethnic heritage. Earlier that winter, the

Patrick R. Guiney, pictured here as a colonel, would rise to the command of the Irish 9th Massachusetts Volunteer Infantry Regiment in 1862 following the death of Colonel Cass at the Battle of Malvern Hill. Courtesy of U.S. Army Military History Institute. Photograph reproduction courtesy Lynn L. Libby, Enola, PA, 2005.

9th participated in a grand Christmas banquet in camp, where many officers "confessed that they were Irish." Most of it was "Blarney, but true of some of them," Guiney noted in a fascinating case of native-born Americans claiming Irish heritage at a time when the stereotype of the natural Irish ability for fighting was seen as an attribute.[34]

Despite this example of admiration for an Irish fighting spirit, several Irish-American officers believed their native-born commanders and politicians were allowing old prejudices to influence their treatment of Irish troops. Some Irish commanders indicated that while native-born Americans may have appreciated the abilities of Irishmen on the battlefield or during camp festivities, such sentiments disappeared when it came to supplying and supporting Irish regiments.

Colonel Thomas Cass, commander of the Irish 9th Massachusetts Volunteers, had voiced such concerns to Governor John A. Andrew in the first summer of war, reminding him that other regiments had gathered tremendous funds from donations from Boston's "wealthy citizens." This money, however, seemed only directed to aid "other favored regiments." Cass cited William Webster's (son of famous Daniel Webster) 12th Massachusetts Volunteers, who had already received nearly three thousand dollars, while the Irishmen of the 9th were struggling to survive on one-third as much. With this money, his men were expected to provide their own arms and uniforms, and the rapid disappearance of resources and

Colonel Thomas Cass, first commander of the Irish 9th Massachusetts Volunteer Infantry Regiment. Courtesy of U.S. Army Military History Institute. Photograph reproduction courtesy Lynn L. Libby, Enola, PA, 2005.

the poor conditions in which they had to train were affecting the morale of the regiment. In addition, Cass complained, "owing to some cause to which we are not a party, we have not yet had quarters assigned to us . . . while Mr. Webster's Volunteers have, to a large number, been already provided for."[35]

Throughout the summer of 1861 Cass had routinely contacted the governor with news that "the city of Boston has contributed something towards the support of the 'six Boston Companies,' but for the 'out of town' companies, nothing has been done."[36] Again and again Cass cited evidence of Boston Brahmins' prejudice against their Irish soldiers. Boston's ruling elite may have been willing to see the Irish serve in the war, but they appeared to have little interest in the condition of these soldiers, favoring instead the sons, fathers, and brothers recruited from their own social circles.

That June Dr. T. H. Smith contacted the governor to complain of similar mistreatment. Smith, his fellow Irish officers, and the men of the 14th Massachusetts were shocked that after they had "left their homes and situation to enlist in a cause So holy, So Just, and So patriotic, when after nearly two months deep anxiety for their country's good, [they] were rejected" and their unit ordered disbanded. Reports that once again Boston's elite had spoken out against the city's Irish soldiers spread through the regiment. "I hope the report that I heard is not true," Smith admonished the governor, "that we were rejected because we were known . . . as an Irish Regiment, and officered mostly by Irishmen."[37]

While the existence of two Irish regiments from Massachusetts (the 9th and the 28th Massachusetts Infantry Regiments) indicates that there was not total opposition among the state's leadership to such ethnic military participation, the anti-Irish rumors circulating within the 14th's camp and its being disbanded despite its having recruited a full regiment indicates that anti-Irish prejudice remained active in the state despite a clear demonstration by Irish-Americans of their willingness to serve.

Not all Bostonians reacted toward Irish service in this manner. Some members of the city took actions to demonstrate their support for the state's newly formed Irish regiments. City leaders hosted a massive gathering celebrating the Irish 9th's reception of its colors, and during his speech honoring the men, Governor Andrew claimed that the country recognized no separation "between its native-born citizens and those born in other countries."[38] In 1861, city fathers agreed that the Irish flag should be raised during Boston's Fourth of July celebrations at Boston Commons while the band played the Irish national anthem and those of several other nations.[39]

Despite such positive actions, the complaints made by Irish officers

Chaplain Thomas Scully and men of the Irish 9th Massachusetts Volunteer Infantry Regiment celebrating mass at Camp Cass, Arlington Heights, Virginia. Courtesy of the Library of Congress. Photograph reproduction courtesy Lynn L. Libby, Enola, PA, 2005.

could call into question the sincerity of Governor Andrew's claim that Bostonians and Americans saw no difference "between its native-born citizens and those born in other countries." Several possibilities explain Governor Andrew's decision to abolish the 14th Massachusetts and Bostonians' lack of dedicated support of their Irish soldiers. For one thing, Andrew was a Republican governor and knew the importance of keeping Republican supporters happy. Increasing the presence in this war of Irish Catholics, a group openly opposed to abolition, would have been politically unwise. Andrew worried over reports he was receiving regarding other Irish regiments, and he feared that Irish soldiers might do more damage to the reputation of the Bay State than any service they could offer the Union. Just one month earlier, Governor Andrew had received disturbing reports about the lack of discipline in the Irish 9th Massachusetts Volunteers, which included suggestions that the men must have native-born officers and the alternative that the unit be disbanded and the Irishmen dispersed among nonethnic units before they disgraced Massachusetts.[40]

This, however, may not have been sufficient reason for Andrew's decision about the 14th Massachusetts. By the end of that summer the governor was receiving glowing reports on the Irish 9th from that same Boston Brahmin-turned-governor's-informant George D. Wells. In June 1861, the regiment whose lack of discipline had horrified him one month earlier had now earned Wells's admiration through its dogged determination to fight in this war. Wells declared the Irish unit "a fine one,"[41] and boasted that in "comparison with the other regiments about us we are saints—Generally the Regiment maintains itself wonderfully well."[42] He still believed, as did their Irish-born Colonel Cass, that the men would always have an independent streak to them that would make unified operations difficult, but with "proper management . . . the men can be made to do and be everything which is really desirable." As he watched the Irishmen around the camp, whom he had previously described as "the sweeping of our jails . . . utterly unfit in every way . . . vicious—vile,"[43] Wells now proclaimed, "I can't imagine better material for a fighting regiment."[44]

Some native-born American images of the Irish were increasingly positive. In the case of Boston and New York, native-born Americans supported Irish regiments, commemorating their service and Irish heritage on Independence Day, turning out in great numbers to send the Irish troops off to war, and writing of Irish bravery in battle in their non-Irish presses. In Boston, Harvard University conferred an honorary doctor of divinity on the city's Archbishop John Fitzpatrick in July 1861.[45] Prominent businessman Amos A. Lawrence, who had been the nativist American party's candidate for governor in 1858, noted, "This is probably the first time [a doctor of divinity degree] was ever bestowed on a Roman Catholic Ecclesiastic at Cambridge." He theorized that it was done in direct response to "the loyalty shown by him and by the Irish who have offered themselves freely for the army."[46]

On the other hand, examples of anti-Irish prejudice persisted despite the outpouring of support from the native-born communities. When the Irish 9th Massachusetts Volunteers marched out of Boston in June 1861, one voice was heard above the cheers, shouting, "There goes a load of Irish rubbish out of the city."[47] In response to such views, the *Pilot* advised that Irishmen ignore such comments because "the Irish race in America have now a permanent grip on the soil; and their healthy blood is diffusing itself so rapidly in every direction that nothing can check it. . . . The suppression of the rebellion absolutely requires the Irish arms."[48] Despite such assurances, the *Pilot* and leading Irishmen still feared nativism and wondered if Irish service would really improve their condition in America. In fact, some doubted that anything would remove the anti-Catholic and anti-Irish prejudice pervading the nation. Even amid the early celebrations and farewell parades, the *Pilot* warned, "let no Irishman think that because . . . he has lost an arm, an eye, or a leg . . . he will be treated decently henceforward."[49]

Despite some native-born American support, many Irish-Americans remained skeptical of whether these changes would be permanent. In August the *Pilot* reported that Secretary of the Navy Gideon Welles was firing immigrant workers from the Charlestown Naval Yard and replacing them with native-born Americans. A disillusioned *Pilot* warned that such actions revealed the government's general view of the Irish as useful "only as food for powder." Even in this early period of considerable, though in some cases limited, Irish-American support for the war and a rather positive response from significant portions of the native-born populace, there was a hint of the frustration to come and the form it would take as Boston's Irish-American leaders insisted, "Let there be no more enlisting in the army of Irishmen, while they are proscribed in the Navy Yards, custom-houses, and other positions in the gift of the government." Thus, as the campaign season of 1862 began, Irish and native-born Americans entered the period with mixed though fairly positive opinion supporting ethnic military service.[50]

That spring the Irish Brigade's preparations for war continued and the men looked forward to testing their mettle in battle. The personnel arriving in camp included a large number of veterans who would help the brigade on its rise to fame as one of the toughest in the army. In early 1862, Irish immigrant and British Royal Marines veteran W. L. D. O'Grady arrived in New York harbor, spotted an 88th New York recruiting poster, and within two hours had signed his enlistment papers, listing "my regiment" as his address. Other Irish Brigade officers shared his military experience and dedication to serving in an Irish Brigade. Captain P. F. Clooney served in the 88th New York and was a veteran of the Irish Brigade of St. Patrick of the Papal States that had fought the army of Giuseppe Garibaldi in 1859–1860. Francis Reynolds served as the Irish Brigade surgeon and had first earned his respected reputation on the British Army medical staff in the Crimean War.[51]

Such experience at the officer level aided the Irish Brigade greatly in 1862 when so many commanders made novice mistakes and earned public criticism. Union General George B. McClellan's Peninsula Campaign opened that March, and for most of the Irish Brigade this would be their first experience in combat.[52] The battles of Fair Oaks, Gaines's Mill, and Malvern Hill cost the unit serious losses, but it also earned the brigade an impressive reputation. Irish and native newspapers reveled in the story that the call to arms for Fair Oaks interrupted a steeplechase organized by General Meagher to boost the spirits of his men and that Father William Corby, chaplain to the 88th New York, insisted "must unquestionably have been the invention of wild Irishmen, who did not know what fear is!"[53]

As for their fighting in the battle, the *Pilot* reported proudly that division commander General Edwin V. Sumner declared, "I know the Irish

Brigade will not retreat" at the most critical point of the Battle of Fair Oaks that May, proclaiming to the Irishmen, "I stake my position on you: if you run, I will have to run also."[54] Indeed, the Irish Brigade was receiving so much praise in the native and Irish press that Captain James B. Turner, an Irish-born officer in the 88th New York, thought, "part of it is deserved and part of it is not—in all probability they have given [the Irish Brigade] more praise than the work we [have] done has deserved." He added quickly, "However, as long as they don't speak ill of us we should be satisfied."[55]

Following the fighting at Fair Oaks, the Irish Brigade received reinforcements in the form of the 29th Massachusetts Volunteers. Originally intended to be an Irish regiment, the Irishmen of the under-strength 29th were used to fill the 28th Massachusetts, so that by the time the newly recruited 29th joined the Irish Brigade in June 1862 their ethnic heritage was more reminiscent of Boston's Puritan roots than its Irish Catholic population. As one member of the regiment recalled, there was a rather uncomfortable moment when General Meagher, expecting to welcome the men with a speech on their shared Irish military traditions, had to make some quick revisions. After all, William H. Osborne recalled, "the Twenty-ninth was essentially an American regiment, very largely composed of and officered by men who were direct descendants of the early settlers of the Plymouth and Bay colonies,—one of its members, indeed, being a lineal descendent of Miles Standish." Meagher recovered quickly, though, warmly welcoming the men of the 29th and expressing gratitude for the reinforcements.[56]

The fighting intensified in late June and continued into July during a series of engagements known as the Seven Days' Battles, which took a toll on the Irish Brigade. As staff officer Captain David P. Conyngham recalled of some of the toughest fighting at Malvern Hill, "McClellan's army [was] saved, but that hill-side is covered with the dying and the dead of the Irish Brigade."[57] During the course of the Seven Days', the Brigade lost approximately seven hundred officers and men, while the Army of the Potomac counted its losses at 15,249.[58]

The fighting was equally costly for the Irish 9th Massachusetts. At Gaines's Mill, one member of the 9th recalled that they quickly ran out of the sixty rounds of ammunition they had been issued that June morning and they took "the ammunition from the boxes of the dead and wounded and fired that also." The Irish 9th fought off three separate assaults that day and lost 231 Irishmen, killed, wounded, and missing. At Malvern Hill, their losses were significant as well and included the death of their commander, Colonel Thomas Cass.[59]

The reformed 69th Pennsylvania, composed primarily of Philadelphia

Irishmen, gained acclaim for its service at the Battle of Glendale on June 30, 1862. The *Pilot* proudly announced that there was "no better fighting material in the army than this regiment," citing in particular the leadership of its commander, Colonel Joshua T. Owen.[60] General Joseph Hooker's report made similar references to Owen and the 69th Pennsylvania's bravery, congratulating them on Owen's heroism and the regiment's "reckless daring."[61]

While the Irish-Americans of the eastern regiments earned fame in the early summer battles of 1862, similar acclaim fell on the Irishmen of the Midwest. In May 1862 the *Detroit Free Press* took pride in publicizing the heroism of Captain Thomas C. Fitzgibbon, commander of the all-Irish Company B of the 14th Michigan Infantry at the Battle of Farmington. The news was republished in Irish papers across the country, and even such native papers as the *Free Press* celebrated the exploits of the Irish soldiers in the war.[62]

In Illinois, the Irish Brigade of the Midwest, commanded by Colonel James A. Mulligan, was preparing to return to duty that year and looking forward to making similar contributions to the war. Delays regarding the unit's official exchange from its previous prisoner-of-war status, however, led to the 23rd Illinois's assignment to Camp Douglas, a Union prisoner-of-war camp. This was hardly the service the Irishmen were hoping for, but Mulligan made use of this assignment by improving the medical care and food provided to the Confederate soldiers held there. Several Chicago newspapers praised them for this service, though it earned them few friends among the Union officers who saw little need to improve the care of a group they saw as the enemy. That June the 23rd Illinois finally got their wish for more active duty and left Camp Douglas for the fighting in Maryland that September, and later they conducted operations against guerillas in western Virginia.[63]

Despite the positive press concerning the service of Irish soldiers, complaints surfaced because relatively few Irishmen were actually volunteering as compared to their numbers in the population. As the population table in chapter 1 demonstrates, the largest Irish-American populations in the United States remained in the eastern cities of New York, Boston, and Philadelphia, but midwestern cities like Chicago and St. Louis, and cities as far west as San Francisco, had significant Irish populations. The criticism that Irish-Americans were not contributing their share of manpower started in the Midwest in the spring of 1862, when an Indiana recruiter complained that the few Irish they could get to volunteer for Irish companies became disgruntled when they discovered they would serve under native officers and refused to muster into service.[64] English Congregationalist minister James William Massie noticed similar trends during his travels across the northern United States in 1862. Failing to find a single Irishman on a train filled with recruits, Massie theorized that the Irish refused to fight because they "habitually dread the freedom of the Negro, lest he should become a competitor in the labor market."[65] At a town meeting in Quincy, Illinois, in July 1862, similar proclamations were made that "the Irish have not done their duty, in the way of volunteering during the present war."[66]

Irishmen across the Midwest strongly denied these charges. They pointed out that nativists "had no objection to the Irish enlisting and fighting, but [non-Irish] did not want to lose the chance of putting their services to the credit of the 'descendents of the Puritans.' "[67] Reprints of the article ran in several eastern papers, including Boston's *Pilot*, in an attempt to challenge similar claims in local communities. Meanwhile, other native presses, including the Philadelphia *Evening Journal* and the Baltimore *Mirror*, published reports that Massachusetts's Governor John Andrew opposed the idea of raising additional Irish regiments, that he refused to commission additional Irish field officers, and that Irishmen were turning away from recruiting stations as a result of this news. The *Pilot* published the governor's rebuttal to this, in which he declared such statements completely false, but the rumors continued.[68]

As the controversy grew, Irish-American leaders voiced a common complaint: Americans did not appreciate Irish military service. "Some of our contemporaries regret the appearance and valor of the Irish in the national army—out of an effeminate horror for blood,—and we can point the finger at correspondents who deplore the fact, seemingly from the same principle, but in reality from Secession motives." Even so, the *Pilot* argued that Irish-Americans should continue to serve out of a sense of duty and honor. They had a responsibility to help save the Union because it had offered Irishmen so much in their hour of need. "The Irish are citizens of the United States," the *Pilot* argued. "By fair contract they owe the country their lives. To their honor let it be said that they have freely and gloriously paid the debt." The editors quickly added that Irish-Americans would continue to fight because they knew their kinsmen across the Atlantic were watching. Irish-Americans' "native country—of which the Irishman never loses sight—will honor them forever for their splendid support of the best government that ever existed."[69] Once again Irish-American leaders were motivating their communities with references to duty and honor, and linking the causes of Ireland and of America.

Amid these mixed reports of Irish involvement in and support of the war, in July 1862 General Thomas Francis Meagher journeyed home to New York to recruit replacements for his dwindling Irish Brigade. His reception echoed the mood expressed by the *Pilot*. In some ways the Irish were remaining true to their pledge to defend American freedom and to preserve a united country for future Irish emigrants. The Fenians were pleased to be gaining so much military experience, and Irish soldiers were grateful to be earning a steady income. Some of these men and their families at home, however, were concerned that the cost of this service might be too great for their communities to handle.

On July 25, 1862, Meagher spoke at a recruiting rally at the 7th Regiment Armory in New York City, once again turning his famous skills as an orator to the cause of linking the advancement of Irishmen with the war for union. He laid out before the audience all that Irish-Americans had already sacrificed for the country. The 69th New York had entered the battle of Fair Oaks that June with 750 men, but was now reduced to 295. The 88th New York left its winter encampment with nearly six hundred men, and now had less than four hundred. The 63rd New York had seen less action and thus suffered fewer casualties, but it too had dwindled to five hundred men. Meagher informed his audience that he needed two thousand recruits to keep the Irish Brigade together as a separate unit serving Irish honor, preserving America as an asylum for future Irish refugees, and demonstrating Irish-Americans' gratitude for all that the United States and its citizens had provided them. Meagher insisted, "It should be the vehement desire and the intense ambition of every Irishman, who has one chord within him that vibrates to the traditions of that old lyric and martial land of his, not to permit its flag, so vividly emblematic of the verdure of it soil and the immortality of its faith, to be compromised in any just struggle in which it is displayed." The audience responded with thunderous cheers that poured out the open windows of the Armory and into the streets.

Despite this tremendous response, not all Irishmen in attendance were feeling grateful to the native-born populace, nor were they going to be motivated to serve as easily as they had the previous summer. After Meagher had explained the Irish Brigade's losses and his need for two thousand new recruits, one member of the audience suggested, "Take the Black Republicans," referring to the Republican abolitionists so many Irish-Americans disliked. After several such outbursts, Meagher shot back, "Any man who makes a remark like that I denounce as a poltroon and coward. Because others shrink from their duty is no reason why you should shrink from yours. You have no business to shift the responsibility upon others."

The audience applauded his response, but they still had questions about how the Irish Brigade had lost so many men that spring. Some asked if this was due to insufficient attention from the government, indicating that perhaps nativists were at work to make sure their own troops received better equipment and more food and supplies than the Irish soldiers. The losses, Meagher explained, were not due to "insufficient food, or clothing, or undue labor, or neglect of any kind, or sickness, but hard fighting of the enemy that had thinned the ranks—fighting that was the glory and pride of Irishmen." In closing, Meagher again reminded Irishmen of the debt they owed America and the importance of preserving the nation for future Irish exiles. Meagher asked his countrymen for "one more effort, magnanimous and chivalrous for the Republic, which to the thousands and thousands of you, has been a tower of impregnable security, a pedestal of renown and a palace of prosperity, after the worrying, the scandals, and the shipwreck that, for the most part, have been for many generations the implacable destiny of our race."[70] The Irish audience responded once more with deafening applause and appeared ready to storm recruiting stations that evening.

Native-born Americans were similarly impressed with Meagher's call for Irish service. After covering the entire evening's events and Meagher's speech in detail, the *New York Times* correspondent reflected, "the meeting . . . adjourned amid the most earnest enthusiasm, evincing as determined patriotism and unswerving loyalty as ever was displayed in a public gathering, and practically demonstrating that the hearts of Irishmen throb with as pure devotion to our flag as ever animated the hearts of a free and noble people."[71] These demonstrations of loyalty from an immigrant population whom Americans had not always trusted to have such sentiments pleased the *Times*.

Sometime during the night, though, much of the Irish-American support faded. The *Times* estimated that perhaps ten thousand people attended Meagher's speech. Even if we assume that number is slightly inflated and recognize that it included those who were not eligible for military service, the number of recruits who actually pledged their service to the Union was far smaller than one might expect from such a large audience. They may have been inspired by Meagher's speech, but, after time to reflect, many Irish-Americans reconsidered their service to a cause about which they were receiving mixed messages. Their hesitation may have been due to a variety of reasons, but one of them lay in reports from Irish-American soldiers to their families that painted a very different picture of life in the Irish Brigade.

Irish-born Captain James B. Turner, an aide to Meagher in the 88th New York, offered an excellent example of this. Turner had little positive to say of military service and made this clear to his father, who had voiced an interest in volunteering to earn a steady income. Turner warned,

As to any idea you may have of joining the Army give it up at once. Unless a man occupies a position among the very highest, the amount of vulgarity, profanity and utter tyranny that exist is to a man of any regiment and religious training such as you are, a perfect hell. Then when I see young strong men about me, who hold commissions, sinking daily and fast under the mingled fatigue, exposure and want of proper nourishment it makes one wish that never a friend of his should be placed in like predicament. Then what must it be in the ranks of even non-commissioned [officers]. It's not like garrison duty. Think of lying, eating, and daily life in a small tent with from seven to ten men none of them the cleanest or with any pretense to education or refinement, then being cursed and cuffed about by some vulgar wretch in authority. . . . No. [The idea of] soldiering in any capacity you must give up.[72]

Turner's descriptions of the rigors of camp life contradicted those Meagher had offered at his recruiting speech four nights earlier. Turner's family, who would have heard the general's speech or read it in the *Irish-American,* must have been surprised at the discrepancy. But Turner's camp descriptions have nothing to do with animosity toward Meagher. Turner had nothing against the general and in fact thought very highly of him, praising Meagher in nearly every letter to his family. Nevertheless, Turner opposed seeing any additional members of his family involved in this war, despite the fact that his father had been unemployed for over a year and could earn significant money through local and state bounties and military pay.

Similar concerns appeared from across the ocean when Frances Sproul opened a letter from her mother-in-law in Ireland. "I am sorry Andrew has gone out," she began, concerned to learn that her son Andrew had joined the 16th Ohio Infantry Regiment. She begged her daughter-in-law, "please, Fanny, let me now if he was compelled or not. . . . If he could [have] stayed at home I think he was wrong for going as he was not too stout."[73] Closing her note, again the mother asked for clarification, failing to understand why her son would have joined, unless he was drafted into the army, and disappointed that he had not explained his decision in his recent letters. James Turner and Matilda Sproul were not alone in their sentiments, which could have discouraged enlistments by an Irish-American population hearing one image of war from leaders like Meagher and a very different story from their loved ones in camp.

Like Turner and Sproul, Andrew and Lucy Greenlees, Irish-American Protestants living in Illinois, supported the Union war effort but had serious reservations about committing to it themselves. Experiencing serious economic setbacks in the summer of 1862, Andrew Greenlees complained of a significant debt and the need to hire himself out on a neighboring farm. He did not indicate, however, considering the army as a solution to these problems. Instead he discussed the new Homestead Act passed by Congress and declared, "this will give farms to thousands that otherwise never would have had one. . . . I will push off as soon as I have the means after paying my debts." As for the war, he and his wife clarified their support for the Union, but she confided to their family in Ireland, "they are beginning to draft men for the army in some of the States. I am afraid they will be drafting here but I hope not. I am very patriotic but I don't want Andrew to have to go unless I could go too and I could not leave the children."[74]

In Laporte, Indiana, Irish-American Catholic Hugh Harlin noted similar concerns about the draft in his community. "There were about twenty-five men going to leave this town for Canada, Ireland, and Germany so as to avoid the [state] draft," Harlin observed in August 1862. He knew that men had more choices if they volunteered, with the opportunity to join a unit of their choice rather then be assigned to a particular regiment, and worried that he might now be drafted and forced to serve among men with whom he had little in common, particularly his Catholic faith. "What a terrible fate it would be," he told his brother, "to die on the battle field and be thrown into a hole like a dog, no priest perhaps, no friends." He was "sorry now [that] I did not go when I was offered the commission." It appears that Harlin might have had not only the chance to serve with fellow Irish Catholics but also the privilege of an officer rank, but he had preferred to avoid service in the Union Army.[75] His experiences, along with those of fellow Irish-Catholics like James Turner, indicates that Irish-American communities across the North had serious concerns about avoiding military service or the mistreatment of Irish Catholics within the army that impacted recruiting efforts in the summer of 1862. Even among Irish Protestants who expressed a strong support for the war, families like the Greenleeses indicated a desire to avoid military service.

Economic opportunities also caused problems for Meagher's recruiting efforts. Many Irish-Americans were beginning to see improvements in the economy by that summer, making the twenty-dollar bonuses offered by Meagher and fifty-dollar state bonuses less attractive to unemployed laborers than they had once been. In addition, the early luster of war was wearing off. Irishmen might read about the feats of their fellow countrymen in papers like the *Pilot* and the *Irish-American,* but these were accompanied by long casualty lists reminding men of the cost of such bravery. Reports of "Sergeant Conlin, Co. I, wounded by a fragment of a shell; Sergt. Daniel J. Reagan, Co. G, mortally wounded, since dead . . ." were taking their toll on the American public as a whole.[76] Just a few years earlier, after all, the Irish had been targeted by nativist organizations that received the support of a surprisingly large number of Americans. As reports came in that their sons and husbands were hungry, were not receiving proper care, or, worse yet, had been killed or maimed in battle, many Irish did not have a lifetime of schoolhouse lessons of American bravery and honor and lengthy generational ties to the nation to bolster their support for the war. Instead, they wondered if any of this would really improve their condition in America and whether there would be any soldiers left for the liberation of Ireland.

The lengthy casualty lists and continued nativist prejudice confirmed these fears. One member of the Irish 9th Massachusetts complained that the *New York Herald*'s coverage of the Battle of Hanover Court House purposefully omitted any reference to the heroism of Irish soldiers in that struggle. "I had, it appears, erroneously labored under the impression, that the age of narrowmindedness, bigotry and intolerance had passed away," he wrote. "I had thought that the heroic valor and bravery of the Irish soldiers had sufficiently manifested itself during the war, to disarm those prejudices that were so long entertained against us, and insure for us that even-handed justice which even those against whom we are combating are forced to accord." Other Irish-Americans complained of still being targeted for their insistence on offering Catholic education for the children of their communities. In Lowell, Massachusetts, Irish leaders reported that "bigotry and injustice still [exist] in New England," citing the city government's refusal to grant a charter to the community's Catholic College or to recognize the local Catholic schools, which recognition would grant students the same privileges in the community as those enjoyed by children in the public schools.[77]

As mentioned earlier, Irish-Americans in Chicago, Illinois, were outraged that reporters covering the fighting before Richmond that spring had knowingly recognized "the bravery and daring of the descendents of Puritans" for acts that had actually been performed by Irish-Americans. Irishmen of Chicago pointed out that regiments such as the 9th Massachusetts were comprised almost entirely of Irish-born and Irish-American volunteers, and yet that unit's casualty lists were cited as exemplifying "the blood of old Massachusetts watering the soil of Virginia." Colonel Cass, the commander of the Irish 9th, "had great difficulty in obtaining permission to fill his regiment with exclusively Irish troops," the Chicago *Post* explained, due to Puritan descendents' fears of arming the Irishmen of Massachusetts. When it came time, however, to recognize dedicated military service, the editors complained that native-born Protestants gave Irish sacrifices "to the credit of the 'descendents of the Puritans.'"[78]

The growing sense among Irish-Americans that their sacrifices would gain them nothing in postwar America contributed to their diminishing support for the war. As Meagher witnessed this development in the summer of 1862, he argued that it was the result of "treachery or treason here among us." By July 29, four days after his celebrated recruiting speech at the 7th Regiment Armory, Meagher had still had so little success that he requested and received an extension on his leave to continue his recruiting efforts. He complained that his difficulties were "numerous, and most vexatious and embarrassing. The Army of the Potomac has to fight desperate open enemies in front," but he was fighting an equally difficult struggle against "an army of implacable conspirators in the rear."

The following week, Meagher and General Daniel Sickles explained the situation in greater detail to a group of New York businessmen. The problems were the result of two factors, the generals argued. On one hand, the average Irish laborer knew that a draft was coming and that he would earn more money if he simply waited and served as a substitute than if he chose to volunteer. The other problem was far more troubling, though, Meagher and Sickles warned. Some members of the Irish-American community and the Democratic party opposed the Lincoln administration— its direction of the war, its abuses of civil liberties, and the influence of Radical Republicans within Lincoln's party—and these Democrats made a determined effort to discourage Irish-American volunteering.[79]

One final factor may have contributed to Meagher's recruiting difficulties. In August 1862, Colonel Michael Corcoran was finally exchanged and the attention of the Irish-American and native-born population focused on the hero of First Bull Run who had refused the parole that would have secured his early release, but would have also prevented his continued service in the war. Newspapers across the country covered his travel through Washington, Philadelphia, and New York. The *New York Herald* and *Daily Tribune* reported that Corcoran was offered a book contract, while all the papers announced his dinner at the White House and President Lincoln's decision to commission him a brigadier general dating from his capture at Manassas. Secretary of War Edwin M. Stanton offered Corcoran command of an existing brigade or the option to recruit a new unit, but Corcoran preferred to lead the 69th New York. This would not be possible, however, because the 69th was now part of the Irish Brigade under Meagher's command, and rumors resurfaced that some Irishmen, including Corcoran, resented Meagher's position, which had been made possible by Corcoran's absence. Whether there was any truth to the rumors, Corcoran requested permission to recruit a new brigade of Irishmen who would preserve America as "the asylum of all the oppressed of the earth."[80]

As Corcoran went about forming his new "Irish Legion," he noted the divisiveness that was resurfacing within Irish-American communities. The very fact that he addressed this divisiveness indicates that it consisted of more than just the negative sentiments of a few hecklers in a recruiting audience or the occasional disgruntled citizen's letter to an editor. In his speech at Willard's Hotel in Washington, DC, which was so well attended that carriages could not move past the crowd gathered around the famous building, Corcoran placed a strong emphasis on the link between Irish military service in the Civil War and a future Irish struggle for independence. Corcoran spoke of the Civil War as "a splendid school for military training," pledging that the "work of the hour is to be done. We must go to it with a will, and when it is over we will make an opportunity for ourselves elsewhere," a sentiment to which the audience responded with thundering applause.[81]

When Corcoran arrived in Philadelphia, he focused once more on a message of uniting Irish-Americans to support the war and called on them to ignore nativist prejudice. In an effort to explain his decision to recruit a new Irish brigade rather than accept an already existing nonethnic brigade, Corcoran proclaimed that when the Irish "gain glory, I want it to be placed to their credit." As for the huge sacrifices, Corcoran agreed that Irish-Americans had already paid their debt to America, but more was necessary. He explained, "I do not press my Irish fellow citizens to enlist because I think they have not done enough. I believe they have done their share; but the country is in danger, and at such a time let us not be comparing differences with each other." In closing, Corcoran further emphasized this point:

Gentlemen, I desire to address myself to my countrymen. I have one word more for them, and that is, not to allow a petty malice, or anything you may have suffered at the hands of individuals, from time to time, either here or in any other state, to interfere with the sacred duty and obligation you owe to the flag. Let the politicians who have been using us long enough stay at home, if they will, but let us go and fight the battles of the nation, and when we come home a grateful nation will extend to us sufficient to meet all our wants.[82]

Dr. Andrew Nebinger, host of the festivities, closed the evening's speeches by predicting that "the day was not far distant when the gratitude of a mighty nation would remember with thanksgiving the names of Corcoran, Shields, Meagher, and the many others on the long roll of Irish-American patriots." Corcoran and Nebinger, between the speeches in Washington and Philadelphia, touched on the key issues that initially motivated and might sustain Irish-American military service: a desire to preserve America for future Irish refugees, a need to gain training for Fenians and their future war for Irish independence, a sense of obligation and gratitude to America, and a desire to prove their loyalty and challenge nativist prejudice. Just as these themes had appeared in Irish-American letters and newspapers since the war began, Corcoran and Nebinger were reinforcing Irish-Americans' dual loyalties to America and Ireland.[83]

While Meagher and Corcoran made very similar recruiting speeches, Meagher lacked the media attention Corcoran received after his recent release, and this contributed to his success as compared to Meagher's recruiting failure. Throughout the period of July and August, Meagher managed to attract just 250 recruits to the Irish Brigade, despite added bounties to tempt the Irishmen of New York. Irish Brigade historian and staff officer, Captain David P. Conyngham, recalled that the result of the few recruits Meagher gathered offered an "almost imperceptible" benefit to the unit.[84] Corcoran, on the other hand, recruited twenty-five hundred volunteers.

Additional factors beyond the media frenzy may have contributed to Meagher's relative lack of success as well. Some Irish-Americans were suspecting that Meagher's leadership, or lack thereof, was contributing to the Irish Brigade's high casualty rates. According to the numbers he offered during the 7th Regiment Armory speech and casualty reports from the battles during the Peninsula Campaign in 1862, the brigade losses from casualties and disease can be estimated at around seven to eight hundred men.[85] Irish-Americans may have trusted Corcoran to secure the kind of victories they needed and the proper care of themselves or their sons, husbands, and fathers that letters and newspaper reports indicated were not provided to the men under Meagher's command. For now, they seemed willing to place their trust in Corcoran's leadership, but continued battlefield losses and changes in the northern war effort would challenge this willingness.

There were sufficient numbers of Irishmen in New York City, Albany, Plattsburgh, and the neighboring areas for both commanders to fill brigades, and Meagher's recruiting difficulties, even among families like the Turners, who respected that general, reveal significant, if minor, changes in Irish-American views of the war in the summer of 1862. As the nation moved unknowingly toward the horrific losses of Antietam and Fredericksburg and the controversial Emancipation Proclamation, opposition to the war escalated, especially in Irish-American communities. They would be among the first to begin a vigorous questioning of the war's direction by the following year and to initiate demands for a peaceful resolution. These responses would be in part reactions to the war's high cost and its shifting focus from union to abolition, but they were also the result of tensions within the Irish-American community that existed due to complaints of anti-Irish prejudice dating back to 1861.

In September 1862, Confederate and Union armies met again outside Sharpsburg, Maryland, near Antietam Creek. This battle would be remembered as the bloodiest day in American history, with more than twenty-two thousand soldiers killed, wounded, or captured within a twelve-hour period. For Irish-American soldiers and their families at home, two key sections of the battlefield shaped their memories of this fight: the struggle of the Irish 69th Pennsylvania in the West Woods and the Irish Brigade's assault on Bloody Lane. The casualties they lost at Antietam and the battle's larger influence on the changing northern war effort, including the Emancipation Proclamation, played a key role in the diminishing Irish-American support for the war.

When the Battle of Antietam began on September 17, Confederate General Robert E. Lee had positioned his Army of Northern Virginia along a series of hills and ridges not quite touching, spanning from the Potomac River on his left, north of the town of Sharpsburg, to the hills overlooking Antietam Creek, south of the town. At dawn Confederate horse artillery under Major John Pelham opened the battle, and Union guns responded with fire on Confederate lieutentant general Thomas J. Jackson's wing near the Dunker Church. As Federal forces pushed forward into a cornfield on the Miller Farm that morning, they met withering Confederate fire. The death toll rose every hour as Union and Confederate soldiers fought desperately. By about 7:00 A.M. General George B. McClellan, commander of the Army of the Potomac, received word that Major General Joseph Hooker's I Corps and Major General J. K. F. Mansfield's XII Corps, despite heavy casualties, had the advantage in the bloody fight in the cornfield.

McClellan decided to reinforce Hooker in the hope of turning the Confederate left flank and ordered Major General Edwin V. Sumner's II Corps to advance across Antietam Creek. At about 7:30 A.M., Sumner's 2nd Division, under Major General John Sedgwick, marched westward. Sedgwick's 2nd Brigade, better known as the Philadelphia Brigade, included the 69th, 71st, 72nd, and 106th Pennsylvania Volunteer Infantry Regiments under the command of Brigadier General Oliver Otis Howard. The 69th Pennsylvania included a large number of Irish-Americans, a fair number of whom were Fenians, and carried a green flag representing their ethnic heritage. Marching forward in three parallel columns, the Irishmen and the other two brigades of Sedgwick's division waded through Antietam Creek at Pry's Ford, followed the sound of gunfire, and pushed forward toward the East Woods.

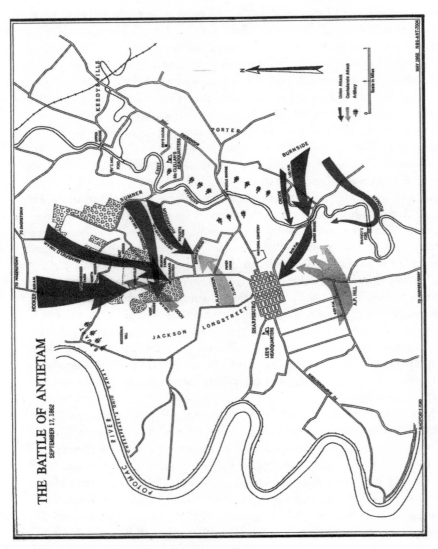

Battle of Antietam, September 17, 1862. *Antietam National Battlefield Handbook.* Washington, DC: Government Printing Office, 1960. Reproduction courtesy of Alann Schmidt, Antietam National Battle-field.

General Sumner, accompanying Sedgwick's men, reached the East Woods within about ninety minutes of receiving McClellan's commands. After reconnoitering the situation, Sumner ordered the 2nd Division into three long battle lines running along the eastern edge of the woods, and then paused as he realized that while the 2nd Division veterans had pushed across the terrain quickly, Brigadier General William French's 3rd Division, newly constituted a few days earlier and right behind Sedgwick when the movement began, had fallen far behind. Frustrated, Sumner pondered the situation. He knew that the Confederates had pulled back across the cornfield and into the West Woods in a disorganized manner, and he wanted to launch an immediate attack before they rallied. He decided to leave word for French to support their advance on Sedgwick's left as soon as his division arrived and then ordered the 2nd Division forward through the East Woods and into the cornfield.[86]

Captain James O'Reilly of Company C of the 69th Pennsylvania recalled the horrifying destruction around them as they advanced through the area where fighting had raged all morning. The County Cavan native noted, "I did pick my steps lest I should trample the fallen foe, but alas it was not always so." All of them lay dead and wounded, and some of Sedgwick's soldiers broke ranks momentarily to give their canteens to the pleading wounded lying among the shredded cornstalks.[87]

Howard's brigade—72nd Pennsylvania, the Irish 69th Pennsylvania, the 106th Pennsylvania, and the 71st Pennsylvania, as deployed from left to right, comprised the third and rearmost line of Sedgwick's division. The entire force received intermittent Confederate artillery fire as it pushed through the cornfield and a clover field adjoining it to the south. Crossing the Hagerstown Pike, they continued forward through an open field and into the West Woods north of the Dunker Church. An eerie calm prevailed. Then a crash of musketry from near the church, coming from the rifles of South Carolinians and Mississippians under Confederate Major General Lafayette McLaws, poured telling volleys into the left flank and rear of Sedgwick's formation, hitting the 72nd and the Irish 69th particularly hard.

While Brigadier General Jubal Early's Virginians slammed Sedgwick's front brigade, McLaws's men continued to hammer the exposed left flank of Howard's Philadelphia Brigade. Howard and Brigadier General N. J. T. Dana, who commanded the brigade immediately forward of the Philadelphians, tried to turn their men to meet the attack, but the woods offered little room for maneuver. As the generals shouted their commands, Sumner rode up and waved his hat and shouted for the men to fall back. But the soldiers could not hear him above the musketry around them. They assumed he intended to rally them for a charge. Fixing their bayonets with a cheer, the men prepared to advance. When they finally realized Sumner's intentions, the onrushing Confederates made even escape difficult.

They slammed into the Philadelphia Brigade first, on the far left of Sedgwick's lines, and the Pennsylvanians began to buckle under the pressure. Colonel Joshua T. Owen managed to maintain some control over his 69th Pennsylvania, but it, too, crumbled in the face of the overwhelming Confederate force turning their flank. One after another, each regiment along the line collapsed. Finally, the entire Philadelphia Brigade broke, heading northward, the only avenue to safety left open to them. Sedgwick fell when three balls slammed into him and, although he managed to remain on the field for nearly an hour, he finally succumbed to the pain. As his men carried him from the field, Howard replaced him and Colonel Owen took command of the Philadelphia Brigade. But neither man could restore order to the chaos raging all along Sedgwick's line.[88]

Facing this overwhelming situation, twin Irish-American brothers, Privates John and Michael Flynn of the 69th Pennsylvania, fled from the West Woods. As they reached the Hagerstown Pike, John Flynn began to climb the fence along the road when a shell fragment hit him. When John could not continue, Michael chose to stay by his brother's side. The Confederates captured him standing next to John's dead body. Michael Flynn remained a prisoner of war until Confederates paroled him a few weeks later, and the Irishman decided he had seen enough of fighting. Michael Flynn deserted the regiment and disappeared from the historical record.[89] Similarly, Private Patrick McConnell, a thirty-year-old father of three, fell unconscious when a bullet bruised his head. He awoke to discover his status as a prisoner and he, too, deserted the 69th Pennsylvania shortly after he was paroled.[90] Much like the Flynn brothers, Sergeant Cornelius Gillen and his brother, Captain Daniel Gillen, both of Company I, endured most of the chaos together. When solid shot crushed "Neal's" leg in the middle of the retreat, Daniel led the remainder of the company to safety and then returned to his brother's side until Confederate soldiers captured him. Neal spent the night of September 17 alone on the battlefield. Union surgeons tried to save him by amputating his leg, but Cornelius Gillen died on September 27. His brother Daniel appears to have suffered a nervous breakdown while in Libby Prison and when Confederates paroled him in early October, he never rejoined his regiment. Michael Flynn, Patrick McConnell, and Daniel Gillen decided that they had sacrificed enough for this war, and their families at home would reach similar conclusions in the coming weeks and months.[91]

Irish-born Lieutenant Colonel Dennis O'Kane succeeded Colonel Owen as commander of the 69th Pennsylvania and he, along with Owen, managed to gather some of the men east of the Hagerstown Pike at the Miller

Farm. Here they reformed around a Union battery and held the position for the remainder of the day, still receiving intermittent Confederate artillery fire. As sounds of fighting moved to the south, the survivors of Howard's brigade, rallied around the Miller Farm and the North Woods, began to count their casualties and look for wounded friends and comrades. The results, gathered over the next few days, horrified them. In approximately thirty minutes in the West Woods, the Irish 69th Pennsylvania lost twenty-one men killed, fifty-seven wounded, and nineteen captured. General Sedgwick's entire division lost nearly half its total strength, an estimated twenty-three hundred men dead, wounded, or captured.[92] Still, though, the battle was not over. To the south another group of Irishmen had begun to earn even more bloody fame.

At approximately 9:30 A.M. on September 17, 1862, the Irish Brigade crossed Antietam Creek at Pry Ford with the rest of Brigadier General Israel Richardson's 1st Division of the II Corps. Many veterans, knowing it would be an exhausting day, paused to fill their canteens. The men advanced at the double-quick toward the Roulette Farm. Brigadier General William H. French's 3rd Division already had pushed forward, slamming into the Confederate center, where they hit elements of Major General D. H. Hill's division. The Confederates spent much of the morning stacking fence rails along the northern and eastern banks of a bending sunken road, creating an excellent defensive position. Many of French's men faced their first combat here, and although they fought well, the Confederate defenders held. Major General Edwin V. Sumner sent Richardson's division, including the Irish Brigade, to support them. Anxious and excited, the Irishmen stopped about six hundred yards from the Sunken Road and, using a rise in the ground to shield them from the Confederate position, dropped their blankets, knapsacks, and everything but the essentials for the day's fight. Seeing the men begin their assault, still marching at the double-quick, Irish chaplain Father William Corby pushed his horse to a full gallop to get out ahead of them. "As they were coming toward me," he recalled, "I had time only to wheel my horse for an instant toward them and gave my poor men a hasty absolution." He then withdrew a short distance to wait for the inevitable time when his services would again be needed by the wounded and dying.[93]

General Meagher planned to advance as close to the rebel line as possible so the "buck and ball" of his men's smoothbores could be used to devastating effect. Then he could order them to close with the bayonet. For the Irish nationalist, it may have seemed like a reenactment of the Irish Brigade at Fontenoy. The 88th New York's Lieutenant James Turner, the County Cavan native turned Jersey City lawyer, recalled the effectiveness of the enemy fire directed at the Irish Brigade as it advanced across the cornfield. "The shot and shell of the enemy poured over our heads and crashed in the hollow to the rear," Turner noted, but the advance was uninterrupted. Only "the close, compact, and strong fences . . . impeded the progress of the men." As the Irishmen pushed on, Turner noted, "the bullets are whirring about, an occasional wounded man falling down and is borne to the rear but we have not yet commenced to fire."[94]

As the brigade crested the slope before the Sunken Road, the fire suddenly intensified. Lieutenant James J. Smith of the 69th New York recalled his first sight of a well entrenched enemy before them. A densely packed line of Confederate infantry, he noted, had deployed in the Sunken Road. A second line stood in ranks in a field behind the road. Confederate batteries formed a third line behind them. All three lines seemed to open on the Irishmen at once, as Smith remembered.[95]

Maintaining their own two-ranked battle line, the Irish Brigade returned the fire with one massive volley pouring into Confederates in the Sunken Road. General Meagher watched the Irish Brigade deliver five or six volleys, and only then personally ordered them to charge. As he later explained, he had his men "push the enemy . . . as they displayed themselves to us, and relying on the impetuosity and recklessness of Irish soldiers in a charge, felt confident that before such a charge the rebel column would give way and be dispersed."[96]

Meagher watched from his horse as the Confederate fire from the Sunken Road and the batteries beyond it "literally cut lanes through our approaching line." Still, the Irishmen pushed on. Lieutenant Colonel James Kelly of the 69th New York led his men forward until two balls slammed into his face, one under his eye and the other crushing his jaw. Despite this, Lieutenant Turner recalled, Kelly remained with the men as long as he could. Nearby, Captain Felix Duffy, acting major of the 69th New York, fell dead.[97] To their left, a succession of color bearers in the 63rd and 88th New York fell, one after another, but each time another man rushed forward to raise the flag. One of the last to grasp the green banner of the 88th New York was Captain Patrick Felan Clooney. Shot through the knee, finding "the pain . . . torturing, terrible," he "seize[d] the colors and hobble[d] along on one leg, waving the green flag that he love[d] so well in front of the line." The Irish-born veteran of the Second Italian War of Independence (1859) had continued his career as a soldier in America, and his moment of glory came at Antietam. He shouted for the men to continue forward with him, and then, in an instant, a ball slammed through his head as another tore open his chest and Clooney fell, his Union blue uniform wrapped in the green of Ireland.[98]

Portions of the Irish Brigade came within thirty feet of the Sunken Road, but they could not break the Confederate line. It seemed to be all they could do simply to hold their position near the crest of the hill and continue firing into the Confederate ranks. Meagher watched the desperate exchange until enemy fire hit his horse, and both slammed to the ground. The pummel of his saddle pressed into Meagher's chest with all the weight of his horse behind it. The general still lived, but as he grew increasingly insensible, his men carried him to the rear. Shortly after this, 1st Division commander General Israel B. Richardson ordered Brigadier General John C. Caldwell's 1st Brigade forward to relieve the Irishmen, who withdrew back behind Caldwell's ranks.[99]

While the Irish Brigade did not personally drive the Confederates from the Sunken Road, the unit received much of the credit for that final victory. Their commanding officers, both Irish-American and non-Irish, heralded their efforts. General McClellan noted that "the Irish Brigade sustained its well-earned reputation" at Antietam, while perhaps the highest praise came from their opponents in the Sunken Lane. One member of the 2nd Mississippi Battalion testified,

> I wish here to bear witness to the gallantry of the men of Meagher's Brigade and the superb courage of their commanding officers on that bloody day. They stood in line on their ridge, in plain view, with three flags as colors—One the Stars and Stripes, one a Pennsylvania [Massachusetts] State flag and one the green flag with the Harp of Erin. Our men kept those flags falling fast, while just as fast they raised again. Several times the deadly fire of our rifles broke the ranks of those men and they fell behind the ridge, but quickly re-formed each time and appeared with shorter lines but still defiant.[100]

On the home front, both the *New York Times* and the *Herald* offered details of the Irish Brigade's assault on the Confederate position, and they included comments on the Irish excitement for the fight, hinting again at the old stereotype of the Irish love of a good brawl. The *New York Herald* described the Irishmen's enthusiasm as they marched in tight formations toward the Confederates. "[T]heir cheers arose in one great surge of sound," the correspondent recalled, "over the noise of battle, over the roar of a wilderness of artillery."[101]

That reputation came at a price, though, and as the remnants of the Irish Brigade gathered to ascertain their losses, the cost shocked even the battle-hardened veterans. Both the 63rd and 69th New York lost 60 percent of their numbers, suffering 202 and 196 casualties, respectively, most cut down within the first five minutes of the battle. The 88th New York lost twenty-seven killed and seventy-five wounded, with the entire brigade suffering 540 casualties.[102] Among these brigade casualties were seventy-five new recruits who had just joined the brigade the day before the battle.[103]

The extremely high casualty rates speak to the Irishmen's courage and steadiness under fire. These losses may have been a credit to the valor and ability of Irish-American soldiers, but they had a devastating effect on their families and communities at home. Criticisms of Meagher increased, captured in the reflections of one Irish sergeant who described Meagher as "a gentleman and a soldier, but . . . he wanted to gain so much praise he would not spare his men."[104] Further problems arose as rumors spread that Meagher had actually fallen from his horse drunk at Antietam, failing his men when they needed him most. As Union Colonel David Hunter Strother of McClellan's headquarters staff noted, "Meagher was not killed as reported, but drunk, and fell from his horse." While none of the Irish Brigade officers supported this account, it circulated through northern newspapers that fall. It would join with other events, including the Emancipation Proclamation, General McClellan's departure from command, and the horrific losses at the Battle of Fredericksburg, all of which would contribute to the increasing concern with which Irish-Americans viewed the Union war effort.[105]

The dramatic losses were not for the Irish Brigade alone. Robert Webb, a Protestant native of Ireland, served in the 12th New York Volunteer Infantry Regiment of the 3rd Brigade of the 1st Division of V Corps, held in reserve during the battle. He survived his eighth engagement and third wound at Antietam, and he hoped this battle would be his last. Shocked by the horror of the battle as he walked the field the next day, Webb insisted he had "never witnessed anything so terrible in my existence. Most of the men lay as if in line of battle, giving evidence of their courage in standing their ground until they were killed. The ground around the field was strewn with the dead and dying. Several did I hear imploring to be shot dead rather than endure the pain of their wounds." As he looked about, Webb saw a whole field that appeared as "one vast Hospital [with] surgeons engaged all over it. Some cutting off limbs, others bandaging wounds. It was certainly the most awful sight that ever I witnessed and may God forbid I shall ever witness another of the same sort." Webb declared, "I think if I live for one or two months more I shall leave it altogether," and added that even the regimental surgeon had advised him to resign from the service. Robert Webb had seen enough of war.[106]

The losses from this fight at Sharpsburg, Maryland, would combine with a series of controversial decisions announced by President Lincoln in the coming months. These actions and reactions are critical to understanding why so many Irish-Americans would see that winter as a turning point, where they had sacrificed too much for a war that offered too little in return.

The first event immediately followed the Battle of Antietam, when Lincoln announced the Emancipation Proclamation that would free all slaves held in Confederate territory as of January 1, 1863. The new law did not free slaves in slave-owning states that had remained in the Union, such as Maryland and Missouri. Nor did it free slaves in lands that had previously been part of the Confederacy but were now held by Federal forces. Despite this, the proclamation had a direct impact on the direction of the war, which evolved from a conflict to preserve the Union to a bloody struggle to abolish slavery and reunite a nation.

Many northerners had never taken a clear stand on slavery, believing that it had little impact on their lives and that they should be far more concerned with saving the Union. For some northerners, including many Irish-Americans, the Emancipation Proclamation indicated that the Lincoln administration had sided with the most radical aspects of the Republican party and Irish-Americans' sworn enemies, the abolitionists. Irishmen linked the abolition of slavery with new labor competition from free blacks in an already difficult market. It meant freedom and a level of respect, though drastically limited, for a group the Irish had prided themselves as being above, no matter how low the Irish seemed to fall within the American socioeconomic system. As the Irish community in America reacted to the losses of Antietam, it learned that the war was moving in a direction it could not support. If Lincoln was going to retain support in the Irish-American community, he needed a victory to validate this controversial decision.

Lincoln's other problem focused on his relief of General George B. McClellan from command of the Army of the Potomac. McClellan had displayed a constant case of what Lincoln called "the slows" throughout the campaign season of 1862, and the president believed he could not win the war with such a conservative commander. His decision, however, was nearly as controversial as the Emancipation Proclamation and, coming on its heels, only added fuel to the fire of complaints across the North.

Much of this unrest was within the Army of the Potomac, whose soldiers loved the commander who seemed so concerned with sparing their lives, compared to the press and politicians at home who always demanded more and more battles. As McClellan passed the Irish Brigade, Meagher ordered the Irishmen to throw down their green battle flags in an act of devotion. McClellan was honored, but insisted that the men retrieve the banners before he passed and obey their orders just as he must accept his. With McClellan's departure, several Irish Brigade officers tendered resignations to protest the president's decision, but Meagher refused to accept them. The Irishmen of the Army of the Potomac would obey their orders, but not without complaint. Several days after McClellan's departure, the New York *World* published the following statement by Meagher:

> Ah! If the gentlemen of the White House could have seen what I saw this morning—could have heard the cheers from those 100,000 soldiers which rent the air and deadened the artillery itself as the parting salute was fired —they would have felt that a mistake or crime has been committed by them, which the Army of the Union will never forgive.[107]

The Lincoln administration had just made the most controversial decisions of the war in a period of two months, following a year of military defeats or limited and very costly successes. To quell the unrest, Lincoln needed a victory.

Again, it should be clarified that this response to McClellan's departure was not universal among Irish-Americans, Protestants and Catholics. Midwesterner Andrew Greenlees, an Irish-born Protestant, declared the general a "miserable slow fellow" who "ought to have been court martialed and shot." Greenlees explained to his family in Ireland,

> The rebels were too quick for him every time. He has been in Command of the grand army of the Potomac for eighteen months, and what has he done, simply nothing or worse than nothing, wasted at least 50 or 70 thousand lives besides hundreds of millions of dollars. He had all the men and munitions of war he asked for, an army of a hundred & fifty thousand men and upwards and yet by his do nothing policy the army stays where it was one year ago on the banks of the Potomac.

McClellan's replacement, Ambrose Burnside, Greenlees predicted, was "a fighting man and a good general [and] it is said he has not sympathy for the rebels but will give them shot and shell in abundance."[108] He may not have been exact in his prophecy of Burnside's abilities, but his views are significant in noting the textures within Irish America and the varied responses from these communities to the defining events of the war.

Amid the controversial decisions of the fall of 1862, Ambrose Burnside marched his Army of the Potomac down toward Richmond on a more easterly path than that used by his predecessors. This required the use of pontoons to construct bridges to take the army over the Rappahannock River. The Federals arrived across from Fredericksburg, Virginia, on 18

November, but the pontoons did not arrive for another week. And Burnside caused further delays with his indecision.

It was during this period that friends departed the Irish Brigade while new regiments joined them. The 28th Massachusetts, an Irish regiment, replaced the 29th Massachusetts, whose native-born Americans bade a fond farewell to the Irishmen they had fought beside that year, though the friendship did not go so far as to accept an Irish Brigade green banner in honor of their service. The commander of the 29th politely declined Meagher's gift, according to some sources because he feared it would brand his men Fenians. Other accounts explained that Colonel Joshua H. Barnes did not believe it would be right for his non-Irish regiment to carry an Irish banner and felt sure that his men agreed. The historical record is unclear as to which story is the more accurate.[109]

In addition to the 28th Massachusetts, the 116th Pennsylvania, commanded by Irish-born Colonel Dennis Heenan and Lieutenant Colonel St. Clair Mulholland, joined the Irish Brigade. This Philadelphia-based regiment had a strong Irish component, but it included a significant German-American and native-born element as well, and it never fought under a green banner. The men of these two new regiments would see some of the hardest fighting of the war at Fredericksburg, and for some, it would be their first and final battle.[110]

Some native-born Americans chose this quiet period of early winter to recognize the sacrifices of the Irishmen. On December 2, a delegation from New York received the tattered national and regimental colors of the Irish Brigade, which were to be replaced with new flags "purely the gift of Americans, in appreciation of the Irish Brigade." The new colors would be a "grateful commemoration of the gallant deeds" of the Irish Brigade that had won "the unqualified praise of all." As New Yorker Henry F. Spaulding explained, the Irishmen would be pleased if they could "see with what enthusiasm their services are appreciated. On the soil of their adoption they have added fresh and enduring pages to the chivalric history of their native land."[111]

Despite the delays and the ever increasing Confederate forces facing him, General Burnside decided to proceed with his plans on December 11, 1862, and he ordered his engineers to begin the construction of the pontoon bridges. On that and the following day, most of the Army of the Potomac crossed the Rappahannock River into Fredericksburg, Virginia. This movement included Meagher's Irish Brigade, which marched across the bridge at the upstream crossing on the morning of December 12. The delays had caused frustration in the ranks, but now that the soldiers were on the move, confidence rose despite the embalmers who rushed toward them, handing them business cards with promises that should any man require "an early trip home" he would be "nicely boxed up and delivered to loving friends by express, sweet as a nut and in perfect preservation." Disgusted by these macabre creatures, several Irish soldiers offered sharp retorts as the brigade marched on and the embalmers sought fresh targets.[112]

At the edge of town, the Irish Brigade headed down Sophia Street to help secure the middle pontoon crossing, and then made camp at the city docks. From commanders' reports, as well as contemporary and modern histories, it appears that the Irish Brigade was absent from most of the looting that occurred in Fredericksburg on December 12, possibly due to their location on the outskirts of town. General Meagher insisted that his men "scrupulously abstained from any act of depredation" such as those carried out by other Union men.[113]

While denying their involvement in the destruction of private property, some of the Irish Brigade officers did admit to acquiring tobacco, though their effort to do so sounded more like a rescue than a theft. County Antrim native St. Clair A. Mulholland, lieutenant colonel of the 116th Pennsylvania, recalled that the men of his regiment dove into the chilly Rappahannock River to secure large quantities of tobacco that southerners had sunk along with the barges rather than surrender them to the Federals. Much of the tobacco was packed so tightly that the centers of the cakes were still dry. As Mulholland recalled, some of the men insisted that those thick plugs actually stopped some Minnie balls and saved Irish lives, but the evidence had, literally, gone up in smoke.[114]

Some Irishmen outside the brigade, however, boasted of their involvement. William White, a member of the Irish 69th Pennsylvania, was thrilled with what he and his comrades gathered. "We could get anything we wanted," he told his parents. "Some fellows got jewelry and silver ware. One fellow in our company got a splendid gold watch. You can get all kinds of groceries, barrels of flour, books, papers, [and] all sorts of goods." White included a proud postscript, boasting that this very letter was on "a sheet of Fredericksburg paper."[115]

The men slept fitfully that night, if at all. The ground had become a soggy mess as the temperature rose that day, turning the previously frozen turf into a quagmire. Private William McCarter of the 116th Pennsylvania recalled that night as "sleepless and most uncomfortable," with the only rest coming after he separated the staves of an old barrel, laid them out, and found some small protection from the damp ground. St. Clair Mulholland fared no better, declaring it "one of the most dismal and miserable [nights] ever experienced." He noted, "The troops [were] massed so close that there was not even room enough for the men to lie down on the ground, and it was a fortunate man who could secure a cracker box to sit upon during the weary hours. Sleep was impossible, it was so cold and chilly."[116] McCarter appears to have been a lucky one, managing an hour's sleep on his broken barrel.

As the men arose on the morning of December 13, they enjoyed a brief breakfast as the fog burned off. It was just over thirty degrees by 7:00 A.M. and, despite the chill, some Irishmen continued to dive for tobacco while others awaited anxiously their orders to march.[117] As McCarter and the rest of the Irish Brigade formed into a column, General Meagher spoke to each regiment rather than simply rallying the brigade with a standard address. Meagher of the Sword was always more of an orator than a general, and despite the fact that most of the Irish Brigade was made of veterans who would not be fooled by stories of glory, the general knew how to reach this audience.

Meagher had his orderlies distribute sprigs of boxwood throughout the ranks, insisting that each man follow his example of tucking some greens into his cap to symbolize the Irish heritage of the unit. The brigade having sent its tattered green flags home to New York before replacements arrived, the boxwood would serve to remind friend and foe alike that these were Irishmen fighting for American union. Once this image of Ireland was set, Meagher reminded the men of their duty to America, too. Shouting over cracking musketry and crashing shells, Meagher told his officers and men,

> In a few moments you will engage the enemy in a most terrible battle, which will probably decide the fate of this glorious, great and grand country—the home of your adoption. . . . [T]his day you will strike a deadly blow to those wicked traitors who are now but a few hundred yards from you, and bring back to this distracted country its former prestige and glory.[118]

With these reminders of their dual loyalties to Ireland and America, the men began their march back up Sophia Street. The fire intensified as they reached each intersection, where the lack of cover allowed Confederate artillery to focus on the clusters of blue. Just past the railroad tracks the column paused as commanders discussed which units would push westward and up through the town first. It was probably at this point, if not sooner, that the confidence instilled by Meagher's speeches began to fade. Even during his talk a shell had crashed in among the men, killing several and, as one officer recalled, "cutting off legs right by our side." Now, as the brigade paused on Sophia Street, the wounded from earlier attacks stumbled past.[119] A wounded soldier covered with blood and missing one

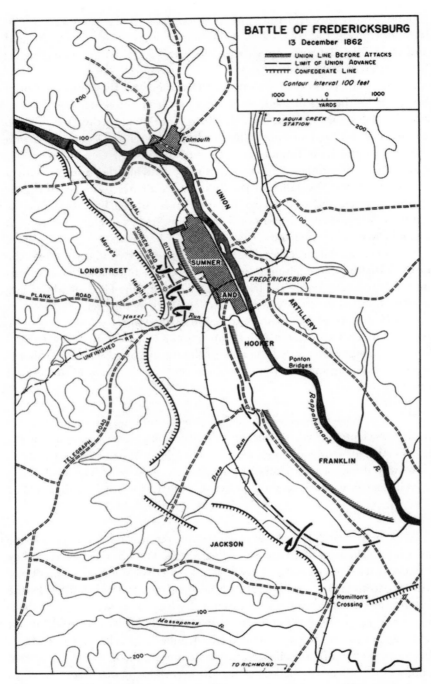

The Battle of Fredericksburg, December 13, 1862. *American Military History*
(Washington: Center for Military History, 1989), 232.

arm shuffled by the brigade until another shell careened down the lane, killing him instantly. Similarly, a Federal officer carried along on a shutter grimaced with pain. A cannon ball had struck his leg above the knee, nearly ripping it off but for a single tendon that refused to tear. Quietly, a sympathetic Irish veteran stepped from the ranks and cut it, and the officer smiled in relief as his leg dropped to the ground and disappeared behind him.[120]

Mixed in with the wounded soldiers, some African-American civilians were still scrambling for safety. Most townspeople had either left or barricaded themselves in cellars, but Private William McCarter saw "colored women rushing out of half demolished houses in the wildest confusion, not knowing which way to run out of the reach of the bursting shells," possibly trying to reach safety and freedom behind the Union lines. McCarter recalled one of the women in particular, carrying a heavy basket with three children clinging to her skirts as they raced down the street. He watched with horror as solid shot slammed into her, killing her and two of the children, leaving the third wounded in the street.[121] St. Clair Mulholland declared the trail of wounded along Sophia Street a scene "not calculated to enthuse the men or cheer them."[122]

Still, amid the terrifying carnage, one soldier's quiet courage may have steeled some nerves. As the men awaited the word to move forward, a German-American soldier passed the Irish Brigade in a wheelbarrow, pushed along by some comrades, with his legs hanging over the side. As the man was coolly puffing on his pipe, the scene might have seemed humorous until the Irishmen noticed that one foot was missing, leaving nothing but a shredded uniform and bloody stump. The soldier went by in determined silence, interrupted only by an occasional sharp command of "Ach, make right!" whenever the barrow would tip to one side or the other. The German's determination brought a smile to the veterans' faces. For one new Irish recruit, though, it was too much and he collapsed in a dead faint.[123]

After about ten or twenty minutes, the Irish Brigade moved forward again along Sophia, with another brief stop, and then they turned onto George Street and pushed up the hill. The air, one soldier recalled, "seemed to be filled with all kinds of hissing and exploding missiles," but still they pressed on.[124] For a short time the terrain offered them cover, but once they crossed Princess Anne Street they reached a plateau and there was little shelter from the Confederate guns behind the city on Marye's Heights. These were the Confederate forces of Lieutenant General James Longstreet's I Corps of the Army of Northern Virginia. Entrenched behind a stone wall, in a sunken lane, infantry lay anywhere from four to eight men deep, and behind them were the guns of the Washington Artillery that the expert Confederate gunner Lieutenant Colonel E. Porter Alexander had carefully emplaced. He had pledged, "A chicken could not live on that field when we open on it," and the day would prove him right.[125]

As the Irishmen continued through the town, coming under increasingly heavy fire, they marched past the charred remains of buildings, over the bodies of dead Confederate defenders and Union attackers, as well as wounded Federals working their way to the rear. At the outskirts of town, near the free-black section called Liberty Town, George Street curved southward and blended into Hanover Street. Lieutenant Colonel Mulholland remembered a moment of strange quiet here, even hearing the mew of a cat sitting on a fence, until Confederate shells disrupted the calm once more. One landed nearby, decapitating Sergeant John C. Marley, who dropped to his knees, headless, still clutching his musket. A ball slammed through three other soldiers, killing them instantly. They dropped to the ground, "stark dead, their faces calm, their eyes mild and life-like, lips unmoved."[126]

The Irish Brigade reached the millrace, a small waterway that ran behind the town and that served as a run-off for Fredericksburg's canal. The 69th and 88th New York, as well as the 28th Massachusetts, crossed using the remains of a bridge, but the process was tedious and they were losing men to ruthless Confederate fire. General Meagher recognized that the crossing was taking too long and ordered the remaining two units, the 63rd New York and the 116th Pennsylvania, to wade across, while two wounded soldiers assisted him in crossing the remains of the bridge. He had injured his knee recently and marching with the men was difficult, but General Hancock had ordered all officers to leave their horses behind. Once across the millrace, which cost the men about thirty minutes and an unknown number of wounded and killed, they formed into line and fixed bayonets.[127]

By this point in the early afternoon, the temperature was nearly sixty degrees.[128] The men saw little of the warming sun, though, as "[n]oonday [was] turned to dusk by the storm and smoke of battle."[129] Meagher continued to have difficulty walking, and as he sent the Irish Brigade forward he decided to head back for his horse.[130] Why Meagher left his men at this moment remains a mystery, and resulted in sharp criticisms in contemporary and modern sources.[131] The general insisted that he "was compelled" to go back for his horse if he was "to be of any further service to the brigade that day."[132] Still, he could have remained along the west side of the millrace, commanding his brigade on foot from that position. Or he could have sent a staff officer back for a horse, leaving him in a position closer to the attack and better able to command. Whatever the motivation behind his actions, the evidence is insufficient to reach a conclusive judgment of the general.

It is significant to note that most of the Irish-American community continued to praise Meagher in their local papers, and none of the brigade officers criticized him for his actions at Fredericksburg during or after the war.[133] Perhaps they all recognized that Meagher's greatest strength was as the voice of the unit, their representative to the Lincoln administration, and one of the most famous leaders in Irish America. Or they sincerely believed that their general would have been with them if at all possible, or they suppressed their doubts in order to present a unified front to those outside their communities. Still, Meagher's absence had been noted, and he was charged with cowardice by native-born officers and journalists at the battles of First Bull Run and Antietam, and now at Fredericksburg. While some Irishmen joined the critics in the postwar period, most of the Irish-American community, soldiers and civilians, continued to defend Meagher in the winter of 1862–1863. How long this could last, though, remained to be seen.[134]

As Meagher headed back toward the millrace, nearly every other Irish Brigade officer continued to advance up Marye's Heights. Just before they started, the 69th New York's Captain John H. Donovan, who had already lost an eye at Malvern Hill, watched "Zooke's brigade advance in fine style, but, God! Mark how they fall; see how its ranks are thinned; still on they go." Then the Irish Brigade pushed forward, beyond the protection of a swale in the ground, and into "a blinding storm of bullets." William McCarter managed to fire for some time until a spent round struck his shoulder and then another clipped his kepi, "leaving it dangling at my ear by a solitary thread." As he continued to load and fire, McCarter watched as shots hit his officers and comrades, leaving some writhing in pain and some calling for their mothers, while others fell in silence. As he rammed another cartridge home, a ball slammed into his right arm. He felt rushing blood, his arm falling limp by his side, and collapsed unconscious to the ground.

Robert Nugent, colonel of the 69th New York, recalled that the "fight was terrific" in front of Marye's Heights. Struggling to keep his command together as an effective force, he began to realize that his was an impossible task. "By virtue of the commanding position of the enemy no attack could have been successful," he insisted.[135] Similarly, Major John Dwyer of the 63rd New York looked out upon the heights and noticed with horror how "the dead were piled in heaps" behind them.[136] St. Clair Mulholland recalled officers in his 116th Pennsylvania falling all around him. A ball ripped through Lieutenant Garrett Nowlen's thigh, while another tore

Private William McCarter, 116th Pennsylvania Volunteer Infantry Regiment. McCarter's first experience in battle was at Fredericksburg, Virginia, on December 13, 1862. It made such a powerful impact on him, physically and psychologically, that he moved to Fredericksburg, Virginia, in the postwar period and chronicled his wartime experiences in *My Life in the Irish Brigade*. Courtesy of the Historical Society of Pennsylvania.

through Lieutenant Robert McGuire's lungs. Mulholland watched, as if in a dream, as an orderly sergeant spun around, blood spraying from a gaping hole in his head, and collapsed to the ground.[137] Shortly after him, Mulholland fell, too, as a ball cut through his right calf.[138]

One of the tragic ironies of this struggle was that some of the Confederates opposing the Irish Brigade on Marye's Heights were fellow Irishmen, many with the same motivations that inspired Irish-American service in the Union Army. The Confederate troops included the Lochrane Guards, an Irish company in Phillips Legion of Georgia, and County Tyrone native Captain Joseph Hamilton, who rose to command Company E of Phillips Legion when so many of its members fell defending the stone wall. St. Clair Mulholland recalled a strong sympathy for the Irish Brigade among those Confederates. Years later he insisted, "behind that rude stone breast work were 'bone of their bone, and flesh of their flesh'—the soldiers of Cobb's Brigade were Irish like [our]selves." They recognized the Irish Brigade advancing, Mulholland claimed, by the boxwood in the Irish Brigade caps, and the Confederate Irish allegedly cried, "'Oh, God, what a pity! Here comes Meagher's fellow!'"[139]

The Confederate Irish were not in brigade-strength as Mulholland remembered, and while some may have found the situation tragic, it did not keep them from firing. Indeed, a soldier serving under Irish-born Colonel Robert McMillan of the 24th Georgia recalled that when his commander

Captain John Dwyer, 63rd New York Volunteer Infantry Regiment. Courtesy of U.S. Army Military History Institute. Photograph reproduction courtesy Lynn L. Libby, Enola, PA, 2005.

recognized a green banner amid the Union ranks advancing, McMillan shouted, "That's Meagher's Brigade! . . . Give it to them now, boys! Now's the time! Give it to them!" The soldier insisted, "never did men better respond to a call. They did give it to them."[140]

Of all the assaults that day, thirteen in total, the 69th New York was among the few Union regiments to get within fifty yards of the stone wall. Despite their efforts, the men failed to take the position and by the end of the afternoon remnants of the brigade made their way cautiously back down the hill, crawling to avoid the still heavy Confederate fire. Many of the wounded, however, could not move without being hit and had to remain among the dead and in the cold night air until the following day.[141]

As the Irish Brigade reflected on their losses that bloody day in December, a dark depression fell over the men. Father Corby, horrified by the suffering of the Irishmen in his care, declared "the place into which Meagher's brigade was sent was simply a slaughter-pen." Brigade historian and staff member Captain David P. Conyngham went further, challenging the very idea that such fighting deserved the title of a military engagement. "It was not a battle—it was a wholesale slaughter of human beings—sacrificed to the blind ambition and incapacity of some parties," namely General Ambrose Burnside. Colonel Robert Nugent of the 69th New York agreed with such descriptions of the battle, characterizing that bloody day at Fredericksburg as a "living hell from which escape seemed scarcely possible."[142] Years later he explained to a comrade from the Irish Brigade that his regiment lost two officers killed and fourteen wounded, including himself, "so that not a single officer of the sixteen that went into the fight escaped unharmed" at Fredericksburg, including Nugent, who suffered a bullet wound through his right side. "From this you will readily perceive that sad havoc was made in the ranks of the 69th on that day," he argued. As one Irishman from Jersey City, New Jersey, summarized the situation the day after the battle, "The Irish Brigade is completely used up. This morning the whole five regiments together only muster 250 men."[143]

The depleted ranks of the Irish Brigade verified these claims. In addition to the loss of officers, the 69th New York lost 112 men killed, wounded, and missing, of the 173 who entered that battle. They were well on their way to earning the reputation of the New York regiment to lose the most men in action.[144] The 116th lost most of its officers and men, while the 28th Massachusetts lost 158 men on the field. The 63rd New York's casualties numbered forty-four officers and men, while the 88th New York's losses totaled 127 officers and men. In days following the battle, the Irish Brigade estimated that it had taken 45 percent losses. The Irish Brigade lost fifty-five officers killed or wounded at Fredericksburg, a devastating loss in leadership considering that this was in addition to the

Colonel Robert Nugent, 69th New York Volunteer Infantry Regiment. Nugent commanded the Irish Brigade in 1863 and in 1864–1865. Courtesy of U.S. Army Military History Institute. Photograph research/reproduction courtesy Lynn L. Libby, Enola, PA, 2005.

twenty-four officers killed and wounded from its Irish New York regiments at Antietam.[145] It would be difficult, if not impossible, for the brigade to recover from this loss, and this may be another reason why the remaining men rallied around Meagher, despite rumors questioning his leadership, desperate for some guidance amid such turmoil.

The mood of the Irish soldiers and their families at home reflected the carnage. On December 27, 1862, the New York *Irish-American* published a letter Captain William J. Nagle of the 88th New York had sent to his father the day after the battle. In it he spoke well of Meagher, but complained that their efforts had been wasted. "Irish blood and Irish bones cover that terrible field to-day," Nagle wrote. "The whole-souled enthusiasm with which General McClellan inspired his army is wanting—his great scientific engineering skill is missing—his humane care for the lives of his men is disregarded. We are slaughtered like sheep, and no result but defeat."[146] John England, an Irish-American serving in the 9th New York, described the carnage of Fredericksburg as "one of the most fruitless, destructive, and disastrous battles ever fought on the old or new Continent" and was shocked at the treatment of the wounded, who are "thought no more of than a pack of used up maimed dogs, and treated no better; and hundreds are stiff and cold in death to-day, who would be living and might recover if properly treated and attended."[147] Summarizing the situation, one soldier wrote, "As for the remnant of the Brigade, they were the most dejected set of Irishmen you ever saw or heard of."[148]

The year ended in a dark mood for many northern Irish-Americans. What had begun so gloriously with the formation of the Irish Brigade found many Irishmen in December 1862 reexamining the direction of the war and their place in it. With the horrendous losses of Irishmen at Antietam and Fredericksburg, combined with Lincoln's controversial Emancipation Proclamation and decision to relieve McClellan, Irish-Americans who had supported the war for union to preserve an American asylum for Irish refugees could no longer conjure these dreams. Those fighting to gain military experience for the future looked about the battlefields and camps, watching their numbers dwindle as they realized that there would be few Irishmen left to fight such wars. Those of a similar mindset at home were shocked to read the casualty reports in the papers that fall, with the lists of killed and wounded filling page after page. For increasing numbers of Irishmen, the cost of this war and its goals was creating a nation that could no longer be their home. It did not require a great leap of logic to question involvement in a conflict that seemed to offer nothing and demand the sacrifice of nearly everything they held dear.

For most, service and support for the war were founded as much in their loyalty to Ireland as in their loyalty to America, if not more so. Whether fighting to secure military experience for a future war of Irish liberation, to save America as a new home for future Irishmen, to show loyal service that challenged negative stereotypes of the Irish, or simply to gain a steady income, growing numbers of Irish-Americans believed that none of these goals would be achieved through this war. Some may have maintained their motivation through pure American patriotism, but for a population largely comprised of recent immigrants, the need to see the war in terms of what it could provide them as Irishmen was greater than the need to see it in terms of their American identity. As they were increasingly unable to do this, the Irish-American support for the Union war effort continued to decline.

Irish neighborhoods in the North that winter rumbled with complaints about the needless sacrifice of Irishmen on the field of battle. Men bitterly criticized the Lincoln administration's new slavery policies and made equally sharp comments on the inequities of state drafts and the rumors of an upcoming national draft. The cracks within Irish-American support for the war burst open during those cold, dark months, foreshadowing an explosion of riots and protests that would characterize Irish frustrations the following year. As 1863 began an Irish soldier captured the mood that permeated Irish-America: "All is dark, and lonesome, and sorrow hangs as a shroud over us all."[149]

4

"The Irish Spirit for the War Is Dead! Absolutely Dead!"

Battles Raging in the Field and at Home, 1862–1863

While the armies battled from the fall of 1862 through 1863, northerners on the home front struggled with conflicts of their own. A vocal minority opposing the war gathered momentum, with some calling for the immediate opening of peace negotiations and others demanding new leadership for the war. This minority included an increasing number of Irish-Americans, despondent over the toll the war was exacting and opposed to the new goals of the Lincoln administration, especially the Emancipation Proclamation and state and federal drafts. Their civilian resistance to government authority became the most violent in American history.

On September 22, 1862, five short days after the Battle of Antietam, President Abraham Lincoln issued the Emancipation Proclamation and changed the course of the Civil War. The proclamation, he explained, would go into effect on January 1, 1863, and declare all slaves in Confederate-held territory "forever free." Radical abolitionists pointed out the limits of this legislation, which freed only those slaves in areas where federal authority could not enforce the law and retained in bondage slaves in such border states as Maryland and Missouri. Despite these limitations, the Emancipation Proclamation marked a significant shift in the Union war aims. What had previously been a struggle to preserve the union was now a war to make a new nation. "The [old] South is to be destroyed," remarked Lincoln, "and replaced by new propositions and ideas."[1]

Boston's Irish paper, the *Pilot*, complained of the change: "We find ourselves after nearly two years . . . engaged in an abolition war."[2] Emancipation, the editors argued, "is violently opposed to the constitution." Furthermore, they went on, it will only increase the resolve of southerners and drag out the conflict. "The natural, the just, the expedient, the proper, the wise, the certain, the infallible means of ending the war is to withdraw its cause [i.e. emancipation] . . . but the cause is deliberately increased," the *Pilot* cried.[3]

The New York Irish complained as well. The *Irish-American* diagnosed the Lincoln administration as suffering from "Negrophilism" and noted "the irredeemable malignity of the Abolition hatred of [the Irish] race."[4] New York's Irish politicians, newspaper editors, and unskilled laborers opposed abolition and charged hypocrisy, citing the prejudice many abolitionists showed Irish-Americans in their own communities while chastising southerners' treatment of slaves. Leading Irish newspapers, especially those popular among the working class, made numerous references to labor competition in the wake of the Emancipation Proclamation. They feared the added economic competition and diminishing social status that could result from the end of slavery. Reports like those in the New York *Weekly Day-Book* reinforced such concerns with claims that Irish laborers would be "degraded to a level with Negroes" by the changes resulting from emancipation.[5]

In Irish-American communities across the North, men and women worked to demonstrate their disapproval of the administration's new law. In New York, several Irishmen targeted the home of prominent abolitionists James Sloan Gibbons and Abby Hopper Gibbons in an act indicating frustration and anger. The Gibbonses had decorated their home with red, white, and blue bunting on the eve of Lincoln's proclamation and awoke the following morning to find pitch all over their front door and steps.[6] Similar acts of violence continued throughout the city as New Yorkers responded to the Emancipation Proclamation, bearing witness to New York Archbishop John Hughes's warning that "we Catholics, and a vast majority of our brave troops in the field, have not the slightest idea of carrying on a war that costs so much blood and treasure just to gratify a clique of Abolitionists."[7] Such statements would soon create an increasingly negative image of Irish-Americans.

Similar reactions to the Emancipation Proclamation occurred in other Irish-American communities. The situation was particularly controversial in the old Northwest, where tensions had been building for months. In the summer of 1862, native-born farmers and manufacturers had begun importing fugitive slaves, freedmen, and contrabands into the labor market, which irritated poor white unskilled workers. Democrats throughout the region warned Irish and German laborers that they would soon "find some, if not all, of these Negroes, bought by their toil, competing with [immigrants] at every turn."[8] Reacting to such fears, on July 8, 1862, Irish stevedores in Toledo, Ohio, rioted along the wharfs to protest the use of African-American strike breakers. Irishmen attacked with rocks and clubs, the black laborers responded with knives and pistols, and in the process an Irishman named Fitzgerald was killed. His comrades retaliated by attacking the black district of Toledo, destroying homes and businesses until the area was a mass of burning rubble.[9]

Into these growing tensions came the Emancipation Proclamation. Democratic papers claimed that abolitionists and Republicans would raise African-Americans to a standard so high that blacks would overtake Irishmen. Under the Republicans, the papers warned, African-Americans would "take the place of white laboring men" and there would be "a nigger's hand in an Irish potato pot, or his mouth covering the nozzle of an Irishman's whiskey bottle."[10] Irishmen heard rumors that some abolitionists insisted that immigrants had no rights in America and proclaimed that Irish Catholics should not be allowed to fight for the Union because "the oath of a Catholic was not to be relied upon." Meanwhile, the *Chicago Times* claimed, "[W]here abolitionism most abounds, the hatred of foreigners is most intense."[11] Such statements were troubling for Irish-Americans. As their interests and the Union cause diverged, increasing numbers of Irishmen were siding with their own communities rather than the Union.

This response was not universally negative, however, throughout the entire Irish-American population of Protestants and Catholics. It appears to have been the trend for Irish Catholics, but Irish-American Protestants like Andrew and Lucy Greenlees, a poor farming family in Illinois, praised the controversial legislation. Reflecting on the new law, Andrew Greenlees declared, "I bless God that I have lived to see this day; out of our apparent evil and distress God in his providence is bringing much good." Perhaps the tragic losses that year had been a blessing, Greenlees explained:

> if success had followed our arms all along we would not have had the emancipation message . . . then when things looked dark came the proclamation of freedom purely as a war measure . . . beneficial to us and injurious to the rebels. Thus you see God wrung as it were this measure of justice to the down trodden from our government against their wills.[12]

Andrew Greenlees' views represent those of a minority when compared with the sentiments of Irish Catholics in the eastern United States as well as the Midwest. Still, it is significant to note the diversity of responses from the Irish-American population and their regional, as well as religious, variations.

In addition to an overwhelmingly negative response to the Emancipation Proclamation from Irish Catholics, even the commander of the Army of the Potomac, General George B. McClellan, considered the law infamous and privately confided to his wife that he "could not make up [his] mind to fight for such an accursed doctrine as that of a servile insurrection."[13] Union General Fitz John Porter found the law disastrous for the morale of the army and saw daily evidence of this in the soldiers around him. "The proclamation was ridiculed in the Army," Porter explained. It "caused disgust, discontent, and expressions of disloyalty to the views of the administration and amount, I have heard, to insubordination."[14] Many of the soldiers, native born and Irish-American, insisted they volunteered to preserve the union, not free the slaves, and they did not approve of this new development in the northern war effort. As the years passed, many native-born northerners would come to accept this goal as they witnessed the brutality of slavery and its impact on the South, but most Irish-American Catholics at home and in the army maintained their opposition to this policy.[15]

Other Irish-American military leaders agreed with McClellan and Porter, including General Michael Corcoran, who confided to a friend, "I must acknowledge that I am not as full of hope and confidence as to the probable ultimate result of this most unhappy contest as when I last saw you" due to "the results of the late battles and anticipated results of the Proclamation."[16] Judge Charles Patrick Daly was equally disgusted by the proclamation, especially since it coincided with a call for the raising of African-American regiments in the Union Army. Daly claimed, "if that were done he would wash his hands of the whole matter. . . . [R]ecruiting was difficult enough now because of the everlasting Negro question." Indeed, Maria Daly reflected that she and her husband were "heartily sick of the whole business" of this war and complained, "There is no law but the despotic will of poor Abe Lincoln, who is worse than a knave because he is a *cover* for every knave and fanatic who has the address to use him. Therefore we have not one devil, but many to contend with."[17]

Irish-American Rowland Redmond, living in New York City, was not entirely opposed to the idea of ending slavery, but he despised the hypocrisy he saw in the abolitionists. "My notion is ameliorate the condition of the slave and then gradual very gradual emancipation." The abolitionists, however, left him outraged and puzzled as to how they could criticize others for the abuse and misuse of African-Americans. "What did these Puritans do when they landed at Plymouth Rock," he asked. "They looted the redmen's fields and immediately set about exterminating him and seizing his lands and the course is pursued up to the present moment!!!"[18] Such comments reveal a growing frustration among Irish-American leaders about the conduct of the conflict, Republicans' new war aim of emancipation, and the way emancipation would affect postwar American society and the position of Irish-Americans within it.[19] Support for the Lincoln administration diminished, as did faith that the union could be saved. Newspapers such as the New York *Irish-American* and the Boston *Pilot* voiced similar frustrations. Meanwhile, native-born Americans responded to these expressions with charges of disloyalty, and their accusations increased with frequency as Irish-American opposition to the war's conduct and aims grew.[20]

The Dalys and other Irish-Americans found the opportunity to voice their opinions later that fall. In the congressional elections of 1862, Democrats registered their displeasure, focusing primarily on the Emancipation Proclamation and their lack of faith in the Lincoln administration. The results were dramatic. Democrats ousted Republicans from thirty-five congressional seats, installed two victorious governors in New York and New Jersey, dominated state-wide races in Illinois, Indiana, Pennsylvania, and Ohio, and declared the race as evidence that the nation "rejected emancipation, arbitrary arrest, and military incompetency."[21]

Boston and much of Massachusetts proved to be the exception; this area lost to the more powerful Republicans, who reelected Governor John A. Andrew. Nonetheless, Democrats held firm to their positions and Peace Democrats called for an armistice. The *Pilot* strongly supported this agenda: "The North cannot subdue the spirit of the South; nor could the South . . . subdue the spirit of the North. . . . Is there no man of potential character in the North to present this principle—this inevitable fact to the people?" Leading elements of Boston's Irish community believed an armistice that would allow a negotiated peace was the only solution to a war that had cost so much and settled so little. "What description of union shall we have from the bayoneting, and sabering, and devastating by the North of the South into peace? A union bursting with all the elements of disunion. . . ? [F]or the sake of the union, let us have an armistice," the *Pilot* demanded.

Like the Dalys in New York, Irish news editors feared that the leaders who held the reins of the nation were totally out of touch with the people. This war, the *Pilot* warned, was under the direction of "extreme politicians of the North and the South—of the Abolitionists and of the 'fire eaters.' The great body of the people of the two sections had never any virulence for each other.—*This war originated with the politicians*," and the people must regain control to secure a peace.[22]

Peace Democrats did not represent the entire party, but even the War Democrats, who believed in the war but under a Democratic administration, spoke out against Lincoln's abuse of power and roundly criticized the administration's military ineptitude. Irish-born Richard O'Gorman expressed such views in his speech before the Democratic Union Association of New York in October 1862. He called for a "vigorous prosecution of the war for Union," while insisting that policies such as the Emancipation Proclamation must end. O'Gorman explained, "The party in power [is] conducting the war in a manner to make Union impossible. The Union for which Democrats fought did not mean such a Union as that between Great Britain and Ireland."[23] O'Gorman's tremendous popularity among New York Irish-Americans, as well as the fact that other Irish leaders voiced similar opinions, indicates a high level of support for such views.

Like O'Gorman, Irish-American Rowland Redmond, living in New York City, was disgusted with northern leadership by November 1862. As he explained,

> I have never until the last year studied the men and politics of the country, both of which I now hold in the most perfect contempt, <u>not one great mind</u> to direct or control the councils of the country and my chief fear now is that through shear [sic] incapacity with its accompanying self-conceit the country may drift into no one knows what.

Pointing to the poor election returns for the Republicans that fall, he declared "what an emphatic condemnation has been pronounced against Mr. Lincoln and his policy and upon his advisors the Radicals." The best solution, Redmond concluded, was for the South to gain its permanent independence, but he doubted the North would let it go. He hoped, though, that "things will turn out better than they at present promise."[24]

As if Democrats were not sufficiently upset over the war, the Lincoln administration's next action could not have been better calculated to encourage further outrage. On November 5, 1862, President Lincoln relieved General George B. McClellan as commander of the Army of the Potomac. It was a popular decision among Republicans and some military personnel, including General Henry Halleck, who complained of McClellan, "There is an immobility here that exceeds all that any man can conceive of. It requires the lever of Archimedes to move this inert mass," the Army of the Potomac.[25] Among Irish-Americans the decision was devastating. The *Pilot* saw Lincoln's decision as tragic, warning, "the fate of the Republic is growing darker every day. . . . The brave general who made the grand army . . . has been removed in disgrace."[26] Such actions offered further evidence of the ineptness of Lincoln's leadership, the editors argued, and they called on Boston's Irish to oppose the president. "At one time we did support Lincoln; but then he had the full promise of constitutionalism about him. He has changed and so have we. It is now every man's duty to disagree with him."[27]

Irish-American soldiers shared that loyalty to McClellan, and many of them expressed a willingness to abandon the war if he was not their leader. Irish-American John England, serving in the 9th New York Infantry Regiment, reflected, "Indeed the spirit and patriotism of this army is dying out every day. This is occasioned by the general humbug that's carried on, the great want of a proper leader, and lastly by the President's Emancipation Proclamation. I'm sorry for the country—grieved that it should come to this."[28] Irish-American enlisted men, officers, community leaders, politicians, and newspaper editors expressed these sentiments with increasing frequency that fall. By late 1862 increasing numbers of northern Irish-Americans shared John England's fears of a civilian and military leadership that had created "tens of thousands of orphans whose fathers had given their blood to this country" and had so dramatically altered the war's aims that many Irishmen were no longer willing to support it.[29]

The cost of the war effort in the spring and summer of 1862 had cast a shadow of reality across the romantic images of war that had filled American minds. For the first time in American history the nation resorted to conscription, which proved extremely controversial. Many considered the draft unconstitutional, including Irish-Americans who had demonstrated a long-standing and staunch loyalty to the Constitution. Even worse, some argued, it was un-American. In a nation of citizen soldiers, a draft should be unnecessary.[30] But by the summer of 1862 Union manpower fell short. This led Congress to pass the Militia Act on July 17, 1862. Sensing how controversial their decision would be, leaders in Washington made the draft law as restrained as possible, explaining that there was no need to put it into effect if states met their quotas. Each district of every northern state had received a statement explaining how many soldiers it had to supply the army that year based on the number of military-aged males in the population. If regions met the quota, there was no need to enact the draft. If they failed to do so, however, the secretary of war could draft militiamen into service for nine months.[31]

The draft proved extremely controversial, with nearly every district in the country complaining that its quota was too high and bombarding Washington with delegations to protest the system. Complaints ranged from charges that the Republican leadership caused heavier quotas to be placed on Democratic districts than on Republican ones to arguments that their state's enlistments had been miscalculated and they were being unfairly required to provide more volunteers when they had already met their quota. Politicians fearing the repercussions of enforcing a draft called for increased bounties. This failed to solve anything, however, as the bounties multiplied at an alarming rate and only added to the controversy.[32]

Despite efforts to avoid conscription, the fall of 1862 found numerous political leaders in Iowa, Wisconsin, Illinois, Massachusetts, Pennsylvania, and other areas preparing to implement a draft. Large numbers of Irish-Americans, and Democrats in general, organized to resist it and demonstrate dissatisfaction with the war. They no longer saw the goals of the war as having any benefit for them.[33]

During the previous two decades, Irish-American politicians, priests, editors, and community leaders had complained that native-born Americans treated Irishmen unfairly. They renewed this argument when the government demanded that more of them risk their lives in a controversial cause, and draft evasions increased. Many native-born Americans took note and began to overlook the heroic service of northern Irish-Americans.

In Iowa, for example, some native papers reported Irish draft evasion, frequently describing the cases in a stereotypical Irish brogue and poor grammar to convey an image of foreign birth and ignorance. Native-born midwesterners read of one Iowa Irishman who sought a medical exemption for "an impediment in wan iv his eyes, which might make him shoot the captain as aisy as not!" Another Irishman from Dubuque, Michael O'Slagerty, reportedly gave himself a hernia to avoid service, though how an individual might deliberately set out to give himself a hernia was not explained.[34] Both stories were covered in the local papers and read by native-born Americans, who became increasingly angry over what they perceived as cowardly acts by individuals who should be showing gratitude to the nation that saved them. As the *Milwaukee Daily News* complained, immigrants "are so absorbed in the contemplation of the <u>duties</u> now to be performed that they have forgotten the <u>rights</u> they have for so many years enjoyed."[35]

Irishmen read these reports as well, and some tried to counter the image of an ungrateful, cowardly immigrant population. After steady streams of Irishmen were arrested trying to escape to Canada to avoid the draft, prominent Irish businessmen in Toledo, Ohio, denounced the draft dodgers. They published and distributed around the city a pamphlet expressing "utter condemnation and detestation of such conduct, so cowardly and treacherous," to demonstrate that not all Irish-Americans were opposed to the war and that many were already serving in the Union Army.[36]

More forceful resistance to the state drafts in the fall of 1862 began among immigrants, especially Irish and German-Catholic Democrats in rural areas across the North. Riots among German-Americans broke out at draft offices in numerous Wisconsin towns. In eastern Pennsylvania, Irish Catholic mining neighborhoods also erupted in violence, as did several communities across the Midwest. Irish Catholics predominated among the protesters, as well as the rural conservative Democrats known as Butternuts in Indiana and Ohio. They carried banners declaring, "We won't fight to free the nigger" and calling for "The Constitution As It Is, The Union As It Was." To suppress the riots, the government sent in the army, backed by the president's September 24 suspension of the writ of habeas corpus and declaration that "all persons discouraging volunteer enlistments, resisting militia drafts, or guilty of any disloyal practice affording aid and comfort to the rebels" would be subjected to martial law. The result was the arrest and imprisonment, without trial, of hundreds of draft protesters, five newspaper editors, three judges, and numerous political leaders.[37] The Irish-American community was shocked. Such policies reminded many of the Penal Codes in Ireland.

Irishmen in Boston voiced concern while community leaders sought to avoid similar violence. The Boston *Pilot* was swamped with questions from readers asking how the state draft would affect the Irish members of the city. The paper explained that neither unnaturalized persons nor those who had made a previous declaration of citizenship were subject to the draft. It went on, however, to emphasize that "the question with all good citizens, and even aliens, will not be how they may escape service in the cause of the Republic . . . but how they may render it the greatest service in their power." The *Pilot* even went so far as to argue that if a noncitizen male were of military age, were of sound mind and body, and did not have family dependent upon him, he had "a moral obligation to enlist in the army of the Union" or at least to provide a substitute for his lack of service.[38] The paper was not alone on this position. Even New York's Archbishop Hughes supported the draft, so long as it was carried out without showing preference to any class, creed, or ethnicity. Hughes saw the draft as a merciful solution to end an otherwise long and bloody conflict, if carried out so that "every man, rich and poor, will have to take his share."[39]

Despite their disgust with the Lincoln administration, the *Pilot* and many Irish leaders still called on Irishmen to serve in the war, at least for the present. Unlike more established members of the immigrant community, however, laboring Irish-Americans were more cautious. Like the German and Irish Catholics of Wisconsin and Pennsylvania, they resented being forced to serve in a war that had cost so many lives, could lead to emancipation and, in turn, would increase competition for employment. Responding to this dichotomy between prominent Irishmen's call for Irish service and the lack of response from the laboring classes, the *Pilot* began a series on "Records of Irish-American Patriotism," where editor Patrick Donahoe highlighted heroic Irish service in the war while running daily recruiting advertisements for the Irish 28th and 9th Massachusetts Volunteers.

Officers of the Irish 9th Massachusetts Volunteer Infantry Regiment at Culpepper, Virginia, 1863. Courtesy of U.S. Army Military History Institute. Photograph research/reproduction courtesy Lynn L. Libby, Enola, PA, 2005.

The *Pilot* also reminded readers of the benefits of volunteering: a $100 bounty from the city, a $25 bounty from the federal government, and $13 in an advance of one month's salary, for a grand total of $138. Irishmen were quickly reminded, too, that even more money was available during their period of service. Twelve months' service in the U.S. Army earned the average enlisted man $156, as well as a $42 allowance for clothing. Men did not need to worry about their families in their absence, either, as the state of Massachusetts, as well as many other states, paid wives and children a $144 allowance during the soldier's absence. Finally, men were entitled to a $75 bonus upon the expiration of service. The grand total from the bounties, salary, and allowances came to $555, which, at nearly a full year's salary, was quite an incentive for the average unskilled Irish laborer. The catch, of course, was that over half that amount depended upon his survival, but for many men, the benefits outweighed the risks.[40]

Despite these announcements, the *Pilot* hesitated to demonstrate overwhelming support for the war effort. Instead, the editors appear to have sensed that much of the native-born American population was unaware of all that Irishmen had sacrificed for the nation and were determined to confront this ignorance. Their focus on financial rewards indicates, too, that many Irish-Americans were no longer inspired by the recruiting pitches of duty and honor, indicating a growing frustration among the

Boston Irish that their service was being ignored and their patriotism questioned.

The efforts to illustrate the financial opportunities of military service failed to attract significant response. Some men were finding sufficient work at home so that the bounties and other financial inducements were not particularly attractive. Other Irishmen avoided service due to rumors that, despite promises in the papers and at recruiting depots, some men and their families were not receiving the promised money. Edward Caney, for example, had enlisted in the Irish 28th Massachusetts in October 1861 with the understanding that the $144 allowance traditionally given to wives and children of enlisted men would go to his destitute, widowed sister and her child because Caney was not married. In the fall of 1862 Caney contacted Governor John A. Andrew and the mayor of his home-town in Lowell to complain that his sister had not received any payment. Mayor Peter Larosua explained that Caney's sister and child did "not come within the law to be reimbursed by the state." Determined, Caney continued his efforts through the spring of 1863, but there is no evidence that he found any success.[41]

To be fair, not all of the stories of poor laborers tricked into enlisting were true. In February 1863 William Burns of the 28th Massachusetts contacted Governor Andrew regarding pay he had never received upon his discharge. Burns claimed that he was horribly impoverished and need-ed the money to pay the medical bills of his "distressed" family. Unfortu-nately for Burns, Governor Andrew received reports that the doctor Burns claimed was caring for his family had not visited them for years, largely because they were not ill, a fact verified by neighbors upon the doctor's inquiry. The matter worsened when a local manufacturer testified that when applying for work in his factory, Burns was "the worse for liquor," claiming that he "would have his pay of the U.S. or he would demand it of Great Britain."[42] Other reports to the governor described Burns as a "shifty, lazy, worthless fellow" who was "full of liquor" on each visit.[43]

While not the most upstanding man, Burns may have had a legitimate complaint. On the other hand, he could have been part of a growing por-tion of the population taking advantage of the bounty system. After the first year of fighting, when the excitement of battle had been replaced by an appreciation for war's economic and personal cost, Union recruiters had difficulty filling the ranks by volunteerism. To encourage enlistments and avoid state drafts, communities turned to a bounty system that of-fered a fee to volunteers upon enlistment. The prices ranged from fifty to one thousand dollars and, while logical in theory, the system would develop into a scandalous practice. Men for whom the war was more a financial opportunity than an issue of ideology used systems like the bounties and other recruiting incentives to their advantage. By the time of the federal draft in 1863, some men had developed manipulation of bounties into a fine art, enlisting in a regiment, gathering their bounty, and then deserting, repeating the practice in district after district. One such bounty jumper was so proficient that he completed the cycle thirty-two times.[44] The army eventually addressed the problem by transporting bounty soldiers under armed guard to the front, but some men continued to escape and reenlist elsewhere for a new bounty, making a nice living in the process.

For Irish-Americans who were unwilling to manipulate the bounty system, and for whom the financial incentives were not sufficient to attract their service, the federal government used other means to encourage enlistment. Understanding the desire of many Irishmen and other recent émigrés to become American citizens, on July 17, 1862, Congress passed a bill that allowed any alien twenty-one years or older who volunteered for military service and was honorably discharged to become a citizen of the United States. Even if he had not previously declared his intent of naturalization, the soldier need only prove that he had lived in the United States for one year. All other immigrants had to declare their intent to become a citizen several years prior to the naturalization process, prove that they had lived the United States for one year, and renounce any allegiance to their former home nation.[45]

By the summer and fall of 1862, wide-ranging incentives existed to attract Irish and other immigrant and native-born working-class Americans into military service. Nevertheless, a manpower problem remained, revealing widespread dissatisfaction among Irishmen over the direction of the war and its goals, and an unwillingness to serve. Irish-Americans argued that this was not a sign of disloyalty but rather of opposition to the Lincoln administration's conduct of the war, the Emancipation Proclamation, and the draft. On the other hand, Americans supporting the war and frustrated with Irish opposition to it could point to local, state, and federal bounties, as well as reforms to naturalization laws, and wonder why, with all of these incentives, large numbers of Irish-Americans still failed to support the Union during its great crisis, unless it was from a lack of patriotism and loyalty to the United States. As a result, Irish-Americans were faced with increasingly frequent charges of supporting secession, discouraging enlistments, and ranking "least of all in the scale of patriotism."[46]

And many of them did oppose the war. Within one month of its strong encouragement of alien military service, the *Pilot* explained, "Aliens are under no obligation to fight our battles; and no one has a right to make the smallest objection to them for refusing to do so. . . . [W]hen a war is raging . . . non-citizens of a country cannot be morally required to expose themselves to mutilation and death for it." The *Pilot* then reminded its readers of all of the past wrongs committed on Irishmen by the native-born public and all that continued to be withheld from them, questioning why an alien would ever wish to offer his service and his life for such a nation. The editors argued,

> It is going too far to *require* an alien—a recent emigrant—to go to battle. We refuse aliens the right of voting, the right of holding office, and if they wanted passports for foreign travel, not one could they get. The aliens who came to vote would be knocked down at the polls, and then imprisoned; the alien who held office, would be hunted from it by every description of violence; and the alien who looked for the protection of our government would not get it. What *right* then have we to be *severe* with aliens for not enlisting?[47]

Similar expressions of frustration came from New York, arguing that Irish-Americans were expected to fight the war in greater numbers than native-born Americans, with the threat of charges of disloyalty and ingratitude if Irish-Americans failed to do so. When the New York *Illustrated News* claimed that General Michael Corcoran had refused to command several Irish regiments that were ready for service, despite expressing a desire to end the celebrations of his release from Confederate prison and return to the work of war, the *Irish-American* and its readers expressed outrage. A Brooklyn subscriber signing himself "An Irishman" angrily challenged these claims and reminded the city's Irish population of its substantial representation in the Union Army. He then asked, "[W]hat [do] Republican papers mean by singling out Irishmen to fight the battles of America? Is it not rather a stigma on this party that it should be forced to call upon foreigners, and especially upon Irishmen, whom they have always denounced as inferior to 'niggers,' to march 'to victory and glory'?" For this Irishman, the state drafts were the direct result of such thinking. "It would be well if Republicans had done their duty in this war as well as Irishmen, both as regards enlisting and fighting," he argued. "[T]here would have been no necessity of having recourse to a draft, while the war would have long since been terminated."[48]

These concerns weighed heavily on Irish-Americans, and they responded with a steady decline of volunteers and support for the war. The Fenian dreams of using the conflict as a training ground for a future liberation of Ireland faded as high casualty rates among Irish regiments thinned the ranks of potential freedom fighters. In addition, increasing numbers of Irish-Americans were unwilling to preserve the nation for future generations of Irish refugees. They disapproved of the changing principles of the Union, especially its opposition to slavery under powerful Republican leadership.

On the morning of January 16, St. Patrick's Cathedral hosted a solemn high mass for the Irish Brigade's dead that symbolized the depression sweeping through Irish-American communities across the North in early 1863. The New York sanctuary filled long before the ceremonies began, with attendants ranging from leading members of the Irish Catholic community to the poorest private's widow, all gathered to honor the deceased. General Thomas Francis Meagher, commander of the Irish Brigade, attended, escorting his wife and joined by officers of his staff.

The ceremony touched on nearly every factor behind Irish-American service. Father O'Reilly, former chaplain of the 69th New York State Militia, spoke of the loyalty of the adopted Irish citizen-soldiers, of their bravery and their dedication to the United States. Most of all, though, O'Reilly emphasized what seemed most important to those in attendance: Ireland and the Catholic Church. "National pride may blind us, political and party passion may disturb our judgments," O'Reilly reflected, but the men of the Irish Brigade would continue to due their duty.

Honoring the Irish Brigade, O'Reilly reminded the audience, "Their bravery and fidelity to their flag, was bravery and fidelity to God. Ireland has a right to be proud of them and of their achievements on many a battlefield."[49] Similar themes were found in Irish nationalist and writer John Savage's eulogy for the ceremony. The mass may have been for the loss of Irish men fighting for America, but the focus was more on the greatness of Irish sacrifice and what it meant for the community. There seemed to be general agreement that Irish sacrifices must be recognized and mourned, and not enough Americans were doing this. As Savage insisted, "if high the praise, be as deep the wail / O'er the exiled sons of the warlike Gael." The Irish-Americans directing the mass, those covering it in the Irish papers, and the veterans later reflecting on it all emphasized their Irish heritage, their Catholic faith, and their determination on that day that the horrifyingly high casualties would not be forgotten.[50]

At the same time mourners were gathering for the Grand Requiem Mass at St. Patrick's Cathedral, the men of the Irish Brigade still in camp were embarking on new orders that did little to lift their spirits. In January 1863, General Ambrose Burnside ordered his Army of the Potomac to prepare for another offensive against the Confederates. The winter weather, combined with the previous month's battle, had left Fredericksburg a sea of mud, and the troops soon found themselves stuck in a dense quagmire. Those who made it back to camp were half-starved and exhausted, shivering from exposure, and their already low morale sank further.

"Thousands of wretched stragglers were crawling here and there," Irish-born John England reported from Fredericksburg, "and report says that about 500 deserted, and about 30 died of cold and exhaustion!" As the men of the Irish Brigade looked around camp that evening, the funereal prose of their leaders at the Grand Requiem Mass did little to warm their spirits. Disgruntled soldiers constructed an effigy of Burnside that they stuck in the mud, while John England noticed, "The spirit and patriotism of this army is dying out every day." Beyond morale, the situation was exacting a physical toll as well. "Death, in his various forms, is amongst us every day; and he must be a cast iron man who escapes sickness." Of the regiments around England, each buried an average of six to seven men a day. "These unfortunate corpses are generally buried with nothing round them but an old blanket," England noted, adding, "Truly, Virginia, Thou art the grave yard of America."[51]

Irish-Americans in the Midwest expressed similar frustrations. January found Andrew Sproul, a Protestant Irish-born soldier in the Union Army, involved in the fighting near Vicksburg, Mississippi. Despite their determined efforts, Sproul predicted, "We never can close the war by fighting for we have too much ground to get over and they have lots of good soldiers and lots to eat and lots of darkeys to work for them and fight for them." One of the biggest problems, Sproul told his wife in Ohio, "is that . . . most of the boys is getting tired and they are down on this Proclamation of the President. The boys are opposed to freeing the negro and that is the cry. They do not want the darkey free." Personally, Sproul supported emancipation, declaring, "I want them all free," but he had little hope left. "It is a hard sight," he explained sadly, "to see so many strong young men cut . . . like a lot of hogs that is fat for the knife and it looks harder than you think." It did not help, Sproul explained, that in addition to all of the slaughter, "the wounded [are] not cared for by one half as they out to be."[52]

In addition to their frustrations over casualties and the political policies of the war, Sproul claimed that the officers offered little in the form of real leadership. His company still lacked a captain as their commander, making do with a First Lieutenant Jones instead. Within the unit, one man, a Siris Anderson, was "bust and gagged" by a Captain Harn, apparently for writing to the *Wayne County Democrat*. The circumstances surrounding the incident are unclear, but it appears that Anderson was a Copperhead, an anti-Lincoln northern Democrat, whom Sproul described as a "rebel." Still, he appears to have had little love for this Captain Harn, insisting that "we have officers as bad as Captain Harn was . . . but I think that you might shake them up all in a bag for they are as bad as he was but they are more sly about it." As the months continued, Andrew Sproul's opinion of the war and the politics surrounding it would not improve.[53]

By the end of February, the disillusionment and anti-Lincoln comments continued in Andrew Sproul's 16th Ohio Volunteer Infantry Regiment. He accused additional members of his company of "running down the government" and declared at least one "as much of a rebel as old Jeff Davis and so is his Brother and a few more from that place." Sproul had little patience for such views, but revealed that "a great many should like to have this war settled but all the Democrats is down on old Abe and his cabinet for trying to free the darkeys."

Meanwhile, his work continued outside of Vicksburg. Sproul was assigned to the Union Army of the Tennessee under General Ulysses S. Grant and participated in the Federals' attempt to destroy the levees and dig a canal that would connect various river systems and allow Union forces a northern approach to the Confederate stronghold at Vicksburg. They would fail, but Sproul and thousands of other Federal troops spent much of the spring of 1863 digging in wretched conditions. As he explained that February, "It is raining hard all day and our tents don't turn the rain and our clothes are all wet and I was at the ditch at work yesterday and they are making it 60 feet wide and I think that it will take 4 weeks yet to complete it and I do not know what will be the result or what they are going to do with us."[54]

Concerns about home compounded Andrew Sproul's frustrations in Mississippi. His wife Frances related requests from acquaintances for the repayment of debts she thought had already been settled, and now it appeared that their mare was lame and due to give birth in a few months. Sproul offered detailed instructions to Frances insisting that the debts were either settled or for no more than she understood, and he insisted that she agree to pay no more. Then the exhausted and concerned Sproul offered even more information on the proper care for the mare during his absence. Both husband and wife sounded frustrated with the distance and the need to face daily obstacles that neither was accustomed to, and as Andrew said good-bye he reminded Frances to "pray for me night and day."[55]

While General Meagher tried to use his time in New York that January and February to recruit replacements for this brigade, he found evidence of the same disillusionment with the war. Irish newspapers spoke of the community mourning its husbands, fathers, and sons, and reflected a resistance to sending more Irishmen into a cause that many had come to question and that was being conducted under the direction of leaders they did not trust. The most popular Irish paper in the city warned Meagher

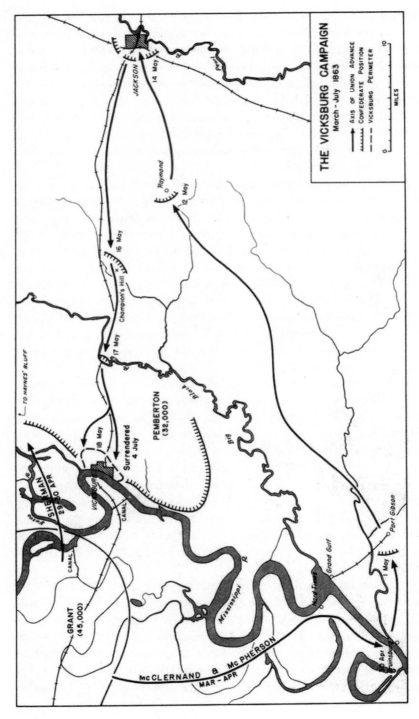

The Vicksburg Campaign, March–July 1863. *American Military History* (Washington: Center for Military History, 1989), 239.

that his recruiting efforts would work only "if men can yet be found to volunteer in a war—the conduct of which reflects anything but credit on those who have undertaken its management."[56]

Some Irish-Americans cited evidence of continuing prejudice when they learned that while the Irish Brigade had all requests to leave the front denied due to manpower needs, other native-born units enjoyed leaves to recuperate, visit families, and recruit replacements. New York's *Irish-American* complained of "favoritism" and "unjust discrimination," and other Irish-American leaders agreed.[57] General Meagher had been trying to secure a leave of absence for the three New York regiments of the Irish Brigade all spring, fearing that without replacements the brigade would be reorganized and he would lose his command. He was positive that if he could just get the men back to the city for a triumphal parade, they would receive the encouragement, rest, and care they needed, while inspiring other Irish-Americans to replenish their ranks. Despite his efforts, the War Department ignored all of the requests.[58]

Trying a new approach, Meagher penned a lengthy letter to Secretary of War Edward M. Stanton on February 19, 1863, in which he recounted the war record of his brigade, its heroic sacrifices, and the Irishmen's devotion to the union. Referring to the fact that regiments from Maine, Massachusetts, and Connecticut had received permission to return home to rest and replenish their ranks, Meagher explained that he asked for no more "than that which has been conceded to other commands, exhibiting equal labors, equal sacrifices, and equal decimation." Secretary Stanton and the War Department seemed unmoved by his testimony.[59]

In actuality, the administration's actions may have had more to do with its military policy and frustration with Meagher than with nativism or ingratitude for Irish military service. The day before Meagher contacted Stanton, the secretary of war had received a concerned missive from General-in-Chief of the Armies Henry W. Halleck. Halleck worried about the number of officers and men receiving leaves of absence, a practice that had drawn over one-third of the northern armies from their commands. As a result, Halleck explained that he would only approve a "very few cases where a refusal would cause great hardship" to officers or men seeking leave for "sickness in family" or "urgent private business."[60] Arriving on the heels of Halleck's letter, Meagher's request for leave was unlikely to have been viewed as worthy of approval. Regiments from other states with similar or lesser records may have received leave prior to the conversation between Stanton and Halleck, but such policies were ending, and it appears that Meagher and the Irish Brigade were subject to the new guidelines. On the other hand, if this was the new policy, why did Stanton not issue a general order announcing it?

There may, indeed, have been some personal animosity behind Stanton's actions, which indicate his diminishing respect for Meagher. During the leave that brought the general home to New York in January 1863, Meagher spent additional time in the city and chose not to return to camp until the following month, technically making him absent without leave. Thirteen days after his leave expired, he finally contacted the adjutant general to explain that he required additional time to recover from wounds to his knee (the injury that had secured his leave) and promised to report for duty in another week. When he finally arrived, Meagher was brought before a military commission, but he managed to explain his absence sufficiently for the review board and was released.

Meagher then embarked on a trip to Washington, his official purpose being to explain his recent actions to the adjutant general, but a secondary purpose may have been to press his case for the Irish Brigade. While in the capital, Meagher met with President Lincoln on February 12, 1863, and called to his attention the plight of the Irish Brigade. After returning from the trip, Meagher wrote his lengthy request of February 19 to the secretary of war. The letter arrived after Halleck's warning to limit leaves of absence, and it was most likely accompanied by reports that Meagher had gone outside official military channels to meet with the president. Stanton probably heard, as well, of Meagher's unauthorized absence, placing him in that category that Halleck had warned Stanton of: applications for leave "supported by pressing solicitations of high officers of the Government and prominent citizens of their own section of the country." Stanton may have viewed Meagher's purpose for his leave, to recover from a knee injury, as an excuse to return home for other reasons, including a hope to raise more volunteers to replenish his regiments before they were consolidated and no longer required the attention of a brigadier general.[61]

Administration and military commanders may have seen Meagher as a general appointed for political purposes who had little respect for military procedure when it impeded his immediate needs and personal ambitions. Henry Halleck complained that "it seems but little better than murder to give important commands" to political generals, a term that had become synonymous with "incompetency" throughout the North by 1863.[62] President Lincoln was tiring of the practice as well. At the beginning of the war, he had seen the political necessity of securing the support of various political factions throughout the North by giving them representation among the Union Army's leadership. By the spring of 1863, however, Lincoln decided that it was more important to have aggressive, capable commanders than to continue appointing political generals. For every such commander selected, Lincoln argued, he had to remove the fighting generals who could win the war.[63]

Meagher was not the first general to take actions that bordered on insubordination or to be accused of this. It may, indeed, have been anti-Irish prejudice that influenced Stanton's decisions, but there is no clear proof of that in this particular case. Meagher insisted, however, that anti-Irish prejudice was behind the administration's position. Despite the silence he received from Washington, Meagher made a similar request for leave to his division commander, General Winfield Scott Hancock, asking for several days to travel to Washington to facilitate his request for rest and recruiting leave for his brigade. Meagher explained that he was anxious to look up his "influential and active friends" in the capital before Congress adjourned and request their assistance as well. Hancock passed the request on to the new commander of the Army of the Potomac, General Joseph E. Hooker. Hooker, reflecting Halleck and Stanton's new policy, explained that he could not approve "the temporary withdrawal of the Irish Brigade from the Army, without positive assurances, that it will be immediately replaced by an equal body of troops."[64]

Meagher did, however, receive some positive reactions from the Lincoln administration. When Meagher asked for support of his Irish Brigade during his meeting with the president in February, Lincoln responded immediately. He contacted Halleck to explain that there had been no promotions within the Irish Brigade and that two of its members, Colonel Robert Nugent and Colonel Patrick Kelly, "have fairly earned promotion." Lincoln argued that both men "hold commissions as Captains in the regular army" and asked his general-in-chief to "examine their records with reference to the question of promoting one or both of them."[65] Thus Lincoln did take steps that spring to indicate his support for Irish soldiers and the formation of additional Irish units.

Unfortunately for the Irish Brigade, the situation became more complicated. In late March 1863, Meagher contacted General Hancock to request a leave because of rheumatism. "The treatment absolutely necessary to my recovery from this attack is such as to necessitate my going to Baltimore or Philadelphia," Meagher explained, ruefully adding that he would not seek treatment in Washington "as I understand, there is a decided objection to officers visiting that city, unless ordered there on duty."[66] When Hancock approved his leave, Meagher traveled not to New Jersey or Pennsylvania but home to New York, where he made a public appearance at a fundraiser for the impoverished in Ireland. Irish-Americans applauded the speakers that evening, who included Archbishop John Hughes, Judge Charles Patrick Daly, Peace Democrat and Irish nationalist Richard O'Gorman, and the future 1864 Democratic candidate for the presidency, General George B. McClellan, among others. It is unclear how much support Meagher gathered from this speech, but it is significant that he did not receive a prominent role that evening, being placed near the end of the list of featured speakers. While Meagher fought a losing battle with the Lincoln administration, it appears he may have also been losing favor within his fellow Irish-Americans.[67]

Meager rejoined his command just in time to accompany them to the battle of Chancellorsville, Virginia, where the depleted Irish Brigade, numbering only 520 men, was positioned in support of the 5th Maine Battery. They suffered 102 casualties in this fight, which reduced the brigade's total force to 418 men, less than half the average regiment of infantry. Meagher reflected on these losses and the fact that he had received no response from the War Department. Not actually wishing to abandon his military career, but desperate to bring attention to the plight of his command and perhaps fearing a demotion should the regiments be consolidated, Meagher approached the Adjutant General's Office to tender his resignation.

On May 8, 1863, Meagher contacted Major John Hancock, an assistant adjutant-general in the War Department, to explain the need to replenish the brigade's losses at the battles of Malvern Hill, Antietam, Fredericksburg, and Chancellorsville. Referring to these matters as well as his previously unanswered or rejected requests, Meagher argued, "the depression caused by this ungenerous and inconsiderate treatment of a gallant remnant of a Brigade that had never once failed to do its duty most liberally and heroically, almost unfitted me to remain in command." Even so, he had wished to stay with his men, despite the fact that he believed "it was to a sacrifice rather than to a victory we were going." Nothing would make him happier, Meagher explained, than "to remain in the companionship and charge of such men." This was now impossible, though, for "to do so any longer would be to perpetuate a public deception, in which the hard-won honors of good soldiers, and in them the military reputation of a brave old race would inevitably be involved and compromised."[68] This message finally received a response: "Your resignation has been accepted by the President of the United States, to take effect this day."[69]

His career, though damaged, was not over. Meagher contacted President Lincoln several weeks later seeking permission to raise three thousand Irish troops from New York City, to which Lincoln agreed with one condition. Ever mindful of governors' frustration with his interference in local issues, Lincoln approved the plan so long as it was done "by the consent of and in concert with [New York] Governor Seymour."[70] Meagher had little success with his recruiting effort, though, and part of that may have been the result of his own reputation.

There were concerns in Irish-American communities regarding his abilities as a commander. As early as 1862, the soldiers and their families

General Thomas Francis Meagher, commander, Irish Brigade,
1862–1863. Courtesy of the Library of Congress. Photograph
research/reproduction courtesy Lynn L. Libby, Enola, PA,
2005.

began grumbling about Meagher's overeagerness on the battlefield, which
contributed to the needless slaughter of his troops. By the fall of 1863,
recent Irish immigrant Maurice Woulfe had found work in Washington,
DC, and was living with family. His work brought him into contact with
large numbers of military personnel, and one was a sergeant who had
served under Meagher. The general, the sergeant insisted, "was a gentleman and a Soldier but . . . he wanted to gain too much praise and he
[would] . . . not spare his men at all." While Meagher may not have had
much luck recruiting, rumors around Washington indicated that Irish-
Americans still comprised much of the fighting force of the Union armies.

A colonel of a Massachusetts regiment informed Woulfe that fall that "there were less Irish in his own regiment than in any other regiment in the Union, and that more than half of them were Irish."[71]

Woulfe does not appear to have been interested in joining any heavy fighting for a cause that may not have meant much to him as a recent immigrant. By November 1863 he secured a position in Washington as an assistant forage master, which he declared quite boring but enjoyable, requiring him to do "nothing at all . . . but to sign bills of forage, order six men that are under my care, [and] keep an account of what is used in the stables." He had little interest in serving more than this, though, and was confident that a lingering illness could help him avoid the draft. As Woulfe explained, "When I spare up some money I will give myself in charge to a good Doctor [and] I am sure if I am drafted that it will exempt me from it."[72]

Certainly Irish were serving, but it appears that Meagher was losing his touch within his own community. Still, he hoped to serve in some way, and in July 1863, he contacted Secretary Stanton to withdraw his resignation and renew his request for a military assignment.[73] This effort was to no avail, and the Lincoln administration may have realized that Meagher no longer enjoyed the support in Irish-American communities that he once had, support the administration needed. They would find another assignment for him, but Meagher would never again lead his famous Irish Brigade in the field.[74]

Irish-American civilian leaders and soldiers expressed outrage at Meagher's resignation, but they responded to it as just another attack on their communities, their men in uniform, and Irish America in general. When individuals argued that the Union was in too precarious a position to allow whole brigades leaves of absence, Irish-Americans pointed to units from other states that secured such periods of rest. So while the government responded to the requests of native-born commanders and expressed concern for their Protestant troops, some Irish-Americans argued, they failed to grant similar attention to Irish Catholic soldiers. Capturing this mood, the New York *Irish-American* charged, "If the Brigade were not so markedly and distinctively *Irish*, they would not have been treated with the positive injustice and neglect to which they have been exposed."[75]

Irish-American community leaders, politicians, officers, and enlisted men resented what they saw as total disrespect from leading Republicans. The *Pilot* reflected, "there is an aching void in our hearts; a sad sense of neglect, if not of wrong done to us and our living comrades; of indifference and coldness toward the memory of our noble immortal dead, whose bones lie on every battle-field from Yorktown to the last and most fatal days at Chancellorsville." The men of the Irish Brigade had fought valiantly and heroically, knowing, as one soldier recalled, that they would be heroes upon their return home. There was, however, little evidence of this. As Captain William J. Nagle of the 88th New York and the Irish Brigade explained, "It was this that made every man determined to excel at Fredericksburg, and prove by our deeds, if any further proof could be necessary, even with our small numbers, how worthy we were of the consideration and kind offices of the government." That May they discovered that their service had achieved none of these aims.[76]

The men of the brigade, Nagle told his father, felt anger, sorrow, and bitterness when they learned of Meagher's resignation, but again, Nagle viewed it within the larger context of the abuse and neglect suffered by Irish-Americans in this conflict. "Am I not right in saying," he asked,

> that in any other country the brigade which had fought and suffered as this has would be gratefully and proudly cherished, its ranks kept full, its deeds of heroism acknowledged and rewarded? We asked neither reward nor favor, only what was right—just to the government, and for the advancement and good of the cause in which we had staked life and reputation. It was denied us, and the Irish Brigade is blotted out of the army of the Union.[77]

Nagle argued that Irish-Americans sought only "what was right" in return for their service, and that he did not view this as a reward or favor, but something Irishmen had earned.

Within camp, the men did offer some direct support for Meagher. The noncommissioned officers of Nagle's regiment went so far as to issue an official statement expressing their regret that Meagher's resignation was the only means possible to maintain the honor and integrity of the brigade. The officers of the 116th Pennsylvania argued that with Meagher's resignation, "we have been deprived of a leader whom we all would have followed to death." Some questioned whether they, too, should resign. As the general departed from camp, they assured Meagher of their support.[78]

Leading members of the Irish-American community expressed their anger more boldly, and in broad terms reaching behind the specific issue of Meagher. Reflecting their disillusionment, the *Pilot* cried, "We are an emigrant race; we did not cause this war; vast numbers of our people have perished in it. . . . [T]he Irish spirit for the war is dead! Absolutely dead!"[79] The editors argued that despite Meagher's countless attempts to strengthen the Irish Brigade, he received no support from the War Department. Secretary Stanton, the editors charged, "has shown his porcine proclivities to their full extent" in this matter, "but not for the first time." Despite the fact that "General Meagher [had] fully informed him of the condition of the gallant brigade . . . Secretary Stanton took no notice of his representations."[80] Such clear disregard for the Irish, the editors warned, would not be forgotten. "The Irish will never forgive this extreme want to decorum. It will remain in their memory with national bitterness, as the deaths of their warriors will with national regret," wrote the *Pilot*. "Such sentiments will have their effect." That effect included diminished Irish support for the war.[81]

Irish-Americans continued to receive disappointing news from the field of battle. Earlier that year the 116th Pennsylvania Volunteers, one of the five Irish Brigade regiments, was so under strength that the army consolidated it into a four-company battalion. Its commander, Irish-born Lieutenant Colonel St. Clair Mulholland, accepted the policy to ensure that the men stayed together and in the Irish Brigade, and he accepted a reduction in rank to remain with them. When Meagher resigned in May, the three New York regiments were consolidated into three two-company battalions, further indicating the dramatic loss of life within the Irish Brigade.

As the Irish Brigade marched toward the quiet town of Gettysburg, Pennsylvania, that July, Colonel Patrick Kelly of the 88th New York led the small remaining fragment of the command, now numbering only about five hundred men. Indeed, as one Irish Brigade officer noted, they were "now a brigade in name only."[82] Although they were few in number, the Irish Brigade contributed to the Union victory at the Battle of Gettysburg, July 1–3, 1863. Moreover, their fight in the famous wheat field represented only one significant element of the Irish-American participation in the fight. Three key aspects of the Union struggle at Gettysburg comprise the core of the Irish-American memory of that struggle.

The first centers on the efforts of a County Cavan native who led his men to the crest of Little Round Top at a crucial moment in the fighting on the second day of the battle. Just two years out of West Point, where he graduated at the top of his class, Colonel Patrick H. "Paddy" O'Rorke and his 140th New York Volunteer Infantry Regiment's efforts have been obscured by the more publicized work of Chamberlain and the 20th Maine.

Born in 1836, O'Rorke was a small child when he and his parents left Ireland for the United States, making their new home in Rochester, New York. At West Point, despite his minority status as a foreign-born and Catholic cadet, O'Rorke enjoyed the respect of his classmates. Evaluating young O'Rorke at West Point, Captain Gouverneur Warren, his instructor and future chief engineer of the Army of the Potomac whose fame also became tied to Little Round Top, declared O'Rorke "a man of noble character," having "nothing of the wild Irish in him." When O'Rorke joined

Cadet Patrick H. O'Rorke, West Point, 1861. Courtesy of U.S. Army Military History Institute. Photograph research/reproduction courtesy Lynn L. Libby, Enola, PA, 2005.

the 140th New York in October 1862, the officers agreed with Warren's assessment, though perhaps with less condescension. Lieutenant Porter Farley insisted that "from the very first [Colonel O'Rorke] commended himself to every one of us, and we date from that day an admiration for his soldierly qualities."[83]

As O'Rorke and the 140th New York marched toward Gettysburg, they suspected this would be a major battle. Rumors raced through the lines that I Corps was already heavily engaged and their commander, Major General John Reynolds, had been killed. Reaching Gettysburg, O'Rorke received a circular from Major General George G. Meade, the new commander of the Army of the Potomac. In it, Meade clarified that this would be a desperate fight, reminding his officers and men that "the whole country now looks anxiously to this army to deliver it from the presence of the foe." As if to clarify this point, Meade gave all commanders the authority "to order the instant death of any soldier who fails in his duty at this hour," and insisted that all of the men hear this order. After the 140th New York heard Meade's orders, O'Rorke turned to address them. While still in the saddle, the Irish colonel warned, "I call on file closers to do their duty and if there is a man this day base enough to leave his company, let him die in his tracks—shoot him down like a dog." As one soldier recalled, this applied to every man, "be he private or officer."[84]

O'Rorke's role at Little Round Top came just as elements of Colonel Strong Vincent's 3rd Brigade, V Corps, began to waver. The 16th Michigan, on the right flank of Vincent's line along a rocky spur of ground midway down the southern and southwestern slope of the hill, had received a series of hard blows from attacking Texans, and they began to pull back toward the crest of the hill. Vincent, seeing the movement, rushed forward to help the Michigan men hold the line, but he fell mortally wounded before the situation stabilized. Intent on holding the eminence, General Warren saw the 140th New York of Brigadier General Stephen H. Weed's brigade cresting the north slope of the hill. O'Rorke explained that his original orders had sent him toward the peach orchard, but after Vincent's brigade headed to Little Round Top, Weed's brigade followed soon after. Warren ordered O'Rorke to take his men to the ledge on Little Round Top where Vincent's brigade still struggled. After the general assured O'Rorke that Warren would take full responsible for this change in orders, the Irishman rushed his 140th New York toward the embattled southern slopes of the hillside. The regiment moved into the fray so quickly that the men did not have a chance to catch their breath as "bullets came flying in among us." The air, one officer remembered, was "saturated with the sulphurous fumes of battle and was ringing with the shouts and groans of the combatants. The wild cries of the charging lines, the rattle of musketry, the booming of artillery and the shrieks of the wounded were the orchestral accompaniments of a scene like very hell itself."[85]

Responding to the desperate situation before him, O'Rorke ordered his men forward, leading the way with his sword and shouting, "Down this way, boys." They never had a chance to form a formal battle line, although the rocky terrain would have prevented this even if time or the Confederates had allowed it. The Texans and Alabamians had thought victory was theirs, but then O'Rorke and his New Yorkers rushed down upon them. At the forefront of the charge, Patrick O'Rorke stopped suddenly and tumbled into the boulders, killed instantly when a southern bullet tore through this neck. Rushing past him, the New Yorkers loaded on the run. Some men did not have time to fix bayonets and used their rifles as clubs, but they had the momentum of running downward into exhausted rebels, which worked to their advantage, and they pushed the Confederates back with a devastating blow.[86] Despite the loss of their colonel, which horrified his men, they managed to stabilize Vincent's right flank and stop the Confederate advance. No single regiment can claim sole responsibility for securing Little Round Top, but Irish-American Patrick Henry O'Rorke and his 140th New York became an essential part of the Gettysburg story that day. The Union had lost a promising young officer and Irish America would mourn another fallen hero, but his actions proved critical to the Federal victory on Little Round Top, and thus the larger battle of Gettysburg.[87]

As the 140th New York's fight ended, a more famous unit of Irishmen entered the battle. Its actions created the second of three parts to the Irish-American memory of the Battle of Gettysburg. It was after 6:00 P.M. when the Irish Brigade moved forward, responding to II Corps commander Major General Winfield Scott Hancock's orders to reinforce General Daniel Sickles's overextended III Corps. Sickles had pushed his men too far forward of the rest of the Union line, and by 5:30 elements of two Confederate divisions began to hit the thin Union lines posted in the wheat field and the peach orchard. Reinforcements from the V Corps did not seem to provide sufficient strength to stop the assaulting southerners.

Responding to Hancock's orders, Brigadier General John Caldwell sent the four brigades of his division, including Colonel Kelly's Irish Brigade, toward the wheat field. They marched southwest from their original position on Cemetery Ridge, wading across Plum Run and making their way through Trostle's Woods, until the Irishmen pushed into the waist-high wheat field owned by George Rose from which so many of them would not return.[88]

Despite their small numbers, the men may have felt more confident in this than in other battles, or at least less fearful for their souls. Before they had advanced into the wheat field, one of the Irish Brigade chaplains, Father William Corby, had climbed onto a boulder so those who could not hear him above the crack of musketry and thundering cannon could see and understand his meaning from his actions. He reminded the Irishmen who could hear him to fight bravely, and to deny any urge to turn and run from the battle. Any soldier who fell in that field, he promised, would receive a Christian burial, but those who ran would be denied such dignities. Then he raised his hand as the men knelt and removed their caps, under flags representing Ireland and the United States, and offered a general absolution for the forgiveness of their sins. "Dominus

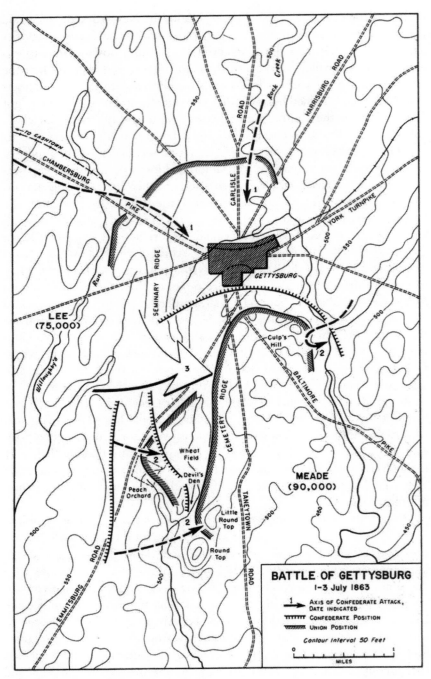

The Battle of Gettysburg, July 1–3, 1863. *American Military History* (Washington: Center for Military History, 1989), 251.

nos Jesus Chrisus vos absolvat," Corby began. Major St. Clair Mulholland, commanding the 116th Pennsylvania, noted that officers joined the men in receiving the blessing, and even General Hancock, watching from his horse, removed his hat and bowed his head. It was, Corby later declared, an absolution for them all—Catholics and Protestants, northerners and southerners, all "who were susceptible of it and who were about to appear before their Judge." Then, as Corby recalled, he watched as the men "plunged into the dense smoke of battle" knowing "that perhaps in less than half an hour their eyes would open to see into the ocean of eternity."[89]

The Irishmen pushed forward into the wheat field, with Colonel Edward Cross's 1st Brigade to their left. Brigadier General S. K. Zook's command to their right, and Colonel John R. Brooke's 4th Brigade following close behind Kelly's men. As they closed with Confederate forces, Colonel Cross and General Zook both fell mortally wounded, but the division's brigades each continued forward. Kelly managed to keep order among the Irish Brigade, leading them through the heart of the wheat field and up a small eminence at its southwest edge generally referred to in battle reports simply as "the Stony Hill." While the men had been at a disadvantage with their smooth-bore weapons firing at long range, as they closed in on the Confederates the "buck and ball" the Irishmen fired found their targets. Years later, Mulholland recalled that their load was one large ball and three buckshot and so powerful at close range that "a blind man could not have missed his mark." The Irishmen inflicted loss, but they sustained severe casualties as well. Mulholland remembered watching "Little Jeff" Carl kill a Confederate soldier within six feet of him while the tall Sergeant Francis Malin, bobbing above the men, fell when a round clipped his head. The hand-to-hand fighting did not last long as the Confederate forces began to pull back and the Irish Brigade seemed to have gained the advantage, sending dozens of prisoners to the rear.[90]

Just as quickly, however, their efforts lost momentum. No longer advancing, they fought in place at the rocky hill. Low on ammunition and with the loss of senior leadership in the brigades on their right and left, the Irishmen realized suddenly, to their horror, that their flanks had become exposed to Confederates advancing upon them from several directions, one thrust moving east from the now fallen peach orchard even threatening their rear. As Kelly explained, "Finding myself in this very disagreeable position, I ordered the brigade to fall back, firing. We here encountered a most terrific fire."[91] Kelly's Irishmen and the other survivors of the 1st Division fought a desperate retreat down the stony hill and back through the wheat field as South Carolinians, Georgians, and Mississippians closed in. St. Clair Mulholland recalled racing through lines of enemy fire that had almost created a gauntlet. "The fire," he noted, "was severe and destructive, and so close were the lines of the enemy between which the men ran, that they finally had to stop firing, as they were hitting each other."[92]

Private Martin "Jersey" Gallagher ran with the rest of the 116th Pennsylvania until a Minié ball tore through his leg, breaking the bone. Lying helpless in the wheat, he was hit another six to eight times before the fighting stopped. Somehow, he survived. Irish-American Private John Ryan, almost eighteen years old and a combat veteran for as many months, remembered "being the whole time exposed to a heavy fire of musketry" during the retreat from Stony Hill and "losing many men from the concentrated fire of the enemy who was on both our flanks."[93] The Irish Brigade managed to regroup and reformed on Cemetery Ridge, north of Little Round Top, where they remained until nightfall.[94]

The Irishmen who survived the fight in the wheat field were exhausted. Private William A. Smith of the 116th Pennsylvania complained to his family that the engagement there "knocked our regiment all to pieces. There is only 9 in my company now . . . [and] but 108 in all in our Regiment with 1 Major—1 Adjutant—and 2 captains in all of them that come out." The 116th Pennsylvania, Smith noted, "had 900 [men] when we left Philadelphia and this fight I think it will finish them off and then there will be no more of the 116 Regt."[95] Indeed, the casualties for the Irish Brigade were heavy, as it lost 202 of the 530 men who entered the fight.[96]

Irish contributions to the Union victory at Gettysburg continued that day with the third major part of the Irish-American memory of the battle. This part involved the Union defense of Cemetery Ridge during Pickett's Charge, when the 69th Pennsylvania Volunteer Infantry Regiment fought desperately to repel the Confederate penetration of the Union line near "The Angle," while just south of them, Captain James McKay Rorty's Battery B, 1st New York Light Artillery, fought heroically to throw back the Confederate assault.

Along with the 71st, 72nd, and 106th Pennsylvania, the 69th Pennsylvania was a largely Irish regiment belonging to Brigadier General Alexander Webb's 2nd Brigade, of Brigadier General John Gibbon's 2nd Division of Hancock's II Corps. Organized in Philadelphia in 1861, the 69th Pennsylvania included many Irish-born or first-generation Irish-Americans. Many were common laborers before the war, including their commanding officer, Colonel Dennis O'Kane, a County Derry native with no formal education who had worked in the restaurant business.[97] The core of the unit came from the city's Irish militia companies, and their green flag was a symbol of their dual loyalties to Ireland and America.[98] Edged with gold trim, the green banner bore an image of the old Irish Harp, with its Maid of Erin, on one side and the coat of arms of Pennsylvania on the other.[99]

GEN. JOSHUA T. OWEN,
Our First Colonel.

COL. DENNIS O'KANE,
Killed at Gettysburg.

LIEUT. COL. MARTIN TSCHUDY,
Killed at Gettysburg.

Brigadier General Joshua T. Owen, 2nd Brigade, 2nd Division, II
Corps; Colonel Dennis O'Kane and Lieutenant Colonel
Martin Tschudy, Irish 69th Pennsylvania of the 2nd Brigade, also
known as the "Philadelphia Brigade." Brigadier General Alexan-
der Webb replaced Owen as the brigade commander shortly
before the Battle of Gettysburg. Sketch from Anthony W.
McDermott, *A Brief History of the 69th Regiment Pennsylvania
Veteran Volunteers, from Its Formation until Final Muster out of
the United States Service.* Philadelphia, PA: D. J. Gallagher &
Co., 1889. Photograph reproduction courtesy of William F. Ural,
M.D., Toad Hall Photography, Southport, NC.

While supporters of the regiment honored them with their green flag,
not everyone in Philadelphia celebrated the unit. When the 69th left the
city in the fall of 1861, there was no parade to encourage the men marching off to war. Instead, Philadelphians hurled rocks and bricks, and when
the 69th joined the Army of the Potomac, their reception was no warmer.
Nicknamed the "Irish Brigade," they were met with "hisses, derisive cries
and shouts of contempt" from their fellow soldiers.[100]

Despite this, the 69th Pennsylvania had fought well in the battles preceding Gettysburg. The morning of July 3 found them posted along Cemetery Ridge at the center of the Union line, already slightly bloodied after fighting off an attack on their position the previous day. On July 2, they inflicted heavy casualties on General Ambrose R. Wright's Georgia Brigade, and many of the dead were still before them in the field. Along with the horse carcasses bloating in the sun, the odor of death would have been nearly overwhelming.[101] Private Anthony McDermott of the 69th Pennsylvania recalled his discomfort on that hot, muggy morning. The "heat [was] almost stifling," he said, and there was "not a breath of air" to offer some relief from the stench around them.[102]

Numbering just 258 officers and men that morning, the ten companies of the 69th Pennsylvania rested behind a low stone farm wall about two feet high. Their far left stopped at a gap in the wall and their far right flank, about 250 yards northward, rested about forty feet from an angle in the stone wall, where the wall took a sharp curve eastward. In the rear center of their line stood a cluster of small oaks and brush. Although they did not know it at the time, the 69th Pennsylvania's line rested near two of the most famous landmarks at the Battle of Gettysburg: "The Angle" and the "Copse of Trees."[103]

Colonel O'Kane did not encourage his men to improve their defensive works, perhaps due to the men's exhaustion, the rocky soil, and their lack of entrenching tools. On the night of July 2, however, he did order them to gather all of the fallen smoothbore and rifled muskets and ammunition lying in the field before them. There were hundreds of Union and Confederate weapons there, discarded during the previous day's fighting, and when they brought them back behind the stone wall, soldiers like Corporal John Buckley set about loading them with what was available. "The ammunition we found to contain three buck-shot and a ball, and . . . I will guarantee it inflicted more harm upon them than upon us. We abstracted the buck-shot from the ammunition and reloaded the spare guns putting 12 to the load, and almost every man had from two to five guns."[104]

About 1:00 P.M. the Confederate bombardment of Cemetery Ridge began, and the Irish Pennsylvanians found themselves in the middle of a fierce artillery exchange as rebel gunners focused fire on the Federal batteries on the crest of the ridge behind the 69th and all along the II Corps line. These included Lieutenant T. Fred Brown's Battery B, 1st Rhode Island Light Artillery, and Lieutenant Alonzo H. Cushing's Battery A, 4th U.S. Artillery. It was a horrifying experience, Private Joseph McKeever explained, recalling that "after the cannonading began, we were all hugging the earth and we would have liked to get into it if we could."[105] The Irishmen of the 69th Pennsylvania could only watch as most of the shells passed overhead and to the rear, but Cushing's battery lost a number of men, including a moment when a single shell hit three limber chests, "destroying several men." Private William White remembered watching as the "shot and shell flew thick and fast" and mourned a friend killed by a shell fragment.[106]

About 250 yards south of the 69th Pennsylvania, another Irish-American volunteer was playing a dramatic role in the battle. In the fall of 1861, Captain James McKay Rorty had broken his promise to his parents in Ireland by reenlisting in the Union Army. His father hoped Rorty would become a merchant, but his loyalty to Ireland and America was overwhelming, and Rorty decided he could serve both causes by fighting in the Union Army. July 3, 1863, found the young Fenian commanding Battery B, 1st New York Light Artillery, and he and his men suffered under the heavy Confederate barrage. Despite the chaos around him, Rorty managed to maintain discipline and kept his men firing. As one Union officer observing him noted, "With guns dismounted, caissons blown up, and rapidly losing men and horses, the intrepid commander moved from gun to gun as coolly as if on a West Point review."[107]

By about 2:00 P.M., Confederate shells had knocked out three of Rorty's four guns and many of his men were wounded or dead. Colonel James E. Mallon of the nearby 42nd New York "Tammany Regiment" watched in astonishment as Rorty stripped off his sword belt and coat, and joined the remaining crew madly working their last gun until Rorty fell fatally wounded.[108] Captain P. J. Downing of the 42nd New York recalled, "Rorty's death is as severe a loss as Ireland has had for a long time. He surpassed everything in the Army of the Potomac [on July 3]. . . . No words can express what he deserves."[109] The exact cause and moment of Rorty's death remain unknown, but he died fighting for the two causes he saw as inextricably linked. As he had pledged in December 1861,

> My political faith as an Irishman has only one article—a firm belief in the future resurrection of Ireland. And whether death meets me, as I hope it will, on an Irish battlefield, or whether it overtakes me battling for freedom [in America], it will ever find me as firm in that faith as it finds the dying Christian in the faith of his own resurrection.[110]

At 3:00 P.M., the Confederate artillery barrage slowed and then there was quiet. Along Cemetery Ridge to the north of Rorty's position, the men of the Irish 69th Pennsylvania watched from the copse of trees as the divisions of Confederate Generals Pettigrew and Trimble emerged from the tree line across the valley off to their right front. But they did not see at first the Virginians of General Pickett's division, whose initial advance from the Pennsylvanians' left front was shielded from view by small ripples of ground. As the Confederates approached the Emmitsburg Road and came into full view of the Union line, Colonel O'Kane addressed the men of the 69th Pennsylvania. He reminded them that this fight would be "upon the soil of our own state," and pledged his faith in their bravery. Like many of the men around him, O'Kane's roots were in Ireland, not the United States. He had been born, had married, and had witnessed the birth of his first two children in County Derry. When O'Kane spoke, though, it is significant that it was of the United States and, more immediately, Pennsylvania. "He knew," Anthony McDermott remembered, "that we were at least as brave as [the Confederates] were, [so] he did not fear but that we would render an account of ourselves this day, that would bring upon us the plaudits of our country," accepting, like his colonel, an American identity.[111] These men had gathered freely under both a green flag and a U.S. national color, representing their ties to both lands. On this day, though, and at this dramatic moment, O'Kane spoke only of America.[112]

In case his speech had not properly fortified the men, the staunch disciplinarian added a warning: "Should any man among us flinch in our duty . . . the man nearest him would kill him on the spot." With that, while the men of the 69th Pennsylvania watched the Confederates advancing, the colonel walked along the line to speak in turn to each company. Crossing Emmitsburg Road and over the fences that bordered it in places broke up some of the Confederate lines, but still they came, colors waving as a slight breeze wafted across the field. In an order reminiscent of Bunker Hill, O'Kane told his men to hold their fire "until the enemy came so close to us that we could distinguish the white of their eyes."[113]

When the Confederates approached to within fifty yards of the stone wall, the 69th Pennsylvania opened with a massive volley. "The slaughter was terrible," John Buckley recalled, "to which fact the ground literally covered with the enemy's dead bore ample testimony." On the left flank of the 69th, where it connected with the 59th New York, Confederate forces made a slight breach in the line. The crisis was short lived, though, because of the timely arrival of Captain Andrew Cowan's 1st New York Battery, which opened fire at near point-blank range and blunted the penetration. The Union line restabilized quickly there.

On the 69th Pennsylvania's right, however, the line began to falter. Several companies of the 71st Pennsylvania that had extended the right flank of the 69th to the bend in the wall that created the angle abandoned their position. The artillerymen who finally had pushed at least two of their cannon up to the wall on the 69th's right flank abandoned their pieces, too. This left a gap of about forty feet of undefended ground between the

69th Pennsylvania and the angle in the stone wall. Portions of Confederate Generals Richard B. Garnett's and Lewis B. Armistead's brigades saw the opening and pushed through, and some Tennesseans and Alabamians from Pettigrew's command may have joined them.[114]

As the rebels' penetration grew, General Webb, their 28-year-old brigade commander, moved the 72nd Pennsylvania forward from its reserve position. In addition, either Webb, O'Kane, or Lieutenant Colonel Martin Tschudy ordered the three right flank companies of the 69th to change front, facing northward to create a right angle in the line that allowed them to fire into the flanks of the Confederates inside the angle. Two companies, A and I, managed to follow these orders, but Captain George Thompson of Company F collapsed dead before he could give the command, a Confederate ball ripping through his head. This left Company F's flank unprotected. Within minutes, Company F lost all of its twenty-two men, killed, wounded, or captured. The Confederates pressed on, contending both with the remaining companies of the 69th Pennsylvania on their right flank and the new threat they faced straight ahead with the arrival of the rest of Webb's men.[115]

Where the Confederates and the Irishmen clashed, Anthony McDermott recalled, the fighting became particularly brutal as the men of Company D turned to face the Confederates threatening to roll up the regimental line. The combatants were so close the Irishmen began swinging their muskets as clubs and McDermott watched as Corporal Hugh Bradley, "who was quite a savage sort of a fellow wielded his piece, striking right and left, and was killed in the melee by having his skull crushed by a musket in the hands of a rebel." Similarly, Private Thomas Donnelly "used his piece as a club, and when called upon to surrender replied tauntingly, 'I surrender' at the same time striking his would be captor to the ground." Private William White recalled this intense fighting pushing them back approximately fifty yards, and many of the men feared they were finished. Just when the Confederates seemed ready to sweep over the last defenders of the 69th, though, fire from the 72nd Pennsylvania as well as a counterattack from the south by the 19th and 20th Massachusetts, 7th Michigan, and the 42nd New York slowed the exhausted rebels.[116] More reinforcements arrived, and, pressed on both flanks, the entire southern assault force wavered, then broke.

As the Confederate lines receded from the fight all along Cemetery Ridge, the survivors of Union regiments like the 69th Pennsylvania looked around in horror. The infantry fight had lasted less than twenty minutes, but its destruction shocked them. Confederate fire struck nearly every officer in the regiment. Colonel Dennis O'Kane was shot through the chest or abdomen and would die from the wounds on July 5. Lieutenant Colonel

Martin Tschudy, killed when a ball tore through his bladder, fell while fighting with either Company D or Company F. Major James Duffy suffered a wound to his thigh that led to his discharge from the army later that year, and he would die of complications from the injury on June 16, 1869. The regiment estimated its total losses as thirty-four killed and sixty-eight wounded, as well as seventeen missing. Combined with the losses of eleven killed and seventeen wounded on July 2, the Irish 69th Pennsylvania suffered over 50 percent casualties at the Battle of Gettysburg.[117]

The Battle of Gettysburg would prove to be one of the North's greatest victories of the Civil War. The image of the fighting Irish at that definitive contest would become an essential part of the memory of Gettysburg. Father Corby's blessing and the Irish Brigade at the wheat field, as well as the defense of Paddy O'Rorke's New Yorkers at Little Round Top and Dennis O'Kane's Pennsylvanians at the angle would become part of the history and the legend of that battle. Miles McDonald, an Irish-American officer in the 63rd New York informed the editors of the *Irish-American* that the Irish Brigade, "by their courage and bravery in the late fights [at Gettysburg], nobly sustained the honor of the land which gave them birth."[118] Over two decades later, poets would still be writing of Father Corby's absolution:

> Old Gettysburg yet lives to tell
> When night each star bend down,
> How rebel hail of shot and shell,
> Plow'd thro' that loyal town.
> And well hath Gettysburg relied
> On soldier boys' brave deed
> While little Round Top points with pride
> To Corby's loyal creed.[119]

For St. Clair Mulholland, commander of the 116th Pennsylvania, Gettysburg became "the battle of the century" and its sacred ground "the National Sanctuary, the Pantheon, the Westminster of the Republic." Veterans of the 69th Pennsylvania were equally protective of that battle and the memory of their role in it. In 1904 they railed against U.S. Congressman Bertie Adams of Pennsylvania, who mistakenly credited the 69th New York, rather than the 69th Pennsylvania, for successfully defending the angle at Gettysburg. Veteran Thomas Furey, former captain of Company B, insisted, "Why every school boy and girl knows it was the Sixty-ninth Pennsylvania Regiment that drove General Pickett back."[120]

While Irish-Americans took pride in their role at the Battle of Gettysburg and engagements elsewhere that year, these victories exacted a heavy toll. When Irish-American Hugh Bradley of the 69th Pennsylvania fell defending the angle at Gettysburg, he left behind a mother and eight siblings in Philadelphia who depended on him as their sole source of income. Irish-born James McKay Rorty had visited with his family in New York City in May 1863, most of them having just arrived from Ireland with their passage covered by his soldier's pay. When Rorty died six weeks later at Gettysburg, they were left with little money, and his father, who had insisted that Rorty abandon army life, never recovered from the loss of his son.[121]

Amid these tragedies, there were serious questions in Irish-American communities about which Americans seemed to be bearing the greatest burden of this war. Indeed, intense debates over conscription raged almost as loudly as the bloody battles of the spring and summer of 1863. As casualties mounted while volunteering declined, Congress had called again for Americans to submit to a draft. With the Enrollment Act passed in March, leaders sought to close some of the loopholes and inequities of the Militia Act and bounty system, while ensuring that the new law filled the Union forces. Understanding the controversy over the draft, political leaders explained that they had included exclusionary clauses in this law to make it a more equitable, democratic call to arms. Section 13 of the Enrollment Act included two means by which a draftee could commute his service. An individual could pay someone to serve in his place or he could pay the government a three-hundred-dollar exemption fee that allowed a draftee to escape service. The price was set, lawmakers explained, to prevent the cost from soaring beyond the reach of many draftees. Their intentions may have been good, or they may have been making sure they and other influential Americans were not affected by the draft. For many Americans it was the latter option. The working poor, for whom three hundred dollars was half a year's wages, were especially outraged, and many saw the exemption as another indicator that the war no longer focused on their interests—citing the recent Emancipation Proclamation, tax increases to pay for the war, and expanding federal authority—and that the classes promoting these changes would not have to serve.[122]

Irish-American soldier John England, for example, argued that he was not opposed to the concept of a draft so much as the inequity of this system. The law, he argued, "was framed for the benefit of the rich and the disadvantage of the poor. For instance—a rich conscript can commute for $300! Now, it is a fact well known to all that there are some rich animals in the northern cities who can afford to lose $300, as much as some poor people can afford to lose one cent." For Irish-Americans in the latter category, the Enrollment Act revealed a war that held nothing for them but prejudice, sacrifice, and death. England warned that the "conscription law, no matter how constructed, can never become popular, for it is the last alternative of an unpopular cause," and a cause in which many working-class Irish-Americans, those most significantly impacted by the bill, would refuse to participate.[123]

In March 1863, when the Enrollment Act passed, Irish community leaders in Boston pointed out that, unlike the previous state drafts, the law targeted aliens. Rumors circulated around the city that immigrants who had declared their intention to become American citizens had sixty-five days after the passage of the Enrollment Act to leave the country, and reviews of the law confirmed this. The *Pilot* complained, "most [aliens] cannot get away in that time. Many of them are here, too, under the advice of Secretary Seward."[124]

Such remarks reflected an ongoing debate in immigrant and Democratic papers about Secretary of State William Seward's response to questions from the British government regarding how the U.S. draft would apply to British subjects. In August 1862, Seward explained, "[N]one but citizens are liable to military duty in [the United States], and . . . this department has never regarded an alien who may have merely declared his intention to become a citizen as entitled to a passport, and consequently, has always withheld from persons of that character any such certificates of citizenship."[125] But the Enrollment Act in March 1863 changed the laws so that "persons of foreign birth who shall have declared on oath their intention to become citizens" and were 20- to 45-year-old males were eligible for the draft. The *Pilot* found such revisions shameful and chastised the secretary of state for tricking the British government into encouraging emigration so that the United States could have fodder for its war while preserving the lives of its more respectable citizens. This was, declared the editors, "a miserable Yankee trick to entice over here 'food for powder.'"[126]

Once again, Irish-Americans who had once supported military service were now challenging this idea. The policies of leading Republicans, including members of the Lincoln administration and the president himself, the *Pilot* argued, exploited Irishmen. These reports discouraged those Irishmen fighting to preserve America as the great Irish hope for the future, as stories of Irish immigrants tricked into military service hardly reinforced the image of the United States as an asylum for future generations of Irishmen.

As the war dragged on and similar events of anti-Irish prejudice surfaced, more and more Irishmen wondered if they were being targeted for service so that native-born Americans could escape the war, which suspicion led some Irish community leaders to clarify their opinions on the draft and the war. They questioned the purpose of the conflict and the wisdom of their sacrifices. In 1863, Archbishop Hughes of New York explained that he had supported the state draft of the previous year only to ensure that all Americans, native born and immigrant, served in the war and that no one was able to escape responsibility. He had "found the number of able-bodied men, fathers, brothers, husbands, in my congregations vastly thinned and the widows and orphans multiplied all around me," and wondered, "was it all voluntary on the part of those who abandoned their homes to defend their country?" Hughes reported that many of his Irish laity claimed they had not gone to war willingly. Instead, they were coerced when their employers temporarily closed their factories at the outbreak of war "to compel . . . Irish and Catholic operatives to enlist, in order that their families would not starve" from their lack of work. Hughes believed that this was all a trick to force Irish Catholic laborers to save the nation while native-born Americans were given Irish jobs when the factories reopened after the Irishmen's departure. "Sooner than witness base tricks upon unfortunate laborers, I was then, and am now, prepared to approve of a thousand conscriptions, openly appointed by the government," Hughes explained. He did insist, however, "that the same shuffling and low trickery shall not be employed to expose the poor to the dangers of battle and leave the wealthy to become wealthier in their quiet homes."[127]

Other Irishmen agreed, focusing their frustration on the three-hundred-dollar exemption clause with headlines reading "Three Hundred Dollars or Your Life" and parodies on popular songs being sung. Abolitionist James Sloan Gibbons, whose home was attacked following the Emancipation Proclamation (and would be again during the New York City draft riots), had written "We Are Coming, Father Abraham" in response to President Lincoln's call for three hundred thousand volunteers in the summer of 1862. Those opposed to exemption parodied his song: "We're coming, ancient Abraham, several hundred strong / We hadn't no 300 dollars and so we came along / We hadn't no rich parents to pony up the tine / so We went unto the provost and there we mustered in."[128]

While many Republican leaders argued that the exemption clause was created with good intentions, to keep the price of a substitute within the reach of more Americans, the working poor did not see it that way. Many Irishmen found such explanations ridiculous and exemplary of how little lawmakers understood the economic realities of the working class. The exemption clause, one Boston Irishman argued, "can have no other effect than to drive into the army, against their will, the poor man. It matters little to them whether the price of a substitute is $100 or $1000, so long as they have not $100 to give." The possibility of alien exemption, he explained, was a false security because it was not being enforced. Relating the story of a newly arrived Irish immigrant who had been enrolled and drafted, the author explained that when he brought the situation to the attention of the provost marshall of the Third District of Boston and offered proof from two citizens that the man was a newly arrived immigrant, the provost claimed that "no evidence short of a protection from the British Consul would secure the man's exemption." The author was shocked at such treatment of an Irish immigrant, who, "like thousands of others, came here with the assurance that he would not be required [to serve]."[129]

These reports by Irish-American laborers and community leaders reveal a growing dissatisfaction with the war and the role Irish-Americans believed the native population demanded of them. Increasing numbers of Irishmen saw their sacrifices as unappreciated, and as a means for allowing native-born Americans to avoid the hardships of war. News reports questioning the quality of Irish military service and accusing the Irish of serving in numbers far below their representation in the populace offered evidence to support the Irishmen's claims. Compounding this problem, news reports indicated that other native-born American prejudices against the Irish continued. In April 1863, the *Pilot,* the *New York Tribune,* the *New York Tablet,* and additional Irish, Catholic, or Democratic papers across the nation reported the destruction of southern towns by Federal forces. Irish Catholics were horrified to read that not only had Protestants from a Maine regiment burned a Catholic church, but also, "not content with thus testifying their hatred of Catholicity, they appeared on the public streets wearing the vestments in mockery of our religion and our feelings as Catholics." The *Tablet* complained that the anti-Catholic New Englanders were largely abolitionists, the group that many Irishmen held responsible for the war and that continued to find opportunities to "do in the South what they have done so often, and so well, in the North,—to plunder, desecrate, and destroy Catholic churches." The *Tablet* warned, "The Government must no longer permit this if it wishes to preserve the respect and good will of the patriotic soldier in the field, and of all sensible, right-minded people at home." The warning was ignored, and the anger among northern Irish Catholics increased as they read other such reports.

Some came from an Irish-American in the 4th New Hampshire Volunteers, who, writing in camp, complained, "[T]he petty insults that we are daily subject to, such as filling our camp with such foolish and lying trash as tracts, &c., we can bear in silence, but when they proceed to such lengths as to destroy our religious institutions, merely to gratify their malignant hatred of such things, we ought to resent it." The soldier asked, "Are we at war with rebels or with the Catholic churches; are we at war with traitors or with Catholicity?" Reflecting on the war and capturing the sentiments of many Irish Catholics that spring of 1863, he argued, "We had thought that this crusade against our religion was at an end, but we are sometimes forced to think that nothing but the existence of the rebellion and the large number of Catholics in our Army prevent a repetition of those scenes that disgraced" Catholic churches and communities in southern towns. "We may be mistaken," he admitted, but warned, "in order to be convinced of our mistake, we must see a stop put to the sacrilegious acts of these church-burning thieves."[130]

These complaints of anti-Catholic actions within the Federal Army, despite impressive service by the Irish Brigade and countless reports of dedicated Irish service, were compounded by similar reports of prejudice against Irish Catholic and other immigrant miners in Pottsville, Pennsylvania. The *Pilot* editorialized on their unsafe conditions, low pay, and limited rights to change this situation, challenging any reports to the contrary. The *Pottsville Miners' Journal,* which appears to have been more the voice of management than of miners, described their laborers as a "debauched, drunken set of rioters, who have no cause whatever for their iniquitous conduct." The *Pilot* fired back, questioning the *Journal's* ability to offer sound judgment when they were nothing but "a truculent, unmanly, indecent, know-nothing and abolition sheet." Reminding their readers again of the dangerous conditions in which the men worked for scrip that was only good to purchase company products, the *Pilot* summarized the situation. Any protest by the miners not only was justified but was "a necessary reaction against murderous mines, gross dishonesty, and absolute selfishness." Furthermore, the *Pilot* warned, the miners' outbreaks would "continue until, by legislation, the mines are made safe, and the operators honest men."[131]

As increasing numbers of Irish-Americans reflected on the recent injustices perpetrated by native-born Americans against Irish men and women, they became more and more opposed to the draft. In the Midwest, a Democratic convention pledged, "we will *resist* to the *death* all attempts to draft any of our citizens into the army." New Yorkers were equally determined, with editor James McMaster of the Catholic *Freeman's Journal* proclaiming for himself and the Irish Catholic community, "when the President called upon them to go and carry on a war for the nigger, he would be d——d if he believed they would go." Irish-Americans across the North made it clear that they had supported a war for union but would never fight to free the slaves, and they certainly would not accept the idea of the government forcing them to serve through a draft. Their reaction to the draft embodied several factors, including their own racism against African-Americans, an almost instinctive cultural response to decades of anti-Irish and anti-Catholic prejudice they had suffered in Ireland and America, and a sense that their faith in the war had been betrayed with the shift from a war for union to one including emancipation. Irish-American and native-born Democratic leaders warned that this sense of betrayal could result in disaster. New York's Democratic governor Horatio Seymour cautioned Republicans about a draft that forced the men to serve and possibly die for a war they opposed. "Remember this," Seymour warned. "The bloody and treasonable doctrine of public necessity can be proclaimed by a mob as well as by a government."[132] The New York City draft riots proved him prophetic. In five days of terror, various groups of New Yorkers, many of them Irish-American Catholic laborers, voiced their opposition to the draft, emancipation, the Republican administration, and the war in general.

The violence began quietly in July 1863, in the wake of the Battle of Gettysburg, which left over forty-seven thousand Americans dead, wounded, or missing from fighting between July 1 and 3.[133] Governor Seymour had promised to fill the state's quotas with volunteers, and even if that proved impossible, he had pledged to go to the courts to challenge the legality of Federal conscription. As a result, many New York workers were surprised on Saturday, July 12, 1863, when they read the names of the first draftees, which included Irish-American Catholics, in the *New York Herald* and other city papers. They resolved that they must take action.

The fact that the riots happened at the same time as the annual Orange Day celebrations probably increased the passionate response within Irish-American communities. These were festivities hosted by Irish Protestants in celebration of the victory of William of Orange's Protestant forces over those of Catholic James II at the Battle of Boyne on July 12, 1690. This was, and remains in Northern Ireland, a period marked by Protestant parades and Catholic protests that frequently erupted in violence. There had been historic clashes in New York in 1836 and 1842, and the worst was yet to come in 1871. Irish-American Catholics' disillusionment with the war and the federal draft combined with the annual religious and ethnic tensions, and contributed to their dramatic involvement in the New York City draft riots.[134]

These factors all converged over the weekend of July 11 and 12, when Irish-Americans and other immigrant and native-born New York laborers, mechanics, and urban poor debated the draft and what action they should take. They began their protest early Monday morning when they refused to show up for work, marched toward draft offices, gathered other laborers with them as they passed, and tore up telegraph lines and other means of communication and transport. They burned draft offices, with the help of Irish fire companies, and then continued to march around various parts

HOW TO ESCAPE THE DRAFT.

"How to Escape the Draft." Coverage of the New York City draft riots in *Harper's Weekly*, August 1, 1863. Provided courtesy HarpWeek, LLC. Photograph reproduction courtesy Lynn L. Libby, Enola, PA, 2005.

of the city demanding that factories close and workers join them in an effort to stop war production and call attention to the injustices of conscription.

Monday's rioting contained a diverse blend of protesters, but artisans and skilled factory workers dominated this day's actions, which would later seem rather focused and somewhat controlled compared to what would follow. Still, these rioters assaulted police officers and African-Americans, whom they blamed for the emancipation, the war, the draft, and the enforcement of these policies. In one of the most infamous attacks that week, the rioters swarmed around the Colored Orphans' Asylum, established by Quaker abolitionists in the 1830s. The rioters looted the building and then set fire to it, striking at what Irish-American Catholics saw as a symbol of the support African-Americans received at Irishmen's expense. While all of the children managed to escape, the building was destroyed as well as a number of the nearby homes. By that evening, though, many of the fire companies that had participated in the violence earlier that morning worked to put out the flames and prevent additional destruction. Many German-American protesters returned home as well to set up patrols of their own neighborhoods, whose safety the police could no longer ensure.[135]

As the riots increased in strength between Tuesday and Thursday, their dynamics shifted. Many skilled laborers stayed in their homes and neighborhoods, satisfied that they had demonstrated their opposition to the draft and now more concerned with restoring order. Those who remained or joined the riots were now predominantly Irish Catholic unskilled laborers and longshoremen, whose motivations differed slightly from the rioters of Monday. The aims of this new group were broader and more violent. Participants targeted African-Americans, Republicans, abolitionists, and anyone or anything associated with them. The rioters saw these groups as influencing the northern war effort toward issues they feared would hurt their communities and their future in America. Abolitionists were attacked and their property was destroyed. African-Americans were dragged from carriages and their homes, and some were lynched in the streets and their bodies mutilated as the rioters struck out at any perceived threat to Irish labor and social influence. Policemen and soldiers trying to suppress the riots also became targets, even if these men were Irish-Americans and Catholics.

The Irish mob did not spare Provost Marshal Robert Nugent, for example, a former member of the 69th New York, due to his role as director of the draft in the city. As they broke into his home, they raced through the rooms, destroying furniture and slashing photographs of Nugent and Thomas Francis Meagher. Interestingly, they left the image of Michael Corcoran alone, indicating perhaps that while Irishmen blamed Nugent for the draft and Meagher for the high casualties that had decimated their neighborhoods, they still trusted Corcoran as a leader. The Irish mob took even more revenge on Colonel Henry O'Brien, an Irishman in the 11th New York Volunteers who had dispersed part of Monday's mob by firing a howitzer in Second Avenue that killed a woman and her child. When the mob found O'Brien the next day, they captured the officer and over the next six hours slowly beat him to death. The violence did not end until Friday, when soldiers fresh from the battle of Gettysburg joined city police to bring an end to the violence.[136]

The draft riots shocked the non-Irish population, while many Irish-American Catholics tried to defend their communities' participation in the violence. One Irish-American soldier defended the rioters' actions as a logical response to the unjust exemption clause. "The government must be very unwise and short sighted," John England argued, "not to see that such a clause benefiting the rich, and injuring the poor would create a tumult, and a general feeling of thorough disgust among the masses whom it affected."[137] The New York *Irish-American* agreed, claiming the Lincoln administration had been warned of "the danger they were risking, and the outbreak of popular resentment and opposition which the obnoxious character of the law would be certain to provoke." Despite this, "they heeded neither advice nor warning; and the deplorable results . . . are all that their disregard of the plainest dictates of common sense has produced."[138]

These arguments satisfied some Irishmen, but few others. The opinions of John England and the editors of the *Irish-American* did little to diminish the outrage of many non-Irish at the role played by Irish men and women in the riots. Nor did it strengthen the position of those who hoped to display Irish-American military service as proof that Irish Catholics were loyal and patriotic, undeserving of nativists' portrayal of them as violent, selfish, and untrustworthy. If anything, the involvement of Irish-Americans in the draft riots, after nearly a year of diminishing support for the war and declining enlistments, reinforced the anti-Irish prejudice so prevalent in the country a decade earlier.

So did the refusal of most Irish-American political, military, or religious leaders to chastise participation in the violence. While insisting that the rioting was wrong, New York Archbishop Hughes argued that some of the week's chaos had to be attributed to unjust Republican policies, as well as anti-Irish and anti-Catholic prejudice. He called on rioters to cease, but saved his most stinging remarks for those who placed exclusive blame on the Irish, as though New York would be a peaceful town if it were not for them. In particular, Hughes challenged abolitionist and New York *Tribune* editor Horace Greeley's claim that all of those arrested during the week's violence were Irish, who must shoulder the blame. Hughes insisted that if only Irishmen were arrested it was further proof that they were "innocuous victims of our municipal laws" and the favorite targets of native-born Americans.[139] The New York *Irish-American* agreed, arguing,

It was supposed that the outbreak of the rebellion, and the patriotism evinced on all sides by Irish-Americans, would put an end to the invidious attacks of [the New York *Tribune* and the Chicago *Tribune*], which, like *Harper's Weekly*, were ever ready to denounce us as "nuisances." But such moderation could not long endure. The moment the Abolition faction began to take breath after the first shock of the secession movement had passed, and the struggle for political preeminence recommenced, the old spirit soon displayed itself and at every check the Radicals experienced, "the Irish" came in for unsparing denunciation for their faithful adherence to the old Democratic faith and traditions of the nation, to which none have been truer than they.[140]

The *Pilot* also concluded that the native-born population must share some of the blame for the week's violence. The editors insisted that all of the rioters, regardless of ethnicity, were wrong to participate in such violence, arguing, "there should be no leniency shown to those who take the law into their own hands, and under the semblance of wrong, wreak their vengeance upon unoffending people, destroying property, and endangering life." Despite this sweeping indictment, the *Pilot* quickly pointed out that the Irish were not the only Bostonians capable of violence, reminding readers of the Protestants' attack several decades earlier on the Charlestown Ursuline Convent, "whose charred walls still stand as a monument of native rioting."

If Irish men and women participated in these riots, the *Pilot* argued, it was because poverty forced them to live where such violence was common. They were as much observers as they were participants. Those who did engage in the violence, the editors explained, were merely "the cat's-paws and tools of actors behind the scenes. The leaders of the riots in New York, as far as we have seen, were not Irish. . . . There is no more law-abiding class in the country, as a general thing, than the Catholic Irish population."

The riots had renewed or reinforced nearly every negative stereotype about the Irish in America. The efforts of some Irish-American Catholics to challenge the rioters were lost in these discussions. Even their countrymen failed to direct major attention to their actions, and as the days, weeks, and years passed the image of violent Irish-American Catholics would come to dominate the memory of the most violent riots in American history. Early native coverage of the event, for example, noted the Irish brogue of participants to support the charge that the vast majority of rioters they observed were Irish, while many reporters failed to note that German- and native-born participants were especially active in Monday's violence. *Tribune* readers learned that on Wednesday night potential victims found safety by answering rioters' question, "Are you for the Union?" with "I am a Democratic Catholic."[141] Similarly, Sixth Avenue railroad director Alfred G. Jones survived the riots by pretending to support the antidraft sentiments of Irishmen who arrived at his depot seeking to attract or force his workers to join their protests. Jones explained, "I promenaded arm in arm with a drunken Irishman, and was let go upon making 'a speech against the draft. . . .' They said I was all right and left me after shaking hands generally."[142]

Beyond this, many of the reports in non-Irish papers and reflections on the events noted by middle- and upper-class New Yorkers characterized the rioters as animals. New York diarist George Templeton Strong, representative of prominent New York Republican businessmen, described the rioters as "[s]talwart young vixens and withered old hags . . . swarming everywhere, all cursing the 'bloody draft' and egging on their men to mischief." Strong characterized the mob as entirely Irish, describing one group of "thirty-four lousy, blackguardly Irishmen with a tail of small boys . . . [and] a handful of *canaille*." To Strong and many other wealthy native-born New Yorkers, the Irish were "brutal, base, cruel, cowards, and as insolent as [they were] base." Reflecting on the riots, Strong mused, "No wonder St. Patrick drove all the venomous vermin out of Ireland! Its biped mammalia supply that island its full average share of creatures that crawl and eat dirt and poison every community they infest."[143]

In addition to characterizing the rioters as largely Irish savages, Republican papers like the *New York Times* had no patience with the theory that their main purpose was to protest the draft. By Tuesday, the second day of the riots, the *Times* reported, " 'Resistance to the draft' was the flimsiest of veils to cover the wholesale plundering which characterized the operations of the day."[144] Indeed, the *Times* chastised anyone who sought to defend the mob. The New York *World,* for example, had concluded, "We charge it plainly upon the radical journals of this City" that by supporting the Lincoln administration and offering no sympathy to Democratic opposition, papers like the *Times* had contributed to the explosion of rage witnessed in New York. The *Times* was disgusted, responding that there was no defense for such violence, nor were they to blame for simply discussing the political and social aspects of this conflict.[145] When a New York laborer and rioter made an effort to explain the mob's perspective, the *Times* was equally impatient. Writing to the paper Monday night as "A Poor Man, but a Man for all that," the rioter argued,

You will no doubt be hard on us rioters tomorrow morning, but that 300-dollar law has made us nobodies, vagabonds, and cast-outs of society, for whom nobody cares when we must go to war and be shot down. We are the poor rabble, and the rich rabble is our enemy by this law. Therefore we will give our enemy battle right here, and ask no quarter. Although we got hard fists, and are dirty without, we have soft hearts, and have clean consciences within, and that's the reason we love our wives and children more than the rich, because we got not much besides them and we will not go and leave them at home for to starve. Until that draft law is repealed I for one am willing to knock down more such rum-hole politicians as [Superintendent of Police John A.] Kennedy. Why don't they let the nigger kill the slave-driving race and take possession of the South as it belongs to them.[146]

Another letter to the editor, signed "A Poor Man," argued against the unfairness of the exemption clause, writing, "If this is not releasing the rich and placing the burden of the war exclusively on the poor, I should like to know what would be." Again the *Times* had no sympathy, explaining that the three hundred dollars paid by the wealthy to escape drafted service is distributed among the poor to induce volunteers, and in the process increases their pay by hundreds of dollars. "Not a single poor man will be drafted now who would not be if this $300 exemption clause were not in the law. But a great many would miss the $300 which now they can obtain as a bounty for volunteering."[147]

Many Irish-Americans doubted the *Times*'s pledge to care for their families and redistribute the wealth among the Irish poor. Following the riots, signs and slogans referring to the Know Nothing activities of the 1850s reappeared. Placards around the city proclaimed, "Sam, Organize!" calling on nativist organizations to return to the activism and prominence they had enjoyed in the previous decade.[148] Awareness of this anti-Irish sentiment was reinforced as Irish-Americans read reports that Irish serving girls throughout the city were being fired in response to the Irish participation in the riots and many native-born Americans' fears of the inherent violence of the Irish in America.[149]

The *Times* was equally impatient with Archbishop John Hughes, who had spoken to a crowd of Irish Catholics on July 16 and proclaimed,

> If you are Irishmen, and the papers say the rioters are all Irishmen, then I also am an Irishman, but not a rioter, for I am a man of peace. If you are Catholics, as they have said, probably to wound my feelings, then I also am a Catholic. . . . They call you rioters, and I cannot see a riotous face among you.

Horrified, the *Times* asked how the crowd of Irish Catholics, whom the *Times* believed dominated the violence of the previous week, could not be called rioters. Perhaps, they mused, the archbishop simply refused to believe that his flock could behave in such a manner. "If the mob had burned the Catholic Orphan Asylum next door to the Bishop's Cathedral," as the Irish mob had burned the Colored Orphan's Asylum that Monday, countered the *Times,* "somebody besides 'the papers' would probably have called them 'rioters.'"[150]

Thus the debate continued, with most Irish-Americans defending the motivations behind the Irish rioters while leading native-born Americans expressed a renewed belief that the Irish were a dangerous, undeserving people who could never be trusted. Nativists ignored the fact that Irish-born Paddy McCafferty helped rescue the young boys and girls from the rioters who destroyed the Colored Orphan Asylum. Nor did they recognize Irish-American officer Robert Nugent, who tried to enforce the draft, or Irish-American Captain Henry O'Brien, who lost his life in an effort to protect New Yorkers' property. Part of this omission, though, may have been due to the attacks on these people by fellow Irish-American Catholics.

The actions by men like Nugent, O'Brien, and McCafferty placed them in the minority, but there were Irish-American Catholic soldiers in the field who shared their position. Peter Welsh, a member of the 28th Massachusetts and the Irish Brigade, actually supported the draft, even with the exemption clause. "No conscription could be fairer" than that proposed in 1863, Welsh claimed, adding, "It would be impossible to frame it to satisfy every one. And those drafted men may never have to fight a battle." Through conscription, Welsh believed, "the war will either be settled or the skulking blowers at home will have to come out and do their share of the fighting." When those "skulkers" included Irish-Americans, Welsh did not change his tone. He commended the use of canister and grape shot in putting down the New York City draft riots, and while regretting that many of the rioters were Irish, he regretted more their actions. "God help the Irish," Welsh prayed. "They are to[o] easily led into such snares which give their enemys [sic] an opportunity to malighn [sic] and abuse them."[151] Welsh was more the exception than the rule, but there were Irish-American volunteers expressing such thoughts.

Andrew Greenlees, an Irish-born Protestant, took a somewhat different view of the draft and the war. From his home in Dayton, Illinois, where he made a living as a farm laborer, Greenlees expressed pride in the United States and the Union war effort, and while he had not seen the need to volunteer, he did pledge to serve if drafted. As he explained to his brother John in Ireland, who had indicated less enthusiasm for the American war, Andrew saw numerous parallels between this war and Irish Protestants' loyalty to the British government. He argued,

I would not expect you to be quite so much interested in the success of our arms as if you were a citizen of our country but surely no good citizen can feel indifferent as to the result had Smith O'Brien and his Confederates succeeded in their designs of rebelling against the British protestant government [in 1848] and establishing in its room a papal tyrannical despotism. How would you have felt on the subject? Would you not have been ready and willing at a moment's notice to shoulder your knapsack and musket and march to the defense of your country's dearest rights? It is so with me.

Andrew Greenlees saw himself as a loyal, active member of the United States. "I am a citizen of this country," he explained to his brother.

> All my interests are here. I look upon this as my country which I love with a true patriot's heart and although it would be very hard for me to leave my family (for I love them dearly) yet should the draft name me (as it has not yet) I will seek no substitute nor no creep hole but march at once to fight and if need be die for my country.

For this antislavery Protestant Irish-American, like many of his fellow Protestant Irishmen, the Union war effort remained quite popular even by the fall of 1863.[152]

There were, however, exceptions to this. Irish-born Joseph Hewitt, living in Cincinnati, Ohio, planned to avoid the draft, and his case is an interesting one as that of a Protestant Irishman who spoke in favor of the Union war effort but showed a clear determination to avoid contributing to it in uniform. In the summer of 1864 he offered a lengthy explanation to his brother in Ireland as to how he might accomplish this, regardless of the draft:

> The drawing [of the draft] was completed during the past week and as luck would have it I failed to draw a prize. However as the lucky drawers of these prizes are required to pay three hundred dollars as commutation money, or furnish a substitute, or serve three years in the rank of the Army I shall not complain as being unlucky. From the way things look at present there is no telling who will be compelled to go into the army or who will keep out of it. It seems at present as if Congress . . . were going to abolish the three hundred dollar commutation "clause" of the "Conscription Bill" and should they do so it will be almost impossible for a poor man to avoid going in the army in case he is drafted. The price of substitutes would go up to such a high figure as to be beyond his ability to purchase one, even now with the clause still in force, they command as high as six hundred dollars and more. [With the] clause abolished I should not be surprised to see them go as high as two thousand or twenty-five hundred dollars. So you see that should Congress make the above change in the Conscription Act and the indications are that they will, a poor man stands an exceedingly good chance, in case he is drafted, of getting into the Army, whether he wants to or not. But as far as brother James and I are concerned—William being unnaturalized is free from the operations of the law—you can tell Father and Mother to give themselves no uneasiness whatever, as neither of us have any idea just now of putting ourselves up as a target for Rebels to shoot at, or of joining the army as long as

money will keep us out of it. Should either one of us be drafted, and not have money enough of our own to purchase a substitute we should experience no difficulty in finding friends that have it and who would cheerfully lend it to us.[153]

A similar determination to avoid the draft came from those hoping to leave Ireland for the United States. In 1863, Irishmen flooded U.S. consulates with requests for passage to America. While some individuals were willing to exchange a pledge of military service for free tickets, many others sought to clarify that if they did go to America, they would not be forced into the Union Army. That August, U.S. Consul E. Eastman reported from Cork, Ireland, "I am often called upon for a certificate to give to Emigrants to exempt them from the draft on their arrival in the United States, which request I have always refused, but explaining to them at the same time that they were not liable to the draft, but still it is not satisfactory to them." The cause of these fears, Eastman theorized, was "the public Press throughout the whole country as well as the Friends of the South [who] use every means to impress the poor and ignorant people that immediately on their arrival in the United States they are liable to be pressed into the Army."[154] Similar reports arrived from U.S. Consul John Young, stationed in Belfast. In December 1863 he reported, "Emigrants going out from this port come to my office to get a passport to prevent them from being drafted. This, of course, is refused."[155]

As for the memory of the riot, many Irishmen accepted the fact that they had to bear a share of responsibility for the riots. What frustrated them, however, were prominent native-born Americans' allegations that inherent Irish brutality really inspired the violence. From the perspective of many Irish-Americas, a clear pattern of disregard and prejudice created the rage. Battlefield carnage had bloodied them and the Emancipation Proclamation was about to unleash a wave of free black workers onto an already tight labor market. Lincoln had removed General George McClellan, the one commander many Irish-Americans trusted to win the war without a needless sacrifice of their lives. State drafts seemed to target the working Irish while wealthy, native-born Americans paid bounties to avoid service. Reports of prejudice by Protestant Americans against Irish Catholics continued, citing the destruction of southern Catholic churches, violence and mistreatment of Irish miners in Pennsylvania, and the federal government's insult to the Irish Brigade in refusing to allow them leave time to return home to rest and recruit replacements to replenish their weakened unit.

Despite all of these tensions, the draft riots resulted in some gains. The rioters' actions had captured the attention of public officials and resulted in the successful, if temporary, halt of the draft. Even when the draft resumed the following month, Irish and other northern laborers were pleased to see that their protest had forced revisions in the way it was applied in their communities. New York Democrats had convinced the Lincoln administration to decrease their quota from twenty-six thousand men to twelve thousand, and the Democrat-dominated Common Council appropriated $3 million to pay bounties and relief to any men drafted. Similar measures were taken in other northern cities as well.[156] Other efforts included the work of Irish-American Judge Charles Patrick Daly, who took charge of the newly formed Working Women's Protective Union in New York late in 1863. The organization financially supported seamstresses and other female laborers, many of them Irish, throughout the war. By 1865 it included the first known Catholic day nursery, or day care program, in the nation.[157]

Yet it is undeniable that the draft riots were also harmful for the Irish. Republican Mayor George Opdyke vetoed the Common Council's appropriation and then further outraged poor laborers when they learned that his son had just purchased his exemption. The final blow came when Republican community leaders, who had vetoed proposals that would greatly assist the Irish poor in avoiding the same military service many Republicans evaded, approved funding to assist victims of the riots and even went so far as to encourage upper-class families to hire African-American rather than Irish domestic servants.[158]

Such actions had several consequences, particularly an increased Irish loyalty to the Democratic party and a continuing decline in Irish military service. Challenging Mayor Opdyke's veto of the Common Council's appropriation, New York's Board of Supervisors created an Exemption Committee with a $2 million budget to purchase substitutes for poor men with dependents or municipal workers. Irishmen across the city took the opportunity to thank the Democratic party for this assistance and send a strong anti-Republican, antiwar statement in the next mayoral election. In the fall of 1863, Irish voters backed antiwar extremist G. Godfrey Gunther, who ran on a platform of peace at any cost and a condemnation of the Lincoln administration. It was Irish Catholic support that secured victory for Gunther.[159]

Originally, Irishmen had supported the Union cause to promote the interests of their own communities and Ireland, with a related but secondary interest in America. But when the interests of Irish America and America diverged, many native-born Americans did not understand these conflicting interests. Irish-Americans might argue that their increasing opposition to the Lincoln administration's conduct of the war and its evolving objectives were not signs of lacking patriotism, but rather loyal opposition. Some native-born Americans agreed, especially northern Democrats, who comprised the main body of opposition to the Republican-directed war effort. Unfortunately for the Irish in America, their acceptance and influence was increasing in a party whose power was steadily declining. As Union war objectives became those of the Republican party, and as larger segments of the population viewed loyalty to the Republican party as loyalty to the Union, an absence of support among many Irish-Americans for the Republicans, the war aims, and military service would be interpreted by many Americans as unpatriotic and disloyal. It would contribute, too, to an image that would endure for decades of the Irish as disloyal, violent, and threatening to all that was good in America.

5

"Hordes of Celts and Rebel Sympathizers"

The Decline and Consequence of Irish-American Support for the War

On a cold Saturday morning in 1863, Sarah McCormick entered the offices of Charles H. Birney, Esquire. She had no money and "appear[ed] to be bad off." As far as she knew, her husband, serving in the Irish 69th New York, had not received any pay recently, or at least he was not sending any home. Charles Birney, treasurer of the Friendly Sons of St. Patrick in New York City, had seen situations like hers since the war began. Susan Callahan, for example, had seven small children and a sick husband "to Provide for." In 1863, she requested from Birney "a little aid to enable me to Purchase some Chamois Leather that I support my family by," adding quickly, "My oldest boy is at the War," perhaps to show that her family had earned the right to assistance.[1]

It was not just women who visited the Friendly Sons. A year earlier Birney had met with Charles James Brennan, a veteran of the Army of the Potomac as well as the British Army, having served in the Crimean War nearly a decade earlier. Brennan had recovered from recent battlefield wounds, but now he was "in great distress" with "no money and no employment." Throughout the war, the Friendly Sons helped countless Irish families waging desperate battles of their own on the home front.[2]

The final three years of the Civil War weighed heavily on Irish-Americans, and they responded with a steady decline of volunteers and support for the war. The Fenian dreams of using the conflict as a training ground for a future liberation of Ireland faded away as high casualty rates among Irish regiments thinned the ranks of potential freedom fighters. In addition, increasing numbers of Irish-Americans were unwilling to preserve the nation for future generations of Irish refugees. They disapproved of the changing goals of the Union war effort, especially its fight against slavery under powerful Republican leadership.

These developments led many Irish-Americans to complain that the war was not securing their futures and those of their families in America and Ireland, but instead hurting them. Those hoping to use heroic Irish military service to prove Irish-American loyalty believed they were not diminishing anti-Irish bigotry among native-born Americans. It appeared that, if anything, increasing numbers of native-born Americans were becoming impatient with Irish charges of mistreatment and prejudice. There was little sympathy for Meagher's efforts to secure leave for the Irish Brigade so the men could visit with their families and replenish their ranks. Another blow came with the loss of one of their most cherished heroes.

The sudden death of 36-year-old Irish nationalist and Brigadier General Michael Corcoran in December 1863 added to the disillusionment within the Irish-American community. That winter had found Corcoran and his Legion encamped in Virginia, and he enjoyed a series of visits from his old friend Thomas Francis Meagher in December. On the night of December 22, Corcoran escorted Meagher to the train station, but in a bizarre accident, Corcoran fell from his horse, lost consciousness, and died. The news spread quickly through Irish-American communities across the North, and St. Patrick's Cathedral in New York was packed for his funeral service, as was the Great Hall of Cooper Institute, where a memorial service was held in January 1864. The *New York Herald* and *New York Times* covered the service, as did many Irish-American papers throughout the country. Despite an inspiring eulogy by Thomas Francis Meagher, members of the Irish-American audience found little comfort in the service.[3] Maria Lydig Daly captured the sentiment and the tensions within the New York Irish-American community. Some Irishmen could not forget, Daly argued, the rumors that it was Meagher who discouraged other Irish leaders from seeking Corcoran's exchange when the Confederates held him as a prisoner. They recalled as well rumors of Meagher's "desertion of [Corcoran] on the field of Bull Run." "In his neighborhood," Daly commented of Meagher, "there can be no good luck for others. . . . Now that Corcoran is gone, he is the representative of the Irish brave—what he has all the time been aiming at!"[4]

Corcoran had held a powerful grasp on Irish Catholic communities in America. Their faith in Meagher had wavered, but Corcoran had held their loyalty with his dramatic stand against the parade for the Prince of Wales before the war and his leadership at the battle of First Bull Run in 1861. Even after that battle, Corcoran defied death during the famous incident involving the C.S.S. *Enchantress*. This was the Confederate ship captured in the fall of 1861 whose officer and crew faced charges of piracy by the Lincoln administration and death sentences. Confederate president Jefferson Davis responded by declaring that he would execute

Brigadier General Michael Corcoran, portrayed in this engraving as colonel of the 69th New York Militia. Courtesy of U.S. Army Military History Institute. Photograph research/reproduction courtesy Lynn L. Libby, Enola, PA, 2005.

a Union officer currently held as prisoner of war for each member of the *Enchantress* hanged by the Union government. Corcoran had been one of the prisoners selected for possible execution, and he made headlines with his bold proclamation that he was ready to make this sacrifice. The Lincoln administration had backed down, but incidents like these, combined with Corcoran's prewar role as a leading Irish nationalist, had made him a figurehead within Irish communities. They had rallied around Corcoran when he returned from prison in 1862 and rushed to join his Irish Legion that year. Even when Irish-Americans' faith in the war faded, they still showed loyalty to Corcoran, as evidenced by the rioters in New York during that bloody week in July 1863, who destroyed images of Meagher and Nugent but left Corcoran's alone. His death in December 1863 delivered a powerful blow to their faith in the Union war effort.[5]

Irish-American nationalists were similarly depressed. Corcoran had been a leading voice among the Fenians since the late 1850s. The war had taken its toll on their ranks, and with Corcoran's death the movement suffered a terrible blow. Fenian officers in the 170th New York, led by Colonel James McIvor, met in camp on December 26, 1863, to mourn his passing and its impact on their movement. "Ireland, the land of his nativity, has met with an irreparable loss," they declared, with the death of "a future leader in the great cause of her redemption from the galling yoke of British tyranny." The Fenian leadership, which was already fractured and whose support for the war always came after the cause of Ireland, increasingly shifted its attention to matters more closely related to Irish independence, including their upcoming Fenian Fair in Chicago in April 1864. Fenians would continue to serve in the war, but their attentions turned increasingly toward postwar actions for Ireland rather than the current fight for America.[6]

Colonel James P. McIvor, 170th New York Volunteer Infantry Regiment. Courtesy of U.S. Army Military History Institute. Photograph research/reproduction courtesy Lynn L. Libby, Enola, PA, 2005.

Along with the Fenians, other Irish-Americans questioned the value of their sacrifices in this war. Like Maria Daly, they criticized Meagher, charging that he had "recklessly exposed the lives of the officers and men of his command," was commonly too drunk to be an effective leader, and used illness to avoid placing himself in harm's way. Clearly concerned, Meagher asked his former command to challenge the charges spreading through the northern home front and in Ireland. The Irishmen of his old Brigade did, but an undercurrent of despair and resentment at the direction of the war and its toll on the Irish continued to run through their communities.[7] And though nearly every member of the unit reenlisted in January 1864, this may have been due more to the bounties and leave time offered to units who pledged continued service than a demonstration of their continuing faith in the war effort. Also, if a sufficiently significant portion of the unit reenlisted, the Irish Brigade, though greatly reduced, would continue to exist as a fighting force.[8]

It was a hard decision that many Union soldiers faced, and Irish-American William White of the largely Irish 69th Pennsylvania refused to succumb to the pressure. As he told his parents in January 1864, "You need not expect me to reenlist. There is not much talk of it in our Brigade. I don't think there is twenty five in the brigade that have reenlisted. Them that did reenlist got their eye shut on the thirty day furlough. I am sure they will not get me again, no matter how they try. "One month later he told them that "the regiment expects to go home every day, I mean them that has reenlisted, but you need not expect to see Cloney or me for we have not the least idea of reenlisting."[9]

The members of the Irish Brigade who reenlisted returned home on January 2, 1864, and saw few signs of the enthusiasm for war that had swept their neighborhoods two years earlier. For months the Irish men of the brigade had dreamed of their return, imagining "the happiness of that day when we would march back through New York; of the welcome we would receive."[10] It certainly was not what they imagined. The city streets were quiet, nearly empty but for the soldiers' families. Only a brief mention appeared in the morning papers, and few native-born Americans saw any reason to celebrate an influx of Irishmen into the city after the previous July's rioting. That very day, January 2, 1864, Republican New Yorker and famous diarist George Templeton Strong complained of Governor Seymour's decision to remove police officials who criticized the rioters. Their actions and Archbishop Hughes's defense of the Irish Catholics of the city, Strong insisted, revealed that Irish-Americans embodied "Babylon, Scarlet Woman, and anti-Christ."[11] Just one year earlier, native-born citizens of New York had sent the state's regiments in the Irish Brigade new flags to honor its sacrifices. Now these regiments returned home to find few but their families waiting to greet them.

Irish-American veterans noted this as a sign of nativist prejudice and declining support for the war in general. The men of the brigade declared that they would "make up for the lukewarmness on the part of the authorities, who were openly and malignantly opposed to the national cause and its supporters, the officers of the Brigade, those who had served and those still in service" by organizing the reception that the city had overlooked. In a grand banquet the officers of the brigade toasted all present and former enlisted members in attendance, many of whom were discharged due to loss of limbs or poor health, in a ceremony celebrating "the blood and brotherhood that united the Chieftains of old to his clansmen."

Despite the efforts at cheer, many speakers that evening could not help but mention what they saw as ingratitude by the city and the country. Thomas Francis Meagher tried to console the men, explaining that though they may "not have the municipal authorities to welcome you at the gates, . . . [or] regiments to go forth in all the finery of military paraphernalia to welcome you after your onerous, tiresome, exacting duties," the men did have the devoted love and gratitude of their wives, their mothers, and their officers. This was a nice sentiment, but some men were not comforted and one colonel raised his glass in a melancholy toast to "[t]he Irish Brigade; what there is left of it."[12]

Because of enlistment bounties, the New York regiments of the Irish Brigade did have some recruiting success during this visit home. Financial inducements attracted other Irishmen into the ranks as the combination of local, state, and federal bounties neared one thousand dollars by 1864. They may have had more luck with recent Irish Catholic immigrants who lacked the family ties and experience in America to have the connections sometimes necessary for employment, and these men, fleeing from desperate conditions in Ireland, turned to the first option they found in the recruiters on the wharfs. Also, while jobs were plentiful in the northern labor market, inflation continued to plague poor common workers. Employment in the U.S. Army was a risky proposition, but the bounties and recruiting posters for Irish units across the North highlighted the financial benefits to enlistment rather than their earlier emphasis on Irish heritage. In 1861, Irish regiments and brigades recruited Irishmen with posters covered in harps, clovers, and calls of "Irishmen to the Rescue" of American union. By December 1863, Captain J. J. Fitzgerald of Mulligan's Irish Brigade enticed Irishmen in Chicago with more tangible incentives. Slogans on his recruiting posters read "Last Chance to Avoid the Draft!" and "$402 Bounty to Veterans! $302 to all other Volunteers!"[13]

Recruiting poster for Mulligan's Irish Brigade, December 1863.
Courtesy of Chicago Historical Society.

Some of those most susceptible to these inducements were indeed the new immigrants desperate for income. By 1863 and 1864, increasing numbers of Irish-Americans and their families in Ireland complained that newly arrived Irishmen in the northern United States were being tricked into military service, encouraged by false pretenses that there would be work for them upon their arrival in the country. These allegations found little or no sympathy among native-born Americans and their newspapers, though, as leading native presses challenged such assertions. The *New York Times* argued that no Irishmen were coerced into leaving their homeland, insisting rather that they came to America voluntarily due to the job opportunities. The *Times* challenged testimony not only from the Irish in America but also that given before the British Parliament by English leaders, including Sir Robert Peel.

Parliament heard testimony in the summer of 1864 that between twenty and thirty thousand Irishmen had been tricked into military service during the past year. Similar reports appeared in *The Illustrated London News* in 1864, along with images of Union Army recruiting stations set up in New York's harbor to entice newly arrived Irish and German immigrants.

The *New York Times* described as absolutely preposterous the British charges that U.S. encouragement of Irish immigration led thousands of British subjects into destitute conditions that forced "no less than thirty-thousand Irish females, who have left home and friends . . . [into] walking the streets of New-York, friendless and deserted." The *Times* countered that neither "thirty thousand, nor thirty, Irish females *willing to work at honest employment* are wandering about the streets of New-York." Indeed, the editors of the *Times* insisted that it was this honest economic opportunity that inspired so many Irishmen to come to America, and the lack of such fortunes in Britain that drove them away.[14]

There was some truth to the *Times* editors' claims. The early 1860s brought heavy rains to Ireland that ruined crops, which in turn ruined the fortunes of farmers and laborers, and led to a dramatic increase in evictions, especially in the midland and western counties. In the first three

"Enlisting Irish and German Emigrants" at Castle Garden, New York, *Illustrated London News*, September 17, 1864. Photograph reproduction courtesy Lynn L. Libby, Enola, PA, 2005.

years of the U.S. Civil War, evictions increased by 65 percent over the previous four years and those in the hardest hit regions almost reached famine conditions. Male emigration in these areas increased dramatically, with County Galway reaching a 422 percent increase over previous years. Anything seemed better than the conditions in Ireland and they inspired thousands of young men to seek every possible means to reach the markets of America, or even the attractive, though extremely risky, pay of the U.S. Army.[15] Even when the crops improved slightly in 1863, many Irishmen simply used this slight improvement to secure the funds to depart Ireland. Recognizing this, the U.S. consul in Cork explained, "instead of checking emigration . . . [it] only affords the means for a much greater increase." Similarly, the Dublin consul reported, "This spring has opened with such an emigration, as has not been known for many years, and new incentives are being given to increase it. In a few days a new line of screw steamers will commence running between Liverpool and New York, and every week to call at Kingstown in this consulate for emigrants."[16]

Among these desperate Irishmen, some were willing to trade service in the U.S. Army in exchange for a free trip to America. Since the second year of the war, the U.S. consular offices in cities like Dublin, Galway, Cork, Belfast, and Derry had been overwhelmed with such requests. Some of the confusion over how the U.S. government may or may not have been recruiting these émigrés could be explained by the U.S. consul in Dublin, Henry B. Hammond. He noticed in the spring of 1862 that "there are many Americans in Dublin at the present time. Most of them are from the States in Rebellion and strange as it may seem, there are many here who give an attentive ear to the falsehoods they utter concerning the Rebellion. Every day numerous applications are made to me for a free passage to America." As Hammond explained, the people requesting this "say they are informed that the Government of the United States is giving free passage to all desiring to Emigrate." An exasperated Hammond insisted, "If the Government has any Agent for that purpose I wish that I might be informed of his whereabouts, that I might send the large numbers who are coming to me, to him." By that summer, Hammond reported thousands of young Irishmen seeking free passage to the United States in exchange for a pledge to serve in the Union Army, and he encouraged the U.S. government to find some way to accommodate them.[17]

By November 1863, those Irish hoping to go to America found an equally strong advocate in U.S. Vice-Consul William B. West, who was serving in Dublin. An enthusiastic West proposed a plan to encourage even greater Irish emigration to America by honoring former Irish Brigade General Thomas Francis Meagher and all Irish-American soldiers. He suggested that the U.S. government set aside "some desirable portion of our territories" as a

> New Ireland, of which no doubt General Meagher would in due time be elected Governor: if desirably located as to climate etc it would be a *point d'appuit* for Irish emigrants, to which they would flock in thousands, and thus regenerate themselves in a Country and on a soil they could really call their own: under a government as free as the air they breathe.[18]

Cases of Irishmen seeking free passage in exchange for service continued throughout 1863 and 1864. Men like Mark Mulligan contacted the U.S. consul at Galway, in the spring of 1863, to secure passage for his son to America. The boy hoped

> to join his brother Christopher Mulligan in the U.S. Army and not having means of paying his passage he wishes to know if you could do anything in the way of forwarding him to his brother as he is inclined to join that Honorable service as soon as he arrives there and as he is out of employment in the alternative he will be under the necessity of joining the British Service.[19]

Others, like James Murphy of County Clare, made similar requests. That same spring he asked if Consul West could tell him "[h]ow I could get out to America or could you send me out as I have a great wish to join the northern army seeing on the papers that they have advanced money for to take out 120,000 persons." To further convince the consul, Murphy pledged, "I would suffer death for North America and the gallant Corcoran," should he receive this opportunity to serve.[20]

Men like Murphy, who included an ideological reference in his request, were fairly unusual compared to the majority, who indicated that only economic factors inspiring their offers. Even Murphy, to be totally accurate, hinted at some desperate condition: "I don't like to tell my situation to you, but if you wish to see me I will go over to Galway very soon and then you will know what I am."[21] Most of these letters to U.S. consuls across Ireland offered a simple exchange of free passage for military service, indicating that the motivations of these émigrés involved economic desperation and a desire to reach America and the North's wartime economy, which was booming by 1864 and 1865.[22]

These recruits' motivations differed from those of Irish-American Catholics at this time. The latter's loyalties split between American and Ireland, and increasingly fell with Ireland. Those men just leaving Ireland, however, had few ties to America and lacked the time in the United States necessary to form any sense of loyalty. Their motivations appear to have been almost entirely financial, though some Irish nationalists may have still hoped to gain military experience. The Fenian newspaper, the *Irish People,* reminded its readers in December 1863 that the Irish immigrant turned Union volunteer would offer "a living example of what a people's army can do—an army officered exclusively by men sprung from the ranks of the people . . . a large portion of whom are Irish-born" with the hope that after the war for union, these experienced Irish warriors would "turn their eyes and hearts fondly towards the land of their birth."[23] There was a split, though, among the Fenians, as they became increasingly concerned about the toll the Union war effort exacted on their ranks. In America and Ireland, increasing numbers of Fenians discouraged enlistments by 1863 and 1864, noting that American Fenian leader John O'Mahony had allowed so many Irish nationalists to enlist in the Union Army that fifty Fenian circles had disbanded for lack of members. James Stephens, Fenian leader in Ireland, insisted that Irish independence was far more important than the war in America and the Irish Republican Brotherhood began to promote the message that it was a crime for Irishmen to leave their homeland to fight in America. Indeed, by 1864 the *Irish People* argued that Irish emigration to America "simply argues the blindest insanity of Irishmen to go there," insisting that Irish emigrants were "Deserters and Traitors." The Fenians would still hope to utilize the experienced Irish-American soldiers and veterans of the Union Army, but many of them, especially those in Ireland, challenged a policy that had such a devastating impact on their ranks.[24] Even O'Mahoney had warned his friends in Ireland as early as 1862 that the situation faced by Irishmen in the U.S. Army, who were suffering "fever, neglect, and mis-government in the swamps of Virginia," offered little salvation for the poor of Ireland.[25]

Despite such warnings, some Irishmen still hoped to find a better life in the United States. Again, their departures appear to have been driven overwhelmingly by economic pressures rather than the ideological loyalties that influenced many Irish-Americans' decisions. Thomas Conroy, a veteran of the U.S. Army and the Mexican War, was Irish born but a citizen of the United States by the time of the American Civil War. As he explained to Consul West in Galway, "my name is on the Record Book in Washington for my Bravery through the Mexican War. I am willing to fight and lose the last drop of my Blood under the stars and stripes once more if the American Consul will do me the favor to grant me a passage home once more." It appears that he had left New York in the spring of 1861, had lost everything he owned when his ship went down off the coast of France, had been trying to sustain himself in Liverpool, and then had traveled to Dublin to seek assistance from his father and friends, only to find that they had already departed for America. He tried to reach other friends in America, but did not receive responses and suspected "most of them are in the northern Army. . . . Honorable Sir, for God's sake, do something for me and get me out of [my] melancholy and heart broken state."[26]

Some of the most desperate to reach America skipped the consul's office and jumped as stowaways onto American ships, including U.S. naval vessels. As late as December 1863, Lieutenant Commander John A. Winslow of the U.S.S. *Kearsarge* complained to Consul Edwin G. Eastman in Cork that he was besieged by young Irishmen begging to enlist to get to America, and though he refused them, several managed to sneak on board as stowaways and were not discovered until they were at sea.[27]

One of the problems that faced those who did enlist, though, was how to send money home. They lacked a secure method for doing this and if they were killed, there was almost no way to get their belongings, including pay and their pensions, to their families unless they lived in America. The tragic case of Michael Murry demonstrates this. In April 1863 he was serving with the Union forces outside Vicksburg, confident that soon they would take the city. He pledged that he was "sending . . . all the money that I have, and you will either receive it in this letter or shortly after." He had not, however, "been paid two hours, and I cant say how it will go." Less than a month later, his father, Edward Murray, received notice that Michael had died in the fighting near Vicksburg. The boy's comrade, Michael Brennan, insisted that Murray had died for an honorable cause, telling Murray's father that his only son

> died without pain, he died defending one of the most holy causes that ever man died for, and a grateful country will yet raise a monument to the memory of the heroes that fought and died for, I may say, the liberty of the human race: for if this country should fail to put down this rebellion it would be death to liberty all over the world.[28]

What concerned U.S. Vice-Consul William B. West in Dublin, however, was that Michael Murray's family had little chance of claiming their son's effects or any pension that might be due them. He forwarded repeated requests to the U.S. government to have

> even half . . . the bounty of $100 paid to the next of kin of soldiers and sailors who have died in our service, and who are residents in this country: the law at present not giving it to non-residents, except widows;

though it is also given to the brothers & sisters of dead soldiers and sailors who are <u>resident in America</u>: the arrears of pay only being given to the parents who are, in Ireland, with scarcely an exception, wretchedly poor, and frequently beg of me to send one of their children to our Country to take the place of a lost one: & a father entreats me to send him out that he might kill ten rebels to revenge the death of his son at their hands!

West argued, "if a free ticket to [the] U.S. would be given to each family who had lost a son in our war, it would be considered a <u>great boon</u>, and the money not only well applied, but highly beneficial to our Country."[29]

Of equal concern to Irish families were reports that their sons were being kidnapped or tricked into serving in the Union Army. In November 1863 Superintendent Daniel Ryan of the Dublin Metropolitan Police reported a case where a local Irish boy had succumbed to the temptations of a large bounty and promises of adventure and steady pay, and now reported unhappily serving with Federal forces in Fortress Monroe, Virginia. The young man, John Egan, had been employed as a shop assistant and now contacted his former employer to beg forgiveness for departing Ireland so promptly and without notice. Egan hinted that the federal agent who enlisted him lived very close to the employer and explained that the agent gave Egan an impressive bounty of $150, or about thirty pounds, for his pledge to join a regiment of New York engineers. As he explained,

I am not the only one. You will find young fellows leaving the finest situations in all parts of Ireland foolishly led to believe the falsifying statements of the Federal Agents. They are enlisting young men every day in fact they are coming out here in thousands and the moment they land they are drafted to the battle field where danger mostly stands. I enlisted in Dublin on the 23rd day of June '63. . . . The reason why I was not called upon sooner to go was the regiment was to be composed to 200 well educated young men. They did not obtain the full amount until 2 days before leaving your employment and I received an order to be ready in a few days which compelled me to leave work, but instead I had to remain 3 weeks, and was compelled to go on Sunday 11th August a day I can assure you dear master I will not forget. I arrived in New York on Monday 12th September and joined my regiment on the 13th. I was but one week in New York when I was ordered to North Carolina where the rebels were concentrated in great numbers.

Egan did not receive much training when he arrived in America. "I did not thoroughly understand the discipline," he explained, "but they can drill you here in the space of 2 days, [and] they do not much mind about marching so as you can handle a rifle you are a United States soldier." Egan did manage to receive a medical discharge from the army and was happy to leave America, which, he insisted, "is not agreeing with me at all. . . . You dare not express an opinion except in favor of [the American] government." He planned to return to New York City, then travel on to England, where he hoped to find work. Not all Irishmen, however, managed such a happy conclusion to their service in the Union Army, and the Dublin Metropolitan Police, along with other British officials, remained busy that fall and through the rest of the war investigating similar reports.[30]

Such accounts in Irish and Irish-American newspapers claimed that even Irishmen in America who were employed risked being kidnapped and forced into military service. These accounts told of Irish-Americans being drugged by recruiters and tricked into enlisting without full knowledge of their actions until they awoke the following morning, at which time it was too late to escape.[31] While some of these reports may have been exaggerated, the numerous accounts in Irish and Irish-American papers and in letters from family in Ireland convinced many Irish-Americans that their friends and relatives in America and Ireland were being tricked into fighting a war and serving an administration they did not support.[32]

Even when General John Dix, commander of the Department of the East, testified to the legitimacy of these charges, the Lincoln administration refused to act. Dix wrote to Secretary of War Edwin Stanton of the illegal actions by recruiters in which "[b]oys have been seduced from their families, drugged, and then enlisted. Two were so sadly drugged that they died." The British government argued that "such conduct was in reality nothing better than murder," but Secretary Stanton simply explained that the administration did not condone or support such actions and was not to blame for them.[33]

But the Lincoln administration had used questionable means to encourage emigration, which led to increased enlistments. Two years earlier, U.S. Consul to Britain Henry W. Lord had informed Secretary Seward that many English subjects were presenting themselves at the American Consulate hoping that they could receive free transport to America in exchange for service in the Union Army. Lord told them that no such policy was in place, but in July 1862 he proposed that Secretary Seward might consider establishing one. Seward forwarded the proposal to Secretary of War Stanton, with a reminder of the government's existing policy on encouraging emigration. In Circular No. 19, dated August 8, 1862, Secretary Seward directed all diplomatic and consular officers of the United

States to make the citizens in their respective countries aware of the fact that "at no former period of our history have our agricultural, manufacturing, or mining interests been more prosperous than at this juncture." Despite inflation, Seward explained, "nowhere else can the industrious laboring man and artisan expect so liberal a recompense for his service as in the United States." He then authorized all consular officials to make this known in their respective countries "in any way which may lead to the migration of such persons to this country," except financial inducements, which would be illegal.[34]

When these men arrived, however, many found that their wages would not support them or their families, and significant numbers turned to military service. One newly arrived immigrant warned his family against believing American advertisers in Ireland who present "misleading scores, telling [Irishmen] what good wares they get [in America], but not telling them what they have got to pay for everything." Living in Lawrence, Massachusetts, the Irishman found that what he could purchase with thirty cents in England was costing him one dollar in America. "My wages," he complained, "are not worth half as much as when we came here first."[35] They also discovered that finding honest employment was not easy for Irish Catholics in New York and other large cities across the North with significant Irish populations facing anti-Catholic bigotry. Nearly every copy of the *Times* published during the war years carried employment advertisements specifying that Catholics were not wanted in American homes. "Cook—Wanted . . . German, English, Scotch or Protestant Irish" read one ad, while another requested the services of a nurse and seamstress, noting "Protestants, English, or Germans preferred." Workers frequently clarified in notices offering their services that they were Protestant or American born. For poor, unskilled, laboring Irish-American Catholics, little seemed to have changed in two years of war. The anti-Irish and anti-Catholic prejudices of antebellum era remained strong in Civil War America.[36]

These situations contributed to the number of recently arrived Irishmen who found their way into the Union Army. Factoring into this as well were the impressive financial incentives for enlistment. As immigrant Thomas McManus explained to his family, "By 'Gor,' the bounty was very tempting and I enlisted the first day I came here." McManus received seven hundred dollars when he joined the 8th Massachusetts, a sum that was the equivalent of several years' wages in Ireland, even more in some counties.[37]

Some Irish immigrants attempted to find ways around hiring prejudices in America by securing civilian employment before departing Ireland. Despite their efforts, some of these men still found themselves wearing Union blue within a matter of weeks or months. This was the case with Irishmen who signed contracts to work with reported American railroad companies for one dollar per day and free passage from Ireland. These men arrived in America only to discover that the contracts were fraudulent and the agents who secured their passage were actually regimental recruiters rather than hiring agents for civilian companies.

It is impossible to know just how many Irishmen suffered from this situation, but the British government was sufficiently concerned in the summer of 1864 that the Lord Lieutenant of Ireland released a formal proclamation warning Irishmen "against the risk and danger" of "accepting offers of Employment as Laborers in the . . . United States of America, whereby they may be entangled in Military Service" in the Civil War "contrary to their own original intention." The U.S. government officially opposed efforts to recruit British citizens into the Union Army and pledged to look into the railroad companies in question, but the British government remained concerned throughout the war that the Lincoln administration was not enforcing this policy and Catholic communities in Ireland became increasingly concerned about the mistreatment of their men arriving in America.[38]

While definitely suffering from wretched economic conditions, these Irish immigrants were not all victims of crafty army recruiters, and the reports from America indicated that the situation was not as bleak as the Lord Lieutenant's proclamation and others indicated. The case of Thomas McManus described above reveals young men who were quite aware of the power they held as potential soldiers, and waited to enlist until they had acquired the best possible deal. In 1864, two Irish-American recruiters named Kidder and Feeney of Boston, Massachusetts, had recruited McManus and approximately a hundred other Irishmen, and paid their passage to the United States in exchange for a pledge to join the Union Army. McManus suspected the recruiters and deduced, "Feeney brought us over here with the intention of making us drunk and enlisting us after, but he was disappointed, for any of us that did enlist, was not with him." McManus, pleased with his decision, explained, "Dear parents, this is a free country, there is no one here forced to [en]list if they don't like."[39]

Edward Cummins, who appears to have traveled with McManus, chose to enlist in the 3rd Massachusetts Cavalry, and the spring of 1864 found him preparing to depart for New Orleans. Cummins appears to have enlisted under Feeney's direction, and noted to his family that recruiting offered a fine income of "about 88 dollars for every man they get, and any man can turn recruiting sergeant." Unlike in many of the cases reported in Irish newspapers and by the British government, Cummins was happy with his decision to enlist and suggested that his father in Ireland consider

By the Lord Lieutenant of Ireland.

CARLISLE.

WHEREAS, in and by Her Majesty's Royal Proclamation, published in the *London Gazette*, on the *Fourteenth* day of *May*, 1861, Her Majesty declared her Royal determination to maintain a strict and impartial neutrality in the contest between the Government of the United States of America and the States styling themselves the Confederate States of America, and Her Majesty did thereby charge and command all Her loving Subjects to observe a strict neutrality in and during the hostilities between the said States, and to abstain from violating or contravening either the Laws and Statutes of the Realm in that behalf, or the Law of Nations in relation thereto, as they would answer to the contrary at their peril.

AND Her Majesty did also thereby warn all Her loving Subjects, and all Persons whatever entitled to Her protection, that if any of them should presume in contempt of that Her Royal Proclamation, and of Her high displeasure, to do any acts in derogation of their duty as Subjects of a Neutral Sovereign in the said contest, or in violation or contravention of the Law of Nations in that behalf—as for example, and more especially [amongst] other things—by entering into the Military Service of either of the said contending parties, as Commissioned or Non-Commissioned Officers or Soldiers—all persons so offending would incur and be liable to the penalties and penal consequences by the Statute of the Fifty-ninth year of the Reign of His late Majesty King George the Third, intituled "An Act to prevent the enlisting or "engagement of His Majesty's Subjects to serve in Foreign Service, and the fitting out or equipping in His Majesty's Dominions Vessels "for Warlike purposes without His Majesty's License," or by the Law of Nations in that behalf imposed or denounced.

AND WHEREAS there is reason to believe that many of Her Majesty's Subjects have been induced to go and embark from various parts of the United Kingdom to the United States of America, by false and delusive promises of Employment upon Railway and other Public Works, in the said United States, and of high and greatly remunerative Wages for their Labor in such Employment, and have after their arrival in the said United States been further induced to enter into the Military Service of the said States, and to serve therein as Soldiers against the said Confederate States of America, contrary to their own original intention, and in contempt of Her Majesty's said Royal Proclamation.

THESE are therefore to warn all such Persons against the risk and danger which they may incur by accepting offers of Employment as Laborers in the said United States of America, whereby they may be entangled in Military Service in the said contest, between the said United States and the said Confederate States of America, contrary to their own original intention and in contempt of Her Majesty's said Royal Proclamation.

And that all Persons who may by entering, under the circumstances aforesaid, into the said Military Service, act in violation and contravention of their duty as Subjects of Her Majesty, and of the Law of Nations in relation thereto, will incur and be liable to the several Penalties and Penal consequences by the said Statute, or by the Law of Nations in that behalf imposed or denounced, and will also, by such misconduct, incur Her Majesty's high displeasure.

Dated at *Dublin Castle*, the *Twenty-fifth* day of *June*, 1861.

By His Excellency's Command,

THOS. A. LARCOM.

DUBLIN: Printed by GEORGE & JOHN GRIERSON, Printers to the Queen's Most Excellent Majesty.

Proclamation by the Lord Lieutenant of Ireland, 12 June 1864. Courtesy of National Archives of Ireland. Photograph reproduction courtesy William F. Ural, M.D., Toad Hall Photography, Southport, NC.

doing this as well. He insisted that his family should not believe reports that Irishmen can be forced to serve in the Union Army. As Cummins explained, "It is a good thing that you cannot be forced to do anything here: and as for forcing us to [en]list, no one could do it, except you were a citizen, and then you would be subject to the draft, and you must be three years in the country before that can be done." The financial incentives were excellent, Cummins added, reminding them that he had received an enlistment bounty of $627 dollars, of which he received four hundred dollars immediately and would earn the rest in his salary in two-month installments. While admitting that inflation was terrible, Cummins encouraged his family to come to America, where his father could "feed himself for 3 dollars a week, and contrary to what I was always let to believe, the men work twice as easy here than at home." "Dear father," he explained, "if you were living once here you would get 4 dollars a month from the State [for enlisting], and if I had a wife and family they would get 12 dollars a month beside my 83 dollars pay & bounty. So you see it is not like the English service." Cummins never indicated any faith in the Union cause or understanding of the issues of the American Civil War. For him, enlistment was clearly an economic decision, and he hoped that "if the war is finished this summer, I can claim my discharge and the remainder of my bounty besides running a chance of confiscated lands down South: & then I will send over the whole family."[40]

Indeed, Catholic communities in Ireland took pride in their boys who outsmarted "Yankee crimping crews" or agents employed to secure enlistments for particular units. Sometimes this was done legally through attractive bounty offers, and sometimes it was done illegally through false financial promises and kidnapping. A popular Irish ballad of this period addressed the concerns of Irish communities and the pride they took in outsmarting the "crimpers." Entitled "The Glorious Victory of Seven Irishmen over the Kidnappers of New York," the song tells of a New York recruiting agent who buys round after round of drinks for young men and then announces, " 'You're listed now as soldiers to defend our country.' " The surprised young men hoped to clarify the situation, explaining, " 'It's not to list that we did come unto America, / But to labour for a livelihood as many done before.' " In the end, the young men defeat the agent and his crew in a brawl, but the popular ballad addresses the concerns felt in Ireland about young men with no ties to the United States being tricked into military service or surrendering to the dire economic straits in which corrupt agents placed them. While they took pride in stories of young Irishmen besting the "crimpers," the concern was real in Ireland and among Irish-American communities in the United States.[41]

Indeed, as the fighting renewed that spring Irish-American spirits on the home front and the battlefield were wavering. During the battles of the Wilderness, Spotsylvania Courthouse, and Cold Harbor in Virginia in the spring of 1864, the Irish Brigade lost over one thousand officers and men, nearly one-third of its renewed strength.[42] Similarly high losses thinned the ranks of the Irish Legion, comprised of the four New York regiments that Michael Corcoran had organized in the fall of 1862. In June 1864, Colonel Patrick Kelly, who had commanded the Irish Brigade at Gettysburg, was shot through the head and fell mortally wounded before Petersburg. He had been with the brigade since the beginning of the

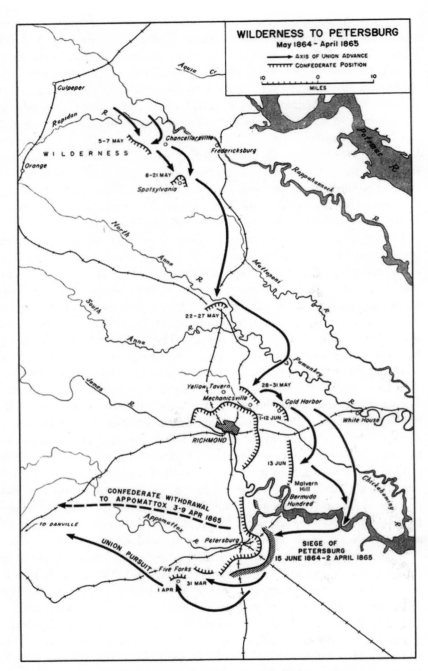

The Battle of the Wilderness through the Fall of Petersburg, May 1864–April 1865. *American Military History* (Washington: Center for Military History, 1989), 268.

war and upon hearing of his death, Irish papers reported that "strong old veteran soldiers wept like children, and wrung their hands in fury."[43] Also killed was Irish-born Captain B. S. O'Neill, who had come to America when the war began "for the sole purpose of joining the Irish Brigade."[44]

At home, the New York *Irish-American* informed its readers of the despair spreading through the ranks, quoting the sentiments of one soldier that his unit "was a Brigade no longer." It appeared that soon the Irish Brigade would exist only in the "recollection[s] of its services and sufferings."[45] As Irish-born St. Clair Mulholland, commander of the 116th Pennsylvania, explained, the losses were so great that "the Irish Brigade was commanded by a captain. Six of the ten field officers who had started with the campaign on May 5th [1864] had been killed and the other four severely wounded."[46]

Due to these drastic losses, the regiments of the brigade were temporarily consolidated into battalions and placed under new command. Many Irishmen considered this yet another "ungracious and ungenerous" act flying in the face of their devoted service.[47] Unfortunately, so many of their officers had died that few could plead the case for the retention of an Irish Brigade composed of Irishmen. Their plight finally came to the attention of Colonel Robert Nugent and several other officers. Their efforts secured the existence of the original three New York regiments in the Irish Brigade for the remainder of the war, though the 28th Massachusetts and the 116th Pennsylvania were assigned to the First Division's 1st and 4th brigades, respectively, and sadly parted ways with their old comrades. Many of the men who replenished the Irish Brigade lacked the determination and experience of many of the Irishmen who had joined the unit two years earlier with ideological rather than economic motivations, and it would be increasingly difficult for the Irish Brigade of 1864 to maintain its superb record. That spring recruits comprised 80 percent of the brigade and it would continue this dependence on a heavy percentage of inexperienced troops for the duration of the war.

Similarly, it suffered from so frequently losing its commanders in combat. Leadership of the brigade shifted from Thomas A. Smyth from March to May 1864, then to Richard Byrnes until he fell mortally wounded leading the Irish Brigade at the Battle of Cold Harbor in June. Colonel Patrick Kelly, who had led the men at the Battle of Gettysburg, resumed command of the Irish Brigade until he, too, fell mortally wounded days later at Petersburg, Virginia. Leadership of the Consolidated Brigade fell to Major Richard Morony and then Major John W. Byron. After Confederate forces captured Byron during the battle of Reams' Station in August 1864 it looked like the unit might be finally and completely disbanded. But new recruits continued to pour in from New York and by November

Colonel Richard Byrnes, commander of the Irish Brigade from May 1864 until his death at the Battle of Cold Harbor. Photo courtesy of U.S. Army Military History Institute. Photograph research/reproduction courtesy Lynn L. Libby, Enola, PA, 2005.

1 an old friend arrived with them. Colonel Robert Nugent was one of the original members of the Irish 69th New York State Militia, but his role enforcing the Conscription Act resulted in outrage from some Irish-Americans during the draft riots. Nugent seems to have reclaimed some of his lost honor, at least among the veterans of the Irish Brigade, by recruiting enough men to have the unit reconstituted in November 1864, with the original three New York regiments mustering 856 enlisted men, and later joined by the Irish 28th Massachusetts and the 7th New York Heavy Ar-

tillery. Nugent would also bring some stability to the unit, remaining as its commander through the end of the war. Still, it would never again be the same fighting force that had made the unit's reputation from Bull Run to Gettysburg.[48]

While these events unfolded in camp and on the battlefields during the campaign season of 1864, on the home front that year the sentiments of most Irish-Americans were increasingly depressed and frustrated. In April, Charles Halpine, creator of the famous fictitious Irish soldier Miles O'Reilly, penned a memorial marking the third anniversary of the organization of the 69th New York. Capturing the mood in "April 20, 1864," Halpine wrote,

> Of the thousand stalwart bayonets
> Two hundred March today
> Hundreds lie in Virginia Swamps
> And hundreds in Maryland clay
> And other hundreds less happily drag
> Their shattered limbs around.[49]

Similar sentiments were expressed in popular songs about Irish soldiers. In "Parody of When This Cruel War Is Over," an Irish soldier mocks the popular war song "When This Cruel War Is Over." The original version tells of a young woman recalling how she first met her hero

General Robert Nugent and staff in the vicinity of Washington, DC, June 1865. Courtesy of the Library of Congress. Photograph research/reproduction courtesy Lynn L. Libby, Enola, PA, 2005.

who volunteered for war, tells of how she misses and fears for him, but emphasizes her belief that he must continue the fight. Mocking the patriotic tale, "Parody of When This Cruel War Is Over" has an Irishman recall when he first impressed his sweetheart at a party. All in attendance envied him "[w]hin they saw my great big bounty / In Green-Backs, all new." As the Irishman leaves New York, however, he sees the excitement of a bounty's wealth and heroics fading: "But now me drame of glory's over / I'm home sick, I fear / I'd give this world for a substitute / To take my place here." The Irish version does not close with the understanding that civilians and soldiers alike must see this war through to victory. It only mentions the hardships of life in camp and on the battlefield, and the fear that the veteran will be betrayed at home when his love forgets him and embraces those who avoided service and stayed at home.[50]

Countless other Irish-American poems and songs complained of nativist prejudice and the injustice of the war. In the popular ballad "What Irish Boys Can Do. Answer to: No Irish Need Apply," Irishmen responded to advertisements excluding Irish workers. The lyrics spoke of Irish heroism in Europe and America, of Irish poets and fighters, but especially of the Irish "in the present war between the North and South." Listing the service of the 69th New York, Meagher, and other Irish-Americans, it asked, "Then, why slur upon the Irish? Why are they treated so? What is it you have against them? . . . Why insult them with the words: No Irish Need Apply?"[51]

In 1864, frustration also appeared among some of the more devoted Irish-American leaders. In the Midwest, for example, General James Mulligan, commander of the Irish 23rd Illinois, complained shortly before his death at the Battle of Kernstown in July 1864, "our cause is gloomy; we will conquer the South about the time the Jews all return to Jerusalem!"[52] Similar complaints came from men serving with Mulligan, requesting that the Irishman stand up for the Irish Catholics in his ranks or seeking permission to transfer to his command. Charges of nativist prejudice, the inspiration behind their requests, surfaced as early as December 1861. One of these came from Captain R. T. Farrell, commander of Mulligan's Chasseurs, 15th Illinois. In the first year of the war, he had written to Mulligan, then commander of that regiment, to report on the progress of the Chasseurs, noting that "we are progressing pretty well." He complained, however, that Illinois Governor Richard Yates "told me and others, long ago, that he would not interfere in the selection of field officers, but I think he is ready to help some of his friends to the position of Colonel. If so, he will find everything but peace." What particularly angered Farrell was not just the fact that Yates did this, but that qualified Irish

Catholics were kept from promotions and assignments due to nativist prejudice. He argued,

> We have presented the name of Captain James McBride, a gentleman of military experience, of American birth, a Catholic and a representative of our American-Franco population for Colonel. He is of Irish descent. Blain [an officer in the 15th Illinois], I think will throw him overboard on account of his religion, as he is an inveterate enemy of Catholicism. Let him do so and to the dogs with his bigotry and the powers that tolerate such accursed intermeddling. We shall have our way or we shall leave.[53]

A few months later, similar reports had arrived from First Lieutenant Gerald B. Walsh, of Company K, 24th Missouri Volunteers, and Captain T. C. Fitzgibbon, commander of Company A, 14th Michigan Infantry. In January 1862, Walsh requested a transfer for himself and his men, nearly all of them Irish Catholics, to Mulligan's command. They asked this, Walsh explained, in part because, as Irishmen, they had nothing in common with the native Missourians in their ranks. More importantly, though, and "paramount to all, we have no chaplain, and this at a time when the exigencies of the service may altogether preclude the possibility of attendance at the Roman Catholic place of worship."[54] By February 1862, Mulligan receive a similar charge from Captain Fitzgibbon of the 14th Michigan, who requested a personal transfer to Mulligan's command because the "regiment is incompletely officered, and to go to battle under them is <u>certain disgrace and death.</u> Besides, they are <u>partially American</u> and bigotedly Protestant. In almighty God's name, if you can possibly do it, get us transferred to you, where we can be with and amongst our own people."[55]

Matters had not improved much by 1863 and 1864. Mulligan continued to receive word, not only of Irishmen's discomfort serving with native-born Protestants but also of more serious charges of prejudice against Irish Catholics serving in his "Irish Brigade" and those serving elsewhere in the Midwest. In early February 1863, Mulligan received another report from R. T. Farrell, insisting that "an Irishman, particularly a Catholic, has a devilish hard road to tread when not in an Irish regiment." Two days later, Irishman Sergeant Major M. W. Toale of the 65th Illinois informed Mulligan that he had been up for a number of well earned promotions endorsed by his commanders, but a higher ranking official always managed to stop him, and Toale suspected it was due to his Irish heritage. He asked Mulligan to "bring me to a regiment where 'nationality' will [not] debar a 'brave man' from holding the position [he] merits, and where '35 miles of water' will no longer separate me from the fellowship of my brother soldiers."[56]

A similar, though more biting, account arrived that March from Private Peter Casey of Mulligan's own 23rd Illinois Volunteers. Casey heard that Mulligan might transfer his command and leave the regiment. This, Casey insisted, would be disastrous for the morale and general protection of the Irishmen serving with him. They would do anything Mulligan ordered, but without him, they would fall apart. Similarly, without him he feared Irish-Americans would never receive the credit due them for their brave sacrifices in the war. It was becoming a cause and conflict he could not support. As Casey explained,

> Black abolitionism is potent in our times. They will not give us a chance of that kind, [and] others not worthy of confidence will fill the high places which is about all they want or care for. The Negro and not the welfare of the country is what most engrosses their minds and perhaps when all is over they will turn their attention to the burning of convents and churches as they have done before.

In the end, Casey prophesized,

> The Irish Catholic so bravely fighting for the country will get no thanks when peace will be proclaimed. This has been always the case heretofore and we need not expect anything better for the time to come. The enemies of our race and religion are numerous everywhere, yet we take a prominent part in the welfare and prosperity of the country. Take the Irish, for instance, from the Army of this Union and this war perhaps will last for fifty years to come. There is not honesty nor bravery enough in the balance to do good fighting. They would reap all the credit and secure to themselves the high places and all the emoluments no matter how it is attained. Let the Irish then do the fighting; we want all the credit.[57]

Increasing numbers of Irish-Americans shared Mulligan's men's attitude, which helped to create a growing antiwar, anti-Lincoln, and anti-Republican sentiment on the home front. Then, just as Irish-Americans in the Northeast complained of signs of anti-Irish Catholic hiring practices and midwestern Irish soldiers' complaints revealed years of anti-Irish bigotry, similar charges of prejudice came from the Irish civilians of the Midwest.

In March 1863, Irish-Americans in Dubuque, Iowa, had reported that the city's Ladies Aid Society refused to aid the wives of Irish Catholic soldiers. When challenged on this policy, the Protestant-dominated organization explained that Irish Catholic widows "had best look to Catholics now for assistance." Journalists uncovered reports that Ladies Aid Society members "insulted . . . and sneered" at Irish Catholics who came to them for help, and many of the Irish women pledged that they would rather go without than receive such harassment.[58]

That same month arguments erupted between native-born and Irish immigrant wives in Tower Hill, Illinois. When Irish Catholic Elizabeth Millican proclaimed that Abraham Lincoln was "black as hell in principle, Jeff Davis was fit to rule over the north, and if [Illinois] Governor Yates sent soldiers to pick up deserters, she hoped 'the soldiers would get their devilish black Brains beat out,'" the community was shocked. When her native-born neighbor Hannah Throne threatened to report Millican to Union military officials, Millican's friend Mary Ann Spahr threatened that, if Throne did, she "would soon be under the sod."[59]

By February 1864, pro-Union Protestant advocates in Mount Pleasant, Iowa, took action into their own hands to eliminate the Irish Catholic influence in their community. Targeting a Catholic parish fair, Protestant activists destroyed what they could around the fair grounds and then addressed the gathered Irish crowd, "damning the Irish with horrible oaths, calling them Secesh, traitors, and every other offensive appellation." The mob's leader was Thomas W. Newman, former probate judge and Baptist Union Army chaplain. As the horrified Irish Catholics looked on, Newman warned *that every Catholic priest and Bishop in America prepare very soon to lose their heads.*[60]

Similar examples of anti–Irish Catholic prejudice appeared in the Northeast as well. By the fall of 1864, Irish papers were filled with reports of various anti-Irish and anti-Catholic actions taken by portions of the native-born population against the Irish in America. The Boston *Pilot* reported that New York's *Rochester Democrat* was publishing slanderous remarks about the Irish. In particular, *Rochester Democrat* editor Robert Carter claimed that "the most ultra, the most rancorous of the Copperhead presses, those which give tone and character to the party, and most fully and openly express its opinions and tendencies are controlled by Irishmen." He continued with an explanation blaming Irish-Americans. Too many Irishmen, he argued, feared African-Americans, "of whom they naturally feel jealous, because they feel themselves to be socially nearly on his level, and are therefore morbidly anxious about his claims to equality." Furthermore, the *Rochester Democrat* explained, Irish Copperheads suffer from an illogical hatred of Protestants. Proof of this, he argued, could be found in their frequent attacks on Protestant churches, clergy, and everything from the New England area in general, which the Irish believe unduly influenced the actions of the nation. Finally, he claimed that Irish criticisms of Lincoln and the war were rooted in their "atrocious abusiveness and personalities." Much of this, Carter explained, was due to "the innate vulgarity of the tribe, and to its imperfect education and entire ignorance of the habits and modes of thought and discussion that prevail among gentlemen." The *Rochester Democrat* warned its readers that "wherever you find a peculiarly virulent [Copperhead] journal . . . you may be sure an Irishman is at work upon it."[61]

Irish leaders in Boston challenged this. The *Pilot* argued that it was true that large numbers of Irish-Americans opposed the Lincoln administration and his reelection that fall, but this was due to their great loyalty to the nation. The Irish challenged Lincoln, the *Pilot* explained, "because they desire to see the Union re-established, peace and prosperity return to bless the land once more, and the Constitution to be restored over all," and they did not believe that Lincoln could accomplish this.[62]

But as Irish community leaders spoke out against the war, increasing numbers of native-born Americans had trouble seeing the Irish as loyal and patriotic. Peace Democrat Irishmen, who called for an immediate end to the war even if it meant a permanent division of the United States, included outspoken New Yorkers Richard O'Gorman and Daniel Devillin. Leading native-born Americans viewed them as an internal threat to the country. John Mullaly, Irish-American editor of the *Metropolitan Record,* sympathized with Peace Democrats and used his paper to condemn the draft, emancipation, and the entire Republican-led war effort as a complete failure that would result in "five hundred thousand more victims to abolitionism." In 1864, Mullaly was arrested and imprisoned on charges of "incendiary, disloyal, and traitorous" acts.[63]

Some Irishmen had feared this result of Irish complaints about the Union war effort. In December 1863, First Lieutenant Thomas F. Wildes contacted Mulligan to emphasize the importance of educating those in Ireland, many of whom would become Irish-Americans, about the Union cause or else all Irish-Americans would face the results: a lasting reputation of the Irish as cowardly, dishonest, and unworthy members of the Union. By 1864, this had already happened, though it was building on years of nativist prejudice. As Christmas 1863 approached, Wildes had warned Mulligan,

> You have doubtless, with me, read the letter of General Thomas Francis Meagher to the editor of the <u>Irishman</u>, Dublin, with great pleasure. But [Irish nationalist William] Smith O'Brien saw fit to come out in a strong denunciatory letter against General Meagher in which he takes the high ground that the South is right in this contest, and in which he cries <u>"shame"</u>! at all Irishmen who have taken up arms in the Union cause. . . . My main object in writing you is to urge you to endeavor by your influ-

ence to induce General Meagher and other distinguished Irishmen, and without intending any "blarney"—yourself included—to sustain a correspondence with the Irishman and other Irish newspapers, that would tend to educate Irish sentiment as regards the true nature of this contest.

It will result in far more harm to the Irishman to come here with false impressions and false notions of our institutions than it will the American. It is already manifesting itself, and unless Irishmen are led to believe different things than Smith O'Brien and others in Ireland, and John Mitchel —somewhere else—would make them believe, they will land in this country, thousands yearly, open enemies of the North and its free institutions, "copperheads" ready made, and thus give a strong pretext for their enemies to rail against them. . . . For Irishmen to come here with the notion, or to entertain the notion at home, that the south is right in this context and the North wrong will result in far more injury to Irishmen than to any one else. They can be taught as well correctly as incorrectly. And there are plenty of their countrymen here [to] whom they will listen as patiently as Smith O'Brien or any Jeff Davis emissary in Ireland.

Wildes suggested that a "National Convention of Irishmen," organized to meet at Chicago or elsewhere that winter of 1863, would be an excellent way to show Irish support for the war and to promote a pro-Union view among the Irish in America and Ireland.[64]

Despite the efforts of Irish officers like Wildes, native papers and official military reports carried an increasing number of cases reporting the poor quality of Irish-American soldiers at the front by late 1863 and 1864. Native-born commanders, formerly full of praise for Irish volunteers, now had few positive comments about the newly arrived Irishmen. The "new" Irish-American soldier, volunteer or draftee, damaged the reputation of the brave Irish soldier and contributed to an increasingly popular caricature of the Irish as ignorant, selfish, and lazy. Few of these men had ideological motivations like those that inspired the service of the young Irishmen who had marched down Great Jones Street in New York City to secure the nation's capital in 1861 or rushed to fill the ranks of Mulligan's Irish Brigade in Chicago. Many of these new Irish soldiers were new immigrants with few, if any, ties to America and served largely for the financial incentives. This was the case not only in the Irish Brigade but also in units like Corcoran's old Irish Legion. The Irish veterans, many of whom had volunteered in the beginning of the war, were excellent, but by the spring of 1864 most of the men were fresh recruits who lacked the ideological fervor that had once inspired the men of the Irish Brigade and Irish Legion.

Following the Battle of Spotsylvania, for example, Irish-born Colonel

Mathew Murphy reported that he could account for sixteen hundred of his men, but "the remainder . . . [were] drunk on the road."[65] After the Battle of Reams' Station in August 1864, Brigadier General Francis C. Barlow, commanding the 1st Division of the Army of the Potomac, complained that when he ordered the Irish Brigade to fill a break in the line during the battle, the Irishmen "behaved disgracefully and failed to execute my orders. They crowded off to our right into the shelter of some woods, and there became shattered and broken to pieces."[66] While there were few impressive performances among all Federal forces engaged at Reams' Station, the poor performance of the Irish Brigade demonstrates the results of the changing dynamic in the motivation and performance of Irish-American soldiers, from largely ideologically to predominantly economically motivated troops, in the final year of the war.

Accusations of large-scale Irish-American desertion surfaced throughout the fall. In November 1864 one federal investigation concluded that new Irish recruits to the famous 69th New York had deserted and given information to Confederates that led to a raid and capture of hundreds of Union officers and men.[67] Such actions by Irish substitutes, conscripts, and bounty men did little to counter the image of the Irish that was being shaped on the home front through riots, protests, and antiwar news editorials.

Just as the reports of increasingly poor conduct among Irish-American soldiers appeared, news of continued anti-Catholic prejudice within the army surfaced as well. In the fall of 1864, the *New York Herald* and the Boston *Pilot* reported that Catholic soldiers in the Union Army were being prevented from seeing Catholic priests, barred from receiving the last rites, and subjected to other attacks upon their faith. In September, Irish-Americans in Boston and New York read the story of a Catholic soldier whose dying wish to see a priest was repeatedly denied, despite his desperate condition. According to reports, the dying soldier explained that he had motherless children who would soon be orphans, and he wished to entrust his earnings to a priest who would see to their financial security. The soldier argued, "I earnestly desire, and have the right to have, the attendance of a Catholic priest and the consolations of the holy religion in which I was born, reared and desire to die." Adding, "I fought and bled under Gen. McClellan and have been a faithful soldier and citizen of the United States," the soldier demanded "to be treated accordingly." Unfortunately, by the time the attendants finally sent for a priest, the soldier had died. The *New York Herald* then reported that a hospital official robbed the dead Irishman in the presence of other officials, who made no effort to stop him. The body was taken to a Protestant cemetery and buried without ceremony. "Is this the time," asked the *Herald,* "if at all, to behave so to Irish Catholic soldiers?" referring to their years of service and perhaps more subtly to the upcoming election.[68]

The *Herald,* a press with strong Democratic party leanings but run by native-born Americans, may have been reporting accurately, or perhaps it was simply stirring up readers in preparation for the fall presidential elections. It could have been expressing genuine frustration over such violations of an immigrant soldier's freedoms, indicating that at least some native-born Americans were interested in protecting the rights of Irish Catholics, or the story may have been politically motivated to agitate Irish Catholic Democratic voters in the final weeks of the presidential campaign of 1864. While the story sounds tragic, three weeks later Boston's Irish *Pilot* published a subsequent letter from U.S. Army surgeon William J. Sloan recounting an official army investigation into the soldier's story that found it to be entirely false, nothing but an angry hoax devised by a disgruntled hospital employee. It is unclear, however, whether the *Pilot* accepted these findings. It merely printed the letter with an editorial noting that the paper was forced to print it under the orders of Major General John A. Dix, commander of the Department of the East.[69] Whether the *Herald* or the *Pilot* believed the official challenge to this story or not, there was enough anti-Catholicism throughout the North and in the Union Army to convince readers that it could be true.

There were some Irish soldiers who remained determinedly faithful to the Union cause despite the antiwar trend in their northern communities by 1864, but most Irish Catholics were losing their faith in this cause. Within the broad Irish Protestant and Catholic community in the United States, however, many Protestant Irishmen and Scots Irish continued to support the war. Like much of the native-born North, by the summer and fall of 1864, and especially after the fall of Atlanta, Georgia, convinced northerners that they could win this war, Irish Protestants maintained or renewed their faith in President Lincoln and the way he directed the war. Irish-born Protestant Abraham Irvine is an excellent example of this. In the summer of 1864, he missed his family, their farm, and Ireland. He saw himself as "a stranger in a strange land" but was determined to continue to fight. Irvine took pride in the facts that he was an Irish-born officer in charge of American troops and that he earned his command of Company E, 76th Illinois Volunteer Infantry Regiment, through dedicated service in "twenty two hard contested battlefields."

Writing to his brother Joseph on June 4, Abraham Irvine was surrounded by the bloody carnage of the battle of Cold Harbor, a battle so horrific that commanding generals Robert E. Lee and Ulysses S. Grant were negotiating the process of removing the overwhelming number of dead and suffering wounded from the field before resuming the fight.

Abraham Irvine, an Irish-born Protestant Union officer. Rank and unit unknown. Courtesy of William and Ruth Irvine, who still live and work on the family farm called "The Hollow" in Keadymore where Abraham Irvine was born and of which he writes in his letter. Photograph reproduction courtesy Irvine Collins, Kissimmee, Florida.

Despite this, Irving insisted that the United States was "the best government that the world ever knew," and pledged,

> Let this proud flag now waving by my tent door be restored to those domes & spires from which treason has ruthlessly & wickedly dragged it, then let that nation tremble whose heart has devised mischief against

"The Land of the free & the home of the brave," with her million brae dauntless and disciplined Army & her Iron Navy. Let despotism everywhere tremble and they who would be free rejoice.

Irvine's family never heard from him again and presumed that he died in the fighting around Richmond, Virginia, in that final year of the war.[70]

While Abraham Irvine continued to maintain his strong faith in the Union cause, Irish-born Catholic John O'Neill simply hoped to survive. He appears to have disobeyed his parents and viewed his service as a form of penance. "Mother it is hard marching, some days & nights 25 and 30 miles through rivers and woods, lying on the bare ground with nothing to cover you but the sky, but enough of that, I deserve it all and more." O'Neill seems to have offended his father in particular: "I suppose Mother, my father does not forgive me yet or else he would write to me, but I cannot help it. I hope he will write to me." There is no mention of the reason behind the fighting or why he continued, only the hope that he would survive. He asked friends to "think of me in their prayers for me, for I need them all for God knows the state I am in and I need all their prayers."[71] The family never heard from John O'Neill again and deduced from other information that he died in the famous Confederate prison at Andersonville. Their one consoling thought came from a Francis Fowler of the U.S. Sanitary Commission, who told the O'Neills that a Roman Catholic priest was present at Andersonville who would have administered to their son daily and at his death.[72]

Irish-American resentment of the Lincoln administration and the Union war effort came to a head during the presidential campaign that year. For months the Irish Catholic press had been supporting Lincoln's challenger and former Army of the Potomac commander, George B. McClellan. The Lincoln administration, the *Pilot* warned, embarked upon "strides of despotism . . . so rapid and gigantic, that we had almost begun to tremble for the liberties of our country." Under the Republicans, they argued, "arbitrary arrests seemed to have paralyzed the people . . . [in a] sullen submission to the imperial will of 'one too powerful man.'" Thankfully, Boston's Irish leaders sighed, a challenger had arisen in the form of George McClellan.

The *Pilot* argued that McClellan's failures as a general were not his own, but rather the results of a jealous Lincoln administration that had long sought to restrain him. Lincoln and the Republicans had tried "to crush him by removing him from the [Army of the Potomac], which has suffered nothing but disaster since McClellan's retirement." Then, the *Pilot* argued, "he was removed because he did not carry out the biddings of the destructives" and failed "to convert the war into a scene of extermination, lit by the glare of burning cities, and horrified by the desolation of sovereign states." What had such actions done for the nation, the Irish press asked?

> The fourth year of the war finds our currency deranged; the necessaries of life at such fabulous figures, that starvation almost impends over the heads of the masses; the good will of Europe gone; our foreign credit far less than that of the Confederates; and above all, it presents the edifying picture of an agrarian sentimental policy which seeks to exalt a degraded, inferior race into equality with the white race, and to tear down personal security and property, the Corinthian pillars of Constitutional liberty.[73]

As the election approached, Irish-Americans read of continuing anti-Irish and anti-Catholic actions by leading northern officials. Despite increasing Irish complaints regarding official army mistreatment of Catholic clergy and the destruction of church property in conquered southern cities, such actions continued in the fall of 1864. The *Pilot* expressed outrage that Brigadier General Mason Brayman, commander of U.S. forces in Natchez, Mississippi, had suspended an area bishop and taken possession of and closed nearby Catholic churches. The editors saw these actions as yet another sign of the Lincoln administration's support of "open and unprovoked infraction of the guarantees of the civil constitution, and an outrageous, unauthorized, audacious, inexcusable and uncalled for aggression upon the Catholic Church."[74] A single newspaper cannot speak for an entire community, but the popularity of the *Pilot* indicated that such views were held by large portions of the Boston Irish-American community.

Accounts of the poor conditions of the troops contributed to this growing frustration. As Irish-born William Reese, living in Youngstown, Ohio, explained, "nearly all of [the veterans] was [sic] very ill [and] they say that Old Abe will never again be able to take them out of the State." Reese seemed to find a solution to these problems in the upcoming election. "I have no doubt but what you have heard ere this that General G. B. McClellan has been nominated for President by the Democratic Party," he explained, "and such an excitement exists [as] you ever saw. The Democratic Party . . . thinks Old Abe is now politically dead and his funeral will take place in November next. . . . But mortification has already set in. Scared of 'Little Mac.'" Reese's thoughts are significant as he is not Catholic but actually Irish Protestant and, as such, unusual in comparison to other Irish Protestants, particularly those from the Midwest.

Clearly, though, Reese despised Lincoln. In his final words to his family in Ireland, he shared a song set to the tune of "Yankee Doodle," promising his friend John, who had fought in the Civil War but since returned to Ireland, that "when you will return to this country you will sing a different Yankee doodle to what we used to sing." The title of this strongly anti-Lincoln, anti-abolition piece, William Reese explained, is "Commonly Called Abe Doodle":

Hurrah for our great President
The world never saw a bigger
In stature he is 6 feet 3,
And equal to a nigger
To tell a joke or split a rail
And write a Proclamation
We guess he is about a mile
A head of all Creation

Chorus:
Now Leaguers all for shoddy bawl
And Abe Doodle Dandy
And Each shall have a nigger wif
As sweet as sugar candy.

When first he went to the White House
He played a clever joke, Sir
By running off from Harrisburgh
In Scotchman's Cap & Cloak, Sir
Soon after that he made a Speech
The best all must agree, Sir
It was "I came to look at You
And you can look at me Sir!"

Chorus:
Now Leaguers all for Abe bawl
Together in a body
Let Union—Constitution slide
But give us Abe & Shoddy.

More than five 100 thousand men
He has butchered up in war, Sir
And for the wooly headed tribe
We'll kill as many more, Sir.
So let poor men as conscripts go
And leave their wives neglected,

Hurrah for Abraham the Great
He must be re elected.

Chorus:
Now Leaguers all for Greenbacks bawl
And Abe Doodle Dandy
And Each shall have a nigger wif
As sweet as Sugar Candy.[75]

While similar sentiments appeared in Irish-American newspapers and letters, other reports of mistreatment of Irish filled the papers. Stories continued to appear alleging that Irishmen were being tricked into immigrating to the United States so that economic difficulties would force them to enlist in the army. In September 1864, the *Pilot* published testimony given before the British Parliament that Irish citizens were still being tricked into immigrating to the United States on promises of profitable employment and then, finding none, enlisting in Union forces in desperation. The *Pilot* cited further evidence to prove that the U.S. political officials knew of such actions but did little to stop them and might even be encouraging them.[76]

One case described young Irishmen responding to an advertisement for employment in Canada. After meeting with the advertiser, the men paid for their passage from Ireland to Canada but nothing more, having been told that work would be easy to find and they would earn plenty of money to cover any immediate expenses. During the trip across the Atlantic, the men were surprised to learn that their destination was New York, not Canada, but the advertiser assured them that transport had been arranged for the final leg of their trip north of the border. When they arrived in New York, however, the advertiser took them to a tavern, paid for some of their food, explained that he had paid for a trip to Long Island, and then disappeared. Having no other funds, the young men used their tickets to travel to Long Island, only to find themselves isolated there, penniless and without friends. In desperation, two of the Irishmen enlisted immediately, while four others made their way back to Manhattan but then found themselves so impoverished that they, too, enlisted. The final member of the group snuck onto an English steamer and returned to Great Britain, where he reported their mistreatment at the hands of American advertisers, whom some British leaders suspected were American Army recruiters.[77]

As Irish Catholic opposition to the war grew and stories like this spread, the president himself took a position on immigrants and their role in the war. In his annual address to Congress in December 1863, Lincoln used his characteristic brevity to confront charges that innocent immigrants in America were being forced into military service. Many of them, Lincoln argued, had been exercising the rights of American citizens for years, faithfully casting their ballots in local, state, and national elections. When they were drafted into military service, however, they disavowed all previous claims of naturalization. The president proposed a law to make the act of voting prevent any plea for exemption on the grounds that the individual was not a citizen. Lincoln's speech illustrates the dual, and dueling, loyalties in Irish Catholic communities throughout the Civil War. When citizenship benefited them, many Irish-Americans claimed it. When it was to their disadvantage, however, some of these same immigrants tried to reject it.[78] And as the war continued, more and more were trying to avoid serving in a conflict they saw as more harmful than helpful to their communities in America and Ireland.

With that said, however, Lincoln called attention to the fact that there were cases in which foreigners had fallen victim to unscrupulous labor contractors and been tricked into military service. In these situations, the president believed the government needed to punish criminal recruiters and ensure the fair treatment of all persons, citizen or alien. After his re-election, Lincoln would further soften his position and clarify that while he strongly encouraged immigration, which served as "one of the principal replenishing streams which are appointed by Providence to repair the ravages of internal war," he opposed any by-product of this system that imposed involuntary military service on immigrants. Many Irish-Americans, however, insisted that Republicans saw the Irish as useful for nothing better "than being reduced to dust and being made food for gunpowder."[79]

As the presidential election of 1864 approached, Union Army victories dramatically increased Lincoln's chances for reelection. On the second of September, General William T. Sherman's forces finally ended their siege of Atlanta, Georgia, and took control of that Confederate stronghold. This victory was soon followed by Admiral David Farragut's celebrated naval victory in the Battle of Mobile Bay and General Philip Sheridan's successes in the Shenandoah Valley. Maria Daly sensed the changing political attitudes in New York City. By late September she was concerned over the growing support for Lincoln. "The events seem to have much lessened the chances of McClellan's success," Daly noted, "although it is not fair that it should be so, for he is as much for the preservation of the Union in its integrity as anyone of the nation."[80]

By August, the Democratic party had risen above its differences to unite behind former General George B. McClellan. Despite their efforts to present a single platform, infighting between the Peace and War factions continued. The party platform included a charge that, because the Lincoln administration had failed to restore the union during its bloody war effort, the demands of justice and humanity called for an immediate cessation of hostilities and meeting of all the states, North and South, to reach a peace compromise. When the party nominated McClellan, however, the War Democrats found him more supportive of their philosophy than outspoken exiled Peace Democrat Clement L. Vallandigham, who wrote the strong resolution for peace. In his acceptance letter, McClellan clarified this challenge to the peace plank, noting, "I both am and shall continue to be unpledged to any man except the real patriots of the land who value the 'Union' above all things on earth."[81] McClellan was not entirely opposed to the peace option. Indeed, he argued that an "honest and frank effort" should be made for peace. If such an effort failed to end the war with the Union reestablished, however, McClellan explained, "then I am of the belief that we must again resort to the dread arbitrament of war."[82] In taking this position, McClellan may have alienated himself from the most devoted Peace Democrats, but he made his candidacy far more attractive to many northern Democrats, who were hesitant to support peace at any cost.[83]

It was a compromise that many northern Democrats could publicly adopt without feeling disloyal to the soldiers in the field. A vote for McClellan, his Irish Catholic supporters in Boston argued, meant union and peace, "for the simple reason that, after his inauguration, the character of the war will have so changed that the southern people will no longer have a sufficient motive to stand out." With Lincoln defeated and his emphasis on abolition gone, the Confederacy "will then see that submission to the Union does not involve the overthrow of their institution, . . . and the nameless horrors of a servile war. . . . On the election of General McClellan . . . a peace party will spring up, as if by magic, in every part of the South."[84] Should this fail to appear, however, the Democratic party was ready to continue the war effort—a stance made clear in every Democratic pamphlet and newspaper across the country. Appealing to Americans as a whole, the Democrats argued, "whether you call yourselves Republicans, Whigs, or Democrats, sink party now deeper than plummet can sound, say good bye to by gones . . . and elect McClellan. . . . In the name of country vote for him!" Such a vote was for the restoration of the union "at all hazards . . . peacefully if we can, forcibly if we must."[85]

Such a policy was overwhelmingly popular among northern Irish-Americans. For those reluctant to join the position the *Pilot* and other papers had adopted earlier, calling for an immediate cessation of hostilities, McClellan's position was a perfect compromise. It allowed Irish-Americans to protest the Republican direction of a war they saw as costing too many Irish lives. Where they saw a trampling of civil rights in the Republican emphasis on abolition and the arrest of those protesting the war, Irish-Americans could vote for McClellan while also maintaining a position as loyal, patriotic Americans dedicated to Union.

As Boston's *Pilot* explained, those who criticized McClellan and the Democrats for their emphasis on peace were misinformed. The general and the party, Irish-American leaders explained, pledged that if elected they would make "immediate efforts for a cessation of hostilities," but only if it included reuniting the nation. Without an agreement on the restoration of the union, McClellan and the Democrats would not agree to peace.[86] Quite simply, the editors argued, "our Irish brethren, in very great numbers, are opposed to the re-election of Abraham Lincoln, because they desire to see the Union re-established, peace and prosperity return to bless the land once more, and the Constitution to be restored over all."[87]

While such reports may have united large numbers of Irish-Americans within the Democratic party, it did not quiet their resentment. In Pottsville, Pennsylvania, for example, Irish laborers, miners, and deserters protested not only their conditions in the mines but also the draft. Army officials witnessed the frustration of large elements of the Irish-American community in Schuylkill County, Pennsylvania, in October 1864 when four to five hundred deserters and drafted men refused to report for service. They attacked cavalry detachments attempting to arrest them, firing upon soldiers and then rushing into the safety of the thickly wooded hills. U.S. Army officers reported that they were predominantly Irish and claimed that they were committing various acts of violence, ranging from breaking into private homes to beating wounded soldiers. Occasionally the rioters would parade through the streets, destroying shops and residences. Officers noted that while Welsh, English, and German laborers were generally law abiding and had reported for service or secured a substitute when drafted, the Irish Catholics continued to resist and resort to violence. Other commanders, however, saw draft resistance and the mine protests as generally embraced by all Pottsville miners and argued, "The lower classes are given to understand by their leaders that the triumph of one political party will be the signal for a revolution [in] the North."[88]

As the fall elections approached, northern Irish-Americans confronted dramatic images of what they could expect from a victory of one candidate over the other. The *Pilot* informed Boston's Irish community that the election of George McClellan would herald a time of "Peace, the Union restored, the Constitution unimpaired; [and] the Constitutional rights of every one preserved." President Lincoln's reelection, however, would ensure suffering due to "[w]ar, fierce, bloody, long, disunion, the Constitu-

"The Chicago Platform," *Harper's Weekly*, October 15, 1864. Provided courtesy HarpWeek, LLC. Photograph reproduction courtesy William F. Ural, M.D., Toad Hall Photography, Southport, NC.

tion violated, Constitutional rights trampled upon, debt overwhelming and increasing, taxes burdensome, beggary, ruin and national death."[89]

Most Irish-Americans were not simply tricked into supporting the Democratic party. The Democrats had proven their loyalty to the Irish over the last several years of war. In New York City and its surrounding counties, Democrats had appropriated millions of dollars to the care of the city's Irish poor. New York's city council, for example, set aside $6 million to aid destitute families of Irish volunteers, caring for those whom many Irish believed would have died had it not been for Catholic, Irish, and Democratic organizations. As Irish-Americans discussed the fall elections, political leaders reminded them that it was the New York County Board of Supervisors that had provided $10 million in bonus money, allowing some volunteers to earn as much as seven hundred dollars upon their enlistment, while relieving the burden of the draft for those who remained opposed to military service. Not only did the Democrats provide similar support in other northern cities but they also appealed to the conservative nature of the Irish in America. The Democrats of the mid–nineteenth century emphasized the importance of individual rights and local control, and they remained sharply critical of reformers who sought to radically alter the racial structuring of American society.[90]

Unfortunately for the Irish, large numbers of native-born Americans saw Irish Democrats as ignorant immigrants who year after year sold their votes for services from the Democratic party. Irish Catholics were regarded as ignorant brutes who knew little better than to do as they were told, and their actions, leading native-born Americans argued, were threatening the very survival of the nation.

One month before the election, for example, *Harper's Weekly* ran an image by famous political cartoonist Thomas Nast entitled "The Chicago Platform." Nast used his skills to warn Americans of the Democratic platform and what it held for the nation if McClellan was elected. Nast's cartoon included caricatures of barefoot Irish children and their parents with apelike features beating victims in the streets while other Irishmen looked on with glee. The warning was that chaos would follow a McClellan victory.[91] Just one week before the election, another Nast cartoon appeared in *Harper's Weekly,* this one titled "Election Day." Nast contrasted Lincoln supporters as soldiers and respectable citizens with those who supported McClellan. The Democratic voter appeared as a filthy, ignorant, and impoverished Irish-American directed to the polls by a reporter from *The London Times,* a paper known for its Confederate sympathies.[92] Although more than 140,000 Irish-Americans were serving in the Union Army and Navy, no Irish-Americans were associated with soldiers and respectability in these images. Both cartoons were tremendously popular throughout the North among native-born Americans. Famous New York City diarist and Republican George Templeton Strong argued that the

Detail from "Election-Day," *Harper's Weekly*, November 12, 1864. Provided courtesy HarpWeek, LLC. Photograph reproduction courtesy William F. Ural, M.D., Toad Hall Photography, Southport, NC.

great weakness in the northern war effort was represented in the "Peace-Democrats, McClellan-maniacs, mere traders and capitalists, and the brutal herd of ignorant Celts and profligate bullies and gamblers and 'sporting men.'" As the election neared, he mocked a gathering of McClellan supporters as "hordes of Celts and rebel sympathizers" and "the liquor dealers, roughs, and brutal Irishy [sic] of the city."[93]

Republicans and large numbers of native-born Americans in general were not alone in criticizing Irish loyalty to the Democratic party. Even Irish nationalist Thomas Francis Meagher began to argue that the Irish were allowing themselves to "be bamboozled into being obstinate herds in the political field."[94] In some ways, Meagher and other critics seem to have had abundant evidence to support these charges.[95] Critics failed to recognize, however, that to many Irish-Americans party loyalty was one of the best methods for promoting their interests. Unfortunately, they were being loyal to the party associated with secession and slavery, an action northern Republicans more often saw as treason than as dissenting opinion. This contributed to the view of Irish-Americans as an ignorant and foolish people on whom the privilege of voting was wasted and whose presence was a threat to the security of the democratic system.[96]

Ironically, Abraham Lincoln and the Republicans had worked to reach out to the Irish and other immigrant laborers in the lower echelons of the Democratic party. Occasionally, however, leading Democratic newspapers twisted Lincoln's words to the point that it would have been better had he remained quiet. When the New York Workingmen's Democratic Republican Association made Lincoln an honorary member, for example, the president took the opportunity to address the common laborers of the North. "None are so deeply interested to resist the present rebellion as the working people," Lincoln argued, and because of this workers must "be aware of prejudice, working division, and hostility among themselves." Referring to the New York City draft riots of July 1863, Lincoln reminded his audience that those events included "the hanging of some working people by other working people. It should never be so. The strongest bond of human sympathy, outside of the family relation, should be uniting all working people, of all nations, and tongues, and kindreds."

Democratic newspapers across the North assailed the president's comments, charging that he had made claims of racial equality and supported miscegenation. New York's *Jeffersonian* argued that the president believed "our citizens of Irish birth are inferior to the negro and that they could be vastly improved by intermixture with the negro." The *Freeman's Journal and Catholic Register,* also in New York, expressed similar horror that the "beastly doctrine of the intermarriage of black men with white women" was being "openly and publicly avowed and endorsed and encouraged by the President of the United States."

Irish-Americans turned out in droves that fall to vote for McClellan.[97] In some areas of New York, including the heavily Irish Sixth Ward, McClellan received 90 percent of the vote, while the entire city went to McClellan with more than a two to one majority.[98] It was not enough. In terms of the popular vote, the election was fairly close, with the president earning just over 55 percent and only 350,000 more votes than he had won four years earlier in a four-way race. On the other hand, McClellan took only three states—New Jersey, Kentucky, and Delaware—with a devastating Electoral College loss of 212 to 21. In many crucial states, Democrats lost control of state legislatures, and they retained only one state governor, New Jersey's Joel Parker. Even New York Governor Horatio Seymour found himself out of power.[99]

Lincoln received strong support from Union soldiers. Never before had so many military men voted. Recent revisions to state constitutions had made this possible, and it had a significant impact on the election. Lincoln received 78 percent to McClellan's 22 percent of the soldier vote, whereas civilians voted 53 percent for Lincoln and 47 percent for McClellan. Most Irish-American Catholic soldiers supported McClellan, but not enough to give him the White House.[100]

The significance of Irish Catholics' support for McClellan and the Democrats' peace platform cannot be overstressed. It is true that Irish-American soldiers were not the only disillusioned troops in the Union Army in 1863 and 1864. Indeed, they had great company in the ranks and across the civilian home front. The majority of those northern civilians and soldiers, however, changed their mind in the fall of 1864 and decided that Lincoln was the man to lead them to victory. Irish Catholics, soldiers and civilians, did not. They remained consistent in their frustration with Lincoln and their opposition to his wartime policies.

McClellan's defeat was a defeat for the Irish, who would pay the price for years to come. Loyalty to Democrats meant opposition to Republicans, many of whom would not forgive or forget this when their party came to dominate the national leadership for the next two decades. That sense of betrayal culminated in President Lincoln's assassination on April 14, 1865, just five days after General Robert E. Lee surrendered his Army of Northern Virginia. For many Republicans, abolitionists, and African-Americans, Lincoln's death at the moment of his victory over slavery made him almost Christlike. Anyone who had criticized or challenged the martyred Lincoln seemed somehow partly responsible for his death.[101]

Despite the fact that the *Pilot,* the *Irish-American,* and other Irish news-papers mourned the loss of the president, prominent native-born Ameri-cans questioned the sincerity of Irish grief. George Templeton Strong reported that dozens of New York families had fired their "Celtic hand-maidens . . . for some talk of rejoicing at Abe Lincoln's death." Similar actions were seen at the city's Gramercy Park House where Irish wait-ers were dismissed "for blind, foolish, Celtic talk approving Lincoln's murder."[102]

With the Union victory, many northern Irish-Americans had little to celebrate. Despite the fact that over 140,000 Irish served in the Union forces, much of the native-born population in the years to come would focus instead on Irish-American participation in draft riots, outspoken criticism of a victorious administration, and unfailing support of the op-position party—the party of the South, secession, slavery, and defeat. A shadow of disloyalty would darken the Irish for years to come, and the history of Irish bravery, loyalty, and devotion to Union would remain bur-ied for decades.

Irish-Americans would preserve the role that Irish soldiers played in the Civil War within their own communities, celebrating the heroic feats of units like the 69th New York, the Irish 9th Massachusetts, and Mulligan's Irish Brigade. The men of the Irish Legion and the Irish 69th Pennsylvania would remember their brave fighting under Corcoran and O'Kane. But it would be years before Irish veterans resurrected the image of bravery and loyalty. In 1870, a British traveler noted the negative reputation that con-tinued to plague Irish-Americans, observing that "in no part of the world are the virtues of the Irish so little appreciated; . . . in no part is the name of Irishman a greater obstacle to a man's success" than in America.[103]

6

"Father Was a Soldier of the Union"

Irish Veterans and the Creation of an Irish-American Identity

During the American Civil War, Irish-Americans' support or criticism of the Union war effort revolved around its impact on their neighbors, their soldiers in the field, and their families in Ireland. As this perspective fueled their criticism of the Lincoln administration and led to declining enlistments by young Irish-American men, native-born Americans railed against them as being disloyal and ungrateful. Irish-Americans insisted that they were loyal citizens protecting their communities from the same prejudices they had faced since their arrival in the United States. In the postwar period they retained their strong sense of local unity and developed an increasingly powerful sense of autonomy in relation to the rest of the population. They came to realize that while their self-reliance led to criticism, it also provided new forms of influence in the United States. With this new power, and in response to the new waves of immigrants pouring into the country from southern and Eastern Europe, Irish-American Catholics would carve out a place for themselves within the nation and its history. There was no more powerful way to do this in postwar America than to clarify, within and outside their communities, their role in the defining American experience: the Civil War.[1]

Their early efforts to secure political power were made possible in large part by their increasing population in America in the late 1860s and early 1870s. By the postwar period, their numbers were so impressive and their practice of voting as a bloc so strong that Democratic politicians' success came to depend upon significant Irish Catholic support. That power was slowly acquired, however, and the Irish would continue to face poor economic conditions and countless social injustices. This reality drove home the lesson, however, of the importance of autonomy, and Irish-Americans

TABLE 6.1

Irish-born Populations in Major U.S. Cities, 1870

City (Ranked in Order of Largest Irish-born Population)	Total City Population	Total Irish-born City Population	Irish-born as Percentage of Total City Population
1. New York, NY	942,292	201,999	21%
2. Philadelphia, PA	674,022	96,698	14%
3. Brooklyn, NY	396,099	73,985	19%
4. Boston, MA	250,526	56,900	23%
5. Chicago, IL	298,977	39,988	5%
6. St. Louis, MO	310,864	32,239	6%
7. San Francisco, CA	149,473	25,864	7%
8. Cincinnati, OH	216,239	18,624	9%
9. Jersey City, NJ	82,546	17,665	21%
10. Albany, NY	69,422	13,276	19%
11. Pittsburgh, PA	86,076	13,119	15%
12. Newark, NJ	105,059	12,481	11%
13. Buffalo, NY	117,714	11,264	10%
14. Milwaukee, WI	71,440	9,784	13%
15. Lowell, MA	40,928	9,103	22%
16. Detroit, MI	79,577	6,970	15%
17. Rochester, NY	62,386	6,078	10%

SOURCE: Francis A. Walker, *The Statistics of the Population of the United States Embracing the Tables of Race, Nationality, Sex, Selected Ages, and Occupations. Compiled, from the Original Returns of the Ninth Census (June 1, 1870), Under the Direction of the Secretary of the Interior* (Washington: GPO, 1872), 386–91.

would learn to wield this newfound weapon with increasing expertise as the century continued.

This isolation, partly imposed on them and partly self-imposed, applied to Irish-American veterans as well and can be see in their limited involvement with traditional veterans' organizations. After the war, the largest and most popular northern veterans' group was the Grand Army of the Republic (GAR), but many Irish-Americans and other foreign-born and nonwhite, non-Protestant veterans formed their own organizations rather than join a GAR post. Most of the Irish Catholics who did join the GAR remained among veterans of a similar ethnic background rather than associating with members of different ethnic and religious backgrounds, which means they tended to belong to units and attend meetings in cities with large Irish-Catholic veteran populations.[2]

This division between Catholic veterans, dominated by Irish and Irish-Americans in the postwar period, and the GAR was the result of several factors. The Catholic Church discouraged its members from joining anti-clerical fraternal organizations requiring members to take oaths and participate in secret rituals. Church leadership saw the GAR as a Masonlike organization that weakened the laity's ties to the church and took actions to keep Catholic veterans out of the organization.[3] When GAR Post 51 of Philadelphia tried to bury a Catholic member with a GAR-directed service in 1871, for example, the archbishop prohibited the action. Three years later another confrontation occurred in Reading, Pennsylvania, when GAR members attending a veteran's funeral service in a Catholic Church refused to remove their GAR badges, leading the priests performing the service to bar the GAR members from the sanctuary and prevent them from joining the funeral procession. On Memorial Day 1882, another conflict erupted between the GAR and the Catholic Church in Milford, Massachusetts. GAR members placed flags at veterans' graves and became enraged when a priest removed the flags from Catholic gravesites and complained that the GAR was too influential in Catholic veterans' lives. In 1885, a similar confrontation occurred between the GAR and the Catholic clergy in Pottsville, Pennsylvania, and tensions increased between the Protestant and Catholic residents.[4]

The nature of the GAR discouraged Catholic veterans' involvement as well. White, native-born, Protestant veterans dominated the organization, and their practices reflected this. Protestant themes ran throughout their *Services* guidelines, all of the GAR chaplains-in-chief through the late 1880s and most of the following decades were Protestants, and Memorial Day services (the most important celebration of the year for the GAR) was celebrated nearly 100 percent of the time in Protestant churches. Even without pressure from the Catholic Church to avoid the GAR and its Masoniclike rituals, most Irish-Catholic veterans would not have felt comfortable or welcome in an organization with such a strong Protestant culture.[5]

Economic status also kept most Irish-American veterans from the prominent organization. There were some exceptions to this rule—with whole posts being comprised of industrial workers or farmers—but members and certainly those who held offices within the organization were middle- and upper-middle-class Americans. While GAR rules required that to become a member an individual only had to have served honorably in the Union Army, many posts came up with local criteria for membership that excluded some individuals. Some posts, for example, withheld membership or blackballed men who had served a year or less. If one did become a member, a man's wartime rank frequently influenced his position within the post, and veteran officers dominated GAR state and national offices as well. Thus officers came to dominate the organization while low-ranking enlisted men comprised the audience rather than leadership of the posts, and since the vast majority of Irish-Catholic soldiers were not officers, they fell into the lower ranks of these organizations if they chose to join them.[6]

Other tensions between the GAR leadership and Irish-American veterans relate to the industrialization of the United States in the late nineteenth century. The new economic system inspired a growing dissatisfaction among industrial workers, which included many Irish-Americans. During the railroad strikes of 1877, for example, the GAR commander-in-chief, John Robinson, insisted that while he supported justice and equal rights, the GAR was opposed to "every attempt at anarchy or insurrection." By the late 1880s, GAR members were offering their services to state governors to put down local strikes and acts of "anarchy." At the same time, a Union Army veteran and GAR member published a history of the Irish-dominated New York City draft riots, *The Volcano under the City*, as a warning of the labor chaos that could reemerge. GAR leaders and much of the GAR's membership expressed shock at the violence of the Pullman and Homestead Strikes and voiced support for management. While giving a glance to "the dignity of labor," the GAR routinely backed the suppression of labor violence and unions in general, discouraging many Irish-American veterans, who were frequently among the striking workers, from joining this group. Finally, the GAR leadership, as former officers and middle- or upper-middle-class businessmen and professionals, were usually Republicans. Most Irish-American Catholic veterans, on the other hand, belonged to the Democratic party, which was increasingly prolabor, and they had lower positions in the military and on the economic ladder. These increasingly Republican, military-officer and pro-management tendencies of the GAR further discouraged Irish-American veterans from joining.[7]

When Irish-Americans did join veterans' organizations, they frequently entered groups dominated by fellow Irish-American, Irish-Catholic, or other foreign-born veterans. Members who had served in the New York regiments, for example, as well as some of those from Massachusetts and Pennsylvania, formed the Irish Brigade Association, open to all veterans of the brigade.[8] Fenian nationalism was another factor that attracted Irish veterans into their own organizations rather than the GAR. The Fenians were a brotherhood of Irish nationalists in America founded in the 1850s with ties to the Irish Republican Brotherhood in Ireland. Their name was a romantic reference to the legendary Fene or Fianna, which tradition held were the great warriors and defenders of ancient Ireland.[9] Many Fenians had served in the Union Army—indeed, most of the Irish Brigade leadership was Fenian—and many of them volunteered in order to acquire military experience that could be used to liberate Ireland in a future war rather than to express any great loyalty to America. Others fled to the United States to escape prosecution in Ireland. In Dublin in the spring of 1864, for example, U.S. vice-consul William B. West reported that 130 Fenians had done this and insisted, "there can be no doubt of the widespread disaffection existing in Ireland, which has been openly asserted in

Parliament, as unprecedented. . . . The emigration mania is still rife as ever, and scarcely a day passes at this Consulate without calls for free passage and for information thereon." Not all of those requests were from Fenians, but West and other U.S. consuls in Ireland continued to note their emigration in their reports. With the Civil War over, Fenian leaders focused their attention on weakening British power and freeing Ireland from British rule, and as West noted in Dublin in October 1865,

> This "Fenian mania" has, I regret to state, induced a great many of our adopted Irish Citizens to visit this country, of which there can be little doubt, and many of them are now suffering most severely and, I might add, justly punished for their folly, in abandoning the comforts and happiness of their American homes for the insane project of aiding Revolution here.[10]

While disapproving of the Fenians, West remained an advocate for Irish men and women related to those who had died for the Union cause. As late as 1869 he was still pushing for the U.S. government to allow immediate family members of deceased Irish soldiers to collected pensions due to them even though they did not reside in America. "The greatest cause of complaint and the only drawback against the almost universal homage paid to the liberality of our Government in regard to our dealings with the families of our soldiers slain in battle," West explained, "has been the refusal to pay this $100 Bounty to the parents in Ireland who had no child in America to receive it, and who, as a general rule, are in a state of pauperism."[11]

Like West, other U.S. consuls disapproved of the Fenians' activities. By the fall of 1865, U.S. consul E. Eastman found Irishmen returning to Cork and claiming U.S. citizenship, which required him to investigate their situation when they reported harassment and arrest by British officials on charges of treason as Fenians. That September he visited John McCafferty in prison, where he was facing charges of treason for documents found on him when arrested. McCafferty revealed that he had served in the Civil War as a Confederate under the name "Morgan," probably General John Hunt Morgan, but claimed to have taken a loyalty oath at Detroit, Michigan, at the end of the war. Whether or not McCafferty was telling the truth is unclear, but Eastman concluded, "I have not the slightest doubt about his being a 'Fenian' sent to this country to make war against Great Britain."[12] The rapid movement of men like McCafferty from service in the American Civil War to a new role in an Irish rebellion sheds further light on the dueling loyalties experienced by recent Irish Catholic immigrants serving in the American war.

Similar events surfaced in Cork, where U.S. consul John Young heard rumors that a number of the individuals arrested as Fenians were U.S. citizens and thus required his attention. Facing this delicate diplomatic situation he decided, "My own course is clear enough to me—I shall make what efforts I can in behalf of those whom I regard as innocent and leave the others to their fate."[13]

As the new consul in Belfast, G. H. Heap, discovered by December 1866, Irish-Americans continued to return to Ireland, but those suspected of any Fenian activity found themselves in British custody right after they landed. Heap found,

> the arrested parties are mostly Irishmen returning home from America against whom no charges are sustained, and they are usually soon released. But they not unnaturally consider it a hardship that, on landing on their native soil after years of absence, they should receive their first welcome from a policeman and their first hospitality in a gaol. This does not tend to diminish the general discontent.[14]

As the Fenians planned, British and American leaders watched closely. Anglo-American relations were tense in the late 1860s, largely due to British sympathies for the Confederacy during the war, and now officials in London feared the outbreak of war between the United States and Britain. Lord Palmerston warned Queen Victoria of the strong possibility that "the Northern States will make demands upon England which cannot be complied with, and will either make war against England or make inroads into your Majesty's North American possessions that would lead to war." English leaders decided the best policy was to strengthen Canadian defenses, but some leaders worried that even this would not be enough, and they feared any attempt to secure their North American possession would prove impossible.[15]

Their fears were not unfounded. The Fenians planned to attack several British North American possessions, including portions of Canada, that they would then hold hostage in exchange for Ireland's freedom. They hoped to frighten the Canadian and English leadership into submission with the fear not only of their force but also of American military strength, which was quite large in 1866.[16] The Fenians planned to purchase large quantities of surplus weapons from the U.S. government, arm their own military force, lead a series of simultaneous attacks on positions within Canada, and utilize the tacit support of many Americans to ensure that the U.S. government did not hinder their efforts. The Fenians hoped their attacks, backed by the United States, would so intimidate the British that they would surrender Ireland rather than wage an expensive war with America and possibly lose all of the British North American possessions.

The Fenians recruited and organized busily in northern communities that year, and while the ranks of their circles filled, it was still difficult to grow large memberships or raise sufficient funds. As the Daniel O'Connell Circle of Summitt Hill, Pennsylvania, reported in March 1866, "Owing to the slack of employment and our clergy's objections to the Fenian Brotherhood causes our Circle to continue small. But we hope in another month or two when employment turns up brisk and money plentier that we will [be] able to add many more to the Circle."[17]

While Fenians recruited in the North, their brothers worked to build ranks in the South as well. It was not an easy process, however, and Fenian recruiters noted a distinct bitterness toward northern Irish-Americans because of their Union service during the war, which hindered their efforts. As Patrick Condon found during a visit to Mobile, Alabama, in March 1866,

Little financial support is to be expected from this district, but you can depend on getting any number of good soldiers. [It is] not easy to organize Irish element here [because] there is much bitterness against the Irish of the North on account of their being regarded by the southern people, Irish included, as the chief cause of the destruction of the Confederacy.

It helped, however, that Irish nationalist John Mitchel was active in their cause, because, Condon explained, "the southern people love Mitchel."[18]

Within the next few weeks, Condon continued his southern journeys and reached New Orleans. There he distributed fliers and posters and delivered a lecture at Mechanics' Institute on the future of the Irish struggle for independence. He noted proudly that the Cleburne Circle in Mobile, Alabama, was growing rapidly, particularly through the efforts of Irish-American Captain John McGrath, former commander in the 8th Alabama Infantry, a unit with a strong Irish flavor. Still, it seemed an uphill battle recruiting members and supporters despite Condon's dedicated efforts throughout the South.[19]

One factor that helped their efforts was the tacit support of their plans coming from leading native newspapers. This support is puzzling considering native-born Americans' general disapproval of Irish nationalist movements and frustration with Irish-Americans' lack of faith in the war in its final years. Native-born northerners were even more frustrated, however, with the support Great Britain had shown the Confederacy during the war, and as prominent American editors learned of Fenian plans, they voiced approval, or at least supported the idea of inciting fear among

Canadians over a potential attack. The New York *Tribune* noted with pleasure, "Our Canadian neighbors have an opportunity of appreciating the conditions of America a year or two ago, when they permitted the bands of Rebel robbers to ride across the border and sack American towns." Even the *New York Times,* popular among native-born Americans and especially Republicans, warned, "Weak as this Fenian movement is we say to-day, unhesitantly, that it needs from America but the same support which the Southern rebellion received from England to give it force that would rock the British kingdom to its foundations."[20]

Similar comments came from Irish-American citizens like William Lalor, who lived near Madison, Wisconsin, in the 1860s. The Roman Catholic emigrated from Ireland in the early 1840s, and the years immediately following the Civil War found him bitter. He lost one of his sons, Patrick Edwin, aged nineteen, "in the late cursed War," and on the Fourth of July 1867, Lalor remained home, having refused to go to town with his family to enjoy the festivities. "I take no interest in it," he explained, "since the miserable war—I would rather see an Irish Fox hunt than all the amusements that were ever got up in the United States."[21] Some things did capture the old farmer's attention, though, and these included the efforts of the Irish nationalists, as he asked his brother in Tenakill, Queens County, Ireland, to "tell me . . . about the Fenians and what their prospects are."

Eight months later, the Fenians' efforts continued to capture Lalor's imagination and he had "high Heavenly hopes that the Irish people will before many years own the land robbed from their ancestors—If the United States government would abolish the neutrality law and allow an armed force to leave here, the British government would be driven out of Ireland within 6 months." Lalor hoped to return to Ireland one day, but suspected "it's not likely I will unless I go back with a Fenian Army."[22]

Other issues also contributed to native-born Americans' limited support for Fenian invasions, including the famous *Alabama* claims. Just following the war, many northern Americans' frustration with Britain focused on its willingness to allow Confederates to construct commerce raiders, most notably the C.S.S. *Alabama*, in British cities during the Civil War. American leaders demanded compensation for the damage British-built raiders did to the U.S. merchant marine and other American merchant vessels. Some, including Massachusetts senator Charles Sumner, argued for additional compensation for "indirect damages" as well, based on his theory that British actions allowed the Confederacy to maintain its war effort long after its defeat at the Battle of Gettysburg in the summer of 1863. Sumner proposed that Great Britain cover the cost of the Union war effort from that date, estimating the charges of compensation at

$2 billion dollars or the surrender of some of the British North American provinces in Canada.[23]

Fenians also received direct and indirect support from top members of the U.S. government. President Andrew Johnson, for example, used Fenian activities to secure Irish support for the Democratic party. During the congressional elections of 1866, Johnson and fellow Democrats around the country spoke of their sympathies for the Fenians' efforts and their support for the cause of Irish freedom. Johnson also made a very public release of Irish nationalist and Confederate supporter John Mitchel, who was being held on charges of treason. This action, as well as Fenian leaders' assumption that the government was aware of their purchase of thousands of weapons from New York and Pennsylvania arsenals, led Thomas Sweeny, Secretary of War of the presumptive Fenian government, to conclude that "the United States government . . . was perfectly well aware of the purposes for which the [arms] were intended," adding, "individuals in eminent positions at Washington" were expressing "sympathy . . . for us."[24]

For those in the ranks, planning and dedication to their cause were strong in 1866. Despite reports of small circle memberships from Pennsylvania, the Fenians of New York seemed to be filling the ranks quickly. That spring of 1866, Irish Catholic Patrick Foley, a native of Ireland living in Waterford, New York, contacted fellow Irishman James Sheehan in Albany. The two men appear to have been strong supporters of the Fenians, and at least Foley was involved in the organizing, and maybe the fighting, of the 1866 raid on Canada. That April he reported to Sheehan,

> Our circle is increased very much since you left. There is pretty near twice the number of members this season that there was last year. There is two or three regiments to leave Troy tomorrow or the day following to join up with Genl. Sweeny. There are also some 40 or 50 men mustered up between Lansingburgh and Waterford. I have said nothing about my name yet, but I suppose if required I will jump in the Ring. We had another special call for money . . . and each man subscribed from 5 to 10 dollars each.[25]

Even after the earliest attacks in the summer of 1866 and the capture of several Fenians, the organization's leaders were positive that they had high-ranking supporters within the U.S. government. After a committee of Fenians met with President Johnson in the fall of 1866, for example, Colonel Michael C. Murphy reported happily, "From the assurances given our committee by the President, and all the officials in Washington, I am convinced that the utmost interest is felt for us, and if a single hair of the heads of the prisoners now held by the English authorities in Canada be injured, it will completely revolutionize the Fenian Brotherhood" by eliciting still more sympathy and support from these concerned parties.[26]

Despite this implied support, the Fenians did not receive any direct backing by the United States government. In fact, as early as 1866 Johnson admitted privately that "the Government, surrounded by difficulties in its internal policy, and anxious to obtain support from any quarter against the violent party in the North" (Radical Republicans), was not interested in getting the country into another war. Some northerners may have been frustrated with Great Britain, but most were not interested in allowing the situation to escalate into a war with Great Britain.

They also faced mixed support from the Irish in America. While older farmers like William Lalor might support the Fenians, recent immigrant Maurice Woulfe, a veteran of the Union Army who served on the frontier in 1867, was disgusted by the entire organization, insisting they were doomed to failure due to their lack of professional military training, regardless of bravery. As he grumbled in 1867,

> I know all this "damned Fenianism" is generated in this Country where there are a Pack of Scoundrels going around picking the pockets of their foolish Countrymen, and then go Sporting & Gambling to Europe & Elsewhere, laughing in their Sleeves at their dupes. James Stephens is now Sporting around Europe at the expense of his Countrymen. But . . . all He or his party ever received off me is a Rotten apple which I threw at his Head in Washington, when I heard him getting along with a lot of damned humbug, about "The Men in the Gap" as he calls the fools in Ireland, and There are others in this Country keeping the game up, as they find it is a good paying business.[27]

Woulfe appears to have been the exception among Irish Catholic soldiers in the postwar U.S. Army. Two years later, in 1869, Company F of the 30th U.S. Infantry Regiment, especially the Irishmen in the unit, celebrated news from the East. "There is great excitement and rejoicing in this Post Among the Soldiers over the rejection of the *Alabama* Claims by the Senate and House of Representatives of the United States," Woulfe noted. "The Soldiers think they will Soon have a Chance of a brush with the English Red Coats, if they do go to War, the English will Certainly Come out of the Scape Second best." For the Irishmen in the ranks, tense relations between the United States and Great Britain, and the possibility of war, indicated an opportunity to weaken the British Empire, which could lead to the liberation of Ireland from British rule.[28]

Even Woulfe had to admit, while serving in Wyoming Territory, that "[t]here is scarcely a soldier in this camp that is not a Fenian. It's just the same all over the U.S. Army. There are a great many men in the Army who Enlisted expressly for the sake of learning the Art of war." Still, Woulfe felt the need to clarify that should his family speak with the local Catholic clergy, who disapproved of the Fenians' activities and Irishmen's membership in any secret society, that he was not involved with them. "But you can tell the Archdeacon Gould," Woulfe added, "that I was never a Fenian or never intend to be one as I have not the least confidence in the organization, or in its leaders, as the fellows are making an independent living by cheating their poor countrymen."[29]

As the Fenians conducted raids into Quebec in 1866, and again in 1870 and 1871 into Quebec, New Brunswick, and Manitoba, they reached the limit of U.S. support. On nearly every raid, the Fenians faced varying degrees of interference from U.S. forces, ranging from federal confiscation of Fenian military supplies to direct action by U.S. forces to halt all Fenian operations. As this happened, some Americans began to join those who had long criticized the Fenians. As this occurred, it became apparent that anti-Irish prejudice was still strong among Americans and their previous praise for the Fenians was not strong enough to support an armed invasion. Reflecting on the Fenian raid of 1866, the *Atlantic Monthly* argued, "all the qualities which go to make a republican, in the true sense of the term, are wanting in the Irish nature," adding that "to the Celtic mind, when anything comes in the guise of a law, there is an accompanying seizure of moral paralysis." Five years later a New Yorker calling himself "Americus" agreed, complaining to the *New York Times* of the outrage and embarrassment felt by "every order-loving citizen" over the "pack of adventurers (possibly jail-birds) who have been driven to our shores under the name of returned Fenians!" Prominent papers such as the *Times* had once encouraged Fenian threats to British power in Canada, but by the early 1870s even those native-born Americans who had voiced their sympathy for the Irish nationalists' cause, including top Republican politicians and prominent native presses, now claimed that such actions contradicted the nation's republican values and were an example of the violence and crime common throughout Irish-American communities.[30] Despite this, Irish-Americans like William Lalor continued to support the Fenians. In 1871 he boasted to family in Ireland that "the released or rather exiled Fenians [arriving in America] . . . are receiving a heartfelt welcome on this side of the Atlantic—this is right."[31] For other Irish-Americans, however, their faith in the Fenians was fading.

Criticisms of the Fenians' actions rose among native-born Americans, but Irish nationalists showed little interest in tempering their activities. As it had been when they fought for the Union cause, their primary focus was on the needs of Irish-Americans and Ireland. Fenians revised outward appearances, though, to avoid some of the criticisms arising from their Canadian expeditions. Despite the determination of the leadership, however, enthusiasm within their ranks and support from the broader Irish-American community dwindled. As Fenian Patrick Walsh, a native of Galway, Ireland, reported from Brazil, Indiana, in January 1877, the O'Donovan Rossa Circle was in bad standing, with only Walsh and a few other members regularly attending meetings and fulfilling their responsibilities in the organization. He insisted that one of the main problems was that too many uncommitted members joined the group, "and every word that was said at meeting was carried outside and members got disgusted and would not attend." Even so, Walsh insisted that there were core members that "are as Red Hot for a fight now as ever."[32] The problem, however, was the continued lack of men, funds, and unity within the organization. Interest in Irish nationalism did not disappear, but rather shifted toward an increasingly powerful group in America. Clan na Gael had formed about a decade earlier and was more moderate in its public image than the Fenians. It maintained a determined focus on freeing Ireland, though, and received significant support from Irish-Americans more comfortable with this group, which appeared to be less radical than the Fenians. By the early 1870s, John Devoy joined Clan na Gael and shaped it into an increasingly powerful voice of Irish-American nationalism.[33]

Any continued support of Irish nationalist organizations, however, sustained nativists' efforts to claim that Irish-Americans encouraged violence, terrorism, and treason rather than freedom and democracy. In 1882, for example, Alexander McClure, a leading Philadelphia Republican and editor of the *Philadelphia Times*, warned Irishmen in the city that they were showing too much loyalty to Ireland, and he urged them to embrace their new home if they hoped ever to find greater acceptance in the United States. Leading native-born Americans cited Irish support of the Clan and the Fenians as proof that "assassination, dynamite, blood-thirsty bluster and delirious lying" were all traits of the Irish "nature" as members of an inferior race.[34]

The 1890s found Irish-Americans continuing this increasingly conservative shift away from radical nationalist movements. They maintained their support for the cause of Irish independence, but frowned on the more aggressive approach of groups like the Fenians.[35] This gradual transition toward a more conservative stability is significant with regard to their dual loyalties to Ireland and America. It reflects an increasing focus on America and Irish Catholics' desire to secure their futures in the United States. They would never abandon their Irish heritage, but the postwar period found them focusing increasingly on their own communities and creating an American-Irish Catholic identity. Their determination to remain both Irish and American meant that they would face continued nativist criticisms, but this group loyalty also helped Irish Catholics increase their power within the American economy, political arena, and military. Achieving this increase in power would be a slow and difficult process, as prejudice continued in the late nineteenth century and Irish-American numerical superiority in these arenas made them targets. However, this numerical superiority also increased the power they could wield.

In the U.S. Army, for example, Irish-Americans comprised over 20 percent of Regular Army troops between 1865 and 1874. They had dominated the enlisted ranks in the early nineteenth century and ranked just behind German-Americans as the second largest ethnic group serving in the Union Army, but relatively few Irish-Americans attained the rank of officer.[36] By the 1880s and 1890s, foreign-born soldiers comprised approximately 34.5 percent of the U.S. Army, with Irish and Germans still holding the majority. Concerned with this large foreign-born influence in the ranks, army leadership began to discourage foreign-born enlistments in the late nineteenth century. Articles appearing in the *Army and Navy Journal* contained strong criticisms of foreign-born soldiers and sailors, and support for this view led to new recruiting policies. In 1891, the adjutant general of the army ordered recruiters to focus their efforts "in the smaller towns and rural districts," rather than in the northern cities that had offered routinely high enlistments, especially by recent immigrants looking for work. By 1894, the U.S. Congress passed a law restricting first enlistments to U.S. citizens or individuals who legally stated their intention to become citizens.[37] All new soldiers also had to speak, read, and write English. Dramatic declines in enlistments ensued and reduced foreign-born elements in the U.S. Army. By 1896 the number of immigrants in the army had dropped from more than one-third to approximately one-fourth of all new soldiers.[38]

Despite these policies, the sheer number of Irish Catholics in the ranks allowed them to secure some independence within the U.S. Army, though this trend was still evolving. Evidence of this power is found in the experiences of Maurice Woulfe in 1868 with the army in Dakota Territory:

> This being Easter Sunday, the Soldiers had great Cracking of Eggs, this morning, as the officers, the Majority of whom are Irish, thought they would Keep up the time honoured Custom of eating Eggs on Easter Sunday Morning by giving Eggs to the men of their Companies. The Irish are [a] very Strong party in this Country, and if they pulled together they

would rule a good deal of the destiny of this Country. But the Irish both here as well as in Ireland are always divided except in case of war, then they generally pull together.[39]

Despite the large number of Irishmen around him, Woulfe still found lingering, and occasionally powerful, examples of anti–Irish Catholic prejudice in the U.S. Army. In 1874, while stationed with the 4th U.S. Infantry Regiment at Fort Bridger in Wyoming Territory, Woulfe engaged in an altercation with his commanding officer. As he explained,

I got into a dispute here on last November with the commanding officer of my company. There was a letter written to the St. Louis paper describing the reception given at the Post to a French Priest who paid us a visit. The letter was not very Complimentary to the officers, and they were raising mischief around the Post trying to find out who wrote the letter. Of course I was suspected, and the Company Commander said in my presence at the Sutler's Store that it was some dirty Catholic Irishman that wrote it. I knew that I was the party meant, but the expression was scarcely uttered when he measured his length on the floor. I then tossed him out of doors, there were two other Officers there who thought to lay me out, but I had too many backers. There were some men present that would not wish for better sport than to give them officers a beating.

Woulfe found himself quickly under arrest, but it appeared that the company commander wished to avoid publicizing this challenge to his authority and he chose not to court-martial Woulfe, though he was reduced in rank.[40] While the event reveals anti-Irish and anti-Catholic prejudice that remained in the army, it also indicates that a sizable number of Irish Catholic "backers" were around Woulfe to support him, symbolizing the power Irish Catholics carried in the army and elsewhere in American society through sheer numbers.

This does not mean that the prejudice or the economic hardship that Irish-American Catholics experienced in the antebellum and war years had disappeared. In New York City, they live in overcrowded areas such as the largely Irish Tenth Ward, where there were 276,000 people per square mile. The stench of the polluted East River and nearby factories permeated the neighborhoods, where their poor conditions, overcrowding, and the residents' inability to leave these areas left them susceptible to the rapid spread of diseases such as smallpox and cholera.[41] These conditions led many Irishmen to New York City's workhouses, charity hospitals, almshouses, prisons, or lunatic asylums. The city had built a whole complex of these facilities on Blackwell's Island in the East River, and

Irish-Americans were overrepresented in nearly every building. In the 1870s, five Irish were arrested to every one German in New York City, proving to some native-born Americans that the problem in their communities was not related to immigration generally but to the Irish in particular. Historians have attributed this Irish condition at least in part to the fact that the Irish-born in the postwar city occupied 50 percent of the worst-paying jobs in New York City while they comprised only 20 percent of the population. As late as 1880, 20 percent of New York City Irish-Americans were still working as unskilled laborers whereas only 4 percent of native-born Americans held such positions. The conditions had a devastating impact on nearly all of the inhabitants. "The atmosphere of the place is death, morally and physically," one individual noted after visiting a New York Irish neighborhood in the postwar era, while Irish-American veterans and their widows pressed pension boards for increases of their monthly allotment due to desperate financial needs.[42]

New York was not the only city in which Irish Catholics made up large portions of the working poor and predominated in the most destitute neighborhoods. In the late 1860s, the *Chicago Evening Post* reported on the large Irish representation in the city's jails, reform schools, charities, and hospitals and revealed continuing anti-Irish and anti-Catholic prejudice. "Scratch a convict or pauper," the *Post* claimed, "and the chances are that you tickle the skin of an Irish Catholic made a criminal or a pauper by the priest and politician who have deceived him and kept him in ignorance, in a word, a savage, as he was born." The *Post* cannot speak for an entire community, but its popularity before and after it published such prejudicial articles indicates that a sizable portion of the Chicago population shared these sentiments. And while the report claimed that at least some of the native-born population viewed Irish-Americans as having the potential for improvement, the editors clarified that such advances could only come when the Irish abandoned their Catholic faith.

Accounts of pandemic Irish poverty appeared in postwar Philadelphia as well. Evidence of this can be found in Philadelphians' references to the overwhelming number of "Celtic" visitors waiting in line at the Bedford Street Settlement House soup kitchen in the 1870s. Similar conditions, and the anti-Irish and anti-Catholic prejudice that significant numbers of native-born Americans continued to demonstrate, plagued impoverished sections of Boston, Baltimore, Cincinnati, and other cities throughout the country.[43]

Accounts of Irish disadvantage came from individuals in Charleston, Ohio, as well. Even though Robert Caulwell had found financial success in America, he discouraged other Irishmen from coming. The fall of 1865 found the Union Army veteran battling horrifying memories of the Civil

War and insisting that America was not the place for Irishmen. As he told his cousin in Ireland,

> I have good pay here But I am tired of this country. Dear cousin, I have been in the army and seen enough. The death of a man was . . . like killing a worm. I [b]een in 17 battles and skirmishes in this war and saw about 5 hundred thousand men killed and [twice] as many wounded. . . . Dear cousin mind your place while you have it, and don't be foolish to be advised to come to this country. I cannot complain but I see them that can do so. If a man makes money here he starves himself.[44]

Irish Catholics comprised a major portion of San Francisco's working class and felt similar pressures in that city by the mid-1870s. Prior to that point, the community had basked in a strong economy and rapid commercial growth. The recession spreading through the country in the 1870s hit San Francisco in 1875, and for the next several years times were extremely difficult for men like Frank Roney. A former Fenian who left Ireland in 1866, Roney endured incredible poverty throughout the late 1870s. Despite this, he would rise to prominence by the late nineteenth century as a labor leader in California, where he organized the powerful and active working force, which included significant Irish representation, into a body that could demand and receive reforms.[45]

Again, this does not mean that anti-Irish bigotry disappeared in American in the late nineteenth century. Numerous examples of it can be found across the United States. In the 1880s, Cincinnati, Ohio, community leaders characterized their Irish residents as "illiterates" who were "full of superstition and semi-barbarism" and whose opinion that "progressive civilization [was] an encroachment upon their superior rights, independence and personal liberty" made them totally unfit for the responsibilities of citizenship. James Bryce echoed this in his book *The American Commonwealth,* arguing that most of the immigrants flooding into the country could never be worthy of the vote, offering evidence of this by arguing that immigrants acquired and immediately sold their vote to the Democratic party just after their arrival in America. In the case of many Irish-Americans, Bryce theorized that the greatest problem was their "suspicion of all government" and total lack of "knowledge of the methods of free government."[46]

Such anti-Irish prejudice continued throughout the late nineteenth century. The *Atlantic Monthly* argued, "A Celt . . . lacks the solidity, the balance, the judgment, the moral staying power of the Anglo-Saxon," all of which many native-born Americans saw as the essential foundation of the American political system. As late as 1911 Charles Davenport, a leading eugenics theorist and biochemist at the University of Chicago, argued that individuals of Irish heritage were by nature more susceptible to "alcoholism, considerable mental defectiveness, and a tendency to tuberculosis," and he even theorized that the increasingly active role played by many Irish-Americans in politics, especially machine politics and the graft associated with it, reflected these racial characteristics.[47]

Examples of nativists' concerted resistance to any gains in Irish-American political influence can be found in several dramatic postwar events. In 1870, Jersey City voters elected several Irish-Catholics to positions within the municipal government. The New Jersey state legislature was so concerned by this that congressional leaders abolished elective government in that community. As late as 1885, when Bostonians elected Henry O'Brien as their mayor, the first Irish Catholic to hold this office, the Massachusetts legislature voted to strip control of the Boston Police Department from the mayor for fear of how the Irish-Catholics would use their new power.[48]

Other examples of anti-Irish prejudice abound in the late nineteenth century, including such controversies as the labor resistance and management crackdowns on the Molly Maguires and the Orange Riots of 1870 and 1871, which involved violence between New York Irish Protestants and Catholics, the former receiving the vast majority of support from the non–Irish-American population.[49] Even when many Irish-Americans did not participate in this violence, sweeping anti-Irish statements were made in prominent publications such as the Philadelphia *Public Ledger,* the Chicago *Tribune,* and New York newspapers such as the *Times,* the *Herald,* the *Tribune,* and *Harper's Weekly.*[50] As one Irish-American veteran complained, "Are we forever to be made the subjects of slander on account of a few?" and prominent Irish-American papers agreed. In their coverage of the Orange Riots, the *Irish World, Irish Citizen,* and *Irish-American* all made reference to Irish-American loyal military service in the American Civil War and insinuated or clearly stated that native-born Americans had cast this memory aside in favor of their nativist prejudice against Irishmen.[51]

It was at this time, in the 1870s, 1880s, and 1890s, that Irish-Americans began to make a concerted effort to create a clear identity for themselves in the United States. They were frustrated by the prejudice they had faced since the first famine immigrants began pouring into American ports despite all they had accomplished in America. Much of the ethnic controversy between native-born and Irish-American leaders involved political power in late-nineteenth-century America. In Boston, Massachusetts, Irishmen complained of their limited political influence. Despite their rising population, they argued, Irish Catholics were significantly underrepresented in city and state government, which was hindering their ability to promote the interests of many Irish-Americans and increase their opportunities throughout the city. Some Irish politicians complained that this resulted not only from Republicans' resistance to growing Irish activism but also from Democratic party leaders, who had benefited from years of loyal Irish support at the polls but refused to incorporate Irish-Americans into influential positions within the party and the municipal government.[52]

Increasing numbers of Irishmen in New York City were making similar charges. The 1870 census returns showed that Irish-Americans had dramatically increased their representation throughout the city, especially in Brooklyn. "And yet," the *Irish World* asked, are Irish-Americans "really a power? The Irish naturalized citizens . . . ought to have one of the leading positions of mayor, or sheriff, or county clerk, or surrogate, or district attorney, or judge of some of the upper courts; but . . . it looks as if 'no Irish need apply.'" This was a problem repeated throughout the nation, the editors argued. "A few of the minor offices, the smaller prizes, the crumbs of the political table are thrown to [Irish-Americans]. The big prizes, the rich dishes, are given to the minority—after whom the majority have to run to beg for favors, which they have at the disposal of their own votes." Indeed, Irish representation in city politics actually declined while the Irish-American population increased. Between 1844 and 1884 this population rose from nearly 20 to 40 percent of New York City, but they held a mere 14 percent of political positions under the city's Democratic leadership based at Tammany Hall while native-born Democrats dominated the party and city political offices. Their determination to publicly challenge this situation indicates Irish-American leaders' awareness of the power they could wield if they spoke as one political bloc.[53]

This growing awareness concerned native-born Americans, who preferred to assume that Irish politicians secured their power through corrupt means. As Irish Catholic community leaders and newspaper editors demanded a more active role within American society, native-born Americans struck back. Native presses like *Harper's Weekly* and *Puck* portrayed Irish-American voters and politicians as ignorant brutes too stupid to use the rights of citizenship wisely, or so inherently corrupt that they preferred to operate within a fraudulent and violent political system than to work in support of honest democracy. Political cartoons portrayed Irish-Americans with simian features as still-evolving human beings who were intellectually incapable of the responsibilities required of citizens. Irish-American caricatures carried whiskey bottles or clubs to indicate a natural proclivity toward violence and drunkenness, and their speech reflected ignorance and foreign birth with a thick brogue and poor grammar.[54]

One of the most powerful examples of this characterization appears in the press coverage of presidential elections in the late nineteenth century. The frequency with which these images appeared in native presses and the continuing popularity of the papers that published the editorials and images slandering Irish-Catholic voters indicates that a significant portion of their readers, native-born Americans, accepted this characterization of Irish-Americans.

In the postwar era, Democrats complained frequently that Republicans would "wave the bloody shirt" at every election to portray their party as the embodiment of loyalty, patriotism, and union, and remind voters that the Democrats were the party of secession, slavery, and the prejudice represented in the recently formed Ku Klux Klan. Routinely, Irish-Americans and the increasingly Irish-dominated New York political machine, Tammany Hall, were portrayed alongside images of the Klan and Confederate veterans rather than symbols of the union that many Irish-Americans fought to preserve. Irish Catholics had served heroically in the war, making countless sacrifices to the Union cause along with their families. A decade later, however, they were better remembered for draft riots and anti-Lincoln rhetoric.

During the presidential elections of 1872 *Harper's Weekly* published a political cartoon that offers a clear example of this. In "A 'Liberal' Surrender: Any Thing to Beat Grant," a *Harper's* political cartoonist mocked the efforts by Democrats to welcome liberal Republicans, disillusioned with the Grant administration, into their party in a desperate attempt for victory. The artist depicts reformer Horace Greeley, usually a strong critic of the Democrats, and Republican Senator Carl Schurz of Missouri surrendering to the Democratic party. Representing the party is the Ku Klux Klan, Confederate veterans, Copperheads, and Tammany Hall and its Irish-American influence. The heroes of the cartoon are the Union veterans, including Ulysses S. Grant and a massive army behind him that is ready to defeat the Republican forces the artist portrays as disloyal. Despite the fact that nearly 150,000 Irish-Americans served the Union cause during the Civil War, many of them fighting under Ulysses S. Grant, there is no effort to associate them with General Grant in this image. Instead Irish-Americans are portrayed as the enemy rather than part of a force of Union veterans prepared to save America once again.[55]

An even more powerful characterization of Irish-Americans as a disloyal, threatening element in American society appeared in the native press coverage of the 1880 presidential election. When the hero of the Battle of Gettysburg, General Winfield Scott Hancock, ran for president as the Democratic candidate that year there were numerous references to his Union Army service as Democrats tried to attract the soldier vote to

"A 'Liberal' Surrender: Any Thing to Beat Grant," *Harper's Weekly*, May 11, 1872. Provided courtesy HarpWeek, LLC. Photograph reproduction courtesy Lynn L. Libby, Enola, PA, 2005.

back their candidate. In combating this, Republican supporters did not challenge Hancock's military record but chose to characterize his loyalty to the Democratic party as a grievous error.

In August 1880, *Harper's Weekly* printed a cartoon representing Irish-Americans as one of Hancock's disreputable Democratic associates, characterized as a Tammany Boss, alongside a Confederate veteran. When Hancock tries to introduce his two "friends" to a fellow Union Army veteran, crippled from his service but proudly wearing a Grand Army of the Republic cap, the veteran informs Hancock, "I prefer to pick my own acquaintances, and advise you to do the same." Once again, despite significant Irish-American representation in the Union Army, including their dedicated service under General Hancock at the Battle of Gettysburg, Irish-American military service was ignored. The native-born veteran is portrayed honorably with a clear indication of the sacrifice he made for his nation in his crutches and missing leg, while there is no indication that the Irish-American might be a veteran. Instead, he is linked with the symbol of past and possibly future disloyalty, the Confederate veteran holding a rifle in one hand and hiding a pistol behind his back with the other.[56]

Similar images appeared in other prominent papers that year, including the popular New York magazine *Puck*. The editors of this press, like those at *Harper's Weekly*, had significant Republican leanings and presented an even stronger argument that the traitors and corruption within the Democratic party were a burden to the misguided, but honorable, Hancock. In July 1880, cartoonist Joseph Keppler portrayed Hancock carrying the Democratic donkey on his shoulders, while his fellow Union Army veteran and Republican presidential opponent James A. Garfield gallops toward the White House on a strong horse representing the Republican party. Among Hancock's burdens are what *Puck's* editors see as the great weaknesses of the Democrats: "secession sympathy," "Copperheadism," "slavery," and "stupidity." Finally, holding the tail of the Democratic donkey, under whose weight Hancock labors, is an Irish leprechaun representing Irish-American Tammany boss John Kelly and his demands for

HOW HANCOCK WILL (NOT) GET THE SOLDIER VOTE.
GEN. HANCOCK. "Colonel, allow me to make you acquainted with two of my friends."
COL. V. "No, thank you, General; I prefer to pick my acquaintances, and advise you to do the same."

"How Hancock Will (Not) Get the Soldier Vote," *Harper's Weekly*, August 28, 1880. Provided courtesy HarpWeek, LLC. Photograph reproduction courtesy William F. Ural, M.D., Toad Hall Photography, Southport, NC.

"Just the Difference," *Puck*, July 28, 1880. Provided courtesy HarpWeek, LLC. Photograph reproduction courtesy Lynn L. Libby, Enola, PA, 2005.

"political spoils." Once again, there is no reference to any honorable Irish-American military service or to Irish-Americans as virtuous citizens of the United States. Instead, *Puck* editors draw a powerful thread linking Irish-Americans with past and present threats to the nation.[57]

Despite the mocking nature of these cartoons, they indicate the threat nativists felt from Irish-American voters. This large voting bloc held tremendous potential in American politics and by the late 1880s, native presses were criticizing both parties for courting the Irish-American vote. Native newspapers portrayed Republicans and Democrats as corrupting the political process when they sought Irish-American political support through illegitimate means. Papers such as *Puck* and *Harper's Weekly* criticized the growing political influence of Irish-Americans by portraying them as corrupt citizens selling their vote or as influence peddlers convincing leaders such as 1884 Republican presidential candidate James Blaine to tolerate Irish violence and corruption in exchange for their support.[58] Irish-Americans' determined self-reliance and their focus on Irish-American interests helped them acquire power and influence within the American political system.

Indeed, Irish-Americans did see some advances in their political power, despite these negative images, and this was largely due to their political unity and activism.[59] By 1868, for example, Irish-born Patrick Collins was elected to the Massachusetts House of Representatives and used his influential post to increase support for Irish Catholics within Boston and around the state. Collins convinced Massachusetts General Hospital, for example, to admit more Catholics and worked tirelessly for Catholic patients in penal and charitable institutions to have the opportunity to hear mass and participate in other Catholic rites. The latter effort took much longer than the opening of Massachusetts General Hospital's doors to Catholics, but it does demonstrate the power Irish-Americans were able to wield through their large, united, and active efforts in the Democratic party and American political life.

Similar advances occurred in New York City and Albany, both of which had enormous Irish populations. By the late nineteenth century, Albany Irishmen were purchasing homes and securing increasingly influential positions in the police and fire departments. They began to fill the seats of the State Assembly, rise to the office of mayor, and even secure

"Ready for Business," *Puck*, July 23, 1884. Provided courtesy HarpWeek, LLC. Photograph reproduction courtesy Lynn L. Libby, Enola, PA, 2005.

"Is This 'The True American Policy?'" *Harper's Weekly*, July 26, 1884. Provided courtesy HarpWeek, LLC. Photograph reproduction courtesy Lynn L. Libby, Enola, PA, 2005.

election to the U.S. House of Representatives. Michael O'Sullivan is an example of this. The Limerick native fled Ireland in 1840 to escape persecution by local Irish Protestants for his Catholic views. In 1861 O'Sullivan organized a company comprised entirely of Irish Catholics and boasted that they were all volunteers and had joined entirely sober, an important point for O'Sullivan to make since he had abstained from alcoholic beverages since 1834. During the war his company joined the 63rd New York Infantry Regiment, which was an original part of the Irish Brigade.

O'Sullivan remained with them until wounds made continued service impossible. The postwar period found him financially successful and still an extremely devout Roman Catholic, carefully noting the attention to the faith paid within the 63rd New York—mass every morning, rosary every evening, and confessions as required. By 1870 he reported proudly to friends in Ireland that Catholicism had found a new home in Albany, New York, over the last thirty years, "making Albany a center" of the faith.[60]

The new opportunities and gradually increasing political power experienced by some Irish-Americans in the late nineteenth century were the result of Irish-American organization and activism. In politics, their newfound influence could be seen in cities like New York, Boston, and Philadelphia, as well as smaller communities like Michael O'Sullivan's Albany, New York. As George Washington Plunkett, one of the most famous Irish-American politicians of this era, explained, they developed, or perhaps expanded, a practice of looking "after their friends. . . . Every good man looks after his friends. . . . If I have a good thing to hand out in private life, I give it to a friend. Why shouldn't I do the same in public life?" Those friends were predominantly Irish in the late nineteenth century, and Plunkett and his successors at Tammany would ensure, slowly but surely, Irish-American dominance of New York City politics from 1871 to 1924.[61]

Reaching beyond political issues, Irish-Americans made a conscious effort to insert themselves into the American memory, and they accomplished this through a major emphasis on their role in the Civil War, which the war generation recognized immediately as a defining moment in American history. Seeing this, Irish-Americans sought ways to teach their communities and native-born Americans about their service in this conflict. Similarly, Irish leaders were outraged in 1894 when nativists in the American Protective Association attacked their war record. Irish-American spokesmen renewed their interest in the formation of an Irish historical organization to refute such attacks with evidence. They wanted to not only promote but preserve for future generations a documentary record of Irish-Americans' role in the United States dating back to the colonial period. Their passionate response to the attack on Irish-Americans' Civil War records played a major role in the birth of the American Irish Historical Society in New York City in 1897.[62]

Similarly, Irish-American veterans themselves played a similar role in educating Americans about the service of Irish Catholics in the Civil War. An example of this came in the immediate aftermath of the war with Captain David Power Conyngham's history of *The Irish Brigade and Its Campaigns,* published in 1867. Conyngham was an Irish revolutionary who had served as one of Meagher's staff officers during the war. He wrote the book "with the sole desire of helping to rescue from obscurity the glorious military record we have earned in America." In the text, he insisted that "the Irish soldier was . . . a patriot, and no mercenary. He had just the same right to fight for America that the native American had." As Conyngham explained,

> The Irish soldier . . . felt that the safety and welfare of his adopted country and its glorious Constitution were imperiled; he, therefore, willingly threw himself into the breach to sustain the flag that sheltered him when persecuted and exiled from his own country, the laws that protected him, and the country that, like a loving mother, poured forth the richness of her bosom to sustain him.

While some of his fellow Irish Catholics might challenge that characterization of native-born Americans as welcoming, Conyngham's description of sacrifice and loyalty combined with Irishmen's determined fighting spirit were common tenets throughout their histories of this war. Indeed, they seized on such stereotypes as a "natural" fighting spirit and turned them to their advantage in an effort to write themselves into the American story.

Irish Brigade veteran and former commanding officer General Denis F. Burke made similar claims when he spoke at the dedication of the monument to the New York regiments of the Irish Brigade at the Gettysburg Battlefield on July 2, 1888. Reminding his audience of the shared bonds between Irishmen and Americans, he said, "Here twenty-five years ago the Puritan and the Celt fought side by side for the Union founded by George Washington and his confreres. . . . And everywhere during our civil war, wherever the Stars and Stripes floated in battle, there were Irishmen fighting for the preservation of this Republic, the only refuge of the oppressed of all lands." Reinforcing this, he continued, "Yes, Irishmen and the sons of Irishmen have stood nobly by the Republic at every critical period in its history. . . . During all the battles, sieges and other operations in which we were engaged, each regiment of this brigade carried two flags, the Stars and Stripes of Free America, and the Green Flag of poor persecuted Ireland." In a powerfully conscious manner, Burke and the audience at the battlefield that day insisted on the inextricable link between the causes of Catholic Ireland and the United States, as well as Irish-Americans' undeniable place within American history.[63]

Another example of Irish-Americans shaping the memory of their role in the American Civil War is Father William Corby's memoir of his military service, first published in 1893. Corby served as the Catholic chaplain for the 88th New York, one of the original regiments of the Irish

Monument to the New York Regiments of the Irish Brigade at Gettysburg National Military Park, Pennsylvania. New York Monuments Commission for the Battlefields of Gettysburg and Chattanooga. *Final Report on the Battlefield of Gettysburg* (Albany, NY: J.B. Lyon Company, 1902), 474.

Brigade. He had been teaching at Notre Dame University when the war began, and he returned to Indiana when he left military service in 1864. He wrote his memoirs "to show the religious feature that existed in the army. In the presence of death, religion gives hope and strength. The Christian soldier realizes that his power comes from the 'God of battles,' not from man." He added, like Conyngham, that he was pleased to see his comrades writing about the service of Irish soldiers, who are "so renowned" because they come "from a fearless race, whose valor has been tested in a war that was incessant for three hundred years, with the Danes and Normans, followed by contests, more or less fierce, for centuries, with England."[64] Like Conyngham, Corby's story referenced the stereotypical fighting prowess of Irish-Americans, but the chaplain also reminded his readers of the loyalty of these Catholic warriors, and Catholics across the United States celebrated the book when it first appeared. The *Catholic Citizen,* for example, described it as "timely," insisting that "every lover of liberty and religion should read it" while another Catholic American boasted, "It stands out" as "a living refutation to the base calumnies of ranting, roaring, noisy, blatherskites, who keep crying 'the country will be crippled by Catholics.' "[65]

St. Clair Mulholland, the Irish-born Catholic commander of the 116th Pennsylvania of the Irish Brigade, was even more active in these efforts to educate Americans about the sacrifices of Civil War veterans. By the turn of the century, increasing numbers of veterans became involved in this movement, and Mulholland and Corby were definitely part of it. For some, enough time had passed to become nostalgic and even to romanticize their dramatic days at war. Part of their motivation, too, was a fear that the next generation was forgetting all they had done.[66] And for Irish Catholics in America, the movement was a concerted effort to challenge the stereotypical image of Irish-Americans as disloyal, weak-minded, ungrateful, and un-American. Mulholland's role in this movement and his impact on the memory of the Irish role in the war was tremendous.

One of his most successful tributes came with the statue of Father William Corby's famous blessing at the Gettysburg Battlefield, erected in 1910. Mulholland directed the project as president of the Catholic Alumni Sodality of Philadelphia, and Catholic leaders across the country took pride in knowing that the statue would "tell the tale of the devotion of Catholic chaplains on the fields where the fate of the Union was being written in pages of blood" and it would serve as "the convincing answer . . . to the false pleading of the sectarian bigots as to Catholic allegiance and sense of citizen duty at times of crisis." For Mulholland, the statue also served to unite Catholics and Protestants in America as a testimony of the faith of their soldiers. In his frequent public talks Mulholland always reminded his audience that when Father Corby offered the blessing on that second day at Gettysburg, Protestants knelt beside Catholics and Corby's prayers were meant for all of the Union soldiers before him, and even the Confederates in the distance. They all received absolution that day. This action, Mulholland insisted, was much like the war itself and the lessons it offered. It transcended ethnicity and faith. The Corby statue became one of the most powerful symbols in America of the identity Irish Catholics created for themselves as loyal, active American citizens who also remained true to their ethnic heritage.[67]

Mulholland's work was not isolated to the Corby monument. In 1905 he had published a history of his regiment, the 116th Pennsylvania, and he worked tirelessly to ensure that another monument appeared at Gettysburg honoring the unit's service in that battle. In 1907, he reached beyond the Civil War, but remained focused on the Irish-American identity in the United States, by helping the Friendly Sons of St. Patrick in Philadelphia erect a statue celebrating Irish-born Commodore John Barry, hero of the American Revolution, in the city's famous Independence Square. The statue was yet another symbol of Irish sacrifice for American union. Mulholland's work itself addresses this blurring of the lines between Irish and American, Protestant and Catholic. For him, the war transcended all of these divisions and he insisted that, in the end, his greatest accomplishment was the knowledge that his children could "make it their proudest boast that 'Father was a soldier of the Union.'" Mulholland's messages of unity and Irish-American loyalty served as a powerful antidote to the images of violence and treason printed in *Harper's Weekly* and *Puck* in postwar America. It seems fitting that when he died in 1910, he had a funeral mass in a Catholic Church as well as a private GAR ceremony in his Philadelphia home. This Irish-born hero of the American Civil War was part of the American identity Irish Catholics carefully crafted in the late nineteenth century that balanced their dual loyalties to Ireland and the United States in a uniquely American way.[68]

Just as Irish-American veterans wrote memoirs or spoke at gatherings about their service during the postwar period, so their families and communities made similar efforts to celebrate Irish and American traditions. These efforts were all part of their attempt to create an Irish-American Catholic identity. Irish Catholic immigrant Stephen Owens offers an excellent example of this. In the spring of 1900 he celebrated St. Patrick's Day with his fellow Irishmen in Clontarf, Minnesota. He was elderly now, but he still went "nearly every day" to mass, which he celebrated with the Reverend Father McDonald, a native of Kilkenny, and enjoyed traditional holidays like St. Patrick's Day. In March 1900, their parish in Clontarf had "a grand time," Owens recalled:

First thing in the Morning, all the Hibernians met in their Hall at ten O Clock in the morning, put on their badges and marched in a body to the Church, the Stars and Stripes on one side of the men and the Harp in the middle of the Green Flag of Ireland on the other side, and the band of music in the front as they marched in to the Church. . . .

From there, with the dual symbols of Ireland and the United States waving down the street toward a Catholic mass, the festivities continued into the evening:

> Our Priest is a Noble Patriot and Irishman, at 5 O clock in the evening we had a grand oration on the life of St. Patrick in our Town Hall by a Lawyer from St. Paul, a city in Minnesota, our capitol of the state, his name was McDermot, very smart orator. After that we all went to supper. After supper again we went to the Hall, it was then we had the time. There was a grand Irish play by the young local Talent of the Parish. They called it Shan Rue in Seven Acts. It was just splendid. The priest was training the young folks since the middle of January. The Hall was crowded with Irish, and some Americans and Norwegians. I bet you did not celebrate like that in Skerries [Ireland].

As for his Minnesota community, Owens boasted, "We are all Irish to the backbone out here."[69] Yet they were American Irish. Their St. Patrick's Day celebrations included American flags and had native-born Americans and other immigrants in attendance. Like Corby in Indiana, Mulholland in Pennsylvania, and countless other Irish Catholics across the country, Stephen Owens's Minnesota community was crafting an identity that was both Irish and American and no longer favored one ethnicity over the other. This process was one of the most powerful legacies of their participation in the American Civil War.

Conclusion

The St. Patrick's Day parade in the largely Irish Catholic community of Clontarf, Minnesota, in 1900 bears a striking resemblance to the 69th N.Y.S.M. regiment marching down Great Jones Street in April 1861, ready to defend the Union. In both cases, flags of Irish green rippled next to the stars and stripes of the United States. And yet, there is a powerful difference between these two events. In 1861 Irish Catholic communities supported the war for union, but their actions during that conflict indicated that their first loyalties were to Ireland and their Irish communities in America. When they perceived the northern war effort as threatening these, their support for the war diminished drastically, though they insisted that they remained loyal Americans who simply disagreed with President Lincoln's direction of the war.

In the postwar period they faced tremendous challenges defending this position as members of a weakened minority party and as a largely immigrant group that had strongly criticized a president who held martyrlike status following his assassination. They continued to dominate the lower levels of the American economy and remained persecuted as Catholics in an overwhelmingly Protestant nation. As the years passed, however, Irish-American Catholics realized the power they held as a largely unified voting bloc within the American democracy. Similarly, their time in America may have influenced their increasing attention to affairs in the United States rather than Ireland. Also, the influx of other Catholic immigrants from southern and Eastern Europe in the late nineteenth century influenced Irish-Americans' efforts to secure their dominance of the American Catholic traditions within the broader American society.

It is extremely difficult to evaluate how, specifically, the military service of Irish-American volunteers affected their lives in postwar America. To argue that it improved their condition and opportunities ignores the fact that Irish Catholics continued to face tremendous challenges in the United States long after the war, and any improvements they enjoyed may have been due more to their time in the country and their adjustment to its cultures and customs. The more significant lesson of the experiences of Irish volunteers in the Union Army from 1861 to 1865 is how their dual loyalties to Ireland and the United States influenced their actions throughout the entire war and well into the postwar period.

When the Civil War began, their communities, dominated by recent immigrants, focused largely on themselves, their needs, and those of their families in Ireland. Their actions directly reflected the way they saw the war affecting them. In the postwar period these dual loyalties continued to exist, but they evolved as Irish-Americans became increasingly involved in politics and carved a niche for themselves within American society and its larger cultural traditions. Now their families and communities reflected shared, balanced traditions grounded in Ireland and the United States. They became Irish Catholics who also considered themselves Americans and were determined to enjoy the rights that identity entailed. Their sense of ethnic and community unity, as not only Irish Catholics but also Americans, gave them a degree of power that they did not request from native-born Americans, but rather took for themselves and wielded with increasing skill. Their dual loyalties to Ireland and the United States, symbolized by the harp and the eagle, carried them through four bloody years of war and political crises, as well as the painful postwar period. By remaining true to those blended traditions, Irish Catholics secured for themselves a unique and powerful role in America's past, present, and future.

Notes

NOTES TO THE INTRODUCTION

1. William L. D. O'Grady to the Commissioner of Pensions, Washington, DC, October 19, 1897, William L. D. O'Grady Pension Records, National Archives and Record Administration (NARA), Washington, DC; see also William L. D. O'Grady to President Grover Cleveland, August 3, 1886, William L. D. O'Grady Pension Records, NARA, Washington, DC. William L. D. O'Grady was a second lieutenant in the Royal Marines Light Infantry when he resigned.

2. In 1745 Irish exiles serving in the French army had formed into le Brigade Royal Irlandois (the Royal Irish Brigade) and earned their fame in a daring bayonet charge against the English that turned the tide at Fontenoy for France. See Russell F. Weigley, *The Age of Battles: The Quest for Decisive Warfare from Breitenfeld to Waterloo* (Bloomington: Indiana University Press, 1991), 207; for more information on the Irish Brigade at the Battle of Fontenoy see Jon Manchip White, *Marshal of France: The Life and Times of Maurice de Saxe* (New York: Rand McNally, 1962), 146–66, and Jacques Boudet, "Fontenoy, 1745," in *Great Military Battles*, ed. Cyril Falls (London: Spring Books, 1964), 50–57.

3. William L. D. O'Grady to the Commissioner of Pensions, Washington, DC, October 19, 1897, William L. D. O'Grady Pension Records, NARA, Washington, DC; see also William L. D. O'Grady to President Grover Cleveland, August 3, 1886, William L. D. O'Grady Pension Records, NARA, Washington, DC.

4. O'Grady Pension File.

5. Terry Golway, *Irish Rebel: John Devoy and America's Fight for Ireland's Freedom* (New York: St. Martin's Griffin, 1998), 37. The Fenians chose their name in romantic reference to the legendary Fene or Fianna, which tradition held were the great warriors and defenders of ancient Ireland.

6. While I am offering a new interpretation of the motivation and service of Irish-American Union soldiers, I have benefited from the outstanding scholarship of my predecessors. The theories they put forth vary, but all should be considered: William L. Burton, *Melting Pot Soldiers: The Union's Ethnic Regiments* (New York: Fordham University Press, 1998); Pia Seija Seagrave, ed., *The History of the Irish Brigade: A Collection of Historical Essays* (Fredericksburg, VA: Sergeant Kirkland's Museum and Historical Museum, 1997); Daniel George MacNamara, *The History of the Ninth Regiment Massachusetts Infantry, June 1861–June 1864*, Christian G. Samito, ed. (New York: Fordham University Press, 2000); Joseph G. Bilby, *The Irish Brigade in the Civil War: The 69th New York and Other Irish Regiments of the Army of the Potomac* (Conshohocken, PA: Combined Publishing, 2000); David Power Conyngham, *The Irish Brigade and Its Campaigns*, Lawrence F. Kohl, ed. (New York: Fordham University Press, 1994); Ella Lonn, *Foreigners in the Union Army and Navy* (Baton Rouge: Louisiana State University Press, 1951); William McCarter, *My Life in the Irish Brigade: The Civil War Memoirs of Private William McCarter, 116th Pennsylvania Infantry*, Kevin E. O'Brien, ed. (Campbell, CA: Savas, 1996). Even

though it is a study of the Confederate Irish, Kelly J. O'Grady's *Clear the Confederate Way! The Irish in the Army of Northern Virginia* (El Dorado Hills, CA: Savas, 2000) offers an excellent commentary on Irish service in the American Civil War as well. These are but a sampling of the studies available on various aspects of Irish-American troops in the Union Army. There is no sweeping study of Irish service to the northern war effort beyond that put forth here.

7. The term "Wild Geese" relates back to seventeenth-century Ireland, referencing Irishmen rebelling against English authority who had to flee their land but continued to fight, often against English forces, in foreign armies. Some sources date the term to the flight of Catholic earls Hugh O'Neill and Rory O'Donnell, but the most common use of the term references the Treaty of Limerick (1691), in which the English allowed Irish Catholic Patrick Sarsfield to sail for France with eleven thousand of his defeated Catholic soldiers. There they would serve James II, the Stuart king living in exile in France. Many of these soldiers, who became known as the Wild Geese, formed the Irish Brigade within the French army, where they earned fame for their dedicated service. Other Irishmen exiled from their homeland over the centuries and serving in foreign armies continued this tradition of the Wild Geese, often forming themselves into units like the Irish Brigade seen during the American Civil War. See Maurice N. Hennessey, *The Wild Geese: The Irish Soldier in Exile* (New York: Devin-Adair, 1989); Frank D'Arcy, *Wild Geese and Migrant Scholars* (New York: Mercier Press,

2001); Kerby A. Miller, *Emigrants and Exiles: Ireland and the Irish Exodus to North America* (New York: Oxford University Press, 1989).

8. *New York Irish-American*, 23 November 1861; Patrick R. Guiney, *Commanding Boston's Irish Ninth: The Civil War Letters of Colonel Patrick R. Guiney, Ninth Massachusetts Volunteer Infantry*, Christian G. Samito, ed. (New York: Fordham University Press, 1998), 60.

9. *Boston Pilot*, 30 May 1863.

10. These characterizations are presented in David T. Knobel, *Paddy and the Republic: Ethnicity and Nationality in Antebellum America* (Middletown, CT: Wesleyan University Press, 1986), 76, 78.

11. Lawrence J. McCaffrey, *The Irish Catholic Diaspora in America* (Washington, DC: Catholic University of America Press, 1997), 7–8.

12. Historian Randall Miller addresses this problem in "Catholic Religion, Irish Ethnicity, and the Civil War," in *Religion and the American Civil War*, eds. Randall M. Miller, Harry S. Stout, and Charles Reagan Wilson (New York: Oxford University Press, 1998), 262.

13. For examples of this see James M. McPherson, *For Cause and Comrades: Why Men Fought in the Civil War* (Cambridge: Oxford University Press, 1997); Earl Hess, *The Union Soldier in Battle: Enduring the Ordeal of Combat*, Modern War Studies (Lawrence: University Press of Kansas, 1997); Gerald Linderman, *Embattled Courage: The Experience of Combat in the American Civil War* (New York: Free Press, 1989); Reid Mitchell, *Civil War Soldiers* (New York: Viking, 1988); Bell Irvin Wiley, *The Life of Billy Yank: The Common Soldier of the Union* (Baton Rouge: Louisiana State University Press, 1952; reprint, 1971).

NOTES TO CHAPTER I

1. One of the best studies of the Ulster Irish is Patrick Griffin's *People with No Name: Ireland's Ulster Scots, America's Scots Irish, and the Creation of a British Atlantic World, 1689–1764* (Princeton, NJ:

Princeton University Press, 2001). For additional information see James G. Leyburn, *The Scotch-Irish: A Social History* (Chapel Hill: University of North Carolina Press, 1962).

2. Leyburn, 241.

3. Griffin, 157–75; see also Kerby A. Miller, *Emigrants and Exiles: Ireland and the Irish Exodus to North America* (New York: Oxford University Press, 1985), 162–63.

4. Leyburn, 318.

5. Ibid., xi.

6. Lawrence J. McCaffrey, *The Irish Catholic Diaspora in America*, rev. ed. (Washington, DC: Catholic University of American Press, 1997), 63–64.

7. Ibid., 169.

8. Ibid., 193–97.

9. Ibid., 171–72.

10. Ibid., 172.

11. McCaffrey, 64–65; and Miller, 171. Miller offers an excellent explanation of this: "Irish Catholic identity, especially of Irish-speakers, was tied to Ireland itself and was inseparable from historical, cultural, religious, and linguistic associations with their homeland." Miller, *Emigrants and Exiles*, 167–68.

12. James Stuart Olson, *The Ethnic Dimension in American History* (New York: St. Martin's Press, 1979), 78; For theories on emigration vs. exile and many Irish Catholics' perspective that they were forced from their homeland by persecution and famine, see Miller.

13. Walter J. Walsh, "Religion, Ethnicity, and History: Clues to the Cultural Construction of Law," in *The New York Irish*, ed. Ronald H. Bayor and Timothy J. Meagher (Baltimore, MD: Johns Hopkins University Press, 1996), 61–62.

14. Ibid., 81–82.

15. Thomas H. O'Connor, *The Boston Irish: A Political History* (Boston: Back Bay Books, 1995), 43–44.

16. Charles R. Morris, *American Catholic: The Saints and Sinners Who Built America's Most Powerful Church* (New York: Vintage Books, 1997), 55.

17. O'Connor, 45. The estimates of the sales are presented by historian Ray Allen Billington, *The Protestant Crusade, 1800–1860*

(New York: Macmillan, 1938), 90–109.

18. Ibid., 45–46.

19. Dennis Clark, *The Irish in Philadelphia: The Generations of Urban Experience* (Philadelphia: Temple University Press, 1973; reprint, Philadelphia: Temple University Press, 1984), 21–22 (page citations are to the reprint edition).

20. Robert Smith, Philadelphia, PA, to James Smith and family, Moycraig, County Antrim, Ireland, 14 August 1844. Smith Family Letters, 1832–1848, D. 1828, Public Record Office of Northern Ireland.

21. William Barnaby Faherty, S.J. *The St. Louis Irish: An Unmatched Celtic Community* (St. Louis: Missouri Historical Society Press, 2001), 35, 63.

22. R. A. Burchell, *The San Francisco Irish, 1848–1880* (Berkeley: University of California Press, 1980), 3, 7.

23. Ellen Skerrett, "The Catholic Dimension," in *The Irish in Chicago*, ed. Lawrence J. McCaffrey (Urbana: University of Illinois Press, 1987), 22–23.

24. *St. Louis Observer*, 10 August 1836; quoted in Faherty, 63.

25. Skerrett, 25.

26. *Chicago Tribune*, 26 February 1855, quoted in Skerret, 26.

27. This is a central argument of works such as Kathleen Conzen's *Immigrant Milwaukee: Accommodation and Community in a Frontier City* (Cambridge: Harvard University Press, 1976).

28. Miller, *Emigrants and Exiles*, 291. For more information on the Irish potato famine see Cormac Ó Gráda, *Black '47 and Beyond: The Great Irish Famine in History, Economy, and Memory* (Princeton, NJ: Princeton University Press, 1999); Christine Kinealy, *The Great Irish Famine: Impact, Ideology, and Rebellion* (Houndmills, Hampshire: Palgrave, 2002); and James S. Donnelly, *The Great Irish Potato Famine* (Phoenix Mill, Gloucestershire: Sutton Publishing, 2001).

29. Thomas Gallagher, *Paddy's Lament, Ireland 1846–1847: Prelude to Hatred* (New York: Harcourt Brace, 1992), 78–79.

30. *Catholic Telegraph*, 18 February 1847; quoted in Robert Francis Hueston, *The Catholic Press*

and *Nativism, 1840–1860* (New York: Arno Press, 1976), 119–20.

31. Boston *Pilot*, 1 May 1847.

32. Boston *Daily Advertiser*, 18 January 1850; quoted in O'Connor, *The Boston Irish*, 63–64.

33. Theodore Parker, "A Sermon on the Moral Condition of Boston" (1849) in *The Collected Works of Theodore Parker*, ed. Francis P. Cobbe (London, 1864), 7:136; quoted in O'Connor, *The Boston Irish*, 64.

34. Boston *Daily Advertiser*, 23 January 1850; quoted in O'Connor, *The Boston Irish*, 64.

35. Ellis Paxson Oberholtzer, *History of the United States since the Civil War*, 5 vols. (New York: Macmillan, 1917–37), 5:732; quoted in Dennis Clark, *The Irish in Philadelphia: Ten Generations of Urban Experience* (Philadelphia: Temple University Press, 1973), 35.

36. Faherty, 68.

37. Faherty, 53.

38. Faherty, 66–67.

39. Henry Allen, Iowa City, Iowa, to Reverend Robert Allen, Dublin, Ireland, 17 March 1856. T.3084. Public Record Office of Northern Ireland.

40. The reader may be familiar with all of these terms except "anti-Bedinism." This refers to the 1853–1854 journey of Papal Nuncio Gaetano Bedini to America to visit parishes experiencing internal discord or tense relations with the Roman Church. Nativists protested against Bedini's representation of the authority of the church within the United States, and they were joined in an unusual union with exiles of the European revolutions of 1848. This latter group railed against Bedini's role in suppressing uprisings and the rather brutal manner in which his orders were carried out in the Papal States during the revolutions of 1848. Both groups characterized Bedini as everything from a threat to republican government to a bloody butcher, leading to his nickname, "The Butcher of Bologna." Nativists and immigrant Forty-eighters protested his visit for different, though occasionally related, reasons, making Bedini's trip so unpopular that he had to make a surreptitious departure from the port of New York in February 1854. For details on Bedini's visit

to America see Tyler Anbinder, *Nativism and Slavery: The Northern Know Nothings and the Politics of the 1850s* (New York: Oxford University Press, 1992), 27–29.

41. Paul Kleppner, *The Third Electoral System, 1853–1892: Parties, Voters, and Political Cultures* (Chapel Hill: University of North Carolina Press, 1979), 68. Kleppner argues, "Stripped to its essentials, this Know Nothing self-description was a crudely expressed listing of native Protestant objections to Catholicism," and "its focus was a perception of Catholicism as aggressively subversive of American values."

42. Anbinder, 92–94.

43. William Shaughnessy, Jackson, Mississippi, to Michael Shaughnessy, Granville, Wisconsin, 3 August 1855. Shaughnessy Family Papers, private collection of Kerby A. Miller, Ph.D., University of Missouri, Columbia.

44. William Shaughnessy, Jackson, Mississippi, to Michael Shaughnessy, Granville, Wisconsin, 31 January 1856. Shaughnessy Family Papers, private collection of Kerby A. Miller, Ph.D., University of Missouri, Columbia. While the brothers may have made this effort, it is significant to note that the family records have the name listed as Shaughnessy throughout, and the name continues to be used without the "O" today.

45. Anbinder, 45. As Anbinder notes, "In early 1855, when membership was at its peak, the vast majority of northern Know Nothings opposed the extension of slavery and adamantly sought repeal of the Kansas-Nebraska Act." Know-Nothing links with Free-Soil ideology are discussed on 227–28.

46. Anbinder, 45.

47. Ibid., 46

48. McCaffrey, 119.

49. Ibid., 119.

50. Edward C. Carter, II, "A 'Wild Irishman' under Every Federalist's Bed: Naturalization in Philadelphia, 1789–1806," in *The Irish: America's Political Class*, ed. James B. Walsh (New York: Arno Press, 1976), 333; for a concurring and more recent assessment of the Whig party's lack of support among immigrants, see the definitive work by Michael F. Holt, *The*

Rise and Fall of the American Whig Party: Jacksonian Politics and the Onset of the Civil War (New York: Oxford University Press, 1999), 117–18.

51. Joel H. Silbey, *The American Political Nation, 1838–1893* (Stanford, CA: Stanford University Press, 1991), 84.

52. Michael Doheny, New York City, New York, to William Smith O'Brien, Ireland, 20 August 1858. Smith O'Brien Papers, MS. 446, I. 3058, National Library of Ireland.

53. Leonard Wibberly, *The Coming of the Green* (New York: Holt, 1958), 163; quoted in Edward M. Levine, *The Irish and Irish Politicians: A Study of Cultural and Social Alienation* (Notre Dame, IN: University of Notre Dame Press, 1966), 47.

54. Patrick Dunny, Philadelphia, Pennsylvania, to Dunny family, Sleaty, County Carlow, Ireland, 30 December 1856. Private Collection of Arnold Schrier, Ph.D., Professor Emeritus, University of Cincinnati.

55. Patrick Dunny, Philadelphia, Pennsylvania, to Dunny family, Sleaty, County Carlow, Ireland, 30 December 1856. Private Collection of Arnold Schrier, Ph.D., Professor Emeritus, University of Cincinnati.

56. James Dixon, Philadelphia, PA, to Catherine Dixon, Castlebridge, Country Wexford, Ireland, 4 September 1855. Private Collection of Arnold Schrier, Ph.D., Professor Emeritus, University of Cincinnati. Dixon's reference to Louisville could be to Louisville, KY, where nativists did lead attacks on Catholics in 1855.

57. Michael F. Funchion, "The Political and Nationalist Dimensions," in *The Irish in Chicago*, ed. Lawrence J. McCaffrey (Urbana: University of Illinois Press, 1987), 62.

58. Details on Hughes are available in numerous works, but two of the best are Richard Shaw, *Dagger John: The Unquiet Life and Times of Archbishop John Hughes of New York* (New York: Paulist Press, 1977) and Charles R. Morris, *American Catholic: The Saints and Sinners Who Built America's Most Powerful Church* (New York: Vintage Books, 1997).

59. George Robertson, *The American Party: Its Principles, Its Objects, and Its Hopes* (Frankfort,

KY, 1855), 2; quoted in Kleppner, 69.

60. Faherty, 49. See chapter 7 on education and the growing independence of the Irish Catholic population of St. Louis for more information on this subject.

61. Burchell, 126–27, 163–64.

62. Donald Bruce Johnson and Kirk H. Porter, *National Party Platforms, 1840–1972*, 5th ed. (Chicago, 1975), 33.

63. The *Liberator*, 25 March, 1842; quoted in Noel Igantiev, *How the Irish Became White* (New York: Routledge, 1995), 10; emphasis original.

64. Boston *Pilot*, 12 February 1842.

65. The *Liberator*, 4 March 1842; quoted in Ignatiev, 13.

66. The *Liberator*, 25 March 1842; quoted in Ignatiev, 12.

67. *National Anti-Slavery Standard*, 24 March 1842; quoted in Ignatiev, 13–14.

68. Ignatiev, 16.

69. *The Irish Patriot: Daniel O'Connell's Legacy to Irish Americans* (Philadelphia: privately printed, 1863); quoted in Ignatiev, 23.

70. Philadelphia *Public Ledger*, 6 July 1843; quoted in Ignatiev, 26.

71. Boston *Pilot*, 9 November 1852.

72. James Brewer Stewart, *Holy Warriors: The Abolitionists and American Slavery*, American Century Series (New York: Hill and Wang, 1976), 14. Stewart argues, "The deepest significance of evangelicalism for abolitionism lay . . . [in] placing the voice of conscience over law, free will over original sin, and human benevolence over divine retribution" in which American Protestantism shaped "a new vision of spiritual and personal liberty."

73. *Catholic Telegraph and Almanac*, 23 October 1852.

74. "Reality vs. Humbug," *U.S. Catholic Magazine* 8 (1849): 17; quoted in Hueston, 185.

75. *Catholic Mirror*, 1 March 1851, 68, and *Catholic Telegraph and Almanac*, 20 March 1852, 5; both quoted in Hueston, 204–5; arguments from the *Pilot* and *Irish American* summarized in Hueston, 205.

76. Robert Smith, Philadelphia, PA, to William Smith, his brother,

Moycraig, County Antrim, Ireland, 22 August 1842. Smith Family Letters, 1832–1848, D. 1828, Public Record Office of Northern Ireland.

77. Hueston, 209.

78. Orestes Brownson, "The Fugitive Slave Law," *Brownson's Quarterly Review*, New Series, 5 (1851): 410–11; quoted in Hueston, 211.

79. Eric Foner, *Free Soil, Free Labor, Free Men: The Ideology of the Republican Party before the Civil War* (New York: Oxford University Press, 1995), 228.

80. Reginald Byron, *Irish America*, Oxford Studies in Social and Cultural Anthropology (Oxford: Oxford University Press, 1999), 55–57.

81. Joseph P. Ferrie, *Yankees Now: Immigrants in the Antebellum United States, 1840–1860* (New York: Oxford University Press, 1999), 70.

82. Historians now argue that the memories of "No Irish Need Apply" have been exaggerated to the point where this is understood as the standard Irish experience. If this were the case, there is little to explain how Irish women came to dominate the household service industry and Irish men found a powerful role in labor unions and the police forces in the late nineteenth century. Nonetheless, to disregard the difficulties faced by Irish immigrants in America would be equally misleading.

83. David R. Roediger, *The Wages of Whiteness: Race and the Making of the American Working Class*, rev. ed. (London: Verso, 1991), 144–46.

84. Richard H. Coolidge, M.D., *Statistical Report on the Sickness and Mortality in the Army of the United States, Compiled from the Records of the Surgeon General's Office, Embracing a Period of Sixteen Years, from January 1839 to January 1855* (Washington, DC: A.O.P. Nicholson, 1856), 627.

85. Francis Paul Prucha, *Broadax and Bayonet: The Role of the United States Army in the Development of the Northwest, 1851–1860* (Madison: State Historical Society of Wisconsin, 1953; reprint, Lincoln: University of Nebraska Press, 1995), 41 (page citations are to the reprint edition).

86. Prucha, 43; Edward M.

Coffman, *The Old Army: A Portrait of the American Army in Peacetime, 1784–1898* (New York: Oxford University Press, 1986), 196–97; and Kenneth J. Hagan, *This People's Navy: The Making of American Sea Power* (New York: Free Press, 1991), 141.

87. Prucha, 43–44.

88. Stanley Lebergott, *Manpower in Economic Growth: The American Record since 1800* (New York: McGraw-Hill, 1964), 541.

89. Coffman, 153–54.

90. Peter F. Stevens, *The Rogue's March: John Riley and the St. Patrick's Battalion* (Washington, DC: Brassey's, 1999), 33. See also Robert Ryal Miller, *Shamrock and Sword: The Saint Patrick's Battalion in the U.S.-Mexican War* (Norman: University of Oklahoma Press, 1989).

91. Coffman, 137.

92. Ibid., 143.

93. Ibid., 179; *New York Freeman's Journal*, 12 April 1846.

94. Coffman, 78–81.

95. Stevens, 56.

96. Ibid., 55.

97. Historian K. Jack Bauer takes a firm stand on that matter, arguing, "Actually, most of the deserters were not Irish. . . ." Bauer, *The Mexican War, 1846–1848* (New York: Macmillan, 1974); reprint, Lincoln: University of Nebraska Press, 1992), 42 (page citations are to the reprint edition).

98. Boston *Pilot* (Massachusetts), 14 September 1847.

99. Stevens, 38.

100. Ibid., 37–38.

101. John Edward Thompson, Fort Duncan, Texas, to his father, Reverend Skeffington Thompson, Killead, Co. Antrim, Ireland, 24 February 1858. U.S. Consular Dispatches, Belfast, Ireland, Film T-368, Reel 3. National Archives and Records Administration, Washington, DC.

102. Michael Doheny, New York City, New York, to William Smith O'Brien, Ireland, 20 August 1858. Smith O'Brien Papers, Ms. 446, I. 3058, National Library of Ireland.

103. Thomas Reilly, Albany, New York, to John M. Kelly, Dublin, Ireland, 24 April 1848. Thomas Reilly Letters, New York State, to Dublin, 1846–1848, MS. 10, 511. National Library of Ireland.

104. Sir Arthur G. Doughty, ed., *Elgin-Grey Papers, 1846–1852* (Ottawa, Canada: J.O. Patenaude, 1937), 1:209, 4 vols., 18 July 1849; quoted in Brian Jenkins, *Fenians and Anglo-American Relations during Reconstruction* (Ithaca, NY: Cornell University Press, 1969), 16.

105. O'Connor, *The Boston Irish*, 83–84.

106. Thomas H. O'Connor, *Civil War Boston: Home Front and Battlefield* (Boston: Northeastern University Press, 1997), 29.

107. Albert J. Von Frank, *The Trials of Anthony Burns: Freedom and Slavery in Emerson's Boston* (Cambridge, MA: Harvard University Press, 1998), 251–52.

108. O'Connor, *Civil War Boston*, 72. For a discussion of the rise of Know Nothing power in Boston and throughout Massachusetts in the 1850s, see O'Connor, *The Boston Irish*, 76–77. In 1854–1855, Know Nothings in Massachusetts "elected all the state officers, the entire membership of the state senate, and all but four seats in the house." In addition, the mayor of Boston and the governor of Massachusetts were Know Nothings. See also Tyler Anbinder, *Nativism and Slavery.*

NOTES TO CHAPTER 2

1. Boston *Pilot*, 3 November 1860.

2. Ibid., 3 November 1860.

3. Ibid., 26 May 1860.

4. Ibid., 3 November 1860.

5. Ibid., 25 August 1860.

6. *New York Herald*, 6 November 1860.

7. The *Pilot*, 16 April 1862.

8. Sidney G. Fisher, *A Philadelphia Perspective: The Diary of Sidney George Fisher Covering the Years 1834–1871*, ed. Nicholas B. Wainwright (Philadelphia: Historical Society of Philadelphia, 1967), 439; quoted in Noel Ignatiev, *How the Irish Became White* (New York: Routledge, 1995), 165–66. See also Dennis Clark, *The Irish in Philadelphia: Ten Generations of Urban Experience* (Philadelphia: Temple University Press, 1973), 73, 120–21; Kevin Kenny, *The American Irish: A History* (New York: Longman, 2000), 125.

9. Richard O'Gorman, New York, New York, to William Smith O'Brien, Ireland, 6 April 1861. William Smith O'Brien Papers, National Library of Ireland.

10. The Fenians chose their name in romantic reference to the legendary Fene or Fianna, which tradition held were the great warriors and defenders of ancient Ireland. See Terry Golway, *Irish Rebel: John Devoy and America's Fight for Ireland's Freedom* (New York: St. Martin's Griffin, 1998), 37.

11. George Templeton Strong, *Diary of the Civil War, 1860–1865,* ed. Allan Nevins (New York: Macmillan, 1962), 51.

12. Letter from Colonel Corcoran to W. B. Field, 6 October 1861, in the private collection of Colonel Kenneth H. Powers; quoted in Joseph G. Bilby, *The Irish Brigade in the Civil War: The 69th New York and Other Irish Regiments of the Army of the Potomac* (Conshohocken, PA: Combined Publishing, 2000), 2.

13. New York *Irish-American*, 23 March 1861.

14. Ibid., 23 March 1861.

15. Marcus Cunliffe, *Soldiers and Civilians: The Martial Spirit in America, 1775–1865* (Boston: Little, Brown, 1968), 228.

16. *Harper's Weekly*, 20 October 1860.

17. Ibid., 20 October 1860.

18. New York *Irish-American*, 23 March 1861.

19. Ibid., 23 March 1861.

20. Tyler Anbinder, *Nativism and Slavery: The Northern Know Nothings and the Politics of the 1850s* (New York: Oxford University Press, 1992), 107.

21. Terry Golway, *For the Cause of Liberty: A Thousand Years of Ireland's Heroes* (New York: Simon & Schuster, 2000), 33.

22. Phyllis Lane, "Colonel Michael Corcoran, Fighting Irishman," in *The History of the Irish Brigade: A Collection of Historical Essays*, ed. Pia Seija Seagrave (Fredericksburg VA: Sergeant Kirkland's Museum and Historical Society, 1997), 13–14.

23. For a nice introduction to the Fenians and excellent analysis of the organization see Leon Ó Broin, *Fenian Fever: An Anglo-American Dilemma* (New York: New York University Press, 1971). See also Oliver Rafferty, "Fenianism in North America in the 1860s: The Problems of Church and State," *History* 84 (April 1999): 257–77.

24. Ibid., 14–15.

25. Michael Doheny, New York City, New York, to William Smith O'Brien, Ireland, 20 August 1858. Smith O'Brien Papers, MS. 446, I. 3058, National Library of Ireland.

26. The *Pilot*, 5 and 26 January 1861.

27. Ibid., 12 January 1861.

28. Ibid., 2 February 1861.

29. New York *Irish-American*, 16 February 1861.

30. Michael Cavanagh, *Memoirs of Gen. Thomas Francis Meagher, Comprising the Leading Events of His Career, Chronologically Arranged, with Selections from his Speeches, Lectures, and Miscellaneous Writings, including Personal Reminiscences* (Worcester, MA: Messenger Press, 1892), 367–68.

31. Russell F. Weigley, "The Border City in Civil War, 1854–1865," in *Philadelphia: A 300-Year History*, ed. Russell Weigley (New York: Norton, 1982), 392. Weigley argued, "If all the North had shared the attitudes of Philadelphia, the South would have had nothing to fear. . . . On the contrary, the attitude of Philadelphia encouraged southerners to believe that if they did secede . . . much of the North would acquiesce in their departure."

32. Samuel and Ann Nimiks, Eden, IA or KS, to William Anderson, Co. Derry, Ireland, 4 February 1861. Anderson Family Letters, Public Record Office of Northern Ireland.

33. John Thompson, Ft. Sumter, SC, to his father, Robert Thompson, Articlave Parish, County Londonderry (Derry), Ireland, 14 February 1861. Public Record Office of Northern Ireland. T. 1585/1–2.

34. John Thompson, Ft. Hamilton, NY, to his father, Robert Thompson, Articlave Parish, County Londonderry (Derry), Ireland, 28 April 1861. Public Record Office of Northern Ireland. T. 1585/1–2.

35. Brian Hutton, "Two Letters from Fort Sumter," *The Irish Sword* 5 (Summer 1962): 183.

36. Cavanagh, 369.

37. Boston *Pilot*, 27 April 1861, 18 May 1861.

38. Ibid., 31 May 1861.

39. New York *Irish-American,* 15 June 1861.

40. Philadelphia *Inquirer,* 14 November 1860.

41. Dennis Clark, *The Irish in Philadelphia: Ten Generations of Urban Experience* (Philadelphia: Temple University Press, 1973), 121. These ties would continue, most famously through Commodore Stewart's grandson and fighter for Irish home rule, Charles Stewart Parnell.

42. *New York Herald,* 2 June 1861.

43. Lawrence Frederick Kohl, introduction to *The Irish Brigade and Its Campaigns,* by David Power Conyngham (New York: Fordham University Press, 1994), xiv–xvi.

44. Lawrence Frederick Kohl and Margaret Cossé Richard, eds., *Irish Green and Union Blue: The Civil War Letters of Peter Welsh, Color Sergeant, 28th Regiment, Massachusetts Volunteers* (New York: Fordham University Press, 1986), 4.

45. Kohl and Richard, 102–3.

46. Ibid., 103.

47. Cavanagh, 369.

48. Paul Jones, *The Irish Brigade* (Gaithersburg, MD: Olde Soldier Books, 1969), 19; Cavanagh, 17–19.

49. Jones, 21–22; Robert G. Athearn, *Thomas Francis Meagher: An Irish Revolutionary in America,* The Irish Americans (New York: Arno Press, 1976), 2.

50. Cavanagh, 74–75.

51. Golway, 116.

52. Ibid., 121.

53. Athearn, 12.

54. Ibid., 13.

55. Ibid., 370–71.

56. For an overview of Halpine's life and work, especially as relating to the Miles O'Reilly character, see John D. Hayes and Doris D. Maguire, "Charles Graham Halpine: Life and Adventures of Miles O'Reilly," *New-York Historical Society Quarterly* 51 (1967): 326–44.

57. Charles G. Halpine, *The Life and Adventures, Songs, Services, and Speeches of Private Miles O'Reilly* (New York: Carleton Publisher, 1864), 159–60.

58. The *Pilot,* 15 July 1865 and 27 July 1861.

59. *New York Herald,* 2 June 1861.

60. Cavanagh, 371.

61. Ronald H. Bayor and Timothy J. Meagher, eds., *The New York Irish* (Baltimore, MD: Johns Hopkins University Press, 1998), 195.

62. Maurice Sexton, Boston, Massachusetts, to Sexton family, Killeen, Donaghmore, County Cork, Ireland, 24 November 1861.

63. Henry O'Mahoney Memoir, unpublished, from the private collection of Kerby A. Miller, Ph.D., University of Missouri, Columbia. O'Mahoney received his honorable discharge in 1865 and his two-hundred-dollar bounty, but he was terribly ill and barely managed to survive.

64. D. P. Conyngham, *The Irish Brigade and Its Campaigns,* Lawrence Frederick Kohl, ed. (New York: Fordham University Press, 1994), 20.

65. Ibid., 21.

66. Ibid., 21.

67. Ibid., 21.

68. Russell F. Weigley, *The Age of Battles: The Quest for Decisive Warfare from Breitenfeld to Waterloo* (Bloomington: Indiana University Press, 1991), 207; for more information on the Irish Brigade at the Battle of Fontenoy see Jon Manchip White, *Marshal of France: The Life and Times of Maurice de Saxe* (New York: Rand McNally, 1962), 146–66; and Jacques Boudet, "Fontenoy, 1745," in *Great Military Battles,* ed. Cyril Falls (London: Spring Books, 1964), 50–57.

69. Joseph G. Bilby, *The Irish Brigade in the Civil War: The 69th New York and Other Irish Regiments of the Army of the Potomac* (Conshohocken, PA: Combined Publishing, 2000), 147–48.

70. *New York Times,* 23 April 1861.

71. Ibid., 24 April 1861.

72. Ibid., 24 April 1861.

73. Cavanagh, 375–76.

74. *Harper's Weekly,* 1 June 1861.

75. For an excellent discussion of the Irish and Catholic traditions behind the early recruitment of Irish-American units, see Randall M. Miller, "Catholic Religion, Irish Ethnicity, and the Civil War," in Randall M. Miller, Harry S. Stout,

and Charles Reagan Wilson, eds., *Religion and the American Civil War* (New York: Oxford University Press, 1998), 261–96.

76. Cavanagh, 378–80.

77. *New York Herald,* 9 May 1861.

78. Ibid., 19 May 1861.

79. Cavanagh, 389; Bilby, 9. See also Richard Shaw, *Dagger John: The Unquiet Life and Times of Archbishop John Hughes of New York* (New York: Paulist Press, 1977), 340–41; and Miller, 269.

80. Cavanagh, 387.

81. Judge Charles Patrick Daly to Charles G. Halpine, 11 July 1861, Folder 21: Letters July 1861, Box 3, Charles P. Daly Papers, Rare Books and Manuscripts Division, New York Public Library, New York (hereafter cited as Daly Papers).

82. Colonel Michael Corcoran to Judge Charles Patrick Daly, 8 July 1861, Folder 21: Letters July 1861, Box 3, Daly Papers.

83. William L. Burton, *Melting Pot Soldiers: The Union's Ethnic Regiments,* 2nd ed. The North's Civil War Series (New York: Fordham University Press, 1998), 127. The 37th New York Infantry originally formed as a militia regiment, the 75th Rifles, back in the 1850s as part of an effort to train Irish-Americans for a future battle to free Ireland.

84. "Americans to the Rescue" Broadside, 1850s Boston, Massachusetts Historical Society, Boston, Massachusetts; and the Boston *Pilot,* 24 August 1861.

85. M. H. MacNamara, *The Irish Ninth in Bivouac & Battle, or Virginia and Maryland Campaigns* (Boston: Lee and Shepard, 1867), 19.

86. Ibid., 5.

87. Ibid., 16.

88. Ibid., 17.

89. Brian C. Pohanka, *James McKay Rorty: An Appreciation* (New York: Irish Brigade Association, 1993), 20–21.

90. *Quincy Herald,* 13 May 1861, *Illinois State Register* (Springfield), 29 April 1861; and A. T. Glaze, *The City of Fond Du Lac* (Fond du Lac: P. B. Haber Printing Company, 1905), 6–7; all quoted in Craig Lee Kautz, "Fodder for Cannon: Immigrant Perceptions of the Civil War—the Old

Northwest" (Ph.D. diss., University of Nebraska, Lincoln, 1976), 67–69.

91. George D. Wells to Governor John A. Andrew, Boston, 16 May 1861. Andrew Collection, Massachusetts Historical Society, Boston, Massachusetts.

92. Harold F. Smith, "Mulligan and the Irish Brigade," *Journal of the Illinois State Historical Society* 56 (1963): 164–66.

93. Burton, 145.

94. Ibid., 94–95.

95. Ibid., 148–49; John H. Campbell, *History of the Friendly Sons of St. Patrick and of the Hibernian Society of Philadelphia, 1771–1892* (Philadelphia: privately printed, 1892), 282.

96. Campbell, 281.

97. Ezra J. Warner, *Generals in Blue: Lives of the Union Commanders* (Baton Rouge: Louisiana State University Press, 1995), 362–63. Although the official reports listed Patterson as "found dead in his tent . . . killed by the accidental discharge of his own pistol," rumors circulated that his death was a suicide.

98. Cavanagh, 363.

99. Monsignor Eugene Murphy, *The First One Hundred Years, 1831–1931: The Parish of St. John the Baptist* (Philadelphia: Church Printing and Envelope Co., 1932), 180–82.

100. Curt Johnson and Mark McLaughlin, *Battles of the Civil War* (London: Roxby Press, 1977; reprint, New York: Barnes and Noble, 1995), 33–34 (page citations are to the reprint edition); for insightful commentary on Patterson see William C. Davis, *Battle at Bull Run* (New York: Doubleday, 1977).

101. William T. Sherman, *Memoirs of General William T. Sherman* (New York: Da Capo Press, 1984), 180.

102. Bilby, 11.

103. William C. Davis, *Battle at Bull Run: A History of the First Major Campaign of the Civil War,* 2nd ed. (Mechanicsburg, PA: Stackpole Books, 1995), 185–86.

104. *Harper's Weekly,* 10 August 1861.

105. Brian Pohanka, *James McKay Rorty: An Appreciation* (New York: Irish Brigade Association, 1993), 6.

106. Bilby, 17.

107. For accounts of the 69th N.Y.S.M. in the Battle of First Bull Run see the reports of Colonel William T. Sherman, *War of the Rebellion: A Compilation of the Official Records of the Union and Confederate Armies* (Washington, DC: Government Printing Office, 1880–1901) (hereafter cited as *O.R.*), vol. 2, pt. 2: 368–71; and Captain James Kelly, 69th New York State Militia, *O.R.*, vol. 2, pt. 2: 371–72, as well as secondary accounts by Davis, 184–88, 218–19; Bilby, 9–17; and Christopher-Michael Garcia, "The 'Fighting' 69th New York State Militia at Bull Run," in *The History of the Irish Brigade: A Collection of Historical Essays,* ed. Pia Seija Seagrove (Fredericksburg, VA: Sergeant Kirkland's Press, 1997), 35–56.

108. *New York Herald,* 22 July 1861.

109. Maria Lydig Daly, *Diary of a Union Lady, 1861–1865,* ed. Harold Earl Hammond (New York: Funk & Wagnalls, 1962; reprint, Lincoln: University of Nebraska Press, 2000), 39 (page citations are to the reprint edition).

110. *Irish-American,* 27 July 1861.

111. Daly, 41.

112. *New York Times,* 28 July 1861.

113. *Irish-American,* 10 August 1861.

114. *New York Herald,* 24 July 1861.

115. Matilda Sproul, Carn Corn, Co. Tyrone, Ireland, to Andrew J. Sproul, Fredericksburg, Ohio, 4 March 1861 and 22 July 1861. Andrew J. Sproul Papers, Southern Historical Collection, University of North Carolina, Chapel Hill.

116. New York *Irish-American,* 23 November 1861.

NOTES TO CHAPTER 3

1. D. P. Conyngham, *The Irish Brigade and Its Campaigns,* Lawrence Frederick Kohl, ed. (New York: Fordham University Press, 1994), 39–40.

2. Michael Cavanagh, *Memoirs of Gen. Thomas Francis Meagher* (Worcester, MA: Messenger Press, 1892), 407.

3. Ibid., 50.

4. Conyngham, 50–54.

5. Cavanagh, 415.

6. Ibid., 412.

7. Ibid., 417.

8. Ibid., 422.

9. Anthony W. McDermott, *A Brief History of the 69th Regiment Pennsylvania Veteran Volunteers, from Its Formation until Final Muster out of the United States Service* (no pub., 1889), 5–7.

10. Patrick Dunny, Philadelphia, PA, to his family, Sleaty, Co. Carlow, Ireland, October 22, 1861. Private Collection of Arnold Schrier, Ph.D., Professor Emeritus, University of Cincinnati.

11. Maurice Sexton, Boston, MA, to brothers and sisters in Killeen, Donaghmore, Co. Cork, November 24, 1861. Private Collection of Arnold Schrier, Ph.D., Professor Emeritus, University of Cincinnati.

12. James L. Bowen, *Massachusetts in the War, 1861–1865* (Springfield, MA: Clark W. Bryan & Co., 1889), 419. The problems of this Massachusetts regiment reveal an early weakness in Irish volunteering that is commonly overlooked in the history of Irish military service in the American Civil War. The traditional interpretation, promoted by leaders in the field such as William L. Burton (*Melting Pot Soldiers*) and Ella Lonn (*Foreigners in the Union Army and Navy*), indicates a rush to service by the foreign-born in an effort to prove their loyalty, gain military experience for a future war for Ireland, or earn a steady income. Actually, ethnic units were having some difficulties filling their ranks as early as August 1861 when Americans north and south were raising regiments to prepare for a long war.

13. Craig Lee Kautz, "Fodder for Cannon: Immigrant Perceptions of the Civil War—The Old Northwest" (Ph.D. diss., University of Nebraska, Lincoln, 1976), 71.

14. *Lafayette Daily Courier,* 5 September 1861; quoted in T. Kevin Griffin, "The 1st Irish, 35th Indiana Volunteer Infantry Regiment, 1861–1865: A Military, Political, and Social History" (M.A. thesis, Butler University, 1992), 26–27.

15. *Detroit Daily Tribune,* 11 September 1861; quoted in Kautz, 73.

16. Reverend Thomas McElroy, C.S.C., "The War Letters of Father Peter Paul Cooney of the Congregation of Holy Cross," *Records of the American Catholic Historical Society of Philadelphia* 44 (June 1933): 53.

17. Kautz, 70–71.

18. *Cincinnati Daily Enquirer,* 13 October 1861; quoted in Kautz, 73–74.

19. James Swales to David Swales, 20 September 1861, James Swales Collection, Illinois State Historical Library, Springfield, Illinois; quoted in Kautz, 77.

20. Conyngham, 62; for additional descriptions of the day, the speakers, and the crowd's reaction see Maria Lydig Daly, *Diary of a Union Lady, 1861–1865,* Harold Earl Hammond, ed. (New York: Funk and Wagnalls, 1962; reprint, Lincoln: University of Nebraska Press, 2000), 79–80 (page citations are to the reprint edition).

21. Daly, 75.

22. Father Bernhard O'Reilly, S.J., to Judge Charles Patrick Daly, 4 September 1861, Folder 15 Letters, Sept. 1861, Box 3, Charles P. Daly Papers, 1816–1899, Rare Books and Manuscripts Division, New York Public Library, New York (hereafter cited as Daly Papers).

23. Daly, 101.

24. Rumors of Meagher's cowardice and problems with alcohol plagued him throughout the war and continue to be addressed by modern historians. Most scholars question any criticism of his courage but continue to report his incompetence and alcoholism. As the war progressed there would be evidence to indicate that this may be a fair criticism, but it is hardly a trait unique to this commander. Inept political generals and whiskey courage were common on many Civil War battlefields for both native-born and immigrant officers and men. To characterize such problems as uniquely Meagher's or as uniquely Irish would be inaccurate.

25. James M. McPherson, *Ordeal by Fire: The Civil War and Reconstruction,* 2nd ed. (New York: McGraw-Hill, 1992), 176.

26. Colonel James A. Mulligan, "The Siege of Lexington, MO," in *Battles and Leaders of the Civil War,* Vol. I, Grant-Lee Edition (New York: Century Co., 1887), 307–13.

27. Harold F. Smith, "Mulligan and the Irish Brigade," *Journal of the Illinois State Historical Society* 56, no. 2 (Summer 1963): 171–74; see also William L. Burton, *Melting Pot Soldiers: The Union's Ethnic Regiments,* 2nd ed. (New York: Fordham University Press, 1998), 136–37.

28. Charles D. B. O'Ryan to Governor Richard Yates, 28 December 1861, Yates Family Papers, Abraham Lincoln Presidential Library. Emphasis in the original.

29. P. O'Marsh to William Gooding, 18 September 1862, Yates Family Papers, Abraham Lincoln Presidential Library. See also Burton, 138–40, for an excellent discussion of this matter.

30. John C. Haines to Governor Richard Yates, 17 September 1862, Yates Family Papers, Abraham Lincoln Presidential Library.

31. Burton, 138–40. Burton's discussion of both the 23rd and the 19th Illinois is superb, offering insights into the political and ethnic tensions within and without these units.

32. This is discussed at length in Reid Mitchell, *The Vacant Chair: The Northern Soldier Leaves Home* (New York: Oxford University Press, 1993), 3–18.

33. Patrick R. Guiney, *Commanding Boston's Irish Ninth: The Civil War Letters of Colonel Patrick R. Guiney, Ninth Massachusetts Volunteer Infantry,* ed. Christian G. Samito (New York: Fordham University Press, 1998), 66.

34. Guiney, 60.

35. Colonel Thomas Cass to Governor John Andrew, 3 May 1861, Volume 25, Ninth Regiment, 1861–1864, Executive Department Letter Series, Massachusetts State Archives.

36. Colonel Thomas Cass to Governor John Andrew, 31 May 1861, Volume 25, Ninth Regiment, 1861–1864, Executive Department Letter Series, Massachusetts State Archives.

37. Dr. T. H. Smith, Fourteenth Massachusetts Volunteers, to Governor John Andrew, 6 June 1861, Volume 25, Ninth Regiment, 1861–1864, Executive Department Letter Series, Massachusetts State Archives.

38. Daniel G. MacNamara, *History of the Ninth Regiment* (Boston: E. B. Stillings and Co., 1899), 4–5; quoted in Thomas H. O'Connor, *Civil War Boston: Home Front and Battlefield* (Boston: Northwestern University Press, 1997), 75.

39. O'Connor, 76.

40. George D. Wells to Governor John A. Andrew, 16 May 1861, John A. Andrew Papers, Massachusetts Historical Society.

41. George D. Wells to Governor John A. Andrew, 20 June 1861, John A. Andrew Papers, Massachusetts Historical Society.

42. George D. Wells to Governor John A. Andrew, 27 June 1861, John A. Andrew Papers, Massachusetts Historical Society.

43. George D. Wells to Governor John A. Andrew, 16 May 1861, John A. Andrew Papers, Massachusetts Historical Society.

44. George D. Wells to Governor John A. Andrew, 20 June 1861, John A. Andrew Papers, Massachusetts Historical Society. Wells makes similar comments throughout his correspondence with Governor Andrew during summer 1861.

45. O'Connor, 78.

46. 20 June 1861, Box 4 of 7, Vol. 1B, 23 September 1858–17 November 1865, Amos A. Lawrence Diaries, Massachusetts Historical Society.

47. O'Connor, 76.

48. The *Pilot,* 24 August 1861.

49. The *Pilot,* 27 July 1861.

50. The *Pilot,* 3, 10 August 1861.

51. Lawrence Frederick Kohl, introduction to *The Irish Brigade and Its Campaigns,* by D. P. Conyngham (New York: Fordham University Press, 1994), x.

52. The exception to this would be the veterans of the 69th New York State Militia Regiment, now the 69th New York Volunteers, as well as other veterans serving in the brigade, such as surgeon Francis Reynolds (introduced above), a veteran of the British Army and of service in the Crimean War.

53. William Corby, C.S.C., *Memoirs of Chaplain Life: Three Years with the Irish Brigade in the*

Army of the Potomac (New York: Fordham University Press, 1992), 60.

54. The *Pilot*, 21 June 1862.

55. James B. Turner to the Turner family, 9 May 1862, James B. Turner Papers, 1861–1876, New York State Library, Albany, New York.

56. William H. Osborne, *The History of the Twenty-Ninth Regiment of Massachusetts Volunteer Infantry, of the Late War of the Rebellion* (Boston: Albert J. Wright, 1877), 142.

57. Conyngham, 216.

58. Ibid., 217.

59. Anon., Ninth Massachusetts Diary, 27 June 1862, *Civil War Times Illustrated* 29, no. 2 (June 1990): 30; and Stephen W. Sears, *To the Gates of Richmond: The Peninsula Campaign* (Boston: Houghton Mifflin, 1992), 230.

60. The *Pilot*, 19 July 1862.

61. Bradley M. Gottfried, *Stopping Pickett: The History of the Philadelphia Brigade* (Shippensburg, PA: White Mane Books, 1999), 93.

62. *Detroit Free Press*, 31 May 1862; quoted in the *Pilot*, 12 July 1862.

63. Smith, 173.

64. Kautz, 140–41.

65. Ibid., 141.

66. *Quincy Herald*, 4 August 1862; quoted in Kautz, 141.

67. *Chicago Post*, 19 July 1862; reprinted in the *Pilot*, 2 August 1862.

68. The *Pilot*, 21 June 1862 and 9 August 1862.

69. The *Pilot*, 19 July 1862.

70. *New York Times*, 26 July 1862; also covered in the *Irish American*, 2 August 1862.

71. *New York Times*, 26 July 1862.

72. James B. Turner to the Turner family, 29 July 1862 and 19 July 1862, James B. Turner Papers, 1861–1876, New York State Library, Albany, New York.

73. Matilda Sproul, Carn Corn, County Tyrone, Ireland, to Andrew J. and Frances Sproul, Fredericksburg, Ohio, 28 July 1862. Sproul Family Papers, Southern Historical Collection, University of North Carolina, Chapel Hill.

74. Andrew and Lucy Greenlees, Dayton, Illinois, to Greenlees family, Magheramorne, Co. Antrim,

Ireland, 7 July 1862. Andrew Greenlees Papers, Public Record Office of Northern Ireland. The Homestead Act of 1862 awarded 160 acres of public land to individuals twenty-one years or older after he or she had lived on the claim for five years. See McPherson, *Ordeal by Fire*, 3rd ed., 404.

75. Hugh Harlin, Laporte, Indiana, to John Harlin, New York, 28 May 1862 and 4 August 1862. The Harlin Family Letters, from the private collection of Kerby A. Miller, Ph.D., University of Missouri, Columbia.

76. The *Pilot*, 14 June 1862.

77. Ibid., 14 June 1862 and 26 July 1862.

78. The *Chicago Post*; quoted in the *Pilot*, 2 August 1862.

79. Robert G. Athearn, *Thomas Francis Meagher: An Irish Revolutionary in America* (Boulder: University of Colorado Press, 1949; reprint, New York: Arno Press, 1976), 115.

80. Phyllis Lane, "Colonel Michael Corcoran, Fighting Irishman," in *The History of the Irish Brigade: A Collection of Historical Essays*, ed. Pia Seija Seagrove (Fredericksburg, VA: Sergeant Kirkland's Museum and Historical Society, 1997), 26; Joseph G. Bilby, *The Irish Brigade in the Civil War: The 69th New York and Other Irish Regiments of the Army of the Potomac* (Conshohocken, PA: Combined Publishing, 2000), 50.

81. *Forney's War Press*, 23 August 1862.

82. *Forney's War Press*, 30 August 1862.

83. *Forney's War Press*, 30 August 1862.

84. Conyngham, 368.

85. *New York Times*, 26 July 1862; and *War of the Rebellion: A Compilation of the Official Records of the Union and Confederate Armies* (Washington, DC: Government Printing Office, 1880–1901), Ser. 1, Vol. 11 (Part II): 24 (hereafter cited as *O.R. (Official Records)*).

86. Joseph L. Harsh, *Taken at the Flood: Robert E. Lee & Confederate Strategy in the Maryland Campaign of 1862* (Kent, OH: Kent State University Press, 1999), 385–87.

87. Don Ernsberger, *Paddy Owen's Regulars: A History of the*

69th Pennsylvania "Irish Volunteers" (Philadelphia: Xlibris, 2004), 307; Stephen W. Sears, *Landscape Turned Red: The Battle of Antietam* (New Haven, CT: Ticknor & Fields, 1983; reprint, New York: Book-of-the-Month Club, 1994), 223.

88. *O.R.*, Series I, Volume 19, Part 1: 306.

89. Ernsberger, 313–14.

90. Ernsberger, 314, 317–18.

91. Ernsberger, 322, and Daniel F. Gillen Pension File. See also William C. White, "Camp on Battlefield" (Antietam), to his parents, Philadelphia, Pennsylvania, 19 September 1862. William C. White Collection, White Box 2, Folder 10, MC17-2-10. The Philadelphia Archdiocesan Historical Records Center, Wynnewood, Pennsylvania.

92. Ernsberger, 324, Sears, 227.

93. Corby, 112.

94. New York *Irish-American*, 18 October 1862. Turner wrote reports to the paper frequently under the name of Gallowglass. See also the excellent editorial discussion of Turner's writings in the *Irish-American* in the series " 'Gallowglass' at Antietam: The Irish Brigade's Fight," Michael Kane, Gerry Reagan, and Joe Gannon, eds., The Irish Brigade Association, thewildgeese.com.

95. James J. Smith, Cleveland, Ohio, to Colonel John C. Stearns and General Henry Heth, Antietam Battlefield Board, 1893. The Carmen Collection, Union: II Corps, V Corps, VI Corps, Folder: II Corps, 1st Division, 2nd Brigade, Meagher. Antietam National Battlefield.

96. *O.R.*, Ser. 1, Vol. 19, Part 1: 294.

97. Ibid.; See also New York *Irish-American*, 18 October 1862.

98. New York *Irish-American*, 18 October 1862.

99. Kevin E. O'Brien, "Sprig of Green: The Irish Brigade," in *The History of the Irish Brigade: A Collection of Historical Essays*, ed. Pia Seija Seagrave (Fredericksburg, VA: Sergeant Kirkland's Museum, 1997), 75–77; *O.R.*, Ser. 1, Vol. 19, Part 1: 293–98; Sears, *Landscape Turned Red*, 245–46; Bilby, 60.

100. *O.R.*, Ser. 1, Vol. 19, Part 1: 58–59. Joseph G. Biusy and Stephan D. O'Neill, eds., *My Sons*

Were Faithful and They Fought the Irish Brigade at Antietam: An Anthology (Highstown, NJ: Longstreet House, 1997), 58.

101. New York Herald, 20 September 1862; see also coverage in the New York Times, 20 September 1862.

102. O.R., Ser. 1, Vol. 19, Part 1: 192; See also Stephen W. Sears, Landscape Turned Red, 243 (page citations are to the reprint edition).

103. Conyngham, 308; see also Bilby, 60.

104. Burton, 126.

105. Sears, Landscape Turned Red, 243–44.

106. Robert D. Webb, Headquarters, Provost Guard, Sharpsburg, MD, to George W. Wilson-Slator, Esq., Cartron Lodge, County Longford, Ireland, 16 October 1862. Robert D. Webb Letters, National Library of Ireland.

107. New York World, 12 November 1862.

108. Andrew Greenlees, Dayton, Illinois, to brother John Greenlees, Magheramorne, Co. Antrim, Ireland, 22 November 1862. Andrew Greenlees Papers, Public Record Office of Northern Ireland.

109. Bilby, 63, offers the account that Colonel Barnes refused the green banner, fearing it would brand them as Fenians, citing P. C. Headley, Massachusetts in the Rebellion: A Record of the Historical Position of the Commonwealth and the Services of the Leading Statesmen, the Military, the Colleges, and the People, in the Civil War of 1861–1865 (Boston: Walker, Fuller, and Co., 1866), 326–27. The account reporting that Barnes simply did not believe it honorable for a non-Irish regiment to carry an Irish banner is from Osborne, 203. Unfortunately, neither Conyngham, Corby, nor Cavanagh mention the incident, which could indicate that it embarrassed them, but equally that they understood and did not think it worthy of mention.

110. St. Clair Mulholland, The Story of the 116th Regiment Pennsylvania Volunteers in the War of the Rebellion, Lawrence Frederick Kohl, ed. (Philadelphia: F. McManus, Jr., 1903; reprint, New York: Fordham University Press, 1996), 10–12; Burton, 150;

Kohl, introduction to Mulholland, xi.

111. Conyngham, 330–36.

112. Mulholland, 35–36.

113. O.R., Ser. 1, Vol. 21: 240–41.

114. Mulholland, 37. For an excellent description of the Federals in the town see Francis A. O'Reilly, The Fredericksburg Campaign (Baton Rouge: Louisiana State University Press, 2003), 118–26, and George C. Rable, Fredericksburg! Fredericksburg! (Chapel Hill: University of North Carolina Press, 2002), 177–84. Both books are essential to any understanding of the Fredericksburg campaign.

115. William C. White, Fredericksburg, Virginia, to his parents, Philadelphia, Pennsylvania, 15 December 1862. William C. White Collection, White Box 2, Folder 19, MC17-2-19. The Philadelphia Archdiocesan Historical Records Center, Wynnewood, Pennsylvania.

116. Mulholland, 37.

117. William McCarter, "Annals of the War," Philadelphia Weekly Times, 8 September 1883.

118. William H. McClelland, letter to the editor, New York Irish-American, 10 January 1863.

119. Ibid.

120. William McCarter, Philadelphia Weekly Times, 8 September 1883.

121. Ibid.

122. Mulholland, 43.

123. Ibid., 43.

124. McCarter, Philadelphia Weekly Times, 8 September 1883.

125. James Longstreet, "The Battle of Fredericksburg," in Battles and Leaders, vol. 3 (New York: Yoseloff, 1956), 79.

126. Mulholland, 45.

127. McCarter, Philadelphia Weekly Times, 8 September 1883; Conyngham, 342; Mulholland, 45; O'Reilly, 310–11; O.R., Ser. 1, Vol. 21: 242.

128. O'Reilly, 127.

129. John H. Donovan, letter to the editor, New York Irish-American, 3 January 1863.

130. O'Reilly, 305.

131. Kelly J. O'Grady, Clear the Confederate Way! The Irish in the Army of Northern Virginia (Mason City, IA: Savas, 2000), 125–30.

132. O.R., Ser. 1, Vol. 21: 242.

133. It is unlikely that the officers would criticize Meagher in

their reports (O.R., Ser. 1, Vol. 21: 240–53), though they did have a chance in newspapers, letters home, and postwar writings. Such critiques are extremely rare among veterans of the Irish Brigade.

134. See Burton, Melting Pot Soldiers, 123–25, for an excellent discussion of Meagher's problems with charges of cowardice here and at the battles of First Bull Run and Antietam. For an Irish criticism of Meagher see Thomas Francis Galwey, "Fredericksburg and the Assault on Marye's Heights," The Catholic World, December 1889, 373; quoted in O'Grady, 126.

135. Robert Nugent, "The Sixty-ninth Regiment at Fredericksburg," in Third Annual Report of the State Historian of the State of New York (Albany, NY: Wynkoop Hallenbeck Crawford Co., 1898), 42–43.

136. John Dwyer, "63d Regiment Infantry," New York at Gettysburg, ed. William F. Fox (Albany, NY: J. B. Lyon Company, 1902), 2:501.

137. Mulholland, 48.

138. St. Clair A. Mulholland Pension File, National Archives, Washington, DC.

139. Mulholland, 56–57.

140. Southern Watchman (Athens, Georgia), 25 February 1863. See an excellent discussion of the Confederate Irish at Fredericksburg in O'Grady.

141. O'Reilly, 316–17.

142. Corby, 132; Conyngham, 343; Bilby, 67.

143. Robert Nugent, New York City, to St. Clair Mulholland, Philadelphia, Pennsylvania, 5 January 1881. St. Clair A. Mulholland Papers, Box 1, Civil War Library and Museum, Philadelphia, Pennsylvania. New York Irish-American, 27 December 1862.

144. Nugent, 43; William F. Fox, Regimental Losses in the American Civil War (Albany, NY: Albany Publishing, 1889), 204.

145. O.R., Ser. 1, Vol. 21: 129; O.R., Ser. 1, Vol. 19, Part 1: 192; Bilby, 70.

146. The Irish-American, 27 December 1862.

147. John England to Ellen Hargeddon, 17 December 1862, John England Letters, U.S. Army, 1814–1862, Manuscripts and

Archives Division, New York Public Library.

148. Conyngham, 350.

149. *Irish-American,* 10 January 1863.

NOTES TO CHAPTER 4

1. James M. McPherson, *Battle Cry of Freedom: The Civil War Era* (New York: Oxford University Press, 1988), 558. McPherson notes, "These words were T. J. Barnett's paraphrase of Lincoln's comments, but the president's sentiments were 'indicated plainly enough,' according to Barnett."

2. The *Pilot,* 10 January 1863.

3. The *Pilot,* 17 January 1863.

4. The *Irish-American,* 8 November 1862, 17 January 1863, 4 July 1863.

5. The *Weekly Day-Book,* 23 January 1863; quoted in Edward K. Spann, "Union Green: The Irish Community and the Civil War," in *The New York Irish,* ed. Ronald H. Bayor and Timothy J. Meagher (Baltimore, MD: Johns Hopkins University Press, 1996), 203.

6. Iver Bernstein, *The New York City Draft Riots: Their Significance for American Society and Politics in the Age of the American Civil War* (New York: Oxford University Press, 1990), 25.

7. This quotation, and variations on it, is offered in several sources: McPherson, 507, Bayor and Meagher, 207.

8. *Quincy* (Illinois) *Herald,* 14 July 1862; quoted in Craig Lee Kautz, "Fodder for Cannon: Immigrant Perceptions of the Civil War—The Old Northwest" (Ph.D. diss., University of Nebraska, Lincoln, 1976), 106–7.

9. *Chicago Times,* 30 September 1862; *Illinois State Register* (Springfield), 29 September 1862, 2 October 1862; quoted in Kautz, 109–10.

10. *Chicago Times,* 30 September 1862, and *Rock Island Weekly Argus,* 28 October, 5 November, 17 December 1862; quoted in Kautz, 109–11.

11. *Chicago Times,* 30 September 1862; *Illinois State Register* (Springfield), 29 September 1862, 2 October 1862; quoted in Kautz, 109–10.

12. Andrew Greenlees, Dayton, Illinois, to John Greenlees (brother), Magheramorne, Co. Antrim, Ireland, 22 November 1862. Andrew Greenlees Letters, Public Record Office of Northern Ireland.

13. McPherson, 559.

14. Stephen W. Sears, *George B. McClellan: The Young Napoleon* (New York: Ticknor & Fields, 1988), 325.

15. James McPherson offers a detailed discussion of Union soldiers and their changing views on abolition as a northern war aim in *For Cause and Comrades: Why Men Fought in the Civil War* (New York: Oxford University Press, 1998): 117–30.

16. General Michael Corcoran to Judge Charles Patrick Daly, 13 January 1863, Charles P. Daly Papers, Manuscripts and Archives Division, New York Public Library.

17. Maria Lydig Daly, *Diary of a Union Lady, 1861–1865,* ed. Harold Earl Hammond (New York: Funk and Wagnalls, 1962; reprint, Lincoln: University of Nebraska Press, 2000), 177, 179 (page citations are to the reprint edition).

18. Rowland Redmond, New York City, to William Young, Ballymena, County Antrim, Ireland, 7 November 1862. Rowland Redmond Papers, Public Record Office of Northern Ireland.

19. The frustration expressed by many Irish-American soldiers, politicians, and community leaders regarding the conduct of the battles of 1862 is addressed in chapter 3. Note particularly Irish-Americans' anger and diminishing support for the war after the Battle of Antietam and especially following the Battle of Fredericksburg.

20. See quotations of abolitionist statements that "the oath of a Catholic was not to be relied upon" following Irish-American protest against black laborers and the Emancipation Proclamation listed above from *Chicago Times,* 30 September 1862; *Illinois State Register* (Springfield), 29 September 1862, 2 October 1862; quoted in Kautz, 109–10.

21. Frank L. Klement, *The Limits of Dissent: Clement L. Vallandigham and the Civil War* (Lexington: University Press of Kentucky, 1970; reprint, New York: Fordham University Press, 1998), 112 (page citations are to the reprint edition); Joel H. Silbey, *A Respectable Minority: The Democratic Party in the Civil War Era, 1860–1868* (New York: Norton, 1977), 143–45.

22. The *Pilot,* 11 October 1862, emphasis original.

23. *New York Times,* 9 October 1862.

24. Rowland Redmond, New York City, to William Young, Ballymena, Co. Antrim, 7 November 1862. Rowland Redmond Letters, Public Record Office of Northern Ireland.

25. McPherson, 568–69.

26. The *Pilot,* 22 November 1862.

27. The *Pilot,* 24 January 1863.

28. John England to Ellen Hargedon, 25 January 1863, John England Letters, Manuscripts and Archives Division, New York Public Library.

29. Bayor and Meagher, 202.

30. This tradition within American society, that celebrates heroic military service while expressing a simultaneous fear of military power, is discussed in several works. For a discussion of Americans' views of the draft in 1862 and the concept of an antidraft American tradition see Eugene C. Murdock, *One Million Men: The Civil War Draft in the North* (Madison: State Historical Society of Wisconsin, 1971), 3–8; for a discussion of the contradictions of the American military tradition see Marcus Cunliffe, *Soldiers and Civilians: The Martial Spirit in America, 1775–1865* (Boston: Little, Brown, 1968), 27, and throughout the book.

31. Murdock, 6; and McPherson, *Battle Cry of Freedom,* 492–94.

32. Murdock, 7.

33. *Chicago Times,* 30 September 1862, and *Rock Island Weekly Argus,* 28 October, 5 November, 17 December 1862; quoted in Kautz, 109–12.

34. *Waterloo Advocate,* 1 August 1862, and *Dubuque Herald,* 10, 29 August 1862; quoted in Kautz, 143–44.

35. *Milwaukee Daily News,* 25 November 1862, emphasis original; quoted in Kautz, 146. For additional examples see *Quincy Herald,* 4 August 1862, and *Waterloo*

Advocate, 12 September 1862; quoted in Kautz, 141–42.

36. Kautz, 144.

37. McPherson, *Battle Cry of Freedom,* 493.

38. The *Pilot,* 23 August 1862.

39. The *Pilot,* 30 August 1862.

40. The *Pilot,* 6 September 1862; and James M. McPherson cites the 1863 Conscription Act exemption clause of three hundred dollars as more than half a year's wages for unskilled workingmen in McPherson, *Ordeal by Fire: The Civil War and Reconstruction,* 2nd ed. (New York: McGraw Hill, 1992), 354.

41. Edward Caney to Governor John A. Andrew, 25 December 1862 and 14 April 1863, and Mayor Peter Larosau to Governor John A. Andrew, 31 December 1862, Executive Department Letters, Vol. W32, 28th Regiment Massachusetts Volunteer Infantry, Massachusetts State Archives.

42. Unidentified letter to Governor John A. Andrew, 16 February 1863, Executive Department Letters, Vol. W32, 28th Regiment Massachusetts Volunteer Infantry, Massachusetts State Archives.

43. Horatio Woodman to Governor John A. Andrew, 13 February 1863, Executive Department Letters, Vol. W32, 28th Regiment Massachusetts Volunteer Infantry, Massachusetts State Archives.

44. McPherson, *Ordeal by Fire,* 353–54.

45. Congressional law published in the *Pilot,* 23 August 1862; and nineteenth-century naturalization requirements in Tyler Anbinder, *Nativism and Slavery: The Northern Know Nothings and the Politics of the 1850s* (New York: Oxford University Press, 1992), 121.

46. *Dubuque Herald,* 8 October 1862; quoted in Kautz, 129.

47. The *Pilot,* 13 September 1862, emphasis original.

48. The *Irish-American,* 11 October 1862.

49. *New York Times,* 17 January 1863; and D. P. Conyngham, *The Irish Brigade and Its Campaigns,* ed. Lawrence Frederick Kohl (New York: Fordham University Press, 1994), 356–59.

50. Conyngham, 359.

51. John England to Ellen Hargedon, 25 January 1863, John England Letters, Manuscripts and Archives Division, New York Public Library.

52. Andrew Sproul, Vicksburg, MS, to wife Frances Sproul, Fredericksburg, Ohio, 26 January 1863. Andrew J. Sproul Papers, Southern Historical Collection, University of North Carolina (hereafter cited as AJSP).

53. Andrew Sproul to Frances Sproul, 26 January 1863 (AJSP).

54. Andrew Sproul to Frances Sproul, 27 February 1863 (AJSP). For information on the canal-digging efforts north of Vicksburg in the spring of 1863 see Michael B. Ballard, *Vicksburg: The Campaign That Opened the Mississippi* (Chapel Hill: University of North Carolina Press, 2004), 174–90.

55. Andrew Sproul to Frances Sproul, 27 February 1863 (AJSP).

56. New York *Irish-American,* 27 December 1862.

57. New York *Irish-American,* 31 January 1863.

58. Ibid.

59. The *Pilot,* 30 May 1863; New York *Irish-American,* 14 March 1863; and Michael Cavanagh, *Memoirs of General Thomas Francis Meagher* (Worcester, MA: Messenger Press, 1892), 28–32. As the evidence outlined in the following paragraphs will demonstrate, Irish-American officers and enlisted men, political leaders, and news editors expressed this frustration.

60. Henry W. Halleck to Edwin M. Stanton, 18 February 1863, Papers of Edwin M. Stanton, Library of Congress, Washington, DC.

61. This possibility is supported by Robert G. Athern, *Thomas Francis Meagher: An Irish Revolutionary in America* (Boulder: University of Colorado Press, 1949; reprint, New York: Arno Press, 1976), 121 (page citations are to the reprint edition).

62. *War of the Rebellion: A Compilation of the Official Records of the Union and Confederate Armies* (Washington, DC: GPO, 1880–1901), Ser. I, Vol. 34, pt. 3, p. 333. Hereafter cited as *O.R. (Official Records)*; and James M. McPherson, *Battle Cry of Freedom,* 328.

63. T. Harry Williams, *Lincoln and His Generals* (New York: Knopf, 1952), 217.

64. Athern, 123; and Assistant Adjutant General S. Williams on behalf of Major General Joseph Hooker to Brigadier General Thomas Francis Meagher, 3 March 1863, Thomas Francis Meagher, M-1064 Roll #187, Letters Received by the Commission Branch of the Adjutant General's Office, 1865, National Archives and Records Administration, Washington, DC (hereafter cited as NARA).

65. Athern, 101.

66. Athern, 124–25.

67. Athern, 125; *New York Times,* 8 April 1863.

68. Brigadier General Thomas Francis Meagher to Major John Hancock, Assistant Adjutant-General, 8 May 1863, Thomas Francis Meagher, M-1064 Roll #187, Letters Received by the Commission Branch of the Adjutant General's Office, 1865, NARA.

69. Conyngham, 405.

70. *O.R.,* Ser. III, Vol. 3, p. 372.

71. Maurice Woulfe, Washington, DC, to unnamed uncle, County Limerick, 25 September 1863. Maurice Woulfe Letters, National Library of Ireland. This name appears as "Wolfe" in some texts but has been spelled "Woulfe" here at the request of Maurice Woulfe's great-nephew, Mr. Timothy Woulfe, to whom I am indebted for granting me permission to use these letters here.

72. Woulfe, Washington, DC, to unnamed uncle, Co. Limerick, 19 November 1863. Maurice P. Woulfe Papers, National Library of Ireland.

73. Brigadier General Thomas Francis Meagher to Edwin M. Stanton, Secretary of War, 13 July 1863, Thomas Francis Meagher, M-1064 Roll #187, Letters Received by the Commission Branch of the Adjutant General's Office, 1865, NARA, Washington, DC; the *Pilot,* 30 May 1863; New York *Irish-American,* 14 March 1863. The author has found no evidence to indicate that Secretary Stanton or anyone within the Lincoln administration announced a general order revising all leave policies.

74. In January 1864, Meagher returned to duty as a major general, assigned to organize a division

comprised of soldiers recovering from wounds, stragglers, and others. In January 1865 he and his division participated in minor operations in North Carolina until he was relieved from duty for drunkenness in February and returned home to New York. Meagher officially resigned this commission in May 1865.

75. New York *Irish-American,* 14 March 1863.

76. The *Pilot,* 30 May 1863.

77. Ibid.

78. Cavanagh, 28–32.

79. The *Pilot,* 30 May 1863.

80. The *Pilot,* 23 May 1863.

81. The *Pilot,* 30 May 1863.

82. Conyngham, 415.

83. Brian A. Bennett, *Sons of Old Monroe: A Regimental History of Patrick O'Rorke's 140th New York Volunteer Infantry* (Dayton, OH: Morningside Books, 1999), 85. Glenn W. LaFantasie, *Twilight at Little Round Top: July 2, 1863 —The Tide Turns at Gettysburg* (New York: Wiley, 2005), 60–61.

84. LaFantasie, 36; Bennett, 227–28.

85. Bennett, 232.

86. LaFantasie, 154.

87. Despite their actions, the 140th New York's defense has been overshadowed by the enormous popularity of Colonel Chamberlain and the 20th Maine. This is due largely to the Pulitzer Prize–winning novel, *The Killer Angels* (1974), and subsequent studies added to this fame until Little Round Top became the most visited site at the Gettysburg National Military Park. While the Maine men deserve recognition, so do Irish-Americans like Patrick O'Rorke and the men of the 140th New York.

88. Glenn Tucker, *High Tide at Gettysburg* (New York: Konecky & Konecky, 1958), 272–74.

89. Tucker, 273; William Corby, *Memoirs of Chaplain Life: Three Years with the Irish Brigade in the Army of the Potomac,* ed. Lawrence Frederick Kohl (New York: Fordham University Press), 183–84; Father William Corby, University of Notre Dame, to Colonel John B. Bachelder, 4 January 1879, *The Bachelder Papers: Gettysburg in Their Own Words,* vol. 3, eds. David L. Ladd and Audrey J. Ladd (Dayton, OH:

Morningside Books, 1995), 2002 (hereafter cited as *BP*).

90. St. Clair Mulholland, *The Story of the 116th Regiment Pennsylvania Volunteers in the War of the Rebellion,* Lawrence Frederick Kohl, ed. (Philadelphia: F. McManus, Jr., 1903; reprint, New York: Fordham University Press, 1996), 125.

91. *O.R.,* Ser. 1, Vol. 27, Part 1: 386.

92. Mulholland, 127–28.

93. Sandy Barnard, ed. *Campaigning with the Irish Brigade: Pvt. John Ryan, 28th Massachusetts* (Terre Haute, IN: AST Press), 95.

94. Edwin B. Coddington, *The Gettysburg Campaign: A Study in Command* (New York: Scribner's, 1968), 406–10; Tucker, 274–81; Mulholland, 127–28; J. Noonan, "The Sixty-ninth New York—History," Kenneth H. Powers Collection, U.S. Army Military History Institute (hereafter cited as USAMHI), Carlisle, Pennsylvania.

95. William A. Smith, Williamsport, Maryland, to his family, 12 July 1863, William A. Smith Letters, Lewis Leigh Collection, USAMHI.

96. *O.R.,* Ser. 1, Vol. 27, Part 1: 386.

97. Background sketches of officers and men of the 69th Pennsylvania from Folder 1, "69th Pennsylvania Infantry Regiment," 6-PA69, Gettysburg National Military Park Library; see also Michael H. Kane, "The Irish Lineage of the 69th Pennsylvania Volunteers," *Irish Sword* 18 (Winter 1991): 184–98; and D. Scott Hartwig, "It Struck Horror to Us All," *Gettysburg* 1 (January 1991): 89–100.

98. Anthony W. McDermott, *A Brief History of the 69th Regiment Pennsylvania Veteran Volunteers* (Philadelphia: D. J. Gallagher & Co., 1889), 5. In April 1861, the 2nd Philadelphia Regiment of State Militia organized and entered the field as the 24th Pennsylvania Volunteers. It drew most of its recruits from Irish militia companies like the Hibernia Greens, Emmet Guards, and Meagher Guards. After service for ninety days, the regiment mustered out in August 1861, and most of them quickly reorganized into a three-year regiment christened the 69th Pennsyl-

vania. See also John H. Campbell, *The Friendly Sons of St. Patrick and the Hibernian Society of Philadelphia, 1771–1892* (Philadelphia: privately printed, 1892), 282.

99. Michael Kane letter, 10 May 1991, Folder 1, "69th Pennsylvania Infantry Regiment," 6-PA69, Gettysburg National Military Park Library (hereafter cited as GNMP). Kane deserves credit for discovering one of the few descriptions of the 69th Pennsylvania's green flag in the New York *Irish-American,* 22 April 1862.

100. Hartwig, 89.

101. Hartwig, 94.

102. Anthony W. McDermott to Colonel John Bachelder, 2 June 1886, *BP*, 1409.

103. Hartwig, 90.

104. Hartwig, 92; Corporal John Buckley to Col. John Bachelder, no date, *BP,* 1402–3.

105. Hartwig, 95.

106. William White, Gettysburg, to his parents, Philadelphia, Pennsylvania, 5 July 1863. William White Papers, Box 2, Folder 22, MC-17-2-22. William C. White Collection, White Box 2, Folder 19, MC17-2-19. The Philadelphia Archdiocesan Historical Records Center, Wynnewood, Pennsylvania.

107. Brian C. Pohanka, *James McKay Rorty: An Appreciation* (New York: Irish Brigade Association, 1993), 16.

108. Pohanka, 14–17.

109. *Irish-American,* 18 July 1863.

110. Pohanka, 8.

111. Anthony McDermott was born in Philadelphia, Pennsylvania, of Irish-born parents.

112. Anthony W. McDermott to Colonel John Bachelder, 2 June 1886, *BP,* 1410; see also sketch of leading officers in 69th Pennsylvania, including Dennis O'Kane and brief history of the unit in 69th Pennsylvania Infantry Regiment 6-PA69, Folder 1, GNMP.

113. Ibid.

114. John Buckley to Colonel John Bachelder, "A Stone from the Wall: A Reminiscence of Pickett's Charge," date unknown, John Buckley Papers, Gettysburg National Military Park, Pennsylvania; Hartwig, 97–98. See also D. Scott Hartwig, "Casualties of War: The Effects of the Battle of Gettysburg upon the Men and Families of

the 69th Pennsylvania Infantry Regiment," *Unsung Heroes of Gettysburg: Proceedings of the 5th Annual Gettysburg Seminar* (Gettysburg, PA: Gettysburg National Military Park, 1996), 4.

115. Ibid.

116. Anthony W. McDermott to Colonel John Bachelder, 2 June 1886, *BP*,1412; William White, Gettysburg, to his parents, Philadelphia, Pennsylvania, 5 July 1863. William White Papers, Box 2, Folder 22, MC-17-2-22. William C. White Collection, White Box 2, Folder 19, MC17-2-19. The Philadelphia Archdiocesan Historical Records Center, Wynnewood, Pennsylvania; Hartwig, "It Struck Horror to Us All," 98–99.

117. Hartwig, "Casualties of War," 5; Hartwig, "It Struck Horror to Us All," 90, 98.

118. New York *Irish-American,* 25 July 1863.

119. *Notre Dame Scholastic,* 20 January 1894, 279; in William Corby, *Memoirs of Chaplain Life: Three Years with the Irish Brigade in the Army of the Potomac,* Lawrence Frederick Kohl, ed. (New York: Fordham University Press, 1992), 402.

120. Philadelphia *North American,* March or May 1904 (page torn).

121. Stephen Rorty Blount, "Foreword" in Pohanka, 3.

122. Murdock, 6–7; McPherson, *Ordeal by Fire,* 354.

123. John England to Mr. Hargeddon, 28 March 1863, John England Letters, Manuscripts and Archives Division, New York Public Library.

124. The *Pilot,* 23 May 1863.

125. The *Pilot,* 30 May 1863.

126. Murdock, 308; and the *Pilot,* 30 May 1863.

127. The *Pilot,* 25 July 1863.

128. Peter Levine, "Draft Evasion in the North during the Civil War, 1863–1865," *The Journal of American History* 67 (March 1981): 816.

129. The *Pilot,* 1 August 1863.

130. The *Pilot,* 25 April 1863.

131. The *Pilot,* 24 March 1863. For an excellent analysis of these labor, class, and ethnic tensions in the Pennsylvania mining regions see Grace Palladino's *Another Civil War: Labor, Capital, and the State in the Anthracite Regions of Penn-*

sylvania, 1840–68 (Champaign: University of Illinois Press, 1990).

132. McPherson, *Battle Cry of Freedom,* 609.

133. McPherson, *Ordeal by Fire,* 358.

134. See Adrian Cook, *The Armies of the Streets: The New York City Draft Riots of 1863* (Lexington: University Press of Kentucky, 1974), 21–22. New York historian and novelist Peter Quinn (*Banished Children of Eve*) deserves credit for recognizing this connection between the draft and Orange Day tensions. We discussed this at length during an interview in May 2001. Examples of these marching season tensions include the time when Irish-American Protestants and Catholics clashed over the distribution of city jobs in July 1836 and state aid to parochial schools in July 1842, but the worst intra-Irish-American conflict came with the Orange Day rioting in July 1871. See Bernstein, 17–42.

135. Bernstein, 17–42.

136. Spann, 204–5; and Bernstein, 36–37.

137. John England to Ellen Hargeddon, 24 July 1863, John England Letters, Manuscripts and Archives Division, New York Public Library.

138. New York *Irish-American,* 18 July 1863.

139. The *Pilot,* 25 July 1863.

140. New York *Irish-American,* 18 July 1863.

141. New York *Tribune,* 17 July 1863.

142. Bernstein, 32.

143. George Templeton Strong, *Diary of the Civil War, 1860–1865* (New York: Macmillan, 1962), 336, 342–43.

144. *New York Times,* 15 July 1863 and 19 July 1863.

145. *New York Times,* 16 July 1863.

146. *New York Times,* 15 July 1863.

147. Ibid.

148. Strong, 343; For an explanation of slogans like "Sam, Organize!" see Anbinder, xiv.

149. New York *Irish-American,* 1 August 1863.

150. *New York Times,* 18 July 1863.

151. Peter Welsh, *Irish Green and Union Blue: The Civil War*

Letters of Peter Welsh, Lawrence Frederick Kohl with Margaret Cossé Richard, eds. (New York: Fordham University Press, 1996), 110, 113, 115.

152. Andrew Greenlees, Dayton, Illinois, to John Greenlees, Magheramorne, Co. Antrim, Ireland, 7 September 1863. Public Records Office of Northern Ireland, T. 2046.

153. Joseph Hewitt, Cincinnati, Ohio, to an unnamed brother, perhaps Moses Hewitt, Co. Armagh, Ireland, 20 June 1864. Joseph Hewitt Letter, 1851–1872, Indiana Historical Society Library.

154. U.S. Consul E. Eastman Report, Cork, Ireland, 27 August 1863. U.S. Consular Dispatches, Cork, 1800–1906, Microfilm T-196. National Archives and Records Administration, Washington, DC.

155. U.S. Consul John Young Report, Belfast, Ireland, 2 December 1863. U.S. Consular Dispatches, Belfast, Ireland, 1796–1906, Microfilm T-386, NARA.

156. Spann, 207–8.

157. Spann, 202.

158. Edwin G. Burrows and Mike Wallace, *Gotham: A History of New York City to 1898* (New York: Oxford University Press, 1999), 897.

159. Spann, 208; and Burrows and Wallace, 896.

NOTES TO CHAPTER 5

1. Joseph Stuart, writing on behalf of Sarah McCormick, to C. H. Birney, Esq. Treasurer, March 14, 1863; Susan Callahan to unknown member of Friendly Sons, ?, 1863; Mary Ann Callahan to unknown member of Friendly Sons, ?, 1863; Box 1, Secretary and Treasurer, ca. 1830–1890, Society of the Friendly Sons of St. Patrick, American Irish Historical Society, New York, New York.

2. Bartholomew O'Connor on behalf of Charles James Brennan, to C. H. Birney, Esq., 2 April 1862; Jane Emiss to Mr. [C. H.] Birney, 1864; Box 1, Secretary and Treasurer, ca. 1830–1890, Society of the Friendly Sons of St. Patrick, American Irish Historical Society, New York, New York. For basic facts on the Friendly Sons in New York see, Richard C. Murphy,

LL.B., and Lawrence J. Mannion, *The History of the Society of the Friendly Sons of Saint Patrick in the City of New York, 1784 to 1955* (New York: Dillon, 1962).

3. New York *Irish-American,* 30 January 1864; see also *New York Herald,* 23 January 1864 and *New York Times,* 23 January 1864.

4. Maria Lydig Daly, *Diary of a Union Lady, 1861–1865* (New York: Funk and Wagnalls, 1962; reprint, Lincoln: University of Nebraska Press, 2000), 271.

5. Most of this is discussed previously in this work, but for a discussion of Corcoran's position within the *Enchantress* affair, see Frank A. Boyle, *A Party of Mad Fellows: The Story of the Irish Regiments in the Army of the Potomac* (Dayton, OH: Morningside, 1996), 169.

6. Minutes of meeting of the officers of the 170th Regiment, New York Volunteers (2nd Corcoran's Irish Legion) at Union Mills, Virginia, 26 December 1863, James P. McIvor Papers, New York Historical Society; Joseph G. Bilby, *The Irish Brigade in the Civil War: The 69th New York and Other Irish Regiments in the Army of the Potomac* (Conshohocken, PA: Combined Publishing, 2000), 96. For some details on the Fenian Fair in Chicago, see John B. Jentz and Richard Schneirov, "Chicago's Fenian Fair of 1864: A Window into the Civil War as a Popular Political Awakening," *Labor's Heritage: Quarterly of the George Meany Memorial Archives* 6 (Winter 1995): 4–19.

7. D. P. Conyngham, *The Irish Brigade and Its Campaigns,* Lawrence Frederick Kohl, ed. (New York: William McSorley, 1867; reprint, New York: Fordham University Press, 1992), 434.

8. Bilby, 95–98.

9. William C. White, Camp near Stevensburg, Virginia, to parents, Philadelphia, Pennsylvania, 13 January 1864 and 24 February 1864. William C. White Collection, MC17, Box 3, Folder 2, Philadelphia Archdiocesan Historical Research Center, Wynnewood, Pennsylvania.

10. The *Pilot,* 30 May 1863.

11. George Templeton Strong, *Diary of the Civil War, 1860–1865,* Allan Nevins, ed. (New York: Macmillan, 1962), 389–90.

12. Conyngham, 432–36.

13. Randall Miller offers an excellent analysis of this in "Catholic Religion, Irish Ethnicity, and the Civil War," in *Religion and the American Civil War,* ed. Randall M. Miller, Harry S. Stout, and Charles Reagan Wilson (New York: Oxford University Press, 1998), 277–78.

14. *New York Times,* 10 July 1864 (emphasis mine); and *The Illustrated London News,* 17 September 1864.

15. Kerby A. Miller, *Emigrants and Exiles: Ireland and the Irish Exodus to North America* (New York: Oxford University Press, 1985), 360.

16. Edwin G. Eastman, Cork, Ireland, to U.S. Secretary of State William Seward, 15 October 1863, U.S. Consular Dispatches, Cork, 1800–1906, National Archives and Records Administration, Washington, DC (hereafter cited as NARA); Henry B. Hammond, Dublin, Ireland, to Seward, 23 April 1863, U.S. Consular Dispatches, Dublin, Ireland, 1790–1906, NARA. For an excellent analysis of this see Joseph M. Hernon, Jr., *Celts, Catholics, and Copperheads: Ireland Views the American Civil War* (Columbus: Ohio State University Press, 1968), 25.

17. Report of Henry B. Hammond, U.S. Consul in Dublin, Ireland, 3 April 1862 and 31 July 1862. U.S. Consular Dispatches, Dublin, Ireland, 1790–1906, NARA.

18. U.S. Vice-Consul William B. West report, U.S. Consulate, Dublin, 28 November 1863. U.S. Consular Dispatches, Dublin, 1790–1906. Microfilm T-199, NARA.

19. Mark Mulligan, Dublin, to Mr. West, U.S. Consul, Galway, 19 May 1863. U.S. Consular Dispatches, NARA.

20. James Murphy, New Quay, Burren, County Clare, to U.S. Consul, Galway, 13 May 1863. U.S. Consular Dispatches, NARA.

21. James Murphy, New Quay, Burren, County Clare, to U.S. Consul, Galway, 13 May 1863. U.S. Consular Dispatches, NARA.

22. For examples other than from the U.S. consuls in Dublin and Galway, see the report of U.S. Consul H. Keenan, former consul

at Cork, in a letter from his new location in Ballibay, County Monaghan, to Secretary of State William Seward, 11 April 1863. Like the others, Keenan notes desperate financial conditions as the impetus behind these requests. U.S. Consular Dispatches, Cork, Ireland, 1800–1906, NARA. In his book *Emigrants and Exiles* Kerby Miller offers a detailed discussion of the economic and ideological factors that led young Irishmen to the United States, and possibly the U.S. Army, during the years of the American Civil War. See 359–61.

23. *Irish People,* 26 December 1863, as quoted in Hernon, 15.

24. *Irish People,* 6 August 1864 and 19 November 1864 as quoted in Hernon, 35–36.

25. Hernon, 24.

26. Thomas Conroy, Dublin, to U.S. Consul, Galway, 28 August 1863. U.S. Consular Dispatches, NARA.

27. John A. Winslow, U.S.S. *Kearsarge,* Cork Harbor, to U.S. Consul Edwin Eastman, Cork, Ireland, 7 December 1863. U.S. Consular Dispatches, Cork, 1800–1906, NARA.

28. Michael Murray, near Vicksburg, Mississippi, to his parents, Ireland, 26 April 1863, U.S. Consular Dispatches, Dublin, 1790–1906, NARA; Michael Brennan, 7th Missouri Volunteers, U.S. Army near Vicksburg, Mississippi, to Edward Murray, Ireland, 30 May 1863, U.S. Consular Dispatches, Dublin, 1790–1906, NARA.

29. U.S. Consul West, Dublin, Ireland, 16 April 1864. U.S. Consular Dispatches, Dublin, 1790–1906, NARA.

30. John Egan, Fortress Monroe, Virginia, to John Keane, Dublin, Ireland, 10 October 1863. Registered Papers, No. 9965, State Paper Office, Dublin Castle. For further discussion on Irish views and actions in Ireland relating to the American Civil War, see Hernon.

31. The *Pilot,* 17 September 1864.

32. Ibid.

33. Ibid.

34. *War of the Rebellion: A Compilation of the Official Records of the Union and Confederate Armies* (Washington, DC: Government Printing Office, 1880–

1901 (hereafter cited as *O.R.*), Ser. III, Vol. 2, 358–59.

35. New York *Irish-American*, 17 September 1864.

36. *New York Times*, 16 January 1863. Similar ads can be found in nearly every issue of the *Times* throughout the war years and afterward.

37. Thomas McManus, Boston, Massachusetts, to Francis McManus, Dublin, Ireland, 17 March 1864, original letter copied by U.S. Consul William B. West, U.S. Consul, Dublin, to Secretary of State William B. Seward, 20 April 1864, U.S. Consular Dispatches, Dublin, Ireland. Microfilm Reel T.199, NARA; James M. McPherson, *Ordeal by Fire: The Civil War and Reconstruction* (New York: McGraw Hill, 1982; reprint, New York: McGraw Hill, 1992), 353 (page citations are to the reprint edition).

38. Chicago and Alton Railroad Company Contract and Lord Lieutenant of Ireland Proclamation, June 1864, Secretary's Office Registered Papers (CSORP) 16765/1864, National Archives of Ireland, Dublin. See also, Hernon, 24–26.

39. Thomas McManus, Boston, Massachusetts, to Francis McManus, Dublin, Ireland, 17 March 1864, original letter copied by U.S. Consul William B. West, U.S. Consul, Dublin, to Secretary of State William B. Seward, 20 April 1864, U.S. Consular Dispatches, Dublin, Ireland. Microfilm Reel T.199, NARA.

40. Edward Cummins, Boston, Massachusetts, to Cummins Family, Dublin, Ireland, 23 March 1864, original letter copied by U.S. Consul William B. West, U.S. Consul, Dublin, to Secretary of State William B. Seward, 20 April 1864, U.S. Consular Dispatches, Dublin, Ireland. Microfilm Reel T.199, NARA.

41. Alf Mac Lochlainn, "Three Ballads of the American Civil War," *The Irish Sword: The Journal of the Military History Society of Ireland* 6 (1963): 29.

42. Conyngham, 459.

43. *Irish-American*, 2 June 1864.

44. St. Clair Mulholland, *The Story of the 116th Regiment Pennsylvania Volunteers in the War of the Rebellion*, Lawrence Frederick Kohl, ed. (Philadelphia: F.

McManus, Jr., 1903; reprint, New York: Fordham University Press, 1996), 269.

45. *Irish-American*, 2 June 1864.

46. Mulholland, 279.

47. See also Bilby, 115.

48. Conyngham, 467; Mulholland, 279; Bilby, 97, 115–20.

49. Manuscript of the poem in Charles G. Halpine Papers, New-York Historical Society; quoted in Edward K. Spann, "Union Green: The Irish Community and the Civil War," in *The New York Irish*, ed. Ronald H. Bayor and Timothy J. Meagher (Baltimore, MD: Johns Hopkins University Press, 1996), 206.

50. *Parody of When This Cruel War Is Over* (Philadelphia: Johnson, n.d.), Rare Books and Special Collections Division, Library of Congress, Washington, DC; and *When This Cruel War Is Over* (New York: Charles McManus, n.d.), Rare Books and Special Collections Division, Library of Congress, Washington, DC.

51. *What Irish Boys Can Do. Answer To: No Irish Need Apply* (New York: H. De Marsan, n.d.), Rare Books and Special Collections Division, Library of Congress, Washington, DC.

52. The *Pilot*, 3 September 1864.

53. R. T. Farrell, Detroit, Michigan, to James A. Mulligan, Chicago, Illinois, 28 December 1861. James A. Mulligan Papers, Chicago Historical Society.

54. First Lieutenant Gerald B. Walsh, near Rolla, Missouri, to Colonel James A. Mulligan, Chicago, Illinois, 13 January 1862. James A. Mulligan Papers, Chicago Historical Society.

55. Captain T. C. Fitzgibbon, Ypsilanti, Michigan, to Colonel James A. Mulligan, Chicago, IL, 10 February 1862. James A. Mulligan Papers, Chicago Historical Society.

56. M. W. Toale, Camp Douglas, Chicago, Illinois, to James A. Mulligan, Chicago, Illinois, 10 February 1863. James A. Mulligan Papers, Chicago Historical Society.

57. Private Peter Casey, 23rd Illinois, New Creek, Virginia, to Colonel James A. Mulligan, Chicago, Illinois, 23 March 1863. James A. Mulligan Papers, Chicago Historical Society.

58. *Dubuque Herald*, 20 and 30 June 1863; quoted in Craig Lee

Kautz, "Fodder for Cannon: Immigrant Perceptions of the Civil War —The Old Northwest" (Ph.D. diss., University of Nebraska, Lincoln, 1976), 199–200.

59. Kautz, 197–98.

60. *Dubuque Herald*, 23 February 1864, emphasis original; quoted in Kautz, 247–48.

61. The *Pilot*, 3 September 1864.

62. Ibid.

63. Spann, 208.

64. First Lieutenant Thomas F. Wildes, 110th Regiment (specifics unknown), Martinsburg, Virginia, to Colonel James A. Mulligan, Chicago, Illinois, 14 December 1863. James A. Mulligan Papers, Chicago Historical Society.

65. *O.R.*, Ser. I, Vol. XXXVI, Part 1, p. 72.

66. *O.R.*, Ser. I, Vol. XLII, Part 1, p. 248.

67. Bilby, 120–21.

68. The *Pilot*, 3 September 1864.

69. The *Pilot*, 24 September 1864. The author has found no record of this order by General Dix.

70. Abraham Irvine, Cold Harbor, Virginia, to Joseph James Irvine, Keadymore, Mountnorris, Co. Armagh, 4 June 1864. T. 2135/1, Public Records Office of Northern Ireland. This is also based on the author's conversations with Irvine's descendents, who still live in the house he describes in the letter, in Keadymore, in 2005.

71. John O'Neill, Spotsylvania Courthouse, Virginia, to Mrs. Doral O'Neill, Portarlington, Ireland, 10 May 1864. O'Neill Family Letters, MS. 18,327C, National Library of Ireland.

72. Francis Fowler, U.S. Sanitary Commission, Washington, DC, to Mrs. Dora O'Neill (mother), Portarlington, Ireland, 24 July 1865. O'Neill Family Papers, MS. 18,327, National Library of Ireland.

73. The *Pilot*, 10 September 1864.

74. The *Pilot*, 17 September 1864.

75. William Thomas Reese, Youngstown, Ohio, to unknown friend named John ?, appears to have been living in County Down, Ireland, 20 September 1864. Private Collection of Kerby A. Miller, Ph.D., Department of History, University of Missouri, Columbia.

76. The *Pilot,* 17 September 1864.

77. Ibid.

78. *Abraham Lincoln: Speeches and Writings, 1859–1865: Speeches, Letters, and Miscellaneous Writings, Presidential Messages, and Proclamations* (New York: Literary Classics of the United States, 1989), 539–42, 650.

79. Ibid.; the *Pilot,* 17 September 1864.

80. Daly, 304.

81. Democratic party efforts for unity in Joel H. Silbey, *A Respectable Minority: The Democratic Party in the Civil War Era, 1860–1868* (New York: Norton, 1977), 116–17; Vallandigham and peace plank, commonly known as the "Second Resolution" of the Chicago Convention of 1864, Frank L. Klement, *The Limits of Dissent: Clement L. Valandigham and the Civil War* (Lexington: University of Kentucky Press, 1970; reprint, New York: Fordham University Press, 1998), 284–85 (page citations are to the reprint edition); McClellan pledge in Stephen W. Sears, "McClellan and the Peace Plank of 1864: A Reappraisal," *Civil War History* 36, no. 1 (1990): 61.

82. Sears, "McClellan and the Peace Plank of 1864," 63.

83. Stephen W. Sears, *George B. McClellan: The Young Napoleon* (New York: Ticknor & Fields, 1988), 376. As a result, as historian Stephen Sears has argued, a pledge of "peace and reunion with honor" became the central theme of McClellan's campaign and popular among Democrats, including many Irish-American soldiers and veterans.

84. Sears, *George B. McClellan,* 376–77 (emphasis mine).

85. Silbey, 138.

86. The *Pilot,* 24 September 1864; and the *Pilot,* 10 September 1864.

87. The *Pilot,* 3 September 1864.

88. *O.R.,* Ser. I, Vol. XLIII, Part 1, pp. 480–82.

89. The *Pilot,* 17 September 1864.

90. Spann, 207.

91. *Harper's Weekly,* 15 October 1864; quoted in Harpweek.com, "Presidential Elections," http://elections.harpweek.com/1Cartoons/cartoon-1864-large.asp?UniqueID=

19&Year=1864, 24 September 2001.

92. *Harper's Weekly,* 12 November 1864 (actually appeared to the public on 2 November 1864 with the paper postdated ten days); quoted in Harpweek.com, "Presidential Elections," http://elections.harpweek.com/1Cartoons/cartoon-1864-Medium.asp?UniqueID=31&Year=1864, 24 September 2001.

93. Strong, 452, 509, 511–12.

94. Spann, 206–7.

95. Paul Kleppner, *The Third Electoral System, 1853–1892: Parties, Voters, and Political Cultures* (Chapel Hill: University of North Carolina Press, 1979), 61. As Kleppner argues, Irish Catholics were the "most strongly and consistently Democratic of the newer immigrant groups" of the mid-nineteenth century.

96. Kleppner, 61.

97. David E. Long, *The Jewel of Liberty: Abraham Lincoln's Reelection and the End of Slavery* (Mechanicsburg, PA: Stackpole Books, 1994), 170–71.

98. Spann, 208.

99. John C. Waugh, *Reelecting Lincoln: The Battle for the 1864 Presidency* (New York: Crown Publishers, 1997), 354.

100. Oscar Osburn Winther, "The Soldier Vote in the Election of 1864," *New York History: Quarterly Journal of the New York State Historical Association* 25 (1944): 458.

101. This argument is supported in Thomas O'Connor, *The Boston Irish: A Political History* (Boston: Back Bay Books, 1995), 94; several historians have made the argument re: Lincoln's martyrdom, including McPherson, *Ordeal by Fire,* 483.

102. Strong, 586.

103. Miller, 324.

NOTES TO CHAPTER 6

1. Randall Miller, "Catholic Religion, Irish Ethnicity, and the Civil War," *Religion and the American Civil War,* ed. Randall M. Miller, Harry S. Stout, and Charles Reagan Wilson (New York: Oxford University Press, 1998), 283.

2. Stuart McConnel, *Glorious Contentment: The Grand Army of the Republic, 1865–1900* (Chapel Hill: University of North Carolina

Press, 1992), 55, 69. In his extensive and acclaimed study of the GAR, McConnell found that this was influenced more by the location of posts than by any concerted effort by the GAR to exclude foreign-born veterans. Since most of the early posts were located in cities, they tended to attract veterans from neighborhoods in which they were located. Thus with many urban districts characterized by their German, Irish, or African-American populations, particular ethnic groups predominated in the GAR posts in the neighborhoods where they were predominant

3. Miller, 284.

4. McConnel, 79–80.

5. Ibid., 79.

6. Ibid., 82.

7. Ibid., 210–12, 81–82.

8. *New York Times,* 15 July 1871.

9. Terry Golway, *Irish Rebel: John Devoy and America's Fight for Ireland's Freedom* (New York: St. Martin's Griffin, 1998), 37.

10. U.S. Vice-Consul William B. West, Report, Dublin, Ireland, 14 October 1865. U.S. Consular Dispatches, Dublin, 1790–1906, Microfilm T-199. National Archives and Records Administration, Washington, DC (hereafter cited as NARA).

11. West Report, Dublin Ireland, 26 June 1869. U.S. Consular Dispatches, Dublin, 1790–1906, Microfilm T-199. NARA.

12. U.S. Consul E. Eastman Report, Cork, Ireland, 24 September 1865 and 30 September 1865. U.S. Consular Dispatches, Cork, 1800–1906, Microfilm T-196. NARA.

13. U.S. Consul John Young Report, Belfast, Ireland, 21 February 1866. U.S. Consular Dispatches, Belfast, Ireland, 1796–1906. Microfilm T-368, NARA.

14. U.S. Consul G. H. Heap Report, Belfast, Ireland, 12 December 1866, U.S. Consular Dispatches, Belfast, Ireland, 1796–1906. Microfilm T-368, NARA.

15. Brian Jenkins, *Fenians and Anglo-American Relations during Reconstruction* (Ithaca, NY: Cornell University Press, 1969), 41–42.

16. The support the U.S. Army could have offered would have been limited due to its reduced size

and various duties relating to Reconstruction and the Indian Wars, but there was a substantial force in uniform immediately following the war.

17. Report of the Daniel O'Connell Circle, Fenian Brotherhood, 24 March 1866. Fenian Brotherhood Collection, Box 2, Folder 4, Item 12, American Catholic History Research Center and University Archives, Catholic University of America, Washington, DC.

18. Patrick Condon, Mobile, Alabama, to Patrick J. Downing, 31 March 1866. Fenian Brotherhood Collection, Box 1, Folder 9, Item 21, American Catholic History Research Center and University Archives, Catholic University of America, Washington, DC.

19. Patrick Condon, New Orleans, Louisiana, to Patrick J. Downing, 30 April 1866. Fenian Brotherhood Collection, Box 1, Folder 9, Item 34, American Catholic History Research Center and University Archives, Catholic University of America, Washington, DC.

20. New York Tribune, 16 November 1865; and New York Times, 28 September 1865; quoted in Jenkins, 43.

21. William Lalor, Dunn, Wisconsin, to Richard Lalor, Tenakill, Abbeyleix, Queens County, Ireland, 4 July 1867. Lalor Family Letters, 1843–1931, National Library of Ireland, Dublin.

22. William Lalor, Dunn, Wisconsin, to Richard Lalor, Tenakill, Abbeyleix, Queens County, Ireland, 10 February 1868. Lalor Family Letters, 1843–1931, National Library of Ireland, Dublin.

23. The Alabama Claims are discussed in Doris W. Dashew, "The Story of an Illusion: The Plan to Trade 'Alabama' Claims for Canada," Civil War History 15, no. 4 (1969): 332–48; Maureen M. Robson, "The 'Alabama' Claims and the Anglo-American Reconciliation, 1865–1871," Canadian Historical Review 42, no. 1 (1961): 1–22.

24. Jenkins, 48, 56; Golway, 58–59.

25. Patrick Foley, Waterford, New York, to James Sheehan, Albany, New York, 20 April 1866. James Sheehan Letters, MS.

24,559, National Library of Ireland.

26. Colonel Michael C. Murphy to Frank B. Gallagher, Esq., 30 October 1866, Folder 14-1-15, Box 1, MC 14, Record Group 14, Papers of the Fenian Brotherhood, Philadelphia Archdiocesan Historical Research Center, Wynnewood, Pennsylvania.

27. Maurice Woulfe, Fort Sedgwick, Colorado Territory, to Michael Woulfe, County Limerick, Ireland, 12 May 1867. Maurice Wolfe Letters, National Library of Ireland.

28. Maurice Woulfe, Fort Fred Steele, Wyoming Territory, to cousin Maurice Woulfe, County Limerick, 30 April 1869. Maurice Wolfe Letters, National Library of Ireland.

29. Maurice Woulfe, Fort Fred Steele, Wyoming Territory, to Batt Woulfe, Cratloe West, County Limerick, 16 November 1868. Maurice Wolfe Letters, National Library of Ireland.

30. The Atlantic Monthly, May 1866, 574, 575; quoted in Matthew Frye Jacobson, Barbarian Virtues: The United States Encounters Foreign Peoples at Home and Abroad, 1876–1917 (New York: Hill and Wang, 2000), 192; and the New York Times, 17 July 1871.

31. William Lalor, Dunn, Wisconsin, to Richard Lalor, Tenakill, Abbeyleix, Queens County, Ireland, 17 February 1871. Lalor Family Letters, 1843–1931, National Library of Ireland, Dublin.

32. Patrick Walsh, Brazil, Indiana, to Jeremiah O'Donovan Rossa, 28 January 1877. Fenian Brotherhood Collection, Box 2, Folder 4, Item 4, American Catholic History Research Center and University Archives, Catholic University of America, Washington, DC.

33. See Golway.

34. Dennis Clark, The Irish in Philadelphia: Ten Generations of Urban Experience (Philadelphia: Temple University Press, 1973), 129; and Lawrence J. McCaffrey, "Forging Forward and Looking Back," in The New York Irish, ed. Ronald H. Bayor and Timothy J. Meagher (Baltimore, MD: Johns Hopkins University Press, 1996), 224.

35. Jenkins, 129, 309, 318–27.

36. Robert M. Utley, Frontier Regulars: The United States and the Indian, 1866–1891 (Lincoln: University of Nebraska Press, 1973), 23–24; and Edward M. Coffman, The Old Army: A Portrait of the American Army in Peacetime, 1784–1898 (New York: Oxford University Press, 1986), 141–43.

37. Coffman, 330–31. Coffman describes this as an effort toward the "the Americanization of the Army."

38. Coffman, 330–31.

39. Maurice Woulfe, Fort D.A. Russell, Dakota Territory, to cousin Maurice Woulfe, Bruff, County Limerick, 12 April 1868. Maurice Wolfe Letters, National Library of Ireland.

40. Maurice Woulfe, Fort Bridger, Wyoming Territory, to cousin Maurice Woulfe, Bowling, Dumbartonshire, Scotland, 8 January 1874. Maurice Wolfe Letters, National Library of Ireland.

41. Edward O'Donnell, "Henry George's New York" (Ph.D. diss., Columbia University, New York, 1996), 144; Philip H. Bagenal, The American Irish and Their Influence on Irish Politics (New York: J. S. Ozer, 1971), 68, 71; both quoted in Golway, 3–5; and Hasia R. Diner, "Overview: 'The Most Irish City in the Union,' The Era of the Great Migration, 1844–1877," in The New York Irish, ed. Ronald H. Bayor and Timothy J. Meagher (Baltimore, MD: Johns Hopkins University Press, 1996), 97.

42. W. L. D. O'Grady's Pension File, National Archives and Records Administration (NARA), Washington, DC; Timothy O'Leary Pension File, NARA, Washington, DC; Peter Welsh Pension File, NARA, Washington, DC; William McCarter Pension File, NARA, Washington, DC; Thomas Francis Meagher Pension File, NARA, Washington, DC; Michael Corcoran Pension File, NARA, Washington, DC; New York Herald, 9 December 1870; Diner, 97.

43. Chicago Evening Post, 9 September 1868; quoted in Lawrence J. McCaffrey, The Irish Catholic Diaspora in America (Washington, DC: Catholic University of America Press, 1997), 103; and Dennis Clark, The Irish in Philadelphia: Ten Generations of

Urban Experience (Philadelphia: Temple University Press, 1973), 130.

44. Robert Caulwell, Charleston, Ohio, to James Caulwell, Tullynure, County Tyrone, Ireland, 4 November 1865. Private Collection of Kerby A. Miller, Ph.D., University of Missouri, Columbia.

45. Neil L. Shumsky, ed., "Frank Roney's San Francisco—His Diary: April 1875—March 1876," *Labor History* 17, no. 2 (1976): 249–51.

46. James Bryce, *The American Commonwealth* (1893; reprint, New York: Macmillan, 1905), 2: 99; quoted in Jacobson, 182.

47. The *Atlantic Monthly,* March 1896, 294–95; and quoted in Jacobson, 192. Eugenics was a pseudo-science that focused on improving hereditary qualities in human beings through selective procreation.

48. Kerby A. Miller, *Emigrants and Exiles: Ireland and the Irish Exodus to North America* (New York: Oxford University Press, 1985), 498.

49. Excellent analysis of the Molly Maguires in Kevin Kenny, *Making Sense of the Molly Maguires* (New York: Oxford University Press, 1998); a solid brief synopsis can be found in Kevin Kenny, "The Molly Maguires," in *The Encyclopedia of the Irish in America,* ed. Michael Glazier (Notre Dame, IN: University of Notre Dame Press, 1999), 623–24; and Kevin Kenny, "The Molly Maguires and the Catholic Church," *Labor History* 37 (Summer 1995): 345–76; for the Orange Riots see Michael A. Gordon, *The Orange Riots: Irish Political Violence in New York City, 1870–1871* (Ithaca, NY: Cornell University Press, 1993), 33; Gordon's book offers an insightful investigation of the riots, the intra-Irish tensions they revealed, as well as the reaction they invoked from native-born Americans concerning Irish Catholics and Irish Protestants within the country; an excellent brief summary of this subject is also available by Gordon, "Orange Riots of 1870 and 1871," in Glazier, *The Encyclopedia of the Irish in America,* 748–49.

50. Kenny, *Making Sense of the Molly Maguires,* 259–60; *New York Times,* 12 July and 16 July

1871; and Gordon, *The Orange Riots,* 749.

51. *Irish-American,* 22 July and 29 July 1871; *Irish Citizen,* 29 July 1871; *Irish World,* 12 July, 22 July, 12 August 1871.

52. Thomas H. O'Connor, *The Boston Irish: A Political History* (Boston: Back Bay Books, 1995), 105.

53. *The Irish World—An Illustrated Supplement to the "Irish World,"* n.d. (estimated late July 1871); and McCaffrey, 223.

54. An excellent analysis of these portrayals with numerous examples can be found in L. Perry Curtis, Jr., *Apes and Angels: The Irishman in Victorian Caricature,* rev. ed. (Washington: Smithsonian Institution Press, 1997), 58–67.

55. *Harper's Weekly,* 11 May 1872; for an outstanding analysis of this and other political cartoons, see Harpcom.com, "Presidential Elections," http://elections.harpweek.com/1Cartoons/cartoon-1872-Medium.asp?UniqueID=17&Year=1872, 24 September 2005.

56. *Harper's Weekly,* 28 August 1880; analysis of this cartoon at Harpweek.com, "Presidential Elections," http://elections.harpweek.com/1Cartoons/cartoon-1880f.asp?UniqueID=25&Year=1880, 24 September 2005.

57. *Puck,* 28 July 1880; analysis of this cartoon at Harpweek.com, "Presidential Elections," http://elections.harpweek.com/1Cartoons/cartoon-1880-Medium.asp?UniqueID=10&Year=1880, 24 September 2005.

58. *Puck,* 23 July 1884; analysis of this cartoon at Harpweek.com, "Presidential Elections," http://elections.harpweek.com/1Cartoons/cartoon-1884-Medium.asp?UniqueID=39&Year=1884, 24 September 2005; *Harper's Weekly,* 26 July 1884; analysis of this cartoon at Harpweek.com, "Presidential Elections," http://elections.harpweek.com/1Cartoons/cartoon-1884-Large.asp?UniqueID=37&Year=1884, 24 September 2005.

59. This theory is supported by Reginald Byron, *Irish America.* Oxford Studies in Social and Cultural Anthropology Series (Oxford: Clarendon, 1999), 67.

60. Michael O'Sullivan, New York City, to Brother John A.

Grace, Dublin, Ireland, 8 September 1870. Private Collection of Kerby A. Miller, Ph.D., University of Missouri, Columbia.

61. William L. Riordan, *Plunkitt of Tammany Hall* (1905; reprint, New York: Dutton, 1963), 5; Kevin Kenny, *The American Irish: A History* (New York: Longman, 2000), 160. As historian Reginald Byron theorized in his studies of the Irish of Albany, New York, the elections of Irishmen to prominent political positions "brought nativism to an end . . . and further bound the loyalty of the Irish to the Democrats. The Irish could no longer be marginalized or treated as a minority, but had now asserted their power as the largest single voting bloc in Albany politics," and as an influential constituency in Boston, New York, and Baltimore leading to similar results in those cities.

62. Bluford Adams, "New Ireland: The Place of Immigrants in American Regionalism," *Journal of American Ethnic History* 24 (Winter 2005): 7.

63. New York Monuments Commission for the Battlefields of Gettysburg and Chattanooga, *Final Report on the Battlefield of Gettysburg,* Vol. 2 (Albany, NY: J.B. Lyon Company, Printers, 1902): 479–80.

64. William Corby, *Memoirs of Chaplain Life: Three Years with the Irish Brigade in the Army of the Potomac,* Lawrence Frederick Kohl, ed. (New York: Fordham University Press, 1992), 6.

65. Corby, xxiii–xxiv.

66. For a detailed analysis of when and why many Civil War veterans wrote their memoirs, see James M. McPherson, *For Cause and Comrades: Why Men Fought in the Civil War* (Cambridge: Oxford University Press, 1997); Earl Hess, *The Union Soldier in Battle: Enduring the Ordeal of Combat,* Modern War Studies (Lawrence: University Press of Kansas, 1997); Gerald Linderman, *Embattled Courage: The Experience of Combat in the American Civil War* (New York: Free Press, 1989); Reid Mitchell, *Civil War Soldiers* (New York: Viking, 1988).

67. *Memorial of the Monument Erected on the Battlefield of Gettysburg to Very Reverend William Corby, C.S.C.* (Philadelphia:

Catholic Alumni Sodality of Philadelphia, 1911), 9; Mulholland's discussion of Catholics kneeling with Protestants from his address covered in Franklin *Evening News* 1907.

68. St. Clair A. Mulholland, *The Story of the 116th Regiment, Pennsylvania Volunteers in the War of the Rebellion,* ed. Lawrence Frederick Kohl (New York: Fordham University Press, 1996), iii.

69. Stephen Owens, Clontarf, Minnesota, to Celia Grimes, Skerries, County Dublin, Ireland, 4 December 1899 and 19 March 1900. Owens/Grimes Letters, 1871–1920, Old Skerries Society, Ireland. Courtesy of Kerby A. Miller, Ph.D., University of Missouri, Columbia.

Selected Bibliography

Manuscripts

United Kingdom

NORTHERN IRELAND

Public Record Office of Northern
Ireland
   Anderson Family Letters
   James Carlisle Letters
   Vere Foster Letters
   Andrew Greenlees Letters
   Abraham Irvine Letters
   William McSparron Letters
   John Mitchel Letter
   William Murphy Letters
   Porter Family Letters
   Redford Family Letters
   Rowland Redmund Letters
   William Richey Letter
   Robert Smith Letters
   William Stavely Letters
   John Thompson Letters

Republic of Ireland

National Archives of Ireland,
Dublin
   Secretary's Office Registered
   Papers (CSORP) 9965/1863
   John Egan Letter
   Secretary's Office Registered
   Papers (CSORP) 16765/1864
   Dispatches of British Ambas-
   sador, Washington, DC
   Dispatches of British Consul,
   Portland, ME
   Chicago and Alton Railroad
   Company Contract
   Lord Lieutenant of Ireland
   Proclamation, June 1864
National Library of Ireland, Dublin
   Henry Allen Letter
   Michael Doheny Letters
   Robert Humphreys Letters
   Thomas J. Kelly Letter
   Keogh Family Letters
   Lalor Family Letters
   William Smith O'Brien Papers
   O'Neill Family Papers
   Thomas Reilly Letters

Sheehan Family Letters
Robert D. Webb Letters
Maurice Wolfe Letters

United States

ILLINOIS

Chicago Historical Society
   James A. Mulligan Papers, 1849–
   1900
   James A. Mulligan Diary
   Peter Casey Letters
   Joseph P. Collins Letter
   John P. Donelan Letter
   R. T. Farrell Letters
   T. C. Fitzgibbon Letter
   Ed. C. Russell Letter
   M. W. Toale Letter
   Unknown author, letter from
   Church of the Immaculate
   Conception, Chicago, IL
   Gerald B. Walsh Letter
   Thomas F. Wildes Letter
Illinois State Archives, Springfield
   Adjutant General Records,
   Administrative Files on Civil
   War Companies & Regi-
   ments, 1861–1865
Abraham Lincoln Presidential
Library, Springfield
   Yates Family Papers, Abraham
   Lincoln Presidential Library

INDIANA

Indiana Historical Society Library,
Indianapolis
   Joseph Hewitt Letters, 1851–
   1872

MASSACHUSETTS

Massachusetts State Archives,
Boston
   Executive Department Corre-
   spondence, 1853–1898.
   Series G01/567X
   9th Regiment Files: Volume 25
   28th Regiment, 1861–1864:
   Volume W32

28th Regiment, 1863–1868:
   Volume 3
   General Orders of Massachu-
   setts Adjutant General
   Office, 1861–1866: Volume
   32
   Special Orders of the Massa-
   chusetts Adjutant General,
   1861–1866: Volume 42
   Bounty Claims Correspon-
   dence, 1904. Series PS1/
   699X
   Soldiers' Naturalizations,
   1864–1884. Middlesex
   County Superior Court. Judi-
   cial Archives
Massachusetts Historical Society,
Boston
   John A. Andrew Papers
   Edward Everett Hale Papers
   John Davis Long Papers
   Horace Mann Papers, I–V
   Broadsides
   Miscellaneous Bound Manu-
   scripts

MARYLAND

Antietam National Battlefield,
Sharpsburg
   Regimental Files:
      63rd New York
      69th New York
      88th New York
      9th Massachusetts
      29th Massachusetts
   Ezra A. Carman Manuscript

MISSOURI

Private Collection of Kerby A.
Miller, Ph.D., University of Mis-
souri, Columbia
   Robert Caulwell Letters
   Henry O'Mahoney Memoir
   Seawright/Reese Letters

NEW YORK

Manuscripts and Archives Division, New York Public Library,

Astor, Lenox, and Tilden Foundations, New York City
  Charles P. Daly Papers
  John England Letters, 1862–1863, U.S. Army Collection
  James Stephens Diary
American Irish Historical Society, New York City
  Society of the Friendly Sons of St. Patrick Collection
New York Historical Society, New York City
  James P. McIvor Papers
New York State Library, Albany
  James B. Turner Papers
Private Collection of Mr. Robert J. and Mrs. Ruth Fitzgerald, Rouses Point
  Harlin Family Letters

NORTH CAROLINA

University of North Carolina, Southern Historical Collection, Chapel Hill
  Andrew J. Sproule Papers, 1845–1890

OHIO

Private Collection of Arnold Schrier, Ph.D., Professor Emeritus, University of Cincinnati
  James Dixon Letters
  Patrick Dunny Letters
  Maurice Sexton Letters

PENNSYLVANIA

The Civil War and Underground Railroad Museum of Philadelphia
  St. Clair A. Mulholland Papers
Gettysburg National Military Park Library
  V6-PA69- 69th Pennsylvania Infantry Regiment
  V17- 116th Pennsylvania Infantry Regiment Monument
  V17- 140th Pennsylvania Infantry Regiment Monument
  Box B-13: John Buckley Papers (69 PA IN)
  Box B-34: *D. Scott Hartwig Collection*: 69th Pennsylvania Volunteer Infantry Regiment
  Gettysburg Newspaper Clippings, Volume 5
Historical Society of Pennsylvania, Philadelphia
  John W. Alloway Diary
The Philadelphia Archdiocesan Historical Research Center, Wynnewood
  Fenian Papers
  William C. White Papers

University of Pittsburgh Library, Archives of Industrial Society, Pittsburgh
  Donohoe Family Letters
The United States Army Military History Institute, Carlisle Barracks
  The John J. Kavanagh Papers
    Memoir of John J. Kavanagh
  Lewis Leigh Collection
    William A. Smith Letters
  Kenneth H. Powers Collection
    J. Noonan History

VIRGINIA

Fredericksburg and Spotsylvania County National Military Park
  Francis Yeager Diary

WASHINGTON, DC

Catholic University of America, American Catholic History Research Center and University Archives (ACUA)
  The Fenian Brotherhood Records
  J. O'Donovan Rossa Personal Papers
Library of Congress, Manuscripts Division
  Allen Landis Letters
  Papers of Edwin M. Stanton
National Archives and Records Administration
  Thomas Francis Meagher, Letters Received by the Commission Branch of the Adjutant General's Office, 1863–1870
  St. Clair Mulholland, Letters Received by the Commission Branch of the Adjutant General's Office, 1863–1870
  Record Group 59: General Records of the Department of State, 1756–1993
  Consular Correspondence
  U.S. Consular Dispatches from Galway, Belfast, Dublin, Cork, and Londonderry
  Record Group 94: Records of the Adjutant General's Office, Book Records of Union Volunteer Organizations
  Michael Corcoran Pension Records
  Michael Corcoran Military Records
  Daniel F. Gillen Pension Records
  William McCarter Pension Records
  Thomas Francis Meagher Military Records
  Thomas Francis Meagher Pension Records

St. Clair A. Mulholland Military Records
St. Clair A. Mulholland Pension Records
Ninth Illinois Infantry Order Book
William L. D. O'Grady Pension Records
Timothy O'Leary Pension Records
One-hundred-Eighty-Second New York Infantry Regimental Order Book
One-hundred-Sixteenth Pennsylvania Infantry Regimental Letter, Order, and Miscellaneous Book
Sixty-Ninth New York Infantry Regimental Descriptive, Letter, Order, and Miscellaneous Book
Sixty-Third New York Infantry Regimental Descriptive and Letter Book
Sixty-Third New York Infantry Regimental Order, Casualty, and Guard Report Book
Thirty-Fifth Indiana Infantry Order Book
Twenty-Eighth Massachusetts Infantry Regimental Letter, Order, Roster, and Miscellaneous Book
Twenty-Ninth Massachusetts Infantry Regimental Descriptive and Consolidated Morning Report Book
Peter Welsh Military Records
Maurice Wolfe Pension Records
Record Group 153: Records of the Office of the Judge Advocate General (Army), Court Martial Case Files, 1809–1914

WISCONSIN

Private Collection of Mr. Michael J. Langhoff, Fox Point
  O'Shaughnessy Family Letters

Newspapers

Boston *Pilot*
The Emerald (New York)
Forney's War Press (Philadelphia)
Frank Leslie's Illustrated Newspaper
Franklin (Pennsylvania) *Evening News*
Grand Army Scout & Soldiers' Mail
Harper's Weekly (New York)

The Illustrated London News
The Irish Citizen (New York)
The Irish World (New York)
New York Daily Tribune
New York Herald
New York Irish-American
New York Times
Philadelphia Inquirer
Philadelphia Public Ledger
Philadelphia Weekly Times
Punch (New York)
Scribner's Monthly
Southern Watchman (Athens, Georgia)
Yorkville (South Carolina) Enquirer

Published Primary Sources

Conyngham, D. P. The Irish Brigade and Its Campaigns, Lawrence Frederick Kohl, ed. New York: William McSorley & Co., 1867. Reprint, New York: Fordham University Press, 1994.

Corby, William. Memoirs of Chaplain Life: Three Years with the Irish Brigade in the Army of the Potomac, Lawrence Frederick Kohl, ed. New York: Fordham University Press, 1992.

Corcoran, Michael. The Captivity of General Corcoran, the Only Authentic and Reliable Narrative of the Trials and Sufferings Endured during Twelve Months' Imprisonment in Richmond and Other Southern Cities. Philadelphia, PA: Barclay, 1862.

Daly, Maria Lydig. Diary of a Union Lady, 1861–1865. New York: Funk and Wagnalls, 1962. Reprint, Lincoln: University of Nebraska Press, 2000.

Doyle, James M. "The Diary of James M. Doyle." Mid-America: An Historical Review 20 (October 1938): 273–83.

Dwyer, John. Address of John Dwyer. New York: Herald Press, 1914.

Fehrenbacher, Don E., ed. Lincoln: Speeches and Writing, 1832–1865. 2 vols. New York: Library of America, 1989.

Frank Leslie's Illustrated History of the Civil War: The Most Important Events of the Conflict between the States. . . . New York: Frank Leslie, 1895.

Galwey, Thomas Francis. The Valiant Hours: Narrative of "Captain Brevet," and Irish-

American in the Army of the Potomac, Colonel W. S. Nye, ed. Harrisburg, PA: Stackpole, 1961.

Halpine, Charles W. The Life and Adventures, Songs, Services, and Speeches of Private Miles O'Reilly (47th Regiment, New York Volunteers). New York: Carleton, Publisher, 1864.

Johnson, Robert Underwood, and Clarence Clough Buel, Battles and Leaders of the Civil War. 4 vols. New York: Yoseloff, 1956.

Jones, Frank. "The Fenian Raid on Canada." The Irish Sword: The Journal of the Military History Society of Ireland 3 (1957): 47–49.

Kohl, Lawrence Frederick, with Margaret Cossé Richard, eds. Irish Green and Union Blue: The Civil War Letters of Peter Welsh. New York: Fordham University Press, 1986.

Ladd, David L., and Audrey J. Ladd, eds. The Bachelder Papers: Gettysburg in Their Own Words. 3 vols. Dayton, OH: Morningside Books, 1995.

McCarter, William. My Life in the Irish Brigade: The Civil War Memoirs of Private William McCarter, 116th Pennsylvania Infantry, Kevin O'Brien, ed. Campbell, CA: Savas, 1996.

McDermott, Anthony W. A Brief History of the 69th Regiment Pennsylvania Veteran Volunteers, from Its Formation until Final Muster out of the United States Service. Philadelphia, PA: D. J. Gallagher & Co., 1889.

McElroy, The Reverend Thomas. "The War Letters of Father Peter Paul Cooney of the Congregation of Holy Cross." American Catholic Historical Society 44 (March, June, and September 1933): 47–69, 151–69, 220–37.

Macnamara, Daniel G. The History of the Ninth Regiment Massachusetts Volunteer Infantry, Christian G. Samito, ed. Boston: E. B. Stillings & Co., 1899. Reprint, New York: Fordham University Press, 2000.

Meagher, Thomas F. The Last Days of the 69th in Virginia: A Narrative in Three Parts. New York: Irish American, 1861.

———. Letters on our National Struggle. New York: Loyal Publication Society, 1864.

Memorial of the Monument

Erected on the Battlefield of Gettysburg to Very Reverend William Corby, C.S.C. Philadelphia: Catholic Alumni Sodality of Philadelphia, 1911.

Mulholland, St. Clair. The Story of the 116th Regiment Pennsylvania Volunteers in the War of the Rebellion, Lawrence Frederick Kohl, ed. Philadelphia: F. McManus, Jr., 1903. Reprint, New York: Fordham University Press, 1996.

"On to Prison." Civil War Times Illustrated 29 (May–June 1990): 30–67.

Osborne, William H. The History of the Twenty-Ninth Regiment of Massachusetts Volunteer Infantry in the Late War of the Rebellion. Boston: Albert J. Wright, Printer, 1877.

Pickett, George E. The Heart of a Soldier: As Revealed in the Intimate Letters of General George E. Pickett, CSA. New York: Seth Moyle, 1913.

Samito, Christian G., ed. Commanding Boston's Irish Ninth: The Civil War Letters of Colonel Patrick R. Guiney, Ninth Massachusetts Volunteer Infantry. New York: Fordham University Press, 1998.

Strong, George Templeton. Diary of the Civil War, 1860–1865, Allan Nevins, ed. New York: Macmillan, 1962.

U.S. War Department. War of the Rebellion: A Compilation of the Official Records of the Union and Confederate Armies. 128 vols. Washington, DC, 1880–1901.

Secondary Sources

Adams, Bluford, "New Ireland: The Place of Immigrants in American Regionalism." Journal of American Ethnic History 24 (Winter 2005): 3–33.

Anbinder, Tyler G. " 'Boss' Tweed: Nativist." Journal of the Early Republic 15 (Spring 1995): 109–16.

———. Five Points: The 19th-Century New York City Neighborhood That Invented Tap Dance, Stole Elections, and Became the World's Most Notorious Slum. New York: Free Press, 2001.

———. Nativism and Slavery: The

Northern Know Nothings and the Politics of the 1850s. New York: Oxford University Press, 1992.

Anbinder, Tyler G. "Ulysses S. Grant: Nativist." *Civil War History: A Journal of the Middle Period* 43, no. 2 (June 1997): 119–41.

Athearn, Robert G. *Thomas Francis Meagher: An Irish Revolutionary in America*. Boulder: University of Colorado Press, 1949. Reprint, New York: Arno Press, 1976.

Ballard, Michael B. *Vicksburg: The Campaign That Opened the Mississippi*. Chapel Hill: University of North Carolina Press, 2004.

Banes, Charles H. *History of the Philadelphia Brigade*. Lippincott, 1876.

Barnard, Sandy, ed. *Campaigning with the Irish Brigade: Pvt. John Ryan, 28th Massachusetts*. Terre Haute, IN: AST Press, 2001.

Bates, Samuel P. *History of Pennsylvania Volunteers, 1861–5*. Harrisburg, PA: B. Singerly, 1870.

Bayor, Ronald H., and Timothy J. Meagher, eds. *The New York Irish*. Baltimore, MD: Johns Hopkins University Press, 1996.

Beaudot, William J. K. "Chief of the Civil War Skull Crackers." *Milwaukee History* 11 (1988): 98–106.

Bennett, Brian A. *Sons of Old Monroe: A Regimental History of Patrick O'Rorke's 140th New York Volunteer Infantry*. Dayton, OH: Morningside Books, 1999.

Beringer, Richard E., Herman Hattaway, Archer Jones, and William N. Still, Jr. *Why the South Lost the Civil War*. Athens: University of Georgia Press, 1986.

Berlin, Ira, Barbara J. Fields, Steven F. Miller, Joseph P. Reidy, and Leslie S. Rowland, eds. *Slaves No More: Three Essays on Emancipation and the Civil War*. New York: Cambridge University Press, 1992.

Berlin, Ira, Joseph P. Reidy, and Leslie S. Rowland, eds. *Freedom's Soldiers: The Black Military Experience in the Civil War*. New York: Cambridge University Press, 1998.

Bernstein, Iver. *The New York City Draft Riots: Their Significance for American Society and Politics in the Age of the Civil War*. New York: Oxford University Press, 1990.

Biusy, Joseph G., and Stephan D. O'Neill, eds. *My Sons Were Faithful and They Fought the Irish Brigade at Antietam: An Anthology*. Hightstown, NJ: Longstreet House, 1997.

Blight, David W. *Beyond the Battlefield: Race, Memory, and the American Civil War*. Amherst: University of Massachusetts Press, 2002.

Bowen, James L. *Massachusetts in the War, 1861–1865*. Springfield, MA: Clark W. Bryan & Co., 1889.

Burchell, R. A. *The San Francisco Irish, 1848–1880*. Berkeley: University of California Press, 1980.

Burton, William L. "Indiana's Ethnic Regiments." *Journal of Popular Culture* 14, no. 2 (1980): 229–41.

———. "Irish Regiments in the Union Army: The Massachusetts Experience." *Historical Journal of Massachusetts* 11, no. 2 (1983): 104–19.

———. *Melting Pot Soldiers: The Union's Ethnic Regiments*, 2nd ed. New York: Fordham University Press, 1998.

Byron, Reginald. *Irish America*. Oxford: Clarendon Press, 1999.

Campbell, John H. *The Friendly Sons of St. Patrick and the Hibernian Society of Philadelphia, 1771–1892*. Philadelphia: privately printed, 1892.

A Century of Faith: Parish of St. Patrick. Philadelphia: privately printed, 1940.

Cimbala, Paul A., and Randall M. Miller, eds. *Union Soldiers and the Northern Home Front: Wartime Experiences, Postwar Adjustments*. New York: Fordham University Press, 2002.

Clark, Dennis. *The Irish in Philadelphia: Ten Generations of Urban Experience*. Philadelphia: Temple University Press, 1973.

Coffey, Michael, ed., with text by Terry Golway. *The Irish in America*. New York: Hypernion, 1997.

Cole, Donald. *Immigrant City: Lawrence, Massachusetts, 1845–1921*. Chapel Hill: University of North Carolina Press, 2002.

Conzen, Kathleen Neils, and David A. Gerber. "The Invention of Ethnicity: A Perspective from the U.S.A." *Journal of American Ethnic History* 12 (Fall 1992): 3–39.

Cook, Adrian. *The Armies of the Streets: The New York City Draft Riots of 1863*. Lexington: University Press of Kentucky, 1974.

Cornish, Dudley Taylor. *The Sable Arm: Black Troops in the Union Army, 1861–1865*. New York: Longmans, Green, 1956. Reprint, Lawrence: University Press of Kansas, 1987.

Cullop, Charles P. "An Unequal Duel: Union Recruiting in Ireland, 1863–1864." *Civil War History* 13 (June 1967): 101–13.

Curti, Merle. *The Roots of American Loyalty*. New York: Columbia University Press, 1946.

Curtis, L. Perry, Jr. *Apes and Angels: The Irishman in Victorian Caricature*. Washington, DC: Smithsonian Institution Press, 1997.

D'Arcy, Frank. *Wild Geese and Travelling Scholars*. Cork, Ireland: Mercier Press, 2001.

Diner, Hasia R. *Erin's Daughters in America: Irish Immigrant Women in the Nineteenth Century*. Baltimore, MD: Johns Hopkins University Press, 1983.

Donnelly, James S. *The Great Irish Potato Famine*. Phoenix Mill, Gloucestershire: Sutton Publishing, 2001.

Dupree, A. Hunter, and Leslie H. Fishel, Jr., eds. "An Eyewitness Account of the New York City Draft Riots, July 1863." *The Mississippi Valley Historical Review* 47 (December 1960): 472–79.

Eagleton, Terry. *Scholars and Rebels in Nineteenth-Century Ireland*. Oxford: Blackwell, 1999.

Ekirch, Arthur A., Jr. *The Civilian and the Military: A History of the American Antimilitarist Tradition*. Colorado Springs, CO: Ralph Myles, 1972.

Emmons, David M. *The Butte Irish: Class and Ethnicity in an American Mining Town, 1875–1925*, reprint edition. Champaign: University of Illinois Press, 1990.

Engerman, Stanley L., and Robert E. Gallman, eds. *The Cambridge Economic History of the United States*. Vol. 2, *The Long Nine-*

teenth Century. New York: Cambridge University Press, 2000.

Ernsberger, Don. *Paddy Owen's Regulars: A History of the 69th Pennsylvania "Irish Volunteers."* 2 vols. Philadelphia: Xlibris, 2004.

Faherty, William Barnaby, S.J. *The St. Louis Irish: An Unmatched Celtic Community.* St. Louis: Missouri Historical Society Press, 2001.

Fallows, Marjorie R. *Irish Americans: Identity and Assimilation.* Englewood Cliffs, NJ: Prentice Hall, 1979.

Ferrie, Joseph P. *Yankees Now: Immigrants in the Antebellum United States, 1840–1860.* New York: Oxford University Press, 1999.

Fisher, Donald M. "Born in Ireland, Killed at Gettysburg: The Life, Death, and Legacy of Patrick H. O'Rorke." *Civil War History* 39 (September 1993): 225–39.

Formisano, Ronald P. "The Invention of Ethnocultural Interpretation." *American Historical Review* 99 (April 1994): 453–77.

Frank, Joseph Allan. *With Ballot and Bayonet: The Political Socialization of American Civil War Soldiers.* Athens: University of Georgia Press, 1998.

Gallagher, Thomas. *Paddy's Lament, Ireland 1846–1847: Prelude to Hatred.* New York: Harcourt Brace, 1982.

Garland, John L. "Michael Corcoran and the Formation of the Irish Legion." *The Irish Sword: The Journal of the Military History Society of Ireland* 17 (1987): 26–40.

George, Joseph, Jr. "Philadelphia's *Catholic Herald*: The Civil War Years." *Pennsylvania Magazine of History and Biography* 103 (1979): 196–221.

Glatthaar, Joseph T. *Forged in Battle: The Civil War Alliance of Black Soldiers and White Officers.* New York: Free Press, 1990.

Glazier, Michael, ed. *The Encyclopedia of the Irish in America.* Notre Dame, IN: University of Notre Dame Press, 1999.

Golway, Terry. *For the Cause of Liberty: A Thousand Years of Ireland's Heroes.* New York: Simon & Schuster, 2000.

———. *Irish Rebel: John Devoy*

and *America's Fight for Ireland's Freedom.* New York: St. Martin's Griffin, 1998.

Gribben, Arthur, ed. *The Great Famine and the Irish Diaspora in America.* Amherst: University of Massachusetts Press, 1999.

Griffen, Patrick. *The People with No Name: Ireland's Ulster Scots, America's Scots Irish, and the Creation of a British Atlantic World, 1689–1764.* Princeton, NJ: Princeton University Press, 2001.

Griffin, T. Kevin. "The 1st Irish, 35th Indiana Volunteer Infantry Regiment 1861–1865: A Military, Political, and Social History." M.A. thesis, Butler University, 1992.

Hackmer, Kurt. "Response to War: Civil War Enlistment Patterns in Kenosha County, Wisconsin." *Military History of the West* 29 (Spring 1999): 31–62.

Harris, Leslie M. *In the Shadow of Slavery: African Americans in New York City, 1626–1863.* Chicago: University of Chicago Press, 2003.

Harsh, Joseph L. *Taken at the Flood: Robert E. Lee & Confederate Strategy in the Maryland Campaign of 1862.* Kent, OH: Kent State University Press, 1999.

Hartwig, D. Scott. "Casualties of War: The Effects of the Battle of Gettysburg upon the Men and Families of the 69th Pennsylvania Infantry Regiment." *Unsung Heroes of Gettysburg: Proceedings of the 5th Annual Gettysburg Seminar* (Gettysburg, PA: Gettysburg National Military Park, 1996), 1–22.

———. "It Struck Horror to Us All." *Gettysburg* 1 (January 1991): 89–100.

Hattaway, Herman, and Archer Jones. *How the North Won: A Military History of the Civil War.* Urbana: University of Illinois Press, 1991.

Hayes, John D., and Doris D. Maguire. "Charles Graham Halpine: Life and Adventures of Miles O'Reilly." *New York Historical Society Quarterly* 51 (1967): 326–44.

Hennessy, Maurice. *The Wild Geese: The Irish Soldier in Exile.* Old Greenwich, CT: Devin-Adair, 1973.

Henthorne, Sister Mary Evangela.

The Irish Catholic Colonization Association of the United States. Champaign IL: Twin City Printing Company, 1932.

Hernon, Joseph M., Jr. *Celts, Catholics, and Copperheads: Ireland Views the American Civil War.* Columbus: Ohio State University Press, 1968.

Hershberg, Theodore, ed. *Philadelphia: Work, Space, Family, and Group Experience in the 19th-Century City.* New York: Oxford University Press, 1981.

Hess, Earl J. *The Union Soldier in Combat: Enduring the Ordeal of Combat.* Lawrence: University Press of Kansas, 1997.

Higham, John. *Strangers in the Land: Patterns of American Nativism, 1860–1925.* New Brunswick, NJ: Rutgers University Press, 1955.

The History of the Catholic Church in Indiana. Logansport, IN: A. W. Bowen & Co., 1898.

Holmes, Richard. *Acts of War: The Behavior of Men in Battle.* New York: Free Press, 1985.

Horowitz, Murray M. "Ethnicity and Command: The Civil War Experience." *Military Affairs* 42 (December 1978): 182–89.

Hueston, Robert Francis. *The Catholic Press and Nativism, 1840–1860.* New York: Arno Press, 1976.

Ignatiev, Noel. *How the Irish Became White.* New York: Routledge, 1995.

Jackson, Alvin. *Ireland, 1798–1998: Politics and War.* Oxford: Blackwell Publishers, 1999.

Jacobson, Matthew Frye. *Barbarian Virtues: The United States Encounters Foreign Peoples at Home and Abroad, 1876–1917.* New York: Hill and Wang, 1999.

———. *Whiteness of a Different Color: European Immigrants and the Alchemy of Race.* Cambridge, MA: Harvard University Press, 1998.

Jenkins, Brian. *Fenians and Anglo-American Relations during Reconstruction.* Ithaca, NY: Cornell University Press, 1969.

Jensen, Richard J. *Grass Roots Politics: Parties, Issues, and Voters, 1854–1983.* Westport, CT: Greenwood Press, 1983.

———. " 'No Irish Need Apply': A Myth of Victimization." *Journal* of Social History 36 (2002): 405–29.

Jentz, John B., and Richard Schneirov. "Chicago's Fenian Fair of 1864: A Window into the Civil War as a Popular Political Awakening." *Labor's Heritage: Quarterly of the George Meany Memorial Archives* 6 (1995): 4–19.

Johnson, John J., ed. *The Role of the Military in Underdeveloped Countries*. Princeton, NJ: Princeton University Press, 1962.

Jones, Paul. *The Irish Brigade*. Gaithersburg, MD: Olde Soldier Books, 1969.

Joyce, William Leonard. *Editors and Ethnicity: A History of the Irish-America Press, 1848–1883*. New York: Arno Press, 1976.

Kaiser, Leo. "Letters from the Front." *Journal of the Illinois State Historical Society* 56 (1963): 150–63.

Kane, Michael H. "American Soldiers in Ireland, 1865–1867." *The Irish Sword* 23 (Summer 2002): 103–40.

———. "The Irish Lineage of the 69th Pennsylvania Volunteers." *The Irish Sword* 18 (Winter 1991): 184–98.

Kautz, Craig Lee. "Fodder for Cannon: Immigrant Perceptions of the Civil War—The Old Northwest." Ph.D. diss., University of Nebraska, Lincoln, 1976.

Kazal, Russell A. "Revisiting Assimilation: The Rise, Fall, and Reappraisal of a Concept in American Ethnic History." *American Historical Review* 100 (April 1995): 437–71.

Kean, Kathleen Cochrane. "George Tipping, the Corcoran Irish Legion, and the Civil War." *Niagra Frontier* 24 (1977): 53–65.

Kelly, Brian. "Ambiguous Loyalties: The Boston Irish, Slavery, and the Civil War." *Historical Journal of Massachusetts* 24 (1996): 165–204.

Kinealy, Christine. *The Great Irish Famine: Impact, Ideology, and Rebellion*. Houndmills, Hampshire: Palgrave, 2002.

Kirlin, Joseph L. *Catholicity in Philadelphia: From the Earliest Missionaries Down to the Present Time*. Philadelphia: John Jos McVey, 1909.

Klement, Frank L. "Catholics as Copperheads during the Civil War." *Catholic Historical Review* 80 (January 1994): 36–57.

———. *The Limits of Dissent: Clement L. Vallandigham and the Civil War*. Lexington: University of Kentucky Press, 1970. Reprint, New York: Fordham University Press, 1998.

Kleppner, Paul. *The Third Electoral System, 1853–1892: Parties, Voters, and Political Cultures*. Chapel Hill: University of North Carolina Press, 1979.

Knox, Oliver. *Rebels and Informers: Stirrings of Irish Independence*. New York: St. Martin's Press, 1997.

Knupfer, Peter B. *Union as It Is: Constitutional Unionism and Sectional Compromise, 1787–1861*. Chapel Hill: University of North Carolina Press, 1991.

Krieg, Joann P. *Whitman and the Irish*. Iowa City: University of Iowa Press, 2000.

LaFantasie, Glenn W. *Twilight at Little Round Top: July 2, 1863—The Tide Turns at Gettysburg*. New York: Wiley, 2005.

Levine, Peter. "Draft Evasion in the North during the Civil War, 1863–1865." *Journal of American History* 67 (March 1981): 816–34.

Leyburn, James G. *The Scotch Irish: A Social History*. Chapel Hill: University of North Carolina Press, 1962.

Linderman, Gerald F. *Embattled Courage: The Experience of Combat in the American Civil War*. New York: Free Press, 1987.

Lochlainn, Alf Mac. "Three Ballads of the American Civil War." *The Irish Sword: The Journal of the Military History Society of Ireland* 6 (1963): 28–33.

Lonn, Ella. *Foreigners in the Union Army and Navy*. Baton Rouge: Louisiana State University Press, 1951.

McAvoy, Thomas T. "Peter Paul Cooney: Chaplain of Indiana's Irish Regiment." *The Journal of the American-Irish Historical Society* 30 (1932): 97–102.

McCaffrey, Lawrence J. *The Irish Catholic Diaspora in America*, rev. ed. Washington, DC: Catholic University of America Press, 1997.

McCaffrey, Lawrence J., ed. *The Irish in Chicago*. Urbana: University of Illinois Press, 1987.

McMahon, Eileen M. *What Parish Are You From? A Chicago Irish Community and Race Relations*. Lexington: University Press of Kentucky, 1995.

McPherson, James M. *For Cause and Comrades: Why Men Fought in the Civil War*. New York: Oxford University Press, 1997.

McPherson, James M., and William J. Cooper, Jr., eds. *Writing the Civil War: The Quest to Understand*. Columbia: University of South Carolina Press, 2000.

Meagher, Timothy J. *Inventing Irish America: Generation, Class, and Ethnic Identity in a New England City, 1880–1928*. Notre Dame, IL: University of Notre Dame Press, 2000.

Meneely, A. Howard. *The War Department, 1861: A Study in Mobilization and Administration*. New York: Columbia University Press, 1928.

Miller, Kerby A. "Assimilation and Alienation: Irish Emigrants' Responses to Industrial America, 1871–1921." *Irish Studies* 4 (1985): 87–112.

———. *Emigrants and Exiles: Ireland and the Irish Exodus to North America*. New York: Oxford University Press, 1985.

Miller, Kerby A., Bruce D. Boling, and David N. Doyle. "Emigrants and Exiles: Irish Cultures and Irish Emigration to North America, 1790–1922. *Irish Historical Studies* 22 (1980): 97–125.

Miller, Kerby A., Bruce D. Boling, and Liam Kennedy. "The Famine's Scars: William Murphy's Ulster and American Odyssey." *Éire-Ireland* 36 (2001): 98–123.

Miller, Kerby A., Arnold Schrier, Bruce D. Boling, and David N. Doyle, eds. *Irish Immigrants in the Land of Canaan: Letters and Memoirs from Colonial and Revolutionary America, 1675–1815*. New York: Oxford University Press, 2003.

Miller, Randall M., Harry S. Stout, and Charles Reagan Wilson, eds. *Religion and the American Civil War*. New York: Oxford University Press, 1998.

Mitchell, Brian C. *The Paddy Camps: The Irish of Lowell, 1821–1861*. Urbana: University of Illinois Press, 1988.

Mitchell, Reid. *Civil War Soldiers: Their Expectations and Their Experiences*. New York: Viking Penguin, 1988.

———. *The Vacant Chair: The Northern Soldier Leaves Home*. New York: Oxford University Press, 1993.

Morrow, Rising Lake. "The Negotiation of the Anglo-American Treaty of 1870." *The American Historical Review* 39 (July 1934): 663–81.

Moskos, Charles C., Jr. "The Military." *Annual Review of Sociology* 2 (1976): 55–77.

Mulkern, John R. *The Know-Nothing Party in Massachusetts: The Rise and Fall of a People's Party*. Boston, MA: Northeastern University Press, 1990.

Mullen, Thomas J. "The Irish Brigades in the Union Army, 1861–1865." *The Irish Sword: The Journal of the Military History Society of Ireland* 9 (Summer 1969): 50–58.

Murdock, Eugene C. "New York's Civil War Bounty Brokers." *The Journal of American History* 53 (September 1966): 259–78.

———. *One Million Men: The Civil War Draft in the North*. Madison: State Historical Society of Wisconsin, 1971.

Murphy, Monsignor Eugene. *The First One Hundred Years, 1831–1931: The Parish of St. John the Baptist*. Philadelphia: Church Printing and Envelope Co., 1932.

Murray, Thomas Hamilton. *History of the Ninth Regiment, Connecticut Volunteer Infantry, "The Irish Regiment," in the War of the Rebellion, 1861–1865. The Record of a Gallant Command on the March, in Battle, and in Bivouac*. New Haven, CT: Price, Lee & Adkins, 1903.

Neely, Mark E., Jr. *The Union Divided: Party Conflict in the Civil War North*. Cambridge, MA: Harvard University Press, 2002.

De Nie, Michael. " 'A Medley Mob of Irish-American Plotters and Irish Dupes': The British Press and Transatlantic Fenianism." *The Journal of British Studies* 40 (April 2001): 213–40.

Oates, Stephen B. *With Malice toward None: The Life of Abraham Lincoln*. New York: New American Library, 1977.

Ó Broin, León. *Fenian Fever: An Anglo-American Dilemma*. New York: New York University Press, 1971.

———. *Revolutionary Underground: The Story of the Irish Republican Brotherhood, 1858–1924*. Totowa, NJ: Rowman and Littlefield, 1976.

O'Connor, Thomas H. *The Boston Irish: A Political History*. Boston: Northeastern University Press, 1995.

———. *Civil War Boston: Home Front and Battlefield*. Boston: Northeastern University Press, 1997.

———. *Fitzpatrick's Boston, 1846–1866: John Bernard Fitzpatrick, Third Bishop of Boston*. Boston: Northeastern University Press, 1984.

O'Flaherty, Very Reverend Patrick Daniel. "The History of the Sixty-Ninth Regiment of the New York State Militia, 1852–1861." Ph.D. diss., Fordham University, 1963.

———. "James Huston, a Forgotten Irish-American Patriot." *The Irish Sword: The Journal of the Military Society of Ireland* 11 (1973): 39–47.

Ó Gráda, Cormac. *Black '47 and Beyond: The Great Irish Famine in History, Economy, and Memory*. Princeton, NJ: Princeton University Press, 1999.

O'Leary, Cecilia Elizabeth. *To Die For: The Paradox of American Patriotism*. Princeton, NJ: Princeton University Press, 1999.

Olson, James S. *Catholic Immigrants in America*. Chicago: Nelson Hall, 1987.

———. *The Ethnic Dimension in American History*. New York: St. Martin's Press, 1979.

O'Reilly, Francis Augustin. *The Fredericksburg Campaign: Winter War on the Rappahannock*. Baton Rouge: Louisiana State University Press, 2002.

Osofsky, Gilbert. "Abolitionists, Irish Immigrants, and the Dilemmas of Romantic Nationalism." *The American Historical Review* 80 (October 1975): 889–912.

Palladino, Grace. *Another Civil War: Labor, Capital, and the State in the Anthracite Regions of Pennsylvania, 1840–1880*. Champaign: University of Illinois Press, 1990.

Peterson, Robert L., and John A. Hudson. "Foreign Recruitment for Union Forces." *Civil War History* 7 (1961): 176–89.

Pohanka, Brian C. *James McKay Rorty: An Appreciation*. New York: Irish Brigade Association, 1993.

Priest, John Michael. *Antietam: The Soldiers' Battle*. New York: Oxford University Press, 1989.

Prendergast, Thomas F. *Forgotten Pioneers: Irish Leaders in Early California*. San Francisco: Trade Press Room, 1942.

Prucha, Francis Paul, ed. *Army Life on the Western Frontier: Selections from the Official Reports Made between 1826 and 1845 by Colonel George Croghan*. Norman: University of Oklahoma Press, 1958.

Rable, George C. *Fredericksburg! Fredericksburg!* Chapel Hill: University of North Carolina Press, 2002.

Rafferty, Oliver. "Fenianism in North America in the 1860s: The Problems for Church and State." *History* 84 (1999): 257–77.

Reid, Whitelaw. *Ohio in the War: Her Statesmen, Her Generals, and Soldiers*. 2 vols. New York: Moore, Wilstach & Baldwin, 1868.

Roediger, David R. *The Wages of Whiteness: Race and the Making of the American Working Class*, rev. ed. London: Verso, 1999.

Rose, Anne C. *Victorian America and the Civil War*. New York: Cambridge University Press, 1992.

Ruffner, Kevin Conley. *Corcoran's Irish Legion in Fairfax County: 1863–1864*. Fairfax: Historical Society of Fairfax County, Virginia, 1997.

Sandburg, Carl. *Abraham Lincoln: The War Years*. 4 vols. New York: Harcourt Brace, 1939.

Seagrave, Pia Seija, ed. *The History of the Irish Brigade: A Collection of Historical Essays*. Fredericksburg, VA: Sergeant Kirkland's Museum and Historical Society, 1997.

Sears, Stephen W. *George B. McClellan: The Young Napoleon*. New York: Ticknor & Fields, 1998.

———. *Landscape Turned Red: The Battle of Antietam*. New Haven, CT: Ticknor & Fields,

1983. Reprint, New York: Book-of-the-Month Club, 1994.

Silbey, Joel H. *The American Political Nation, 1838–1893.* Standord CA: Stanford University Press, 1991.

———. *The Partisan Imperative: The Dynamics of American Politics before the Civil War.* New York: Oxford University Press, 1985.

———. *A Respectable Minority: The Democratic Party in the Civil War Era, 1860–1868.* New York: Norton, 1977.

Silbey, Joel H., Allan G. Bogue, and William H. Flanigan, eds. *The History of American Electoral Behavior.* Princeton NJ: Princeton University Press, 1978.

Smith, Daniel Scott. "The Social Demography of Union Military Service by Whites during the Civil War: The Roles of Nativity and Region." Paper presented as part of the symposium "Social Demography and the American Civil War" at the annual meeting of the American Historical Association, Chicago, 7 January 2000.

Smith, Harold F. "Mulligan and the Irish Brigade." *Journal of the Illinois State Historical Society* 56 (1963): 164–76.

Stackpole, Edward J. *The Fredericksburg Campaign: Drama on the Rappahannock.* 2nd ed. Mechanicsburg, PA: Stackpole Books, 1991.

Stampp, Kenneth M. *America in 1857: A Nation on the Brink.* New York: Oxford University Press, 1990.

Terrell, W. H. H. *Indiana in the War of the Rebellion.* Indianapolis IN: Douglass & Conner, 1869.

Thernstrom, Stephan. *The Other Bostonians: Poverty and Progress in the American Metropolis, 1880–1970.* Cambridge, MA: Harvard University Press, 1973.

———. *Poverty and Progress: Social Mobility in a Nineteenth-Century City.* Cambridge, MA: Harvard University Press, 1964.

Vinyard, JoEllen McNergney. *The Irish on the Urban Frontier: Nineteenth-Century Detroit.* New York: Arno Press, 1976.

Walsh, Francis Robert. "The Boston *Pilot*: A Newspaper for the Irish Immigrant, 1829–1908." Ph.D. diss., Boston University, 1968.

———. "The Boston *Pilot* Reports the Civil War." *Historical Journal of Massachusetts* 9 (January 1981): 5–17.

Walzer, Michael, Edward T. Kantowicz, John Higham, and Mona Harrington, eds. *The Politics of Ethnicity.* London: Belknap Press of Harvard University Press, 1982.

Weigley, Russell F. *Philadelphia: A 300-Year History.* New York: Norton, 1982.

Weitz, Mark A. "Drill, Training, and the Combat Performance of the Civil War Soldier: Dispelling the Myth of the Poor Soldier, Great Fighter." *The Journal of Military History* 62 (April 1998): 263–89.

Whisterer, Frederick. *New York in the War of the Rebellion, 1861–1865.* 5 vols. Albany, NY: D. B. Lyon Co., 1912.

Wiebe, Robert J. *The Search for Order, 1877–1920.* New York: Hill and Wang, 1967.

Wilkinson, Warren. *Mother May You Never See the Sights I Have Seen: The Fifty-Seventh Massachusetts Veteran Volunteers in the Last Year of the Civil War.* New York: HarperCollins, 1990.

Willauer, G. J. "An Irish Friend and the American Civil War: Some Letters of Frederic W. Pim to His Father in Dublin, 1864." *The Journal of the Friends' Historical Society* 53 (1972): 62–75.

Williams, T. Harry. *Lincoln and His Generals.* New York: Vintage Books, 1952.

Wilson, David A. *United Irishmen, United States: Immigrant Radicals in the Early Republic.* Ithaca, NY: Cornell University Press, 1998.

Winther, Oscar Osburn. "The Soldier Vote in the Election of 1864." *New York History: Quarterly Journal of the New York State Historical Society* 25 (1944): 440–58.

Wittke, Carl. "The Ninth Ohio Volunteers." *Ohio Archeological and Historical Quarterly* 35 (April 1926): 402–17.

Woodham-Smith, Cecil. *The Great Hunger: Ireland, 1845–1849.* New York: Old Town Books, 1969.

Woodworth, Stephen. *While God Is Marching On: The Religious World of Civil War Soldiers.* Lawrence: University Press of Kansas, 2003.

Young, Warren L. *Minorities and the Military: A Cross-National Study in World Perspective.* Westport, CT: Greenwood Press, 1982.

Index

I Corps (Army of Northern Virginia), 127–128
I Corps (Army of the Potomac, Union Army), 113, 161
II Corps (Army of the Potomac, Union Army), 113, 163, 168
II Corps (Army of the Potomac, Union Army), 1st Division, 117
II Corps (Army of the Potomac, Union Army), 1st Division, 1st Brigade, 165
II Corps (Army of the Potomac, Union Army), 1st Division, 4th Brigade, 165
II Corps (Army of the Potomac, Union Army), 2nd Division, 2nd Brigade, 167
III Corps (Army of the Potomac, Union Army), 163
V Corps (Army of the Potomac, Union Army), 163
V Corps (Army of the Potomac, Union Army), 1st Division, 3rd Brigade, 120, 162
XII Corps (Army of the Potomac, Union Army), 113
1st New York Battery, 170
1st New York Light Artillery, Battery B, 166, 169
1st Rhode Island Light Artillery, Battery B, 168
1st U.S. Infantry, 37
2nd Mississippi Battalion, 119
2nd Philadelphia Regiment of State Militia, 72–73, 277n98
2nd Wisconsin Volunteer Infantry Regiment, 76
3rd Irish Volunteer Infantry Regiment, 79, 83
3rd Massachusetts Cavalry, 205
4th New Hampshire Volunteer Infantry Regiment, 176–177
4th U.S. Artillery, Battery A, 168–169
5th Maine Battery, 156
5th Massachusetts Volunteer Infantry Regiment, 65

5th New York Volunteer Infantry Regiment, 68
7th Michigan Volunteer Infantry Regiment, 171
7th New York Heavy Artillery, 210–211
8th Alabama Volunteer Infantry Regiment, 239
8th Massachusetts Volunteer Infantry Regiment, 204
9th Connecticut Volunteer Infantry Regiment, 80
9th Massachusetts Volunteer Infantry Regiment: 13th Massachusetts, 69; Andrew and, 99; Cass and, 97–98, 100, 109; celebration of the mass, 99; celebrations of, 98, 232; chaplain, 99; commander, 96, 97; departure from Boston, 100; discipline, 99–100; ethnicity of members, 109; existence of, 98; fighting within, 95; Gaines's Mill, 102; Guiney (Patrick R.) and, 94, 96; Hanover Court House, 109; MacNamara and, 69; Malvern Hill, 102; money for, 97–98; morale, 97–98; officers, 145; pride in, 69; Sully and, 99
9th New York Volunteer Infantry Regiment, 134, 142
9th Regiment, New York State Militia, 46
11th New York Volunteer Infantry Regiment, 180
12th Massachusetts Volunteer Infantry Regiment, 97
12th New York Volunteer Infantry Regiment, 120
13th Massachusetts Volunteer Militia, 69, 71
14th Massachusetts Volunteer Infantry Regiment, 98, 99–100
14th Michigan Volunteer Infantry Regiment, Company A, 213

14th Michigan Volunteer Infantry Regiment, Company B, 103
15th Illinois Volunteer Infantry Regiment (Mulligan's Chasseurs), 212
16th Michigan Volunteer Infantry Regiment, 162
16th Ohio Volunteer Infantry Regiment, 107, 151
19th Massachusetts Volunteer Infantry Regiment, 171
20th Maine Volunteer Infantry Regiment, 160, 277n87
20th Massachusetts Volunteer Infantry Regiment, 171
21st Pennsylvania Volunteer Infantry Regiment, Company A, 74
23rd Illinois Volunteer Infantry Regiment ("Irish Brigade of the West"): Camp Douglas, 103; Casey and, 214; Chicago, 72; commander, 103, 212; Lexington, 90–91; Maryland fighting, 103; McClellan and, 91; Mulligan (James A.) and, 72, 91, 103; reorganization, 91; surgeon, 90; western Virginia fighting, 103; Yates and, 90
24th Georgia Volunteer Infantry Regiment, 131
24th Missouri Volunteer Infantry Regiment, 213
24th Pennsylvania Volunteer Infantry Regiment, 72–73, 85, 277n98
28th Massachusetts Volunteer Infantry Regiment (Irish Brigade): 29th Massachusetts, 123; Burns (William) and, 146; Caney and, 146; casualties, 132; commander, 83; ethnicity of members, 102; existence of, 98; Fredericksburg, 128, 132; Irish Brigade, 210; Murphy 28th

28th Massachusetts Volunteer Infantry Regiment (*cont'd*): (Mathew) and, 83; problems with, 271n12; reassignment, 209; recruitment, 85, 144; Welsh and, 54, 185

28th New York Volunteer Infantry Regiment, 68

29th Massachusetts Volunteer Infantry Regiment (Irish Brigade), 102, 123, 144

30th U.S. Infantry Regiment, 242

35th Indiana Volunteer Infantry Regiment, 86

37th New York Infantry ("Irish Rifles"), 68, 270n83

42nd New York "Tammany Regiment," 169, 171

59th New York Volunteer Infantry Regiment, 170

63rd New York Volunteer Infantry Regiment (Irish Brigade): 3rd Irish, 83; Antietam, 118, 119; casualties, 105, 119, 132; Dwyer and, 129, *131*; Fredericksburg, 128, 129, 132; McDonald and, 172; O'Sullivan and, 256–257; size, 88, 90

65th Illinois Volunteer Infantry Regiment, 213

69th New York Volunteer Infantry Regiment (Irish Brigade): Antietam, 119; Arlington Heights, 67; casualties, 105, 119, 132; celebrations of, 232; chaplain, 149; Corcoran and, 110; departure from New York, 88, 90; desertions, 218; Donovan and, 129; Duffy (Felix) and, 118; Fair Oaks, 105; Fredericksburg, 128, 129, 132; Gettysburg, 172; Halpine and, 211; headquarters, 67; Kelly (James) and, 118; leader, 83; Meagher (Thomas Francis) and, 83–84; memorial verse about, 211; Nugent and, 83, 129, *133*, 180, 210; recruitment, 83; size, 87–88; Smith (James J.) and, 118; "What Irish Boys Can Do. Answer to: No Irish Need Apply," 212

69th Pennsylvania Volunteer Infantry Regiment (Philadelphia Brigade): 24th Pennsylvania, 73, 85, 277n98; 69th Regiment, NYSM, 73; Antietam, 113, 115, 116–117; Army of the Potomac, 167; Bradley and, 173; casualties, 113, 117, 172; celebrations of, 232; commander, 103, 116; desertion, 116; ethnicity of members, 85, 102–103, 113,

166; Flynn brothers and, 116; Fredericksburg, 124; Gettysburg, 166–173; Gillen brothers and, 116; Hooker on, 103; McConnell and, 116; McDermott and, 168; O'Kane and, 116; O'Reilly (James) and, 115; Owen and, 103, 116; *Pilot* on, 103; reenlistment, 194; White and, 124, 194

69th Regiment, New York State Militia, 62–68; 69th Pennsylvania, 73; abolitionism, 53; American flag, 62, 78; Bull Run, First Battle of, 69, 74, 75–80, 82–83, 84; casualties, 77–78; chaplain, 67, 78; commander, 50; Corcoran and, 62–63; departure from New York, 62–63, 64–65; dual loyalty, 63; enlistment terms, 68, 79; ethnicity of members, 44, 66; Fenians, 49, 58; Fort Corcoran, 67, 77; Fort Seward, 67; fund for families of the regiment, 63–64; Georgetown, 65, 66; green banner, 77; *Harper's Weekly* coverage, 46, 76–77; headquarters, 65; historian of, 82; *Irish-American* coverage, 78; Irish Zouave company, 58; Irish Zouaves, 66–67; *James Adger* (ship), 65; Lincoln's visit, 67; Louisiana Tigers, 85; Meagher (Thomas Francis) and, 83; Mooney and, 67; native-born Americans, 63–64, 66; *New York Herald* coverage, 78, 79; *New York Times* coverage, 63–64, 65–66, 78–79; offer to serve Union, 62; O'Reilly (Bernard) and, 78, 149; parade for, 62–63, 64, 263; Prince of Wales incident, 44–49; public support for, 63–64; quartermaster, 53; reception on return from the war, *44*; reenlistment, 79; reorganization, 83; Sherman and, 75, 77; size, 66; the South, 53; surgeon, 272n52; Tully and, 53, 60; U.S. Constitution, 53; visitors, 68; Washington, DC, 65; Wild Geese, 63

71st Pennsylvania Volunteer Infantry Regiment (Philadelphia Brigade): Antietam, 113, 115; ethnicity of members, 166; Gettysburg, 166, 170

72nd Pennsylvania Volunteer Infantry Regiment (Philadelphia Brigade): Antietam, 113, 115; ethnicity of members, 166; Gettysburg, 166, 171

76th Illinois Volunteer Infantry Regiment, 219

79th New York Volunteer Infantry Regiment, 76

88th New York Volunteer Infantry Regiment (Irish Brigade): Antietam, 117, 118, 119; Baker and, 83; Burke (Dennis) and, 1; casualties, 105, 119, 132; chaplain, 94, 101, 258; Clooney and, 118; Corby and, 94, 101; Fredericksburg, 128, 132; green banner, 118; Kelly (Patrick) and, 160; leader, 83; Nagle and, 133, 159; O'Grady (W. L. D.) and, 101; size, 88, 90; Turner and, 102, 106, 117

90th Illinois Volunteer Infantry Regiment ("Irish Legion"), 93, 111

98th Pennsylvania Volunteer Infantry Regiment, Company A, 74

106th Pennsylvania Volunteer Infantry Regiment (Philadelphia Brigade): Antietam, 113, 115; ethnicity of members, 166; Gettysburg, 166

116th Pennsylvania Volunteer Infantry Regiment (Irish Brigade): casualties, 132, 166; commander, 123, 160, 165, 260; consolidation of, 160; Fredericksburg, 124–125, 128, 129, 132; Gettysburg, 165, 166; Heenan and, 123; history of, 261; McCarter and, 124, *130*; Meagher's resignation, 159; Mulholland and, 260, 261; reassignment, 209; size, 160

140th New York Volunteer Infantry Regiment: fame, 277n87; Fredericksburg, 5; Gettysburg, 160–163; O'Rorke and, 160

170th New York Volunteer Infantry Regiment, 193

Abolitionism: 69th Regiment, NYSM, 53; anti-Catholic prejudice, 176; Boston, 25; dissolution of the Union, 52–53; Emancipation Proclamation, 136; evangelicalism, 268n72; Greenlees (Andrew) and, 138; Hughes (John) and, 25–26, 137; *Irish-American*, 137; Irish Americans, 24–28, 40, 42, 105, 121; Irish Catholics, 99, 138; Irish laborers, 42; Lincoln and, 136; New York City draft riots, 180; O'Connell and, 24–25, 26; *Pilot*, 25, 43, 52–53, 136–137; Republican Party, 42; U.S. Constitution, 43

Adams, Bertie, 172
Advertiser (Lowell newspaper), 80
African Americans: call for raising African-American regiments, 139; competition with Irish Americans, 4, 43, 188; Emancipation Proclamation, 4; Fredericksburg, 127; free blacks in Boston, 31; Irish Americans, 104, 138, 215; Irish miners in Pottsville, 26; Irish soldiers, 104; New York City draft riots, 180; riot against African American temperance reformers (1842), 28–29; strike breakers, 137–138
Alabama, C.S.S., 240, 242
Alamance, Battle of (1771), 8
Albany, New York: elections of Irishmen to prominent political positions, 255–256, 283n61; Famine Irish, 30; Irish population, 13t, 234t
Alexander, E. Porter, 128
Alien and Sedition Acts (1798), 20
Allen, Henry, 17
American Commonwealth (Bryce), 248
American Irish Historical Society, 257
American Protective Association, 257
Anderson, Siris, 150
Andersonville prison, 221
Andrew, John A.: 9th Massachusetts, 99; 13th Massachusetts, 71; Caney and, 146; Cass and, 97; differences between native- and foreign-born servicemen, 98–99; election as governor, 140; Irish soldiers, 99; opposition to Irish regiments, 104
Anti-Catholic prejudice: abolitionism, 176; among Federal forces, 176; Beecher (Henry Ward) and, 11; Beecher (Lyman) and, 11–12; destruction of Southern Catholic churches, 176, 187, 222; the draft, 176–177; employment ads excluding Catholics, 204; Greenwich Village Riot (1824), 10; Irish Brigade, 177; Know Nothings, 19; labor markets, 204; nativism, 10; New England, 176; New York City draft riots, 181; persistence of, 100, 204; *Six Months in a Convent,* 11; transfer into ethnic units, 91; Union Army, 91, 176–177, 213–214, 218–219, 222; United States Army, 34–35, 36
Anti-Irish Catholic prejudice: anti-Irish prejudice, 10; Boston,

10–12; Irish Americans' view of the war, 13; Midwest, 214–215; nativism, 12–13; New York City, 12; Northeast, 215–216; Philadelphia, 10, 12–13; Pottsville, Pennsylvania, 177; United States Army, 246
Anti-Irish prejudice: anti-Irish Catholic prejudice, 10; Boston, 8, 69, 98, 249; Cincinnati, 248; the draft, 176–177; the East, 5, 71; famine immigrants, 249; *Harper's Weekly,* 46, 249, 250, 251, 252, 261; Illinois, 70; Jersey City, 249; Massachusetts, 98; the Midwest, 5, 71; native-born Americans, 80–81, 191; in native units, 91; New England, 109; New York City, 188; New York City draft riots, 181; *New York Herald,* 249; *New York Times,* 79, 249; "No Irish Need Apply," 250, 268n82; persistence of, 100, 204; in *Puck,* 250, 252–254, 261; transfer into ethnic units, 91; *Tribune,* 249; Union Army, 91, 213–214; United States Army, 38; the West, 5, 71; Wisconsin, 70–71
Anti-Lincoln sentiment: "Commonly Called Abe Doodle," 223–224; Irish Americans, 214; Millican's, 215; *Pilot,* 216; responsibility for his death, 231
Anti-Republican sentiment, 189, 214
Antietam, Battle of (1862), 113–120; I Corps (Army of the Potomac, Union Army), 113; II Corps (Army of the Potomac, Union Army), 113; XII Corps (Army of the Potomac, Union Army), 113; 63rd New York, 118, 119; 69th New York, 115; 69th Pennsylvania, 113, 115, 116–117; 71st Pennsylvania, 113, 115; 72nd Pennsylvania, 113, 115; 88th New York, 117, 118, 119; 106th Pennsylvania, 113, 115; Army of Northern Virginia, 113; Army of the Potomac, 113; casualties, 117, 119–120, 134; Corby and, 117; desertion, 116; Hooker and, 113; Irish Brigade, 82, 113, 117–118, 119, 156; Lee and, 113; Mansfield and, 113; map of, *114;* McClellan and, 113, 115; Meagher (Thomas Francis) and, 117, 118, 119, 129; O'Grady (William) and, 1; O'Kane and, 116–117; opening, 113; Pelham and, 113;

Sedgwick and, 113, 115, 116, 117; Sumner (Edwin V.) and, 113, 115, 116, 117; support for the war, 120–121, 134, 275n19; Turner on, 117–118
Antislavery activists, 19
Antiwar sentiment, 178, 214
Armistead, Lewis B., 171
Army, Confederate. *See* Confederate Army
Army, Union. *See* Union Army
Army, United States. *See* United States Army
Army and Navy Journal, 245
Army of Northern Virginia, 113, 127–128, 231
Army of the Potomac: I Corps, 113, 161; II Corps, 113, 163, 168; II Corps, 1st Division, 1st Brigade, 165; II Corps, 1st Division, 4th Brigade, 165; II Corps, 2nd Division, 2nd Brigade, 113; XII Corps, 113; 69th Pennsylvania, 167; Antietam, 113; Burnside and, 73, 149; chief engineer, 160; commander, 73, 94, 113, 155, 161; Fredericksburg, 123; Halleck on, 141; Hooker and, 155; McClellan and, 94; Meade and, 161; Seven Days' Battles, 102; unrest within, 121; Warren and, 160
Atlanta, siege of, 225
Atlantic Monthly (magazine), 243, 248

Baked Meats of the Funeral (Halpine), 59
Baker, Henry, 83
Balfe, John, 86
Ballentine, George, 35–36
Banks, Nathaniel, 90
Barlow, Francis C., 218
Barnes, Joshua H., 123, 274n109
Barry, John, 261
Beauregard, P. G. T., 51, 73, 75
Bedini, Gaetano, 267n40
Beecher, Henry Ward, 11
Beecher, Lyman, 11–12
Bell, John, 9
Bennett, James Gordon, 43
Birney, Charles H., 190
Blaine, James, 254
Boston: abolitionism, 25; anti-Irish Catholic prejudice, 10–12; anti-Irish prejudice, 8, 69, 98, 249; Boston Brahmins, 98–99; Charlestown Naval Yard, 101; Fenians, 49; first Irish Catholic mayor, 249; free blacks, 31; Irish American political power, 257; Irish political influence, 249–250; Irish population, 5,

Boston (cont'd): 7, 13t, 234t; Irish
volunteers, 3; Know Nothings,
41, 269n108; Lincoln adminis-
tration, 140; Meagher (Thomas
Francis) in, 84; money raised
in, 97; nativism, 16; nonman-
ual jobs, 31; recruitment for
69th New York, 83; Ulster
Irish, 8; violence in Irish
Catholic areas, 12
Boston Recorder (newspaper), 11
Bowen, James, 62
Boyne, Battle of (1690), 10, 178
Bradley, Hugh, 171, 173
Brayman, Mason, 222
Brennan, Charles James, 190
Brennan, Michael, 201
Breslin, John, 75
Brigade Royal Irlandois (Royal
Irish Brigade). See Irish Brigade
of France
Brooke, John R., 165
Brooklyn, New York, 13t, 234t
Broughaw, John, 74
Brown, T. Fred, 168
Brownson, Orestes, 29–30
Bryce, James, 248
Buchanan, James, 21
Buckley, John, 168, 170
Buckner, Simon Bolivar, 35
Buffalo, New York, 13t, 30, 234t
Bull Run, First Battle of (1861),
75–80; 69th Regiment, NYSM,
74, 75–80, 82–83, 84, 85;
Beauregard and, 73; casualties,
77–78; Conyngham and,
82–83; Corcoran and, 76–77,
78, 191; Johnston and, 73;
Louisiana Tigers, 85; Meagher
(Thomas Francis) and, 77, 78,
89, 129; Patterson (Robert)
and, 73; Rorty and, 70; Sher-
man and, 77; unpreparedness
of Union Army, 74
Bull Run, Second Battle of (1862),
82
Burke, Denis .F, 258
Burke, Dennis, 1
Burke, Joseph W., 72
Burns, Anthony, 40
Burns, William, 146
Burnside, Ambrose E.: Army of the
Potomac, 73, 149; Conyngham
on, 132; effigy of, 150; Freder-
icksburg, 122–123, 132;
McClellan and, 122; Patterson
(Robert) and, 73
Butler, Benjamin, 90
Butternuts, 144
Byrnes, Richard, 209, 210
Byron, John W., 209

Caldwell, John C., 119, 163
Callahan, Susan, 190

Caney, Edward, 146
Carl, "Little Jeff," 165
Carrell, George, 14
Carter, Robert, 215
Casey, Peter, 214
Cass, Thomas: 9th Massachusetts,
97–98, 100, 109; Andrew and,
97; permission to organize a
regiment, 68–69; photograph,
97
Catholic Alumni Sodality of
Philadelphia, 260
Catholic Church in America:
authority with the U.S.,
267n40; destruction of South-
ern Catholic churches, 176,
187, 222; Grand Army of the
Republic, 234–235; humanitar-
ianism, 27; nativism, 267n40;
power of, 23; socialism, 27. See
also Anti-Catholic prejudice
Catholic Citizen (newspaper), 260
Catholic Diary (Boston newspaper), 25
Catholic Mirror (Baltimore newspaper), 28
Catholic Telegraph and Advocate
(Cincinnati diocesan newspa-
per), 16, 27, 28
Catholicism: Irish Americans, 5;
Irish Catholics, 9; retention of,
18–19; Sherman and, 35; slavery, 19, 29, 41
Caulwell, Robert, 247–248
Cavanagh, Michael: on Friendly
Sons of St. Patrick, 73–74; Irish
banner incident, 274n109;
Meagher (Thomas Francis)
and, 65; Memoirs of Gen.
Thomas Francis Meagher, 83
Chamberlain, Joshua Lawrence,
160, 277n87
Chancellorsville, Battle of (1863),
156, 158–159
Charleston, Ohio, 247–248
Chicago: 23rd Illinois, 72; Democ-
ratic Party, 23; Irish Catholics,
14, 22–23; Irish population,
13t, 234t; Know Nothings, 15,
23; nativism, 15; postwar con-
dition of Irish Americans, 247
Chicago Evening Post (newspaper),
247
"Chicago Platform" (Nast), 228,
229
Chicago Times (newspaper), 138
Christian Spectator (newspaper),
11
Cincinnati, 13t, 234t, 248
Cincinnati Daily Enquirer (news-
paper), 87
Citizenship, 147, 225, 245
City politics, 250
Clan na Gael, 244

Clontarf, Minnesota, 261–262
Clooney, Patrick Felan, 101, 118
Cobb's Brigade, 131
Cold Harbor, Battle of (1864):
Byrnes and, 210; Irish Brigade,
207, 209, 219
Collins, Patrick, 254–255
Columbian Artillery, 40, 41, 69
"Commonly Called Abe Doodle"
(Reese), 223–224
Condon, Patrick, 239
Confederate Army: commerce
raiders, 240–241; Confederate
POWs at Camp Douglas, 103;
Corcoran capture, 78; Freder-
icksburg troops, 130–132; Irish
Americans in, 76, 130–132,
237, 239; sympathy for Irish
Brigade, 131; veterans, 251
Connolly, Edmond L. T., 89
Conroy, Thomas, 200–201
Conscription. See Draft, the
Conscription Act (Enrollment Act)
(1863), 173–174, 210
Constitution: 69th Regiment,
NYSM, 53; abolitionism, 43;
the draft, 142; Irish Americans,
43; Rorty and, 70
Conyngham, David P.: First Bull
Run, 82–83; Fredericksburg,
132; Irish banner incident,
274n109; The Irish Brigade
and Its Campaigns, 257–258;
Malvern Hill, 102; Meagher's
(Thomas Francis) recruitment
efforts, 112; photograph, 48
Cooney, Peter Paul, 86
Copperheads, 150, 215–216
Corby, William: 88th New York,
94, 101; absolution administered at Gettysburg, 163–165,
172, 260–261; Antietam, 117;
campaigning in Virginia,
94–95; as chaplain, 94; Fredericksburg, 5, 132; Gettysburg,
163–165, 172, 260–261; Irish
banner incident, 274n109;
memoirs, 258–260; photo-
graph, 95; statue of, 260–261
Corcoran, Michael, 44–50; 69th
New York, 110; 69th Regi-
ment, NYSM, 62–63, 66;
ancestry, 49; Bull Run, First
Battle of, 76–77, 78, 191; capture by Confederates, 78;
cheers for, 84; court martial,
62; C.S.S. Enchantress,
191–192; Daly (Charles
Patrick) and, 68; Daly (Maria
Lydig) and, 88–89; death, 191,
192; Democratic Party, 49;
dual loyalty, 45, 49, 59; Emancipation Proclamation, 139;
engraving of, 192; ethnic

units/regiments, 74; Fenians, 49, 58–59, 192–193; Fields and, 45; *Illustrated News* story about, 148; Irish Americans, 191–192; Irish Legion, 192, 207, 217; "Irish Legion," 111; Irish nationalism, 45, 49; Irish Republican Brotherhood, 44; on Irishmen serving in the U.S. Army, 60; linkage of Irish and American independence, 111; marriage, 49–50; Meagher (Thomas Francis) and, 47, 89, 112, 191; Murphy (James) and, 199; Nebinger and, 111–112; New York City draft riots, 180, 192; *New York Herald* on, 110; O'Meara and, 93, 94; as "political general," 90; Prince of Wales incident, 44–45, 47, 48–49, 62, 191; recruitment efforts, 110–111; release in prisoner exchange, 110; reported book offer, 110; Revenue Police, 49; Ribbonmen, 49; Sherman and, 75; Stanton and, 110

Cowan, Andrew, 170
"Crimping crews," 207
Croghan, George, 33
Cross, Edward, 165
Cummins, Edward, 205–207
Curtis, George William, 30
Cushing, Alonzo H., 168–169
Cutler, Enos, 32

Daily Advertiser (Boston newspaper), 16
Daily Tribune (newspaper), 110
Daly, Charles Patrick: 69th Regiment, NYSM, 68; Cass and, 68; on departure of the 69th New York, 88; Emancipation Proclamation, 139; fundraiser for impoverished in Ireland, 155; impatience for war, 68; Meagher (Thomas Francis) and, 89; wife, 62; Working Women's Protective Union, 188
Daly, Maria Lydig: Corcoran and, 88–89; effect of First Bull Run, 78; flag for 69th Regiment, NYSM, 62; Lincoln and, 139; Meagher (Thomas Francis) and, 88–89, 191, 194; political attitudes in New York City, 225
Dana, N. J. T., 115
Davenport, Charles, 248–249
Davis, Jefferson, 191–192, 215
Democratic Party: *American Commonwealth,* 248; Butternuts, 144; care of Irish poor, 228; Chicago, 23, 72; congressional

elections (1862), 140; continuance of the war, 226; Copperheads, 150, 215–216; Corcoran and, 49; criticism of reformers, 228; Doheny and, 21; Emancipation Proclamation, 140; Fenians, 241; individual rights, 228; infighting, 225–226; Irish-American volunteering, 110; Irish Americans, 188–189, 228–229, 230, 231–232, 233, 250, 283n61; Irish Catholics, 42, 281n95; Irish support for, 20–21; Ku Klux Klan, 251; local control, 228; Mulligan (James A.) and, 72; New York City, 188, 228; New York Democrats, 188; *New York Herald,* 219; newspapers allied with, 230; northern Democrats, 226; outreach to immigrants, 20–21; Peace Democrats, 140, 155, 216, 225–226; power of, 189; presidential election (1864), 225–232; secession, 251; slavery, 21, 251; Tammany Hall, 250; War Democrats, 140, 225–226
Democratic-Republicans, 20
Democratic Union Association of New York, 140
Detroit, 13t, 234t
Detroit Daily Tribune (newspaper), 86
Detroit Free Press (newspaper), 103
Devillin, Daniel, 216
Devoy, John, 244
Dix, John A., 203, 219
Dixon, James, 22
Doheny, Michael: American politics, 21; Democratic Party, 21; on departure of 69th Regiment, NYSM, 65; dissolution of the Union, 50; Fenians, 21, 38; Irish American political participation, 21; Irish nationalism, 50; O'Brien (William Smith) and, 21; Republican Party, 21; volunteers preparing to liberate Ireland, 38–39
Donahoe, Patrick, 144
Donnelly, Thomas, 171
Donovan, John H., 129
Dougherty, Daniel, 53
Douglas, Stephen A., 42–43
Downing, P. J., 169
Draft, the, 173–189; aliens, 147–148; anti-Catholic prejudice, 176–177; anti-Irish prejudice, 176–177; bounty system, 142, 146–147, 173; British subjects, 174; constitutionality, 142; debates over, 173;

dichotomy between Irish leaders and laboring classes, 144; draft riots, 143–144 (*see also* New York City draft riots); encouragement of emigration to United States, 174; England (John) on, 173; evasion, 108, 143; exemption clause, 4, 173–174, 175–176, 180–181, 183–184, 186; factory closings, 175; Greenlees (Andrew) and, 185–186; Hewitt and, 186–187; "How to Escape the Draft," *179;* Hughes (John) and, 144, 175; implementation, 142–143; Irish American response, 177–178; Irish Americans, 147; New York City director of the draft, 180; New York City draft riots (*see* New York City draft riots); Nugent and, 180, 185; Pennsylvania, 143; *Pilot,* 147–148; Pottsville miners, 227; provisions, 142, 144; quotas, 142, 188; requests for exemption prior to emigrating from Ireland, 187; Seymour and, 178; by states, 108, 148; substitutes, 4, 175; suspension of the writ of habeas corpus, 144; temporary halt in New York City, 188; waiting for, 110; Wisconsin, 143
Druyts, John Baptist, 17
Dual loyalty: 69th Regiment, NYSM, 63; change in war's aims, 60; Corcoran and, 45, 49, 59; decision to serve the Union, 70; encouragement of military service, 54; ethnic units/regiments, 59–60; first loyalties of Irish Americans during the war, 263; Irish Americans, 4, 52, 199–200; Irish miners in Pottsville, 26; Irish soldiers, 3–4, 6, 80–81, 237; Irish volunteers, 3; linkage of Irish and American independence, 1, 52, 54–55, 58, 60, 104, 111; MacNamara and, 69–70; Meagher (Thomas Francis) and, 51, 59; native-born Americans, 80–81; postwar period, 264; Prince of Wales incident, 47; Rorty and, 70; support for the war, 134–135; symbols of, 264; Union Army, 5; Welsh and, 54–55
Duffy, Charles Gavan, 56
Duffy, Felix, 118
Duffy, James, 172
Dunne, Dennis, 93–94

Dunny, Patrick, 21–22, 85
Dwyer, John, 129, *131*

Early, Jubal, 115
East, the: anti-Irish Catholic prejudice, 215–216; anti-Irish prejudice, 5, 71; Know Nothings, 18; Northeast, 18, 215–216; tolerance for Irish immigrants, 15
Eastman, Edwin G., 187, 201, 237
Egan, John, 202–203
"Election Day" (Nast), 229
Elgin, James Bruce, 8th Earl of, 39
Emancipation Proclamation (1862/1863), 136–141; abolitionism, 136; African Americans, 4; announcement, 4; call for raising African-American regiments, 139; congressional elections (1862), 140; Corcoran and, 139; Daly (Charles Patrick) and, 139; Democratic Party, 140; effective date, 136; Gibbons' home, 175; Irish-American support for the war, 113, 120, 134; Irish Americans, 4, 121, 147, 187; Irish Catholics, 139; Irish soldiers, 150; labor markets, 187; Lincoln and, 4, 121, 134, 136; McClellan and, 138–139; New York City, 137; New York City draft riots, 178; O'Gorman and, 141; Ohio, 137–138; *Pilot*, 136; Protestant Irish Americans, 138; provisions, 136; radical wing of the Republican Party, 121; Union Army, 139; war's aims, 136; working poor, 173
Emmet Guards, 277n98
Enchantress, C.S.S., 191–192
England, John: 9th New York, 134, 142; the draft, 173; Fredericksburg, 150; New York City draft riots, 180–181; removal of McClellan from command, 142
Enlistment in Union Army: citizenship, 147, 245; enlistment bonuses, 206–207; enlistment terms, 68, 74, 79; Irish Americans, 147; rate of, 147–148. *See also* Reenlistment in Union Army
Enrollment Act (Conscription Act) (1863), 173–174, 210
Ethnic pride, 3
Ethnic units/regiments: Corcoran and, 74; difficulties filling ranks, 271n12; dual loyalty, 59–60; Irish Americans, 101; Irish regiments, 1–2, 3, 4, 104;

Irish soldiers, 1–2, 59, 213; native-born Americans, 70, 72, 100, 101; Union Army, 72; United States Army, 38, 70
Evening Journal (Philadelphia newspaper), 104

Fair Oaks, Battle of (1862), 101–102, 102, 105
Farley, Porter, 161
Farmington, Battle of, 103
Farragut, David, 225
Farrell, R. T., 212–213, 213
Federalists, 20
Feeney (Boston recruiter), 205
Fenians, 236–244; 29th Massachusetts, 123, 274n109; 69th Regiment, NYSM, 49, 58; *Alabama* claims, 240, 242; arrests by British, 237–238; attacks on British North American possessions, 238–239, 243; Boston, 49; Cleburne Circle, 239; Corcoran and, 49, 58–59, 192–193; Daniel O'Connell Circle, 239; Democratic Party, 241; Doheny and, 21, 38; Irish Americans, 242, 244; Irish casualties, 200; Irish Republican Brotherhood, 38, 44, 236; Irish volunteers, 3; Johnson and, 241–242; leadership, 193; military experience as training ground for war against England, 54, 55, 80, 105, 148, 190; military service to, 2; Mitchel and, 239; name, 236, 265n5, 269n10; native-born Americans, 239–240, 243; New York City, 49; New York State, 241; *New York Times*, 240, 243; newspaper of, 200; O'Donovan Rossa Circle, 244; Philadelphia, 49; postwar actions for Ireland, 193; recruitment by, 239; Rorty and, 70; the South, 239; split among, 200; *Tribune*, 239–240; uncommitted members, 244; Union Army, 236; United States Army, 243; United States government, 241–242; West and, 236–237
Fields, W. B., 45
Fighting Irish. *See* 69th Regiment, New York State Militia
Fisher, Sidney G., 43
Fitzgerald, J. J., 195
Fitzgibbon, Thomas C., 103, 213
Fitzpatrick, John, 100
Flynn, John, 116
Flynn, Michael, 116
Foley, Patrick, 241
Fontenoy, Battle of (1745), 1, 63

Foster, Eden B., 40
Fowler, Francis, 221
Frank Leslie's Illustrated, 44
Fredericksburg, Battle of (1862), 122–134; I Corps (Army of Northern Virginia), 127–128; 28th Massachusetts, 128, 132; 63rd New York, 128, 129, 132; 69th New York, 128, 129, 132; 69th Pennsylvania, 124; 88th New York, 128, 132; 116th Pennsylvania, 124–125, 128, 129, 132; 140th New York, 5; African Americans, 127; Alexander and, 128; Army of the Potomac, 123; Burnside and, 132; casualties, 120, 132–134, 150; Cobb's Brigade, 131; Confederate troops, 130–132; Conyngham on, 132; Corby and, 5, 132; Donovan and, 129; Dwyer and, 129; embalmers, 123–124; England (John) and, 150; Hancock and, 128; Irish Brigade, 5, 82, 123, 132–133, 156; looting, 124; map of, *126*; Marley and, 128; McCarter and, 124–125, 127, 129, *130*; Meagher (Thomas Francis) and, 123–125, 128–129; Mulholland and, 124–125, 128, 129–130; Nowlen and, 129; Nugent and, 129, 132; O'Grady (William) at, 1; O'Rorke and, 5; support for the war, 134, 275n19; White and, 124; winter weather, 149
Free Soilers, 19, 20, 29
Freeman's Journal and Catholic Register (New York newspaper), 34, 177, 230–231
Fremont, John C., 21
French, William H., 115, 117
Friendly Sons of St. Patrick (New York City), 73–74, 190
Friendly Sons of St. Patrick (Philadelphia), 73–74, 75, 261
Fugitive Slave Act (1854), 40
Furey, Thomas, 172

Gaines's Mill, Battle of (1862), 101, 102
Gallagher, James E., 95
Gallagher, Martin "Jersey," 166
Gallowglass, 273n94
Garfield, James A., 253
Garibaldi, Giuseppe, 101
Garnett, Richard B., 171
Garrison, William Lloyd, 24, 26
Gettysburg, Battle of (1863), 160–173; I Corps (Army of the Potomac, Union Army), 161; II Corps (Army of the Potomac,

Union Army), 163, 168; II Corps (Army of the Potomac, Union Army), 1st Division, 1st Brigade, 165; II Corps (Army of the Potomac, Union Army), 1st Division, 4th Brigade, 165; III Corps (Army of the Potomac, Union Army), 163; V Corps (Army of the Potomac, Union Army), 163; V Corps (Army of the Potomac, Union Army), 1st Division, 3rd Brigade, 162; 1st New York Light Artillery, Battery B, 166, 169; 1st Rhode Island Light Artillery, Battery B, 168; 4th U.S. Artillery, Battery A, 168–169; 7th Michigan, 171; 16th Michigan, 162; 19th Massachusetts, 171; 20th Maine, 160, 277n87; 20th Massachusetts, 171; 42nd New York, 169, 171; 69th New York, 172; 69th Pennsylvania, 166–173; 71st Pennsylvania, 166, 170; 72nd Pennsylvania, 166, 171; 106th Pennsylvania, 166; 116th Pennsylvania, 165, 166; 140th New York, 160–163; Armistead and, 171; Bradley and, 171, 173; Brooke and, 165; Brown and, 168; Buckley and, 168, 170; Caldwell and, 163; Carl and, 165; casualties, 178; Cemetery Ridge, 166–173; Chamberlain and, 160, 277n87; Corby and, 260; Corby's absolution, 163–165, 172, 260–261; Cowan and, 170; Cross and, 165; Cushing and, 168–169; Donnelly and, 171; Downing and, 169; Duffy (James) and, 172; Furey and, 172; Gallagher (Martin "Jersey") and, 166; Garnett and, 171; Georgia Brigade, 168; Hancock and, 163, 165, 251; Irish Brigade, 5, 160–173; Kelly (Patrick) and, 160, 163, 165, 207, 209; Little Round Top, 160, 162–163, 172; Malin and, 165; Mallon and, 169; map, 164; McDermott and, 168, 170, 171; Meade and, 161–162; Mulholland and, 165–166, 172; O'Kane and, 166, 168, 170, 171, 172; O'Rorke and, 160–163, 172; Pettigrew and, 169, 171; Pickett's charge, 169–170; Reynolds (John) and, 161; Rorty and, 166, 169; Ryan (John) and, 166; Smith

(William A.) and, 166; Thompson (George) and, 171; Trimble and, 169; Tschudy and, 171, 172; Union victory, 160; Vincent and, 162; Warren and, 162; Webb and, 166, 171; Weed (Stephen H.) and, 162; wheat field, 163–166, 172; White and, 169, 171; Wright and, 168; Zook and, 165
Gettysburg National Military Park, 259
Gibbons, Abby Hopper, 137
Gibbons, James Sloane, 137, 175
Gillen, Cornelius, 116
Gillen, Daniel, 116
Glendale, Battle of (1862), 103
"Glorious Victory of Seven Irishmen over the Kidnappers of New York" (ballad), 207
Grand Army of the Republic (GAR), 234–235, 281n2
Grant, Ulysses S.: Cold Harbor, 219; elimination of prejudice against Catholic soldiers, 36; Irish American soldiers, 251; "A 'Liberal' Surrender: Any Thing to Beat Grant," 251, 252; mandatory religious services, 35; Riley (Bennet) and, 36–37; Union Army of the Tennessee, 151; Vicksburg, 151
Great Famine (1845–1855), 7
Great Migration (1717–1775), 7, 9
Greeley, Horace, 181, 251
Greenlees, Andrew: abolitionism, 138; the draft, 185–186; indebtedness, 107–108; removal of McClellan from command, 122
Greenlees, Lucy, 107–108
Greenwich Village Riot (1824), 10
Guiney, Patrick R., 95–96, 96
Guiney, Robert, 94
Gunther, G. Godfrey, 188

Haggerty, James, 68, 76, 78
Haines, John G., 93–94
Hale, John P., 30
Halleck, Henry W.: leaves of absence, 153, 154; Lincoln and, 155; McClellan and, 141; Mulligan (James A.) and, 92; political generals, 154; Stanton and, 153–154
Halpin, William G., 87
Halpine, Charles G., 59, 211
Hamilton, Joseph, 130–131
Hammond, Henry B., 198
Hancock, Winfield Scott: Fredericksburg, 128; Gettysburg, 163, 165, 251; "How Hancock Will (Not) Get the Soldier Vote," 253; Meagher (Thomas

Francis) and, 155, 156; presidential election (1880), 251–254
Hanover Court House, Battle of, 109
Harlin, Hugh, 108
Harn (a Captain), 150
Harper's Weekly (magazine): anti-Irish prejudice, 46, 249, 250, 251, 252, 261; "The Chicago Platform," 228, 229; coverage of 69th Regiment, NYSM, 76–77; coverage of the 69th Regiment, 46; "Election Day," 229, 229; "How Hancock Will (Not) Get the Soldier Vote," 253; "How to Escape the Draft," 179; Irish political power, 21; "Is This 'The True American Policy?'", 256; "A 'Liberal' Surrender: Any Thing to Beat Grant," 251, 252; political influence of Irish Americans, 254; presidential election (1864), 229; presidential election (1872), 251; Republican Party, 253; San Patricios (St. Patrick's Battalion), 46
Heaney, Elizabeth, 50
Heap, G. H., 238
Heenan, Dennis, 72, 123
Heintzelman, Samuel P., 76
Henry, James, 23
Hewitt, Joseph, 186–187
Hibernia Greens, 72, 277n98
Hibernian Guard, 71
Hill, D. H., 117
Homestead Act (1862), 273n74
Homestead strike (1892), 236
Hooker, Joseph E.: I Corps (Army of the Potomac, Union Army), 113; on 69th Pennsylvania, 103; Antietam, 113; Army of the Potomac, 155; Irish Brigade, 155
"How Hancock Will (Not) Get the Soldier Vote" (cartoon), 253
"How to Escape the Draft" (cartoon), 179
Howard, Oliver Otis, 35, 113, 115
Hueston, Francis, 29
Hughes, Angela, 14
Hughes, John: abolitionism, 25–26, 137; absolution flags of units going to war, 66; the draft, 144, 175; fundraiser for impoverished in Ireland, 155; Irish Catholics, 25; Lincoln administration, 67; Mooney and, 67; New York City draft riots, 181, 184; sister, 14
Hunter, David, 59, 76

Illustrated London News (newspaper), 197, *197*
Illustrated News (New York newspaper), 148
Inquirer (Philadelphia newspaper), 53
Iowa City, Iowa, 17
Ireland: arrest of Fenians, 237–238; "crimping crews," 207; early 1860s, 197–198; Famine, 15–17, 30, 37, 57; fundraiser for impoverished in Ireland, 155; Irish Catholics in, 49; Revenue Police, 49; Ribbonmen, 49; Union Army recruiting in, 202; volunteers preparing to liberate it, 38–39
Irish-American (New York newspaper): abolitionism, 137; coverage of 69th Regiment, NYSM, 78; discrimination against Irish soldiers, 153, 158; effect of war reports on readers, 108; Irish-American loyal military service, 249; Irish Brigade morale, 209; Irish contributions to the war, 148; in Irish volunteers, 60; on Irishmen serving in U.S. Army, 50; Lincoln administration, 140, 181; Lincoln's assassination, 232; McDonald on Gettysburg, 172; Meagher's recruiting speech, 107; New York City draft riots, 181; Orange Riots, 249; preparation for war, 53; soldiers' support for Meagher, 133–134; temperance movement, 28
Irish Americans: abolitionism, 24–28, 40, 42, 105, 121; African Americans, 104, 138, 215; American-Irish Catholic identity, 245; American political doctrines, 27; anti-Lincoln sentiment, 214; anti-Republican sentiment, 214; antiwar sentiment, 214; autonomy in relation to the rest of the population, 233–234; Bible reading in public schools, 23; Bryce on, 248; Catholicism, 5; cities with largest population of, 5; citizenship, 225; city politics, 250; competition with African Americans, 4, 43, 188; in Confederate Army, 76, 130–132, 237, 239; conservative nature, 228; Corcoran and, 191–192; definition of, 5; Democratic Party, 188–189, 228–229, 230, 231–232, 233, 250, 283n61; dichotomy between Irish leaders and laboring classes, 144; the draft, 147; draft evasion,

143; dual loyalty, 41, 52, 199–200; efforts to insert themselves into American memory, 257–262; Emancipation Proclamation, 4, 121, 147, 187; enlistment, 147; ethnic neighborhoods, 48; ethnic units/regiments, 101; Fenians, 242, 244; first loyalties, 263; focus on America, 244–245; Free Soilers, 29; illegal voting, 22; image among native-born Americans, 80–81, 100, 189; influx of other Catholic immigrants, 263; ingratitude, 46–47; Irish-American Catholic identity, 261–262; labor markets, 30; labor skills, 30–31; leaders in the North, 50, 52, 53; Lincoln administration, 90, 135, 136, 139–140, 147, 221, 233; Lincoln and, 121, 156–160; Lincoln's assassination, 232; linkage of Irish and American independence, 52, 104; local unity, 233; loyalty of, 216, 232; loyalty to United States, 62; Meagher (Thomas Francis) and, 129, 156–160; nativism, 40, 184–185; patriotism, 147; in political cartoons, 250; political influence, 254; political participation, 19–24; political unity and activism, 254–257; population, 13t, 234t; population increase, 233, 245, 250; postwar condition of, 246–248, 263–264; preservation of cultural heritage, 47–48; presidential election (1860), 50; presidential election (1864), 221–222, 225–232; presidential election (1872), 251; presidential election (1884), 254; proslavery movement, 40; public funds for parochial schools, 23; radical wing of the Republican Party, 24, 110, 121; Republican Party, 105, 158, 189; reputation, 232; response to secession crisis, 51–53; response to the draft, 177–178; secession, 147; self-confidence, 93; self-interests, 13; sense of ethnic and community unity, 264; shadow of disloyalty, 232; share of manpower in Union Army, 103–104; shift away from radical nationalist movements, 244; slavery, 40; socioeconomic condition, 31; stereotypes of, 184–185, 260; support for the Union, 51, 73; support for the

war (*see* Support for the war); temperance movement, 28; U.S. Constitution, 43; United States Army, 33, 36–38; volunteers preparing to liberate Ireland, 38–40; as voting block, 263; Young Ireland, 58
Irish Brigade: anti-Catholic prejudice, 177; Antietam, 82, 113, 117–118, 119, 156; Bull Run, Second Battle of, 82; casualties, 101, 102, 105–106, 112, 119–120, 132–134, 156, 207–209; Chancellorsville, 156, 158–159; Cold Harbor, 207, 209, 219; commander, *133*, 209, *210*, 211; Confederate sympathy for, 131; consolidation of, 209; despair in the ranks, 209; discipline and order, 94; experience at officer level, 101; Fair Oaks, 101–102, 102; Fredericksburg, 5, 82, 123, 132–133, 156; Gaines's Mill, 101; Gettysburg, 5, 160–173; Grand Requiem Mass, 150; Hanover Court House, 109; historical renown, 88; Hooker and, 155; Irish Catholic immigrants, 195; Kernstown, 212; leadership, 209; leave for, 191; leaves of absence, 153–155, 158; life in, 106–107; looting by, 124; Malvern Hill, 82, 101, 156; mass for its dead, 149; McClellan and, 121; McClellan on, 119; Meagher (Thomas Francis) and, 123; members, *95;* morale, 150, 209; new/replenishment/economically-motivated troops, 209, 217–218; New York regiments, 160, 209, 210, 258, *259;* Nugent and, 210–211; Peninsula Campaign, 101, 112; Petersburg, 207–209; press coverage, 119; promotions within, 155; Reams' Station, 209, 218; reception for returning veterans, 195; reconstitution, 210; reenlistment, 194–195; regimental colors, 123; regiments in, 83, 123, 153, 210 (*see also* 28th Massachusetts Volunteer Infantry Regiment; 29th Massachusetts Volunteer Infantry Regiment; 63rd New York Volunteer Infantry Regiment; 69th New York Volunteer Infantry Regiment; 88th New York Volunteer Infantry Regiment; 116th Pennsylvania Volunteer Infantry Regiment); reputation,

101, 119; retention of Irish character, 209; Seven Days' Battles, 102; Spotsylvania Courthouse, 207, 217–218; studies of, 2; surgeon, 101; training, 94; Wilderness, 207
Irish Brigade and Its Campaigns (Conyngham), 257–258
Irish Brigade Association, 236
Irish Brigade of France (*Brigade Royal Irlandois*): Fontenoy, 1; formation of, 265n7; Irish traditions, 63; memories of, 69; O'Grady (William) at, 1
Irish Brigade of St. Patrick of the Papal States, 101
"Irish Brigade of the West." *See* 23rd Illinois Volunteer Infantry Regiment
Irish casualties: 28th Massachusetts, 132; 63rd New York, 105, 119, 132; 69th New York, 105, 119, 132; 69th Pennsylvania, 113, 117, 172; 69th Regiment, NYSM, 77–78; 88th New York, 105, 119, 132; 116th Pennsylvania, 132, 166; Antietam, 117, 119–120, 134; Bull Run, First Battle, 77–78; Chancellorsville, 156; Fenians, 77–78; Fredericksburg, 120, 132–134, 150; Irish Brigade, 101, 102, 105–106, 112, 119–120, 132–134, 156, 207–209; support for the war, 108–109, 120–121, 134, 190; Wilderness to Petersburg, 207–209
Irish Catholics: abolitionism, 99, 138; California, 22; Catholicism of, 9; Chicago, 14, 22–23; conservatism, 29; Democratic Party, 42, 281n95; Emancipation Proclamation, 139; focus on America, 244–245; Fugitive Slave Act, 40; Hughes (John) and, 25; in Ireland, 49; Irish Catholic identity, 266n11; Irish immigration, 9, 10; Lincoln, 231; Meagher (Thomas Francis) and, 191; native-born Americans, 229; presidential election (1860), 42–43; presidential election (1864), 231; proslavery movement, 19; Protestant Americans, 28, 29–30, 41; reputation, 251; St. Louis, Missouri, 13–14, 17; San Francisco, 14, 23–24; slavery, 19, 29, 40; tolerance for, 22; Ulster Irish, 8–9, 17–18; Union Army, 5; United States Army, 245–246. *See also* Anti-Irish Catholic prejudice

Irish Citizen (newspaper), 249
Irish immigration, 7–10; 1820s, 10; 1860s, 197–198, 199–200; cities, 30; economic desperation, 199–200; encouragement of emigration to America, 174, 198–199, 203–204; Famine Irish, 15–17, 30, 37, 249; free trip to America in exchange for military service, 198–199; Great Migration (1717–1775), 7, 9; Irish Catholics, 9, 10; motivations, 7–8; Napoleonic Wars (1796–1815), 9; promises of employment, 224; recruitment, 1; requests for exemption from the draft prior to emigrating from Ireland, 187; tricking Irishmen into military service, 196–197, 203, 207, 224–225; Ulster Irish, 7–9; War of 1812, 9
Irish Legion: celebrations of, 232; Corcoran and, 192, 207; motivations of enlistees, 217; regiments in, 207
"Irish Legion." *See* 90th Illinois Volunteer Infantry Regiment
Irish men, 268n82
Irish militias: 2nd Philadelphia Regiment of State Militia, 72–73, 277n98; 9th Regiment, New York State Militia, 46; 13th Massachusetts Volunteer Militia, 69, 71; 69th Regiment, New York State Militia (*see* 69th Regiment, New York State Militia); disbanding by nativists, 46, 69; expenses incurred by militiamen, 45; native-born Americans, 69; Philadelphia, 72, 74
Irish nationalism: Clan na Gael, 244; Corcoran and, 45, 49; Doheny and, 50; heroes of, 14; Irish Americans' shift away from radical nationalist movements, 244; Meagher (Thomas Francis) and, 55, 56–58; native-born Americans, 239; nativism, 244; Young Ireland, 56
Irish News (newspaper), 58
Irish People (newspaper), 200
Irish Protestants. *See* Protestant Irish Americans; Ulster Irish
Irish regiments. *See* Ethnic units/regiments
Irish Repeal Movement, 24, 26, 57
Irish Republican Brotherhood: Corcoran and, 44; Fenians, 38, 44, 236; fighting in America a crime, 200
"Irish Rifles." *See* 37th New York Infantry

Irish soldiers: African Americans, 104; America as an asylum for future Irish refugees, 60; Andrew and, 99; appreciation of their services/sacrifices, 104, 145–146, 260–261; benefits of volunteering, 145–146, 201–202; Boston Brahmins, 98–99; bounty jumping, 147; bounty system, 146–147; camp life, 107; casualties (*see* Irish casualties); Conyngham on, 258; crediting their sacrifices to native-borns, 109; "crimping crews," 207; demonstration of loyalty to United States, 134; desertion, 116, 218; discrimination against, 153, 158; dual loyalty, 3–4, 6, 80–81, 237; economic necessity, 2, 54, 60–61, 134; Emancipation Proclamation, 150; enlistment bonuses, 206–207; ethnic units/regiments, 1–2, 59, 213; failure to acknowledge their heroism/sacrifices, 67, 109, 149; fighting prowess, 38, 74, 77, 96, 109, 120, 258, 260; goals, 4; Grant and, 251; gratitude and loyalty to America, 2, 41, 60, 112; "How Hancock Will (Not) Get the Soldier Vote," 253; illiteracy rates, 4; illness, 222; image of Irish Americans among native-born, 80–81; Irish American officers, 245; Irish rebellion, 237; Lincoln and, 155; linkage of Irish and American independence, 1, 54–55, 60; loyalty of, 47, 53, 74; Meagher (Thomas Francis) and, 133–134, 274n133; memories of historic glory, 69; military experience as training ground for war against England, 54, 55, 80, 105, 112, 134, 148, 190; money promised to families, 146; motivations for joining Confederate Army, 76, 81, 218; motivations for joining Union Army, 2–3, 4, 53–62, 65, 69–70, 76, 105, 106, 112, 134; new/replenishment/economically-motivated troops, 209, 217–218; non-resident next-of-kin, 201–202; nonethnic units/regiments, 1, 213; number in Union Army, 2, 157–158, 229, 232, 245, 251; obligation to enlist in the Union Army, 144; preservation of the Union as an asylum for future Irish refugees, 2, 41,

Irish soldiers (*cont'd*): 112; recency of immigration, 3, 54; reenlistment, 70, 79, 194–195; respect from fellow citizens, 59; Scott and, 53; source materials about, 4–5; tricking into military service, 146, 174, 196–197, 203, 224–225; veterans' families, 237; veterans' organizations, 234, 236; violation of a dead one, 218–219

Irish women, 31, 268n82

Irish World (newspaper), 249, 250

Irish Zouaves, 58, 66–67

Irishmen, definition of, 5

Irvine, Abraham, 219–221, *220*

Irvine, Joseph, 219

"Is This 'The True American Policy?'" (cartoon), *256*

Jackson, Andrew, 20

Jackson, Claiborne Fox, 67

Jackson, Thomas J., 113

Jackson Rifles, 74

James II, King of England and Ireland, 10, 178, 265n7

Jay's Treaty (1795), 20

Jefferson, Thomas, 20

Jeffersonian (New York newspaper), 230

Jersey City, New Jersey, 234t, 249

Job market. *See* Labor markets

Johnson, Andrew, 241–242

Johnston, Joseph E., 73, 75

Jones, Alfred G., 182

Jones, Robert, 32

Jones (a First Lieutenant), 150

"Just the Difference" (cartoon), *254*

Kansas-Nebraska Act (1854), 40, 267n45

Kearsarge, U.S.S., 201

Kelly, James, 118

Kelly, John, 253

Kelly, P. D., 79

Kelly, Patrick: 88th New York, 160; death, 207–209; Gettysburg, 160, 163, 165, 207, 209; Lincoln and, 155; Petersburg, 209

Keppler, Joseph, 253

Kernstown, Battle of (1864), 212

Kidder (Boston recruiter), 205

Know Nothings: Americanization, 18; anti-Catholic prejudice, 19; antislavery activists, 19; Boston, 41, 269n108; Chicago, 15, 23; ethnic neighborhoods, 48; ethnicity of members, 18; extension of slavery, 267n45; Free Soilers, 19; immigration, 18; Irish political power, 21;

Kansas-Nebraska Act, 267n45; Massachusetts, 18, 41, 269n108; murders of Irishmen, 22; nativism, 19; New England, 18; Northeast, 18; Order of the Star-Spangled Banner, 18; purposes, 18, 267n40; Republican Party, 19; San Francisco, 23; Yates and, 92

Ku Klux Klan, 251

Labor markets: anti-Catholic prejudice, 204; availability of work, 33; competition between Irish and African Americans, 4, 43, 188; dismissal for voting against Lincoln, 232; domestic servants, 188, 268n82; Emancipation Proclamation, 187; firings for participating in New York City draft riots, 184; Grand Army of the Republic (GAR) strike breakers, 236; Irish Americans, 30; Irish women, 31, 268n82; New York City, 204, 247; poor Irish laborers, 42; replacement of immigrant workers with native-born Americans, 101; unskilled laborers, 33, 247

Labor unions, 268n82

Ladies Aid Society (Dubuque, Iowa), 214–215

Lalor, Patrick Edwin, 240

Lalor, William, 240, 243

Lamoriciere, Christophe-Louis-Leon Juchault de, 46

Larosua, Peter, 146

Lee, Robert E.: Antietam, 113; Army of Northern Virginia, 113, 231; Cold Harbor, 219; on involvement with Episcopal Church, 35; surrender, 231

Lefferts, S. E., 70–71

Lexington, Battle of, 90–91

"A 'Liberal' Surrender: Any Thing to Beat Grant" (cartoon), 251, 252

Life and Adventures of Private Miles O'Reilly (Halpine), 59

Limerick, Treaty of (1691), 265n7

Lincoln, Abraham: 23rd Illinois, 91; abolitionism, 136; annual address (1863), 224–225; anti-Lincoln sentiment (*see* Anti-Lincoln sentiment); assassination, 231–232; call for volunteers, 62; controversial decisions, 120; Daly (Maria Lydig) and, 139; Democratic newspapers, 230; on Douglas, 43; Emancipation Proclamation, 4, 121, 134, 136; Halleck and, 155; impatience for

action, 74; Irish Americans, 121, 156–160; Irish Catholics, 231; Irish Protestants, 219; Irish soldiers, 155; Kelly (Patrick) and, 155; McClellan and, 121, 141; Meagher (Thomas Francis) and, 154, 155, 156; Millican on, 215; Mulligan (James A.) and, 72; New York City draft riots, 230; Nugent and, 155; "political generals," 90, 154; presidential election (1860), 42; Seymour and, 156; tricking Irishmen into military service, 224–225; visit to 69th Regiment, NYSM, 67; working people, 230

Lincoln administration: Boston, 140; civil liberties, 110, 144; controversial decisions, 122; encouragement of emigration, 203–204; failure to acknowledge heroism/sacrifices of Irish soldiers, 67; failure to restore the Union, 226; hopes for reenlistments, 68; Hughes (John) and, 67; illegal recruitment methods, 203; *Irish-American*, 140, 181; Irish Americans, 90, 135, 136, 139–140, 147, 221, 233; Massachusetts, 140; McClellan and, 221; "Negrophilism," 137; New York City draft riots, 178; New York Democrats, 188; *Pilot*, 140, 144–145, 174, 221; radical journals' support for, 183; removal of McClellan from command, 122, 187; reorganization of 69th Regiment, NYSM, 83; slavery policies, 135; suspension of the writ of habeas corpus, 144; War Democrats, 140

LNRA (Loyal National Repeal Association), 26

Lochrane Guards, 130

London Times (newspaper), 229

Longstreet, James, 127

Loomis, Gustavus, 35

Lord, Henry W., 203

Louisiana Tigers, 85

Louisiana Zouaves, 76

Lovejoy, Elijah, 15

Lowell, Massachusetts, 13t, 234t

Loyal National Repeal Association (LNRA), 26

Lytle, William Haines, 72

MacNamara, M. H., 69–70

Maguire, George, 14

Mahan, John W., 95

Mahoney, Dennis, 86–87

Malin, Francis, 165

Mallon, James E., 169
Malvern Hill, Battle of (1862): 9th
    Massachusetts, 102; Conyng-
    ham on, 102; Donovan and,
    129; Irish Brigade, 82, 101,
    156
Manassas Junction, 75
Mansfield, J. K. F., 113
Marley, John C., 128
Massachusetts: 69th New York, 83;
    anti-Irish prejudice, 98; Boston
    (see Boston); Know Nothings,
    18, 41, 269n108; Lincoln
    administration, 140; Milford,
    235; Ursuline Convent
    (Charlestown), 11–12, 182
Massachusetts General Hospital
    (Boston), 235, 255
Massie, James William, 103–104
McAdams, Peter, 74
McBride, James, 213
McCafferty, John, 237
McCafferty, Paddy, 185
McCarter, William: 116th Pennsyl-
    vania, 124, 130; Fredericks-
    burg, 124–125, 127, 129, 130;
    My Life in the Irish Brigade,
    130; photograph, 130
McClellan, George B.: 23rd Illinois,
    91; as an Irishman in charge,
    85; Antietam, 113, 115; Army
    of the Potomac, 94; Burnside
    and, 122; Emancipation Procla-
    mation, 138–139; fundraiser
    for impoverished in Ireland,
    155; Halleck and, 141; Irish
    Brigade, 121; on Irish Brigade,
    120; Lincoln administration,
    221; Lincoln and, 121, 141;
    Meagher (Thomas Francis)
    and, 121; Peace Democrats,
    226; Peninsula Campaign, 101;
    Pilot, 221–222; presidential
    election (1864), 221, 225–228,
    229–231; removal from com-
    mand, 120, 121–122, 134,
    141, 187, 221–222; Strother
    and, 120; "the slows," 121;
    War Democrats, 226
McClure, Alexander, 244
McConnell, Patrick, 116
McCormick, Sarah, 190
McDermott, Anthony, 168, 170,
    171
McDonald, Miles, 172
McDowell, Irvin, 74–75, 76
McGee, Thomas D'Arcy, 56
McGrath, John, 239
McGuire, Robert, 130
McIvor, James P., 193, 193
McLaws, Lafayette, 115
McManus, Terence Bellew, 14, 84
McManus, Thomas, 204, 205
McMaster, James, 177

McMillan, Robert, 131–132
Meade, George: Army of the
    Potomac, 161; elimination of
    prejudice against Catholic sol-
    diers, 36; Gettysburg, 161–162;
    O'Rorke and, 161–162
Meagher, Thomas, Sr., 55
Meagher, Thomas Francis: 29th
    Massachusetts speech, 102;
    69th New York, 83–84; 69th
    Regiment, NYSM, 83; Anti-
    etam, 117, 118, 119, 129; in
    Boston, 84; Bull Run, First Bat-
    tle of, 77, 78, 89, 129;
    Cavanagh and, 65; cheers for,
    84; Conciliation Hall speech,
    56–57; Conyngham and, 48;
    Corcoran and, 47, 89, 112,
    191; courage, 272n24; cow-
    ardice, 129, 272n24; 274n134;
    criticisms of, 120; Daly (Charles
    Patrick) and, 89; Daly (Maria
    Lydig) and, 88–89, 191, 194;
    death report, 78; drunkenness,
    78, 89, 272n24; 276n74; dual
    loyalty, 51, 59; Duffy (Charles
    Gavan) and, 56; education,
    55–56; faith in, 191; Fredericks-
    burg, 123–125, 128–129;
    fundraiser for impoverished in
    Ireland, 155–156; Hancock
    and, 155, 156; incompetence,
    272n24; Irish Americans, 129,
    156–160; Irish Brigade, 123;
    Irish Catholics, 191; Irish loy-
    alty to Democratic Party, 230;
    Irish nationalism, 55, 56–58;
    Irish News, 58; Irish uprising
    (1848), 90; Irish Zouaves, 58,
    66; leave for the Irish Brigade,
    191; leave of absence request,
    155; leaves of absence for Irish
    Brigade, 153–155; Lincoln and,
    154, 155, 156; linkage of Irish
    and American independence,
    58; loyalty to the United States,
    51–52; marriage, 58; mass for
    Irish Brigade's dead, 149;
    McCarter and, 125; McClellan
    and, 121; McGee and, 56;
    "Meagher of the Sword," 57;
    memoirs, 65; military experi-
    ence as training ground for war
    against England, 55; Mitchel
    and, 56; Nagle and, 133–134;
    New York City draft riots, 180;
    nickname, 57; North Carolina
    campaigns, 276n74; O'Brien
    (William Smith) and, 56;
    O'Connell and, 55–56; O'Gor-
    man and, 56; oratorical skills,
    125; photograph, 157; as
    "political general," 90; profes-
    sions, 58; reception for return-

ing veterans, 195; recruitment
    efforts, 66, 83, 104–107, 108,
    110, 112, 151–154, 155–156;
    resignation of his commission,
    156, 158, 159, 160, 276n74;
    return to duty, 276n74; rights
    of Southern secessionists,
    50–51; Sherman and, 75–76;
    Sickles and, 110; soldiers' sup-
    port for, 133–134, 274n133;
    Stanton and, 153–154, 158;
    Treanor and, 84; Turner and,
    106, 107; unauthorized leave of
    absence, 154; Van Dieman's
    Land, 58, 84, 90; West and,
    198; "What Irish Boys Can Do.
    Answer to: No Irish Need
    Apply," 212; Young Ireland,
    56–57
Meagher Guards, 72, 277n98
Memoirs of Gen. Thomas Francis
    Meagher (Cavanagh), 83
Men, Irish, 268n82
Metropolitan Record (newspaper),
    216
Midwest, the: anti-Irish Catholic
    prejudice, 214–215; anti-Irish
    prejudice, 5, 71; draft riots,
    143; nativism, 71; tolerance for
    Irish immigrants, 15
Milford, Massachusetts, 235
Military draft. See Draft, the
Militia Act (1862), 142, 173
Millican, Elizabeth, 215
Milwaukee, Wisconsin, 13t, 234t
Milwaukee Daily News (newspa-
    per), 143
Mirror (Baltimore newspaper), 104
Mitchel, John: Fenians, 239; John-
    son and, 241; Meagher
    (Thomas Francis) and, 56; San
    Francisco, 14; southerners,
    239; treason charges, 241; Van
    Dieman's Land, 84; Young Ire-
    land, 56
Mitchell, Reid, 95
Mobile Bay, Battle of (1864), 225
Molly Maguires, 249
Mooney, Thomas, 67
Morgan, Edwin, 62
Morgan, John Hunt, 237
Moroney, Richard, 209
Morse, Samuel F. B., 10–11
Mount Pleasant, Iowa, 215
Mulholland, St. Clair A.: 116th
    Pennsylvania, 123, 160, 165,
    261; Confederate sympathy for
    Irish Brigade, 131; Fredericks-
    burg, 124–125, 128, 129–130;
    Gettysburg, 165–166, 172;
    losses suffered by Irish Brigade,
    209; remembrance of sacrifices
    made by Irish American sol-
    diers, 260–261

Mullaly, John, 216
Mulligan, James A.: 23rd Illinois,
72, 91, 103; Democratic Party,
72; Farrell and, 212; Halleck
and, 92; Lexington, 90–91;
Lincoln and, 72; Mulligan's
Chasseurs, 212; Mulligan's
Irish Brigade (see Mulligan's
Irish Brigade); photograph, 91;
POWs at Camp Douglas, 103;
prisoner of war, 91; transfers to
his command, 213–214; Wildes
and, 216
Mulligan, Mark, 199
Mulligan's Chasseurs (15th Illi-
nois), 212
Mulligan's Irish Brigade: celebra-
tions of, 232; commander, 91;
Fitzgerald and, 195; motiva-
tions of enlistees, 217; recruit-
ing poster, 196
Murphy, James, 199
Murphy, Mathew, 83, 218
Murphy, Michael C., 241–242
Murray, Michael, 201
My Life in the Irish Brigade
(McCarter), 130

Nagle, William J., 133–134, 159
Nast, Thomas, 229
National Union Guard, 87
Native Americanism, 92
Native-born Americans: 69th Regiment, NYSM, 63–64, 66; antebellum descriptions of the
Irish, 4; anti-Irish prejudice,
80–81, 191; differences
between native- and foreign-
born servicemen, 98–99; dual
loyalty of Irish soldiers, 80–81;
ethnic units/regiments, 70, 72,
100, 101; Fenians, 239–240,
243; illiteracy rates, 4; image
of Irish Americans, 80–81,
100; Irish American ingratitude, 46–47; Irish American
linkage of Irish and American
independence, 52, 60; Irish
Catholics, 229; Irish militias
to, 69; Irish nationalism, 239;
Irish regiments, 3, 4; Peace
Democrats, 216; power of
Irish politicians, 250; preservation of cultural heritage,
47–48; Prince of Wales incident, 64; replacement of immigrant workers, 101
Nativism: American Protective
Association, 257; anti-Catholic
prejudice, 10; anti-Irish
Catholic prejudice, 12–13;
Boston, 16; Catholic Church's
authority within the U.S.,
267n40; Chicago, 15;

Columbian Artillery, 41, 69;
courting Irish-American vote,
254; disbanding of Irish militias, 46, 69; early nineteenth
century, 10; elections of Irishmen to prominent political
positions, 283n61; ethnic
neighborhoods, 48; Famine
migrations, 15–19, 37; Greenwich Village Riot (1824), 10;
Irish American ingratitude, 47;
Irish-American poems and
songs, 212; Irish Americans,
40, 184–185; Irish nationalism,
244; Irish resistance to adopting American traditions, 48;
Know Nothings, 19; loyalty of
Catholics to America, 36; the
Midwest, 71; naturalization,
42; peak, 35; promotions of
Irish Catholics, 213; Republican Party, 42; Taylor and, 21;
temperance movement, 28;
United States Army, 33–34;
Ursuline Convent
(Charlestown, Massachusetts),
11–12; the West, 15
Naturalization, 24, 42, 147
Nebinger, Andrew, 111–112
New England: anti-Catholic prejudice, 176; anti-Irish prejudice,
109; Know Nothings, 18;
Ulster Irish, 8
New Jersey: Jersey City, 234t, 249;
Newark, 13t, 234t
New York Association for Improving the Condition of the Poor,
60
New York City: anti-Irish Catholic
prejudice, 12; anti-Irish prejudice, 188; Board of Supervisors, 228; Common Council,
188; Democratic Party, 228;
Democrats, 188; director of the
draft, 180; dismissal for voting
against Lincoln, 232; draft
riots (see New York City draft
riots); Emancipation Proclamation, 137; Exemption Committee, 188; Fenians, 49; fundraising for 69th New
York, 83; Greenwich Village
Riot (1824), 10; Hibernian
Hall, 49, 62; Irish American
political power, 257; Irish population, 5, 7, 13t, 234t; Irish
volunteers, 3; Irish women, 31;
labor markets, 204, 247;
Orange Riots (1870, 1871),
249; political attitudes in, 225;
political positions under Tammany Hall, 250; postwar condition of Irish Americans,
246–247; presidential election

(1864), 231; Sixth Ward, 231;
volunteering in, 68
New York City draft riots (1863),
178–185; abolitionists, 180;
African Americans, 180; anti-
Catholic prejudice, 181; anti-
Irish prejudice, 181; antiwar
sentiment, 178; Corcoran and,
180, 192; the draft, 178;
Emancipation Proclamation,
178; England (John) on,
180–181; exemption clause of
the draft, 18–181, 183–184;
firings for participating in, 184;
gains from, 187–188; Hughes
(John) and, 181, 184; Irish-
American, 181; Irish loyalty to
the Democratic Party,
188–189; Lincoln, 230; Lincoln administration, 178;
Meagher (Thomas Francis)
and, 180; memory of, 187;
New York Herald, 178; New
York Times, 183–184; Nugent
and, 180; Pilot, 182; removal
of police officials critical of
rioters, 194; Republicans, 180;
Seymour and, 194; stereotypes
of Irish Americans, 182–183,
184–185; Strong and,
182–183, 194; targets of rioters, 180; temporary halt to the
draft, 188; Tribune, 182; Volcano under the City, 236
New York Fire Zouaves, 78
New York Herald (newspaper):
anti-Catholic prejudice in
Union Army, 218–219; anti-
Irish prejudice, 249; Bennett
and, 43; on Corcoran, 110;
Corcoran's funeral, 191; coverage of 69th Regiment, NYSM,
67, 78, 79; Democratic Party,
219; Hanover Court House
coverage, 109; Irish Brigade at
Antietam, 119; New York City
draft riots, 178; violations of a
dead immigrant soldier,
218–219
New York Irish Republican Union,
39
New York Observer (newspaper),
11
New York State: Albany (see
Albany); Brooklyn, 13t, 234t;
Buffalo, 13t, 30, 234t;
Meagher (Thomas Francis)
and, 83; New York City (see
New York City); Rochester,
13t, 30, 234t
New York Tablet (newspaper), 176
New York Times (newspaper): anti-
Irish prejudice, 79, 249; Corco-
ran's funeral, 191; coverage of

69th Regiment, NYSM, 63–64, 65–66, 78–79; employment ads excluding Catholics, 204; Fenians, 240, 243; Irish Brigade at Antietam, 119; on Irish patriotism, 106; New York City draft riots, 183–184; Republican Party, 183, 240; tricking Irishmen into military service, 196–197

New York Workingmen's Democratic Republican Association, 230

Newark, New Jersey, 13t, 234t

Newman, Thomas W., 215

Nimiks, Samuel, 51

"No Irish Need Apply," 250, 268n82

Nowlen, Garrett, 129

Nugent, Robert: 69th New York, 83, 129, 133, 180, 210; Bull Run, First Battle of, 78; death report, 78; draft director, 180, 185; Fredericksburg, 129, 132; Irish Brigade, 133, 210–211; Lincoln and, 155; New York City draft riots, 180; photograph, 133, 211; recruitment efforts, 210; retention of Irish character of Irish Brigade, 209

Oberholtzer, Ellis Paxson, 16–17

O'Brien, Henry, 180, 185, 249

O'Brien, John Paul Jones, 34, 37

O'Brien, William Smith, 21, 43, 56

O'Connell, Daniel: abolitionism, 24–25, 26; Garrison and, 24, 26; Irish Repeal Movement, 24, 26; Loyal National Repeal Association, 26; Meagher (Thomas, Sr.) and, 55; Meagher (Thomas Francis) and, 55–56; politicization of Irish people, 20; Young Ireland, 55

O'Donnell, Rory, 265n7

O'Donohue, Patrick, 14

O'Gorman, Richard: 69th Regiment, NYSM, 68; Emancipation Proclamation, 141; fundraiser for impoverished in Ireland, 155; Meagher (Thomas Francis) and, 56; native-born Americans, 216; Peace Democrats, 216; prediction of war, 43; sins of America, 43; support for the war, 140–141; Young Ireland, 56

O'Grady, W. L. D., 101

O'Grady, William, 1–2

Ohio: anti-Irish prejudice, 248; Butternuts, 144; Charleston, 247–248; Cincinnati, 13t, 234t, 248; Emancipation Proclamation, 137–138

O'Kane, Dennis: 2nd Philadelphia,

72; 69th Pennsylvania, 116; Antietam, 116–117; death, 171; Gettysburg, 166, 168, 170, 171, 172; sketch of, 167

O'Mahoney, Henry, 61–62

O'Mahoney, John, 68, 200

O'Marsh, P., 93

O'Meara, Timothy, 93–94

O'Neill, B. S., 209

O'Neill, Hugh, 265n7

O'Neill, John, 221

Opdyke, George, 188

Orange Riots (1870, 1871), 249

Order of the Star-Spangled Banner, 18

O'Reilly, Bernard, 78, 89, 149

O'Reilly, James, 115

O'Reilly, Miles (fictional character), 59, 211

O'Rorke, Patrick "Paddy": 140th New York, 160; Farley on, 161; Fredericksburg, 5; Gettysburg, 160–163, 172; Meade and, 161–162; photograph, 161; Warren and, 160–161

O'Ryan, Charles D. B., 90, 92–93

Osborne, William H., 102

O'Slagerty, Michael, 143

O'Sullivan, Michael, 256–257

Owen, Joshua T., 103, 116, 167

Owens, Stephen, 261–262

Palmerston, Henry John Trimble, 3rd Viscount, 238

Parker, Joel, 231

Parker, Theodore, 16

"Parody of When This Cruel War is Over" (song), 211–212

Patterson, Francis E., 73, 271n97

Patterson, Robert, 73, 75

Patterson, Robert Emmet, 73

Peel, Robert, 196

Pelham, John, 113

Peninsula Campaign (1862), 101, 112

Pennsylvania: draft riot, 143; Meagher (Thomas Francis) and, 83; Philadelphia (see Philadelphia); Pittsburgh, 13t, 234t; Pottsville, 227, 235; Reading, 235; Schuylkill County, 227

Petersburg, Siege of (1864), 207–209, 208

Pettigrew, James J., 169, 171

Philadelphia: anti-Irish Catholic prejudice, 10, 12–13; attitude toward secession, 269n31; Fenians, 49; Irish American political power, 257; Irish militias, 72, 74; Irish population, 5, 7, 13t, 234t; Irish volunteers, 3; Kensington district, 12; postwar condition of Irish Ameri-

cans, 247; recruitment for 69th New York, 83; riot against African American temperance reformers (1842), 28–29; support for the Union, 73; volunteering in, 72

Philadelphia Brigade, regiments in. See 69th Pennsylvania Volunteer Infantry Regiment; 71st Pennsylvania Volunteer Infantry Regiment; 72nd Pennsylvania Volunteer Infantry Regiment; 106th Pennsylvania Volunteer Infantry Regiment

Philadelphia Times (newspaper), 244

Phillips Legion, 130

Pickett, George E., 169–170

Pierce, Franklin, 17

Pilot (Boston newspaper): on 69th Pennsylvania, 103; abolitionism, 25, 43, 52–53, 136–137; anti-Catholic prejudice in Union Army, 176, 218, 222; anti-Irish Catholic prejudice in Pottsville, 177; anti-Lincoln sentiment, 216; armistice, 140; benefits of volunteering, 145–146; Brayman's suspension of a bishop, 222; denial of underrepresentation of Irish Americans among volunteers, 104; on departure of 9th Massachusetts from Boston, 100; discrimination against Irish soldiers, 158; on disobeying American political doctrines, 27; the draft, 147–148; effect of war reports on readers, 108; Emancipation Proclamation, 136; Enrollment Act, 174; on Fair Oaks, 101–102; Great Famine charity relief, 16; immediate cessation of hostilities, 226–227; Irish contributions to the war, 159–160; Lincoln administration, 140, 174, 221; Lincoln's assassination, 232; loyalty of Irish soldiers, 36; New York City draft riots, 182; obligation to enlist in the Union Army, 144; popularity, 222; presidential election (1864), 227–228; recruiting advertisements, 144; removal of McClellan from command, 141, 221–222; Republican Party, 174; on Republicans, 42; on Rochester Democrat, 215; secession, 52–53; on Stanton, 159; support for the Union, 50, 105; on supporters of a runaway slave, 40; temperance movement, 28; treatment of

Pilot (cont'd): Irish veterans, 59, 100; tricking Irishmen into military service, 224; violations of dead immigrant soldier, 219

Pittsburgh, 13t, 234t

Plunkett, George Washington, 257

Political cartoons, 250

Porter, Andrew, 76

Porter, Fitz John, 139

Post (Chicago newspaper), 109

Pottsville, Pennsylvania, 227, 235

Pottsville Miners' Journal (newspaper), 177

Price, Sterling, 90

Prince of Wales incident, 44–49; 69th Regiment, NYSM, 44–49; Corcoran and, 44–45, 47, 48–49, 62, 191; dual loyalty, 47; native-born Americans, 64; Strong and, 44

Proclamation by the Lord Lieutenant of Ireland (1864), 206

Proslavery movement, 19, 40

Protestant Americans, Irish Catholics and, 28, 29–30, 41

Protestant Irish Americans: Emancipation Proclamation, 138; support for the war, 5, 186, 219

Public Ledger (Philadelphia newspaper), 249

Puck (magazine): anti-Irish prejudice in, 250, 252–254, 261; "Just the Difference," 254; political influence of Irish Americans, 254; "Ready for Business," 255; Republican Party, 252–253

Pullman strike (1894), 236

Purcell, John, 66

Reading, Pennsylvania, 235

"Ready for Business" (cartoon), 255

Reams' Station, Battle of, 209, 218

Recruitment for Union Army: 28th Massachusetts, 85, 144; 69th New York, 83; Boston, 83, 205; Corcoran and, 110–111; illegal methods, 203, 205; in Ireland, 202; Lincoln administration, 203; Meagher (Thomas Francis) and, 66, 83, 104–107, 108, 110, 112, 151–154, 155–156; Mulligan's Irish Brigade, 196; Nugent and, 210; O'Grady (William) and, 210; Pilot, 144; posters, 195, 196; Stanton and, 203; tricking Irishmen into military service, 146, 174, 196–197, 203, 207, 224–225

Redmond, Rowland, 139, 141

Reed, Rebecca, 11

Reenlistment in Union Army: 69th Pennsylvania, 194; 69th Regiment, NYSM, 79; Irish Brigade, 194–195; Lincoln administration hopes, 68; Rorty and, 70; White and, 194

Reese, William, 222–224

Regulators, 8

Reilly, Thomas, 39

Repealers. See Irish Repeal Movement

Republican Party: abolitionism, 42; anti-Republican sentiment, 189, 214; birth of, 20; change in war's aims, 139–140, 189; congressional elections (1862), 140; Doheny and, 21; Free Soilers, 20; Grand Army of the Republic, 236; Harper's Weekly, 253; Irish American ingratitude, 47; Irish Americans, 105, 158, 189; Know Nothings, 20; loyalty to, 189; nativism, 42; naturalization, 24; New York City draft riots, 180; New York Times, 183, 240; Pilot, 174; Pilot on, 42; presidential election (1860), 24; Puck, 252–253; radical wing, 24, 110, 121; removal of McClellan from command, 141; Whigs, 20

Reynolds, Francis, 101, 272n52

Reynolds, John, 161

Ribbonmen, 49

Richardson, Israel B., 117, 119

Riley, Bennet, 36–37

Riley, John, 36, 37, 38

Robinson, John, 236

Rochester, New York, 13t, 30, 234t

Rochester Democrat (newspaper), 215–216

Roney, Frank, 248

Rorty, James McKay: 1st New York Light Artillery, Battery B, 169; Bradley family, 173; Bull Run, First Battle of, 70; dual loyalty, 70; Fenians, 70; Gettysburg, 166, 169; reenlistment, 70; Sherman and, 77; U.S. Constitution, 70

Rose, George, 163

Royal Irish Brigade (Brigade Royal Irlandois). See Irish Brigade of France

Runyon, Theodore, 66

Russell, William Howard, 89

Ryan, Daniel, 202

Ryan, John, 166

St. George, Sister Edmund, 11

St. Louis, Missouri: Catholic Orphans' Association, 14; first foreign-born mayor, 14; Irish Catholics, 13–14, 17; Irish population, 13t, 234t; Irish Protestants, 13–14; public education, 23; support for Lincoln, 67

St. Louis University, 14, 17

San Francisco: education debate, 23; Irish Catholics, 14, 23–24; Irish population, 13t, 234t; Know Nothings, 23; postwar condition of Irish Americans, 248

San Patricios (St. Patrick's Battalion), 36–37, 46

Sarsfield, Patrick, 49, 265n7

Savage, John, 149

Schurz, Carl, 90, 251

Schuykill County, Pennsylvania, 227

Scots Irish, 5

Scott, Winfield: on loyalty of Irish soldiers, 53; Patterson (Robert) and, 75; time for war preparations, 68; unpreparedness prior to Battle of First Bull Run, 74

Scully, Thomas, 99

Secession: Democratic Party, 251; Irish American response, 51–53; Irish Americans, 147; Philadelphia attitude, 269n31; Pilot, 52–53; rights of Southern secessionists, 50–51; South Carolina, 50

Sedgwick, John: II Corps (Army of the Potomac, Union Army), 2nd Division, 2nd Brigade, 113; Antietam, 113, 115, 116, 117

Seven Days' Battles, 102

Seward, William, 174, 203–204

Sexton, Maurice, 60–61, 85

Seymour, Horatio: the draft, 178; Lincoln and, 156; loss of governorship, 231; New York City draft riots, 194

Sharpsburg, Maryland, 113. See also Antietam, Battle of

Shaughnessy, George, 18–19

Shaughnessy, Michael, 18–19

Shaughnessy, William, 18–19

Sheehan, James, 241

Shenandoah Valley campaign (1864–1865), 225

Sheridan, Philip, 225

Sherman, William Tecumseh: 69th Regiment, NYSM, 75, 77; Breslin and, 75; Bull Run, First Battle of, 77, 225; Catholicism of, 35; Corcoran and, 75; Meagher (Thomas Francis) and, 75–76; Rorty and, 77

Shields, James, 88, 111

Sickles, Daniel, 110, 163

Sigel, Franz, 90

Six Months in a Convent (Reed), 11

Slavery: Catholicism, 19, 29, 41; Democratic Party, 21, 251; Irish Americans, 40; Irish Catholics, 19, 29; Know Nothings, 267n45; proslavery movement, 19, 40

Sloan, William J., 219

Smith, E. Kirby, 34

Smith, James J., 118

Smith, Robert, 12–13, 28–29

Smith, T. H., 98

Smith, William A., 166

Smyth, Thomas A., 209

Snowhook, William, 93–94

South, the: 69th Regiment, NYSM, 53; destruction of Catholic churches in, 176, 187, 222; Fenians, 239; northern Irish-Americans, 239

Spahr, Mary Ann, 215

Spaulding, Henry F., 123

Spenser, John C., 32

Spooner, Thomas, 19

Spotsylvania Courthouse, Battle of (1864), 207, 217–218

Sproul, Andrew J., 80, 150–151

Sproul, Frances, 107, 151

Sproul, Matilda, 79, 107

St. Patrick's Battalion (San Patricios), 36–37, 46

Stanton, Edwin M.: Corcoran and, 110; Dix and, 203; Halleck and, 153–154; illegal recruitment methods, 203; Meagher (Thomas Francis) and, 153–154, 158; *Pilot* on, 159

Stephens, James, 242

Stewart, Charles, 53

Stowe, Harriet Beecher, 11

Strong, George Templeton: Lincoln's assassination, 232; New York City draft riots, 182–183, 194; presidential election (1864), 229–230; Prince of Wales incident, 44

Strother, David Hunter, 120

Sullivan, Pat, 61

Sumner, Charles, 240

Sumner, Edwin V.: II Corps (Army of the Potomac, Union Army), 113; Antietam, 113, 115, 116, 117; Fair Oaks, 101–102

Support for the war: Antietam, 120–121, 134, 275n19; casualties among Irish soldiers, 108–109, 120–121, 134, 190; change in war's aims, 60, 81, 110, 112–113, 121, 139–140, 190, 263; Corcoran's death, 192; crediting Irish sacrifices to native-borns, 109; destruction of Southern Catholic churches,

176, 187, 222; dual loyalty, 134–135; Emancipation Proclamation (1863), 13, 113, 120, 121, 134; failure to acknowledge heroism/sacrifices of Irish soldiers, 67, 109, 149; Fredericksburg, 134, 275n19; its effect on families, 13; its effect on Ireland, 13; Lincoln administration abuse of civil liberties, 110; money promised to families of soldiers, 146; O'Gorman and, 140–141; *Pilot*, 50, 105; Protestant Irish Americans, 5, 186, 219; removal of McClellan from command, 120; self-interests, 13; tricking into military service, 146

Swales, James, 87

Sweeny, Thomas, 241

Taylor, Zachary, 21, 34, 36

Temperance movement, 28–29

Thompson, George, 171

Thompson, John, 37–38, 51

Thompson, Skeffington, 38

Throne, Hannah, 215

Toale, M. W., 213–214

Townsend, Elizabeth, 58

Treanor, B. S., 84

Tribune (Chicago newspaper), 15, 249

Tribune (New York newspaper): anti-Catholic prejudice in Union Army, 176; anti-Irish prejudice, 249; editor, 181; Fenians, 239–240; impatience for war, 68; New York City draft riots, 182

Trimble, Isaac R., 169

Tschudy, Martin, *167*, 171, 172

Tully, Joseph B., 53, 60

Turner, James B.: 88th New York, 102, 106; on Antietam, 117–118; Gallowglass, 273n94; life in the Irish Brigade, 106–107; Meagher (Thomas Francis) and, 106, 107; Union Army's treatment of Irishmen, 108

Twiggs, David, 35, 37

Tyler, Daniel, 76

Tyler, John, 12, 26, 34

Tyler, Robert, 26

Ulster Irish: blending into majority population, 17; Boston, 8; Carolinas, 8, 9; definition, 5; Democratic-Republicans, 20; Federalists, 20; immigration to America, 7–9; Indian peoples, 8; Irish Catholics, 8–9, 17–18; Lincoln and, 219; New England, 8; Pennsylvania, 8, 9;

Presbyterian Scotsmen, 7; Protestantism, 5; Regulators, 8; Virginia, 8, 9

Ulster Scots. *See* Ulster Irish

Ulstermen. *See* Ulster Irish

Union Army: anti-Catholic prejudice, 91, 176–177, 213–214, 218–219, 222; anti-Irish prejudice, 91, 213–214; Army of the Potomac (*see* Army of the Potomac); benefits of volunteering, 145–146; bounty jumping, 147; bounty system, 146–147; call for raising African-American regiments, 139; conscription (*see* Draft, the); destruction of Southern Catholic churches, 176, 187, 222; dual loyalty, 5; Emancipation Proclamation, 139; enlistment (*see* Enlistment in Union Army; Reenlistment in Union Army); ethnic units/regiments, 72; Fenians, 236; foreign-born soldiers, 235; free trip to America in exchange for military service, 198–199; inducements for enlisting, 195–196; Irish American officers, 245; Irish Brigade (*see* Irish Brigade); Irish Catholic volunteers, 5; Irish Catholics, 5; Irish share of manpower, 103–104, 157–158; Irish soldiers in (*see* Irish soldiers); leaves of absence, 153; motivations for joining, 2–3, 4; native-born commanders, 96; number of Irish in, 2, 157–158, 229, 232, 245, 251; Peninsula Campaign, 101, 112; "political generals," 90, 154; presidential election (1864), 231; railroad companies, 205; recruiting in Ireland, 202; recruitment (*see* Recruitment for Union Army); Shenandoah Valley campaign, 225; training, 68, 202–203; treatment of Irishmen, 108; unpreparedness prior to Battle of First Bull Run, 74

Union Army of the Tennessee, 151

U.S. Catholic Magazine, 27

United States Army, 31–38; anti-Catholic prejudice, 34–35, 36; anti-Irish Catholic prejudice, 246; anti-Irish prejudice, 38; Catholic chaplains, 37; desertion, 32, 34, 36, 46; ethnic units/regiments, 38, 70; Fenians, 243; flogging, 32, 37; immigrants in, 31–32, 35–37; Irish Americans in, 33, 36–38, 39; Irish Catholics, 245–246; Irish fighting prowess, 38; mili-

tias (*see* Irish militias);
nativism, 33–34; punishment,
32, 37; recruitment, 32; religious freedom, 34; San Patricios (St. Patrick's Battalion),
36–37, 46
Ursuline Convent (Charlestown,
Massachusetts), 11–12, 182

Vallandigham, Clement L., 226
Vicksburg Campaign (1863): Grant
and, 151; map, *152;* Murray
(Michael) and, 201; Sproul
(Andrew) and, 150
Victoria, Queen, 58, 238
Vincent, Strong, 162
Volcano under the City (Union
Army veteran), 236

Walbach, John DeB., 34
Wales, Prince of (later Edward VII).
See Prince of Wales incident
Walsh, Gerald B., 213
Walsh, Patrick, 244
Warren, Gouverneur, 160–161, 162
Wayne County Democrat (newspaper), 150
"We Are Coming, Father Abraham" (Gibbons), 175
Webb, Alexander, 166, *167,* 171
Webb, Robert, 120
Webster, Daniel, 97
Webster, William, 97

Weed, Stephen H., 162
Weed, Thurlow, 62
Weekly Day-Book (New York periodical), 137
Welles, Gideon, 101
Wells, George D., 71–72, 99–100
Welsh, Peter, 54–55, 185
West, the: anti-Irish prejudice, 5,
71; nativism, 15; tolerance for
Irish immigrants, 15
West, William B.: encouragement
of Irish emigration to America,
198–199; Fenians, 236–237;
Meagher (Thomas Francis)
and, 198; remittances to families of deceased foreigners,
201–202
"What Irish Boys Can Do. Answer
to: No Irish Need Apply" (ballad), 212
"When This Cruel War Is Over"
(song), 211–212
Whigs, 20
White, William: 69th Pennsylvania,
124, 194; Fredericksburg, 124;
Gettysburg, 169, 171; reenlistment, 194
Wild Geese: 69th Regiment, NYSM,
63; as an inspiration, 69; definition, 3; history of, 265n7
Wilderness, Battle of (1864), 207,
208
Wildes, Thomas F., 216–217

Wildey, John, 78
William of Orange, 10, 178
Winslow, John A., 201
Wisconsin State Militia, 70–71
Women, Irish, 31, 268n82
Working Women's Protective
Union, 188
World (New York newspaper),
122, 183
Woulfe, Maurice, 157–158,
242–243, 245–246
Wright, Ambrose R., 168

Yates, Richard: 23rd Illinois, 90;
appeasement of Irish Americans, 93–94; Farrell and,
212–213; Haines and, 93;
Know Nothings, 92; Millican
on, 215; O'Ryan and, 92–93
Young, John, 187, 238
Young Ireland: "Battle of Widow
McCormack's Cabbage Patch,"
57; Irish Americans, 58; Irish
nationalism, 56; Irish Repeal
Movement, 57; members, 56;
O'Connell and, 55

Zook, S. K., 165
Zouave regiments: Irish Zouaves,
58, 66–67; Louisiana Zouaves,
76; Meagher (Thomas Francis)
and, 58, 66; New York Fire
Zouaves, 78

About the Author

SUSANNAH URAL BRUCE is Assistant Professor of History at Sam Houston State University in Texas. She is the editor of the forthcoming *Ethnicity and the American Civil War* and author of the forthcoming *Hood's Texans: A History of the Texas Brigade and Southern Society in the American Civil War.*